Contemporary Anthropology of Religion

Series editors
Don Seeman
Department of Religion
Emory University
Atlanta, GA, USA

Tulasi Srinivas
Department of Liberal Arts and Interdisciplinary Studies
Emerson College
Boston, MA, USA

Contemporary Anthropology of Religion is the official book series of the Society for the Anthropology of Religion, a section of the American Anthropological Association. Books in the series explore a variety of issues relating to current theoretical or comparative issues in the study of religion. These include the relation between religion and the body, social memory, gender, ethnoreligious violence, globalization, modernity, and multiculturalism, among others. Recent historical events have suggested that religion plays a central role in the contemporary world, and Contemporary Anthropology of Religion provides a crucial forum for the expansion of our understanding of religion globally.

More information about this series at
http://www.springer.com/series/14916

Knut Rio · Michelle MacCarthy · Ruy Blanes
Editors

Pentecostalism and Witchcraft

Spiritual Warfare in Africa and Melanesia

Editors
Knut Rio
University of Bergen
Bergen, Norway

Ruy Blanes
University of Bergen
Bergen, Norway

Michelle MacCarthy
University of Bergen
Bergen, Hordaland Fylke
Norway

Contemporary Anthropology of Religion
ISBN 978-3-319-56067-0   ISBN 978-3-319-56068-7 (eBook)
DOI 10.1007/978-3-319-56068-7

Library of Congress Control Number: 2017940340

Cover design by Thomas Howey
Photo: © Jan Sochor/Alamy Stock Photo

Printed on acid-free paper

This Palgrave Macmillan imprint is published by Springer Nature
The registered company is Springer International Publishing AG
The registered company address is: Gewerbestrasse 11, 6330 Cham, Switzerland

Acknowledgements

This volume is the result of two workshops, the first held at the University of Bergen in June 2014 and the second at the American Anthropological Association meeting in Washington D.C. in November 2014. Both meetings were funded by the project *Gender and Pentecostal Christianity: A comparative analysis of Gender in Pentecostal Christianity with focus on Africa and Melanesia* led by Professor Annelin Eriksen at the University of Bergen. The project is funded by the Norwegian Research Council and this book is an important part of the dissemination of that project.

The book is also supported by the ERC Advanced Grant project *Egalitarianism: Forms, Processes, Comparisons* led by Professor Bruce Kapferer at the University of Bergen, through the work put into it by Myhre, Bertelsen, and Rio who have all been part of this project also. The conceptual combination of Pentecostalism and Egalitarianism provided an important starting point for this book project, and Eriksen and Kapferer have provided a lot of inspiration for this work.

We also want to thank the editors of the bookseries 'Contemporary Anthropology of Religion', Don Seeman and Tulasi Srinivas, for their support of this project from the start, and Alexis Nelson and Kyra Saniewski at Palgrave MacMillan for professional and generous handling of the manuscript. We are also grateful for valuable comments from the anonymous reviewer.

We also thank The University of Bergen for a generous grant that made it possible to publish the book with Open Access. This makes it more likely that people in the regions of Africa and Melanesia can also access the book and take interest in these issues that are of global relevance.

Contents

Editors and Contributors

About the Editors

Knut Rio is Professor of Social Anthropology at the University of Bergen, Norway, and is responsible for the ethnographic collections at the Bergen University Museum. He has worked on Melanesian ethnography since 1995, with fieldwork in Vanuatu. His work on social ontology, production, ceremonial exchange, witchcraft and art in Vanuatu has resulted in journal publications and the monograph *The Power of Perspective: Social Ontology and Agency on Ambrym Island, Vanuatu* (2007). He has also co-edited *Hierarchy. Persistence and Transformation in Social formations* (with Olaf Smedal, 2009), Made in Oceania. Social Movements, Cultural Heritage and the State in the Pacific (with Edvard Hviding, 2011), and The Arts of Government: *Crime, Christianity and Policing in Melanesia* (with Andrew Lattas, 2011).

Michelle MacCarthy is an Assistant Professor in the Department of Anthropology at Saint Mary's University in Halifax, Canada. She was previously a Postdoctoral Fellow in the Department of Social Anthropology at the University of Bergen (where she undertook the research and writing of the chapter in this book), and where she was a contributor to Annelin Eriksen's Norwegian Research Council–funded project on gender and Pentecostalism in Africa and Melanesia. She completed her PhD at the University of Auckland in 2012. Her monograph, entitled Making the Modern Primitive: Cultural Tourism in the

Trobriand Islands (2016), examines tropes of primitivity and authenticity and mechanisms of cultural commoditization. She recently co-edited (with Annelin Eriksen) a special issue of The Australian Journal of Anthropology on Gender and Pentecostalism in Melanesia (August 2016).

Ruy Blanes is a postdoctoral researcher on the Gender and Pentecostalism project. He has been postdoctoral researcher at the Institute of Social Sciences of the University of Lisbon and Visiting Fellow at Leiden University (2007–2010) and London School of Economics and Political Science (2007–2013). He has worked on the anthropology of religion, identity, politics, mobility, and temporality. His current research site is Angola, where he explores the topics of religion, mobility (diasporas, transnationalism, the Atlantic), politics (leadership, charisma, repression, resistance), temporalities (historicity, memory, heritage, expectations) and knowledge. He has published articles in several international journals and edited volumes on the corporeality in religious contexts (Berghahn, 2011, with Anna Fedele) on spirits and the agency of intangibles (Univ. Chicago Press, with Diana Espírito Santo), and on 'Prophetic Trajectories' (Berghahn). He is also a board member of the APA (Portuguese Anthropological Association) and co-Editor of the journal *Advances in Research: Religion and Society*, edited by Berghahn.

Contributors

Barbara Andersen Massey University, Auckland, New Zealand

Bjørn Enge Bertelsen University of Bergen, Bergen, Norway

Aletta Biersack University of Oregon, Eugene, OR, USA

Ruy Blanes Spanish National Research Council, Santiago de Compostela, Spain; Consejo Superior de Investigaciones Científicas, Madrid, Spain

Tom Bratrud University of Oslo, Oslo, Norway

Annelin Eriksen University of Bergen, Bergen, Norway

Peter Geschiere University Of Amsterdam, Amsterdam, The Netherlands

Michelle MacCarthy Spanish National Research Council, Santiago de Compostela, Spain; Department of Anthropology, Saint Mary's University, Halifax, Canada

Knut Christian Myhre University of Oslo, Oslo, Norway

Katrien Pype KU University of Leuven, Leuven, Belgium; University of Birmingham, Birmingham, UK

Knut Rio Spanish National Research Council, Santiago de Compostela, Spain; University of Bergen, Bergen, Norway

Koen Stroeken University of Ghent, Ghent, Belgium

Thomas Strong Maynooth University, Maynooth, Ireland

CHAPTER 1

Introduction to Pentecostal Witchcraft and Spiritual Politics in Africa and Melanesia

Knut Rio, Michelle MacCarthy and Ruy Blanes

Ninety-seven books on the topic of "spiritual warfare" line one of the shelves in my office. All but a dozen of these have been published in the last ten years. Most of them present some form of "deliverance ministry" and are full of dramatic and triumphant stories. Others are sounding the alarm about "territorial spirits" and make suggestions about identifying them and praying against them.
Clinton E. Arnold, *Three crucial questions about spiritual warfare.*[1]

Introduction

In October 2013, a group of six men and one woman, armed with sticks and stones, invaded the church of Muxima—the most important Catholic pilgrimage site in Angola. In the middle of Sunday Mass, they proceeded to destroy the statue of Our Lady of Muxima. Before they could complete their mission, however, they were cornered and pinioned to the floor. The group belonged to a Pentecostal church known as the Prophetic Church of Judaic Bethlehem's Ark. According to media reports, they wanted to destroy the statue because they had identified it as a potent symbol of witchcraft-fueled idolatry. They had carried out

K. Rio (✉) · M. MacCarthy · R. Blanes
University of Bergen, Bergen, Norway

K. Rio et al. (eds.), *Pentecostalism and Witchcraft*, Contemporary Anthropology of Religion, DOI 10.1007/978-3-319-56068-7_1

their attack to mark their position in a larger spiritual battle. Not only is Muxima a key pilgrimage site for the Catholic Church, it is also believed to be a powerful spiritual site at which several prophets (Christian and non-Christian) carry out their work and obtain their power, be it "good" or "bad" (see Blanes, this volume).[2]

A similar case occurred in Port Moresby, Papua New Guinea (PNG), and this gained considerably wider media exposure. In late 2013, the devout Christian Speaker of Parliament, Theodore Zurenuoc, tried to expunge a number of spirit carvings from Parliament House. These had been intended to represent the country's cultural diversity, but he referred to them as "ungodly images and idols" (Eves et al. 2014; Silverman 2015). Zurenuoc (2013) claimed that the images represented "ancestral gods and spirits of idolatry, immorality and witchcraft." Workers attacked the carvings with chainsaws in an effort to purge these "demons" from Parliament House. Zurenuoc sought to replace the "blasphemous" carvings in the Grand Hall of Parliament with what he called a "National Unity Pole," which incorporated carvings of images from the Bible, the PNG constitution, and the word "unity" in each of the country's 800 or so vernacular languages; it also depicted an eternal flame, "symbolizing the light that comes from the Word of God" (Zurenuoc 2013). The Unity Pole was meant "to usher in an era of morality and prosperity by renouncing Satan and rebirthing the country as godly" (Silverman 2015, p. 361).

The cases of Muxima and the PNG parliament demonstrate the energy and determination with which Pentecostals target public spiritual sites that they associate with witchcraft and evil. On behalf of the nation, the city, or the neighborhood they make into tangible enemies those symbols that are deemed bad for health, security, unity, prosperity, and development. They go on crusades and engage in warfare against invisible demons that they believe corrupt public displays and agencies. They ask: who is *really* running the church; who is *really* in charge of the nation; who is *really* benefitting from business deals? When they pronounce the answers, they often identify "witchcraft" and "sorcery" as their targets.

This book is about such recent trends in what we might call *spiritual politics* in Africa and Melanesia. In using this concept, we suggest that much of current politics, governance, and public debate is rooted in a world of invisible powers—of witches, spirits, and demons (see also Marshall 2009). Indeed, Africanists have long been keen to point out that the concept of political power in these regions is often difficult to disentangle from concepts of sorcery and witchcraft (Geschiere 1997). This notion also draws on Harry West's (2005) observation in his monograph on Mozambique that there has been a reopening of the space of the occult by the church, and that this has involved a radical redefinition of the potent space of governance. West's work, in turn, follows Achille Mbembe's (2001) insistence that an understanding of the development of African democracy requires that attention is paid to alternative "languages of power" that emerge from people's daily lives. The sorcery discourse described by Harry West (2005, p. 3) is just such a language of power that demands to be included in policy-making and governance: "[s]o long as policymakers and citizens speak mutually unintelligible languages of power, the project of democracy is impossible." West suggests that for his informants, *uwavi* (sorcery) is a distinctive way of seeing and understanding the world, and for them, sorcerers move in a realm beyond the visible world. From this vantage point, they envision the world differently to ordinary people. According to the PNG parliamentary Speaker, ritual art had carried this type of demonic spiritual agency and language of power right into the heart of national politics and had to be destroyed, because it had the potential to undermine democracy. In the case of the Muxima church vandalism, the statue was also seen as a vessel for witchcraft that would have a corrupting influence on worshippers. In a similar vein, Adam Ashforth emphasizes that in a system that recognizes witchcraft as a major force, "spiritual insecurity" must be considered as a key element in the formation of democracy (Ashforth 2005, p. 18; see also Van Dijk 2001; Badstuebner 2003; Blanes, this volume).

Thus, in a sense, this is where anthropologists and Pentecostal churches share a particular perspective. Given their sensitivities to the detail of daily life and discourse, anthropologists acknowledge that there is a gap between official politics and grassroots concerns—and especially so when witchcraft and sorcery are involved. Pentecostals have become successful across Africa, Melanesia, and the rest of the world because they also acknowledge this gap as both an existential problem and a governmental problem. Unlike policymakers, politicians, development agencies, and NGOs, the Pentecostal churches take seriously the idea that a different platform of power exists from that of policy and government. As a remedy, they have designed a form of evangelism that might be termed confrontationist, which has as its foundation a direct attack on the power of the invisible realm itself through "spiritual warfare," "spiritual mapping," "discernment," and "healing." This is the source of their considerable appeal—that they enter into a hidden world of sorcerers and witches as matters of life and death. As Harry West (2005, p. 10) observes, the importance of their message is that they "see the unseeable" in order to "know the unknowable, and … make sense of the senseless."

Sorcery, Witchcraft, and Pentecostalism

Before addressing these issues more fully below, it will be helpful to clarify the concepts of "sorcery" and "witchcraft" as they are used throughout to explore the regions of Africa and Melanesia. While each term has particular anthropological connotations and definitions, they are unified in that they both encompass harm to persons or their belongings inflicted by human or spiritual beings. The implication of sorcery or witchcraft in illness, bad luck, or death means that the infliction is not related to accidents or chance encounters, to viruses, bacteria, or other types of occurrence. Sorcery and witchcraft are human-centric, relational ways of understanding health, well-being, and social processes.

When this human-centric definition of the two concepts is acknowledged, it can be seen that Christianity is both deeply allied with these phenomena and, at the same time, adversarial in regard to them. Christianity shares the human-centric belief that misfortune is caused by the malevolent intentions of others, and Christianity's remedy—doing good in the world—takes place through acts of prayer, renunciation, redemption, and sacrifice. In Christianity, demons, the devil, and Satan take hold inside a human being, and Christians find in sorcery and witchcraft the same kind of parasitical anthropomorphic agencies: thus, they find it natural to confront these forces as extensions or translations of their own demons. Although there is little written about the devil, Satan, or demons in the Bible, many Christian theologies, and especially the Pentecostal theologies that are the subject of this book, are consumed with working out how evil operates in human relations and in attempting to remedy this by engaging in "spiritual warfare." In a broad sense, then, Christianity reformulates sorcery and witchcraft in an effort to keep illness and death within the reach of human agency. It makes the attempt to do so by importing such concepts into their existing demonology.

Through this entanglement of Christian demonology and local beliefs, the concepts of sorcery and witchcraft have become almost universally accepted. They not only translate local beliefs, but also shape these beliefs according to the particular history of that translation (see Bertelsen, this volume). This history is marked by a number of factors and perspectives to do with Christian conversions, modernity, life in the colonies, and relations between masters and servants, but also perspectives on an alternative source of power, on where wealth and prosperity comes from, and on how social life works. In Africa and Melanesia, as outlined in the various chapters in this collection, sorcery and witchcraft are powerful concepts that gain considerable attention and energy in both political and economic arenas, as well as in religion and ritual. They no longer feature only in anthropological conferences, or in churches and church crusades, but also in courts of law, in policy documents, and in media coverage.

To begin with, then, some definitions are in order. The concepts used throughout this book are close to the prototypical definitions given in early colonial anthropology (see Turner 1964). Here, "witchcraft" refers to unconscious cannibalistic acts wherein a creature takes hold of a person and dictates that they should prey on and steal other people's vital substances. "Sorcery" is often considered to be different: it refers to conscious acts of poisoning or hurting someone by the use of magic remedies or techniques. In analyses of African settings, witchcraft is often synonymous with "power," and is therefore implicated in any display of high status, wealth, government, or violence:

> The close link between witchcraft and political power expresses, therefore, a deep mistrust of politics and power that is characteristic of these societies. But this is combined with the insight that power, and therefore the occult forces, are indispensable to the very functioning of society. (Geschiere 1997, p. 200)

In Melanesia, this association with power encompasses other factors, and it is difficult to translate "occult forces" and "politics" from Geschiere's Cameroon example to the Melanesian context. That is, there are few cases in Melanesia where successful politicians or businessmen have been suspected of controlling "occult forces" as the source of their influence. Rather, the general impression is that such high profile characters would be considered targets by envious witches. Traditionally, leadership in Melanesia has not been tied to titles, possession, and power but more to fluid notions of guardianship or administration. "Big Men" have been described primarily as managers of wealth: they are organizers of ceremonies and aggregate place, village, or lineage (see Strathern 1991b; Robbins 2007). In many cases in the past, in fact, it was reported that sorcery was an instrument of legitimate Big Man control (see Malinowski 1926; Zelenietz and Lindenbaum 1981; Stephen 1996; Dalton 2007, p. 43), and thereby to some degree it was similar to Geschiere's *djambe* concept of power in Cameroon (Geschiere 1997). But in contemporary Melanesia we instead read about witches as being sick, old, ugly, and unskilled, as well as envious and greedy. In this context, they are perhaps more figures of anti-power (see Knauft 1985; Kelly 1993; Lipuma 1998).

In all the various usages—be it in ethnography, documents of law or policy, or in Christian campaigns—the two forms of doing injury to others are complementary and closely related to one another. The concepts have retained their strength in a globalized world because of the durable position of a Christian human-centric worldview that hinges on the concept that a person is always under attack from evil influences. Thus, the person is in need of protection. Indeed, this is becoming a global truism that effectively cancels out the diverse beliefs and pluralist practices previously glossed under the concepts of witchcraft, sorcery, and divination (see Stroeken, this volume). The various chapters of this volume follow ways in which this global discourse of demonology proceeds when adopting and encompassing the heterogeneous phenomena of the world into its vocabulary, and the contributors highlight what happens when people place locally specific forces of life and death within universalist Pentecostal demonology and its confrontational methodology.

The topic will be of particular interest to anthropology—with its regional models of society and person, and its plural cosmologies and ontologies—since synchronized indigenous Pentecostal movements directly denounce such regionalism and pluralism and engage in profound and effective practices of unification and universalization. Indeed, this book follows Pentecostalism in its effort to bypass regionalism. Our comparison between Africa and Melanesia thus starts off from the cultural specificity of witchcraft and sorcery, but simultaneously highlights how Christian evangelism "pentecostalizes" witchcraft and sorcery as universal concerns of life and death, good and evil.

Pentecostal Universalism and Global Spiritual Warfare

A major theme of this work is how the movement of Pentecostalism changes the parameters of social life by penetrating deeper into the minutiae of everyday life than earlier Christian churches, state governance, or market relations have managed to achieve. The key to its success lies in Pentecostalism having taken control of the forces of life and death, with universality as a key technique.

By Pentecostalism, we refer to Christian beliefs and practices that emphasize connectivity with the Holy Spirit, and to Christian movements that typically value prophecy, visions, prayer, healing, and deliverance from evil spirits. This is a necessarily broad definition of Pentecostalism, precisely because it enables us to accommodate the diversity and heterogeneity of traditions, expressions, materializations, and manifestations framed within the umbrella term of Pentecostalism in the social science study of religion. In this respect, we are less interested in canonical definitions of Christian denominations, and more in the dynamics and fluidity of their practices and ideologies, in which the above-mentioned connectivity seems to play a central role. Indeed, as seen in several of the following chapters, one need not be directly associated with a Pentecostal church or congregation to be filled with the spirit. Therefore, Pentecostal churches themselves downplay denominational divisions. They often also downplay the centrality of their pastor, their church building, and the Bible, and tend to move out into public spaces in parades, crusades, healing missions, and into targeted neighborhoods: they use prayer tents, street occupations, public squares, and rural crossroads. They are known to oppose traditional forms of leadership, ritual regimes, and hierarchical social structures. They also encompass popular social movements that seem to be intensely preoccupied with the idea of evil as spatially and territorially inherent in people's lives. Their notion of "spiritual warfare" addresses particular neighborhoods, companies, or persons, and even whole continents or nations, as harboring evil and being subject to ritual cleansing. These Pentecostalists also move into political spheres, actively engaging in political campaigns and forming parties, but they also build schools and social infrastructure and have become a driving force behind new economic developments, such as microcredit loans, savings accounts, or ostentatious consumption; they also become involved in the moral constitution of state apparatuses such as policing (O'Neill 2010; Rio 2011; Trnka 2011) or healthcare (see Andersen, this volume).

Pentecostalism often focuses on witchcraft as the localization of evil, especially in our two regions of Melanesia and Africa, and its therapeutic cleansing operates through the investigation, examination, and healing of the individual as a site for the penetration of evil. The concepts of "deliverance" or "discernment" seem now to be used in both African and Melanesian contexts, in ways that bypass former Christian usages. They emphasize equally a need to investigate the body, the house, the street, markets, stores, or the nation, as sites for various forms of transgression. As such, Pentecostal movements are action-oriented in the search for remedies for transgression. Thus, Pentecostalism's project is a universalizing one—and its lively rituals, its "prophetic time" (Robbins 2004) , its preoccupation with creating a better future for its followers by detaching from the past (Meyer 1998), and its general theological and governmental content are remarkably uniform across the globe (see Marshall 2009, 2014). Our point here is not that Pentecostalism becomes a universal reality or a unitary phenomenon across the world, but that its ideology is universalist and that its technique for proceeding into local environments is to replace local vocabularies and local explanations with universalist concepts.

The crux of Pentecostal universalism seems to lie in its handling of witchcraft or demons. Spiritual warfare is the Christian version of taking a stand against invisible evil forces (see Beam 1998; Murphy 2003). The foundation for this ideology is the belief that evil spirits intervene in human affairs, and this is as relevant to the movement in the context of the USA or Scandinavia as it is in Africa or Melanesia. However, Pentecostal universalism has taken inspiration from experiences in non-Western settings. One of the pioneers in the field of spiritual warfare is C.P. Wagner, who served as a missionary in Bolivia before he became a professor at California's Fuller Theological Seminary in the School of World Mission. Many of the theologians who have worked on spiritual warfare seem to have brought back from other world regions to the USA a recognition that demons and evil spirits constitute a major challenge to Christian practice. This was a development of the 1980s, and Wagner (2012, p. 12) comments that when a congress on world evangelization was held in Manila in 1989, with thousands of participants from across the world, the three most attended workshops were on the Holy Spirit and spiritual warfare. Another member of this group, Ed Murphy, a former missionary in Latin America, explains their general attitude as follows:

> We are at war. As to the origin of this war, all we know is what the Bible tells us. It began in the cosmic realm, evidently before the creation of man, in an angelic rebellion against the Lordship of God.
>
> The experienced deliverance minister can compel evil spirits to tell the truth. I do so all the time. We obtain from them the information we need to proceed with the deliverance and then expel them to the place where Jesus wishes to send them.
>
> We need to condition ourselves, so to speak, to put on our spiritual warfare eyeglasses to correctly view present reality. (Murphy 2012, pp. 54–55)

Such evangelism proceeds by building universal examples from situations in parts of the world where witchcraft and forces of the invisible dominate people's daily lives. The examples are fed into in a systematic global struggle against the demonic. The demonic, as well as the warfare against it, is presented as an ontological starting point, where Pentecostal energy is dedicated to discerning the presence of Satan in social life anywhere. This always takes place as a war with competing ontological regimes—of science, reason, and the state. Murphy claims:

> By demonization I mean that Satan, through his evil spirits, exercises direct partial control over one or more areas of the life of a human being.
>
> When dealing with the potentially demonized, the typical Western, analytical, reasoned approach towards evangelism will be ineffective. Only a gospel of power will set them free. (Murphy 2012, p. 59)

These globetrotters of so-called third wave Pentecostalism list successful struggles against demons and witchcraft from across the planet, from Thailand to Greece to the Bermuda Triangle (see Wagner 2012, pp. 75–93). In one of the many books edited by Wagner, there are texts by people who have served as missionaries around the world and who have helped people against the demonic hold of traditions and shamanism (see Pennoyer 2012). John Louwerse, professor at Life Bible College in Los Angeles, reports from his stay in West Papua among the Yali in Pass Valley:

> It is a wonderful, humbling experience to be used by God to reach a hidden, Neolithic tribe in the jungles of Irian Jaya and to see in a multi-individual Christward movement approximately 98 percent of a tribe of 3,500 members change allegiance, acknowledging the lordship of Christ over their lives. We have seen multiple thousands healed and freed from demonic forces that had sway over their lives. The Lord chose to use human vessels in the ministry of healing and deliverance to bring honor to His name and to leave a deep impact upon our lives. We witnessed how the results of power evangelism drastically changed the core of their worldview and subsequently every subsystem of their culture. (Louwerse 2012, p. 272)

Similarly, Donald Jacobs, executive director of the Mennonite Christian Leadership Foundation in Landisville, Pennsylvania, who served in Tanzania and Kenya and participated in the East African Revival—an independent Pentecostalist movement going back some 60 years—stated,

> [a] mong East African believers, it matters little whether the spirit is a demon, a nature spirit, or an ancestral spirit. Each and all must go when ordered by Jesus Christ to leave … As I reflect on my learnings as a missionary in East Africa, I recall that the demon cults and the ancestral spirit cults put phenomenal energies into cataloging the demons. They had elaborate ways of finding out the precise name, nature, and power of each demon. They were identified by means of color, smell, area of origin, and fine tastes, such as whether the demon prefers Lifebouy soap over Lux or cotton clothes over synthetics. In that culture, when a person becomes demonized the experts can, within minutes, describe the demon in great detail. Perhaps by so doing, they increase their power over these forces. It struck me strangely at first that when people in that culture become believers in Jesus Christ they abandon the need to classify spirits in this way. All evil spirits, they know, are subservient to Christ. (Jacobs 2012, p. 281)

Here lies the considerable social power of Pentecostalist movements: they offer intelligible techniques for confrontation. At the same time, they lift invisible powers out of their local heterogeneous framings and thereby counteract all claims to local specificity or relativism (see Stroeken, this volume). In other words, they fully embrace the invisible world and take control of it. They describe the different forms of life and creatures that exist in it; they offer techniques for taming them and making the invisible visible. They do not make the mistake that politicians, development agencies, or NGOs make by closing off the invisible or ignoring it; instead, they fully realize the potential for government that lies in the invisible realm itself. In addition, they import the idiom of warfare—so powerfully evocative and potent in the contemporary world—into the realm of the private, into the family, and into the self. As is often pointed out in Pentecostal healing, demonic control is always personal. It never comes from the cultural system, from the state, or from globalization. It always concerns the micro-relations of the family, the church congregation, or the village—and demons seek out the inner self as their dwelling place.

A case in point here is what might be termed "migrant" or "diasporic Pentecostalism," which stems from the proselytizing and congregational intents of migrants. This is the case, for instance, in "African churches" in Europe, which have adopted what Simon Coleman (2006, p. 2) describes as "part culture": that is, Pentecostalism "presenting worldviews meant for export but often in tension (and therefore in strategic, parasitic articulation) with the values of any given host society." Within this framework, new epistemologies of witchcraft and deliverance appear, addressing directly the morality of a Western lifestyle and its effects on a "Pentecostal ethos." This, for instance, is what Rijk van Dijk (1997, 2004) describes in relation to the Ghanaian Pentecostal diaspora in the Netherlands, what Maïté Maskens (2013) refers to in her study of African ministries and evangelisms in Brussels, and that Kristine Krause (2008) points out in her study of healing tactics among Ghanaians in London. In these cases, processes include the re-signification of witchcraft and sources of evil, as well as new spiritual mappings and deliverance strategies. This is what Hermione Harris (2006, p. 83), in her study of the Yoruba Christian diaspora in the UK, calls "dynamic metaphors of spiritual power." However, as Emmanuel Akyeampong (2000) observes, this is not a one-way route, but rather a common determination of the "Pentecostal enclave" (Brodwin 2003), and an adaptation of the Pentecostal universal spiritual struggle across migrant diasporic trajectories and homelands. Van Dijk (1997) exemplifies this in his description of the emergence of prayer camps in Accra that specialize in European deliverance, addressing the vulnerabilities, crises, and dangers to which the African migrant is exposed. Clearly, there is a seamless transition at work here, in terms of crossing over issues of culture, tradition, and belonging, making Pentecostalism an intercultural and international movement.

In its approach to witchcraft, Pentecostalism also problematizes relativism and translation. Pentecostals regularly cure people of ailments caused by "demons," "poison," "dirt," and "evil," which are invisible inflictions caused by relationships that are troublesome. It is rare to hear that these universalized terms and new techniques of healing may be ineffective against local or territorial spirits or witches. As will be seen in the following chapters, such universalization is in part what neutralizes the affliction, since it draws out and cancels the problematic specificity of the illness. Along with "new life" and "breaking with the past," the illness also becomes new: it is brought into the universalist ontology, where "evil," "Satan," and "demons" feature with full force as part of an invisible reality. Those people that we observe in our respective field locations, be it in PNG or Ghana, have often already dealt with and resolved the issue of translation, and they have replaced local terms with a universal demonic vocabulary. Both the contents of the occult space and the methodology for controlling it have been made formally universal, so to speak, and in the process, they have bypassed other local experts such as oracles and diviners. But, as noted in chapters by Stroeken and Myhre in this volume, in the same moment they have also created a problematic new field, with new creatures and new logics of operation, and new forms of violence needed to deal with them. The term "Pentecostal witchcraft" was therefore coined by Sasha Newell (2007) in an effort to describe how Pentecostal churches in Ivory Coast, in their attempt to combat witchcraft, were instead drawn into the witchcraft world. He argues (Newell 2007, p. 462) that Pentecostal Christianity and witchcraft are equally totalizing discourses, with "competing imaginations of power, wealth and illness," and in their effort to engage with the world of spirits, demons, and witches, "Pentecostalism is itself an alternative form of witchcraft discourse" (2007, p. 461). This observation has spurred important reflections throughout the present collection.

Regional Comparisons in a Universalizing Movement

Two ethnographic regions have been chosen as the field sites for the present endeavor—Africa and Melanesia. Both regions have figured prominently in the anthropology of witchcraft and sorcery. To both regions, the colonial era brought Christian missionaries, and they are tied together historically through British, French, and German colonialist personnel and evangelic organizations. The two regions are also closely connected in that charismatic movements have built strongholds through "breakaway churches"—that is, through indigenous churches with charismatic leaders who are believed to be in direct contact with the Holy Spirit. These are movements associated with independence and liberation, and in Melanesia and Africa their emergence and popularity took off during a time of national independence movements—in the 1960s and 1970s. Before this, church strategies for dealing with dark forces had been wide-ranging and mixed. Most early missionaries, in both Africa and Melanesia, tended to simply forbid belief in and talk about local concepts in the hope that they would become obsolete when replaced by a Christian discourse. Often this backfired so that witchcraft fears, sorcery practices, and healing became more or less clandestine spheres outside and separate from the church. The great leap made by Pentecostal churches during the independence movements was to conform to witchcraft beliefs through what Meyer calls "diabolisation" (Meyer 1999; West 2005; Macdonald 2015); that is, they brought the occult and evil within reach of church practices, which is when Pentecostal movements gained in popularity across the two regions.

The chapters that follow demonstrate the pervasive nature of the Pentecostal influence on all aspects of life in these regions. To some extent, a third region in these global connections is the USA, since American evangelists have been prominent, both in person and on television broadcasts, in the spread of charismatic Christianity in recent decades in both Africa and Melanesia; as such, this region should perhaps have been included. However, we have chosen here to focus on the effects of their charismatic presence in our two regions, and on the localization of their ideas and visions.

One interesting connection between Africa and Melanesia is outlined in speculation about whether the term for witchcraft—*sanguma*—in PNG's national language (Tok Pisin) was adopted from German missionaries who had visited South Africa, where the concept of *sangoma* encompassed oracles and healers. Such connections remain potent. During a recent outburst of occult forces in the capital of Vanuatu, a news report on national television claimed that a self-proclaimed vampire-sorcerer in one of the neighborhoods had imported his sorcerous remedies from East Africa (see Rio 2011). An underlying current in these types of discussion in Melanesia is that witchcraft and sorcery are the burden of the "black man," belonging to a dark time before the coming of Christian light, and that Melanesia is also in this primordial sense bound together with the African continent. However, the purpose of this volume is not to support or extend either the anthropological or the popular discourses that have tended to essentialize these two regions by combining their witchcraft with their original blackness. The purpose, rather, is to add to an understanding of this discourse as deeply rooted in a global Christian worldview—the most recent manifestations being found in developments in Pentecostal movements. These popular and energetic movements have often, like anthropologists, embraced sorcery and witchcraft as a social arena for understanding societies in these regions and, therefore, they are also perceived to be the means by which to change them. The domain of "the occult" has become the primary target for governance in the Pentecostal search for a "new life," a redeemed past, and a healthy future.

In terms of the anthropology of the two regions, they are asymmetric with respect to the connection between Pentecostalism and witchcraft or sorcery. In relation to Ghana, Mozambique, South Africa, Congo, Angola, and Tanzania there are large numbers of monographs and articles written over many decades that describe the interventions of Church movements into the spiritual terrains of healers, oracles, sorcerers, and witches. How modernity, capital, power, and prosperity interrelate with this spiritual and dangerous terrain has been a central topic in African anthropology. On Melanesia, however, there are few publications on the connection between the Church and witchcraft (however, see Barker 1990; Lattas 1993; Eves 2000, 2010; Jorgensen 2005), seemingly reflecting a different ethnographic reality. However, it is safe to say that the arrival of a wave of Pentecostal Christianity over recent decades has also changed the landscape of witchcraft and sorcery in this region (Newland 2004; Eriksen 2009a; Rio 2014; Macdonald 2015). There are reports that a new form of aggressive opposition is taking hold between church movements and witchcraft, and in the last decade, the issue of witch killing and torture in Melanesia has caught the attention of both the media and anthropologists. Scholars have understood this in relation to increased pressures on land and resources, an absence of state involvement, and increasing violence toward women (Gibbs 2012), as well as rising rates of HIV (Haley 2010). In June 2013, a conference was organized at the Australian National University, titled *Sorcery and witchcraft-related killings in Melanesia: Culture, law and human rights perspectives*, marking a widespread acknowledgment that new forms of torture and aggression toward witches were generally on the rise in the region (Forsyth and Eves 2015). The focus was on what to do with witch killings through law and governance, and the conference volume provides direct advice on matters of state policy. What is missing from this Melanesian literature, in our view, is a perspective on the underlying dimensions of religious change and worldviews in these new forms of violence, although Dan Jorgensen's (2005, 2014) accounts of "spiritual warfare" in the Mountain Ok area of PNG, serves as an exception. His work highlights the cultural ruptures that have taken place in PNG over the last 20 years (see also Robbins 2004). In 1992, a well-orchestrated upsurge of third wave evangelism and apocalyptic thinking took off in the Mountain Ok area, which had a considerable influence on people's lives and thinking. Jorgensen (2005) specifically addresses a local movement called "Operation Joshua" and the centrality of "spiritual warfare" within it. The focus of this movement was to attack directly invisible evil forces such as witchcraft and sorcery through "spiritual mapping," "healing," and "crusades." Through this confrontational, aggressive, and effective form of evangelism numerous charismatic movements and campaigns found their way into PNG, Fiji, the Solomon Islands, and Vanuatu.[3]

The Telefolmin of PNG have now experienced the third wave Pentecostal evangelism for 20 years, and Jorgensen refers to a new tendency that he has observed: young boys with little status—but armed with guns and intoxicated with alcohol and/or drugs—carry out witch torture and interrogations. Jorgensen asks what motivates the mobs of boys to carry out torture and kill their fellow villagers. Here, it should be recalled, the period when the boys were growing up was marked by an intense Pentecostal activity, in a nationwide Manichean epoch in which evil was targeted through individualized searches for moral ruptures. The torture they carry out is obscene and staged as public drama (Jorgensen 2014, p. 278). Jorgensen relates this to a "traveling package"—an undefined epidemiology of fears and concepts that travels long distances. Concretely, for PNG it is an "anti-witch package," which sets into motion the detection and labeling of witchcraft and evil, as well as the accordingly prescribed reaction and punishment. Jorgensen argues that this package "is a template for the use of torture and violence against suspected witches—rather than a set of ideas about witchcraft per se" (2014, p. 277). For Jorgensen, this is an alien, foreign template that the boys have willingly adopted because they are without other means of power or influence in their society. They have been left behind by the mining economy, by state programs, and by their families, and they live in a society that is increasingly violent. Jorgensen adds, in discussion with those concerned with the suffering brought about by vigilante groups, "[w]itchcraft was not the topic: violence was" (2014, p. 282). He recommends that we focus on what it means to be "useless" in this context and how the boys' situation may have led them to violence.

We draw on this example here because this situation, now widespread across Melanesia, is suggestive of what is at stake across pentecostalized areas. We need to fully realize what Pentecostal Christianity does when it engages in spiritual warfare—in the long run and across regions and cultural distinctions. It works with a universalist template, but this template is attractive to followers, we would argue, contra Jorgensen, because it *is* about witchcraft per se—because it specifically addresses and attacks *their* witchcraft. What has become clear from many African cases and the Pentecostal literature itself is that the Pentecostal movement, in its many forms and expressions, produces and invigorates a space for invisible powers, and it is into this space that Pentecostalism directs its attention and energy. The boys in Telefolmin, growing up in an intense period of Pentecostal spiritual warfare, were raised within this universalist spiritual politics. If we see this in light of recent events in Vanuatu and PNG (see chapters by Bratrud and Strong, this volume), the role of youth in determining evil is not necessarily tainted by a notion of local youth marginality; rather, it may be tied to a larger global theme of youth being connected to hope, truth, and futurity. With this volume we wish to emphasize that there is no way we can remove either Pentecostalism or witchcraft from these analyses, since they provide people with hard-wired cosmological and moral parameters and horizons; neither can we remove global and historical connections, since the Pentecostal movement is a well-organized, synchronized, and unitary movement in terms of its demonology, its diabolization, and its techniques of governance.

It is to be hoped that the concept of Pentecostal witchcraft in Melanesia will benefit from the present exposure to African materials, but also that the African materials will benefit from exposure to the Melanesian cases. This book presents fresh ethnographic materials in order to highlight and interrogate the nature of ongoing religious globalization around these issues of the person, of good and evil, equality and hierarchy, and power and agency.

The context for this volume is a long history of implicit and explicit comparisons between ethnography from Africa and ethnography from Melanesia—two classic anthropological regions. In the early days of such comparisons, models were drawn from the African materials, which were then applied wholesale in an attempt to make sense of, for example, group integration and kinship among recently explored anthropological regions such as the PNG Highlands in the 1960s (Lambek and Strathern 1998, p. 3). We hope here to reopen comparisons between the regions. The understanding of spiritual warfare and reprisals for alleged occult activity across Melanesia can not only benefit from a long-standing anthropological literature on similar themes in Africa, but perhaps add something new to the discussion that can inform further analysis of the African material (see also Myhre et al. 2013).

Peter Geschiere recently summarized previous studies comparing witchcraft in Africa and Melanesia (2013, pp. 166–172). He starts with Max Marwick's 1964 work on the different "social directions," as he terms it, taken by witchcraft and sorcery in Africa and Melanesia. He asserts that "in Africa these belief systems seem to reflect tensions within a community, whereas in Oceania they more commonly express tensions *between* communities" (Marwick [1964]1970, p. 281). His contrastive generalizations are based on the closer examination of the African ethnographic material, and he bemoans the relative lack of in-depth case studies on which to draw in the Melanesian literature. A studied response was a long time in coming, but Michele Stephen, in her conclusion to *Sorcerer and Witch in Melanesia* (1987), argued against the distortion of the "Africanist guidelines" imposed on the interpretation of occult aggression in Melanesian studies. Yet here, too, clear distinctions were advanced, wherein the Melanesian sorcerer would always be social while the witch would be entirely asocial, with cases not fitting the distinction chalked up to "social change." In any case, whatever the shortcomings of her analysis, this comparison made clear, as Geschiere notes, "the spuriousness of trying to oppose the region to Africa as more or less homogeneous blocks" (2013, p. 167).

Current theoretical debates about the nature of different ontologies is germane to this project of comparison, which, in contrast to the comparison of wholesale analytic models has instead turned to "partial connections" à la Strathern (1991), or the "controlled equivocations," of Viveiros de Castro (2004), where the focus is on essential differences between cultural areas and the irreducibility of cultural practices and concepts. With respect to Pentecostalism and witchcraft, we agree with Geschiere (2013, p. 171), who argues that "assuming ontological differences can easily lead to a fetishisation of difference and a neglect of the continuous borrowing and hybridization that shape cultural responses to similar issues." This point is particularly pertinent in our case, since one of the major concerns of Pentecostalism is to cancel out relativist distinctions in its approach to evil demons as one unified universal presence. On the other hand, we also find that Englund and Leach's (2000, p. 230) warning against "meta-narratives of modernity" is pertinent, as the narratives themselves often tend to blur and suppress regional or ideological variations. The case of Pentecostal movements is particularly interesting in this respect, since they root their meta-narratives of modernity in local environments (see Blanes, this volume). It is important here to keep in mind that the Pentecostalist movements generally do not feature as alien, foreign, or as having introduced particular beliefs; rather, they uphold indigenous motivations. Thus, we do not propose a new unified model of the modern world, but rather describe and compare the way in which one such universalist and globalizing "meta-narrative of modernity," the narrative of Pentecostalist demonology, tends to operate in these two regions.

Africa and Melanesia: A Comparison

In this final section of our introduction, we aim to indicate some relevant lines for comparison of pentecostalization in the two regions explored by the contributors to this book. We hope to convey that Pentecostalist values and practices create certain patterns that are of social importance across the regions. If we downplay *en bloc* regional comparisons, since they often lead to generalizations and regional essentialisms, we may instead focus on specific themes in our various cases across the two regions. As indicated above, one key theme is the idea of equality and the equal distribution of wealth; another is the importance of spiritual politics and spiritual warfare, and thus an emphasis on government and control. Below, we discuss these two themes in relation to the existing literature and the chapters that follow.

Pentecostal movements are egalitarian, communitarian, and even nation-like, with a focus on unity, close integration of members and, in ideological terms, at least, egalitarian structures of leadership. On Malawi, Harri Englund (2003, p. 91) observes:

> The expectation among Pentecostal Christians in Chinsapo is that the radical equality of human beings before God translates into an equal distribution of wealth among the brothers and sisters in Christ.

What Englund calls a "radical promise of equality" among Pentecostals is inseparable from their enthusiastic search for signs of inequality, despite vast discrepancies in opportunity and situations of unchanging poverty. It has also been noted in African contexts that Pentecostalism directly addresses and attacks material inequality by moralizing upwards against excessive consumption and accumulation (Meyer 1998; Smith 2001; Parish 2003; Newell 2007; Haynes 2012). Indeed, such issues of wealth, sharing, equality, and prosperity are crucial aspects for comparison of the meta-narrative of Pentecostalism. It is striking that envy, as the coveting of others' consumer items, has become a key moral issue associated with witchcraft and sorcery. Private and individualist rights of ownership have become the naturalized moral state that is being attacked by grudging, ugly, or occult agents of envy and desire for wealth. As noted by Smith (2001, p. 588) on Nigeria, the growth of Pentecostalism "is (paradoxically) associated both with popular discontent over poverty and inequality *and* with people's aspirations to achieve wealth and prosperity."

This picture also involves a particularly intense focus on the dynamics of integration and the exclusion of foreignness, as well as on domestication and a suspicion of signs of differentiation. For Pentecostals, the witch signals a threat to the egalitarian body in two ways: both by being a concealed, intangible, and non-transparent form of presence in the person, and by coveting others' possessions. Given that the witch creature has been added to the normal person, inside the body or by remote control, the witch is both "other" and "same," and within the focus on equality this becomes problematic. By its greed and envy, the witch also entails a form of accumulation that resists the transparent distribution of wealth and the egalitarian ethos of the congregation. It might be expected that this would lead to different issues of conflict in different localized settings. We could argue through the various contributions in this volume that envy articulates the claim to equality that is fundamental both to consumerism and to the relationship between men and God.

Bjørn Enge Bertelsen in Chap. 2 presents an interesting case in point from Mozambique. Here, witchcraft—in the form of the abduction of and feasting on local village children—concerns a group of German Pentecostals who came to live in the area some 20 years ago. According to people's stories today, they kidnapped and consumed the children, who are now missing. Bertelsen speculates that this relates to the notion that the German Pentecostals constantly emphasized sharing, brotherhood, and sameness. In a sense, they produced a form of intimacy so intense that it became consumptive. Here, the witch is an "other," or an outside threat that has become intimate and internal. Witchcraft in this sense is a reflection of intimacy as enforced, or as its double (see Geschiere 2013). Bertelsen asks if perhaps the egalitarian ethos of independence, sameness, and togetherness also attracts the notion of the "other same" as demonic?

This question is also raised in Thomas Strong's account in Chap. 3 from the Eastern Highlands of PNG. Contrary to the popular discourse in Melanesia that witches are backwards and ugly, witchcraft here constitutes a spiritual world where everything is highly ordered, ostentatious, and modern. The domain of witches, which exists in parallel with the village society, is a modern city with offices, stores, buses, discos, a parliament, schools, and a university—where the lowest of men lead parallel existences as salaried employees, where a poor elderly woman is an air hostess, and big talkers are lawyers. Witches are already the people that these Papua New Guineans would like to become. If they are feared and condemned, they also, in this discourse, represent what people desire. Against a background of rotting grass houses and unruly youth, witches inhabit a wealthy and ordered modernity. When describing witches, people are describing things they want or positions they believe are desired by co-villagers. The kind of acquisitive and individualistic subjectivity that the witch symbolizes appeals to people, while also scaring them to death, so they persecute witches and torture them into giving up their doubles and demons. The narrative of the sacrifice of Jesus and his blood given up for human kind is used to break off the connection between the two worlds, and for calling witches back from the modern city world to take part in village issues. There is a striking parallel in these cases from Mozambique and PNG, as the common denominator seems to be the importance of a Pentecostalist ethos of modernity, a foreignness of the same, and the horrific terror of both too much sharing or a lack of sharing.

Still, with Strong's comments on an imagined and desired parallel consumer society in mind, a culture of consumerism is clearly outlined for certain African societies in ways that we have not yet seen in Melanesia (see Ferguson 1999; Roitman 2005; Weiss 2009). In places like urban Cote d'Ivoire consumer objects and brands form entire symbolic systems—so that, for example, Timberland shoes versus Sebago shoes, in Newell's (2007, p. 473) example, becomes an existentially meaningful contrast. We get a sense that this is very different from the signification that consumer objects take in Melanesian societies. However, despite these contrasts, it is perhaps interesting to think more broadly about the way consumerism and witchcraft have become part of larger modes of moral signification. Indeed, this is the angle that Ruy Blanes takes in Chap. 4, when he describes sorcery in urban Angola. He goes one step further with an "occult economy" analysis in showing how sorcery is becoming a paramount index of value in urban Angola. Like the Dow Jones index that daily sets a standard for the universal stock exchange, *ndoki* sorcery is a similar index for measuring spiritual value in pentecostalized neighborhoods of Luanda. It orders and measures the moral parameters of social life and becomes a tool in the spiritual mapping of the city and in the ongoing processes of rumors, scapegoating, and accusations. There are also converging points between this value index and the value index of consumerism—since money and goods that are withheld or redistributed are also valued or devalued by the *ndoki* index.

Whereas in most traditional Melanesian examples the value index of witchcraft is negative, in the sense that it prohibits and destroys work and productivity, the *ndoki* index is a positive scale that sets the value of consumption independently of any production. This has many similarities to what Katrien Pype in Chap. 5 calls "a witchcraft complex," by which she means a total institution that harbors references, connectivity, and contradictions along many planes. As we move from Luanda in Angola to Kinshasa in Congo, Pype finds processes very similar to those described by Blanes. Her point is that the very terms of Pentecostal witchcraft are changing. The prevalent idea among Pentecostals in Kinshasa is no longer that witchcraft is about "a break with the past"—that is, a break with the rural, with kinship obligations, with traditions of fetishes, or with the older generation—as described in Birgit Meyer's work two decades ago (Meyer 1998). Now, the Pentecostals formulate "a break with the future" and with technologies of connectivity. ICT goods and modern technologies such as mobile telephones, the internet, and television play a key role in debates about ***kindoki*** witchcraft; these technologies are now targeted as objects of an electronic modernity that helps mediate the power of the devil. Pentecostal reflections on communication technologies force us to perceive the ways in which contact with social and spiritual Others can be initiated, mediated, or broken off, in a worldview in which a person is under attack from foreign influences and in need of protection. Here, it would seem that the Pentecostals articulate a global template that is about fear of abusive connectivity and fear that invisible evil forces are inclined to follow lines of communication opened up by new technologies. In Kinshasa's Pentecostal discourse, the SIM card, for instance, has become a reference to the soul, and "to unlock a SIM card" means to deliver someone from witchcraft. The technologies are merely shells for hidden occult forces, and the Christian mobilization against this form of connectivity is now just as global as the multinational companies that develop the technologies.

In Melanesia, there are many references to the inherent moral perils in new technologies, but it is perhaps not the technologies themselves or the companies behind them that are demonized to the same degree. This may be because there is a less developed culture of consumerism. Brands are very limited—many are Chinese or Australian products—and their importance in consumer desire is mostly limited to fulfilling kinship network obligations rather than individual consumption. Even in urban places like Port Vila, Honiara, or Port Moresby, the standard tins of beer, cartons of cigarettes, bags of rice, or shorts and t-shirts figure as currencies that certainly have an exchange value, but they do not come with the phantasmagorical promise of individual pleasure, future happiness, or self-fulfillment that has become normal in consumerist worlds. In Michelle MacCarthy's Chap. 6, we realize that the angle toward consumerism is quite different from Blanes' and Pype's urban African examples. In the Trobriand Islands, technology and material possessions may be a source of envy, with Trobriand witches perhaps representing the moral perils of individual consumption, but the main issue with witches is that they hinder productivity. Indeed, the notion that the witches are so "hungry" that they feed on corpses indicates the danger of becoming "greedy" and refusing to share freely and meet all reciprocal exchange obligations. When women are born again as Pentecostals and renounce their evil powers of witchcraft, they shun the antisocial capacities they have carried within them since early childhood, transforming their physical bodies as well as their social space as worship opens up new avenues for women's sociality. This includes prayer groups, open-air preaching, and a focus on productive responsibilities to the nuclear family, and the church community. For witches, it is taboo to touch a broom or coconut husks (used for cleaning saucepans or making fires for cooking), thus indicating that they are immune to the normal work that women do. Tidiness, productivity, order, and female beauty are central qualities in the Pentecostal church and qualities that are resisted by witches. Witches in the Trobriands used to be anonymous and had hidden relational capacities. Now, women may suddenly start confessing inside Pentecostal churches—admitting that they are hiding witchcraft capacities inside their body. By confessing and clearing the place taken up by the witch creature, they leave this space to Jesus. In addition to confession, the means for doing this is also to convert to a life of righteous, "clean," production. This also involves commerce, as work with the banana leaf bundles that used to constitute the most important women's wealth (a classic ethnographic case of gendered exchange) shifts into making new products for the tourist market (MacCarthy, n.d.). This in many ways converges with Newell's (2007) point about Cote d'Ivoire: that the focus of Pentecostals with regard to witchcraft is on material success and money, which thus intertwines with moral issues raised around capitalism. The attention, then, is on the convergence of faith and financial success (Newell 2007, p. 479).

The relationship between sorcery and the economy is also the concern of Knut Myhre in Chap. 7. He describes how Chagga-speaking people in Tanzania understand the phenomenon of the albino murders that have become a national concern in recent years. According to news reports albinos are targeted for their body parts, which are used in witchcraft to bring people good luck. Body parts, and especially albino body parts, have become part of an informal economy, portrayed in the media as a perverted trade. Myhre's argument goes in a different direction to the occult economy argument proposed by Comaroff and Comaroff (1999). The latter proposed that discourses about witchcraft, cannibalism, blood-sucking, and organ-snatching in Africa are metaphoric ways of addressing and critiquing the "real" economy of capitalism. Myhre's important point here is that the circulation of body parts is not necessarily *about* the economy, but may instead be something equally as "real" as the economy: that is, it is about life itself and modes of being, since, for the Chagga, "witchcraft and life fold out of and into each other." (Myhre, this volume 168). A severed arm found outside a church is discussed as a case in point, and Myhre demonstrates that the arm features in church discourse not as a commodity but in the transformed capacity of a body part that is central in the circuity of the life force. In witchcraft the arm is turned against the circuity of life. Witchcraft is not a reaction to an external imposition or phenomenon, but an internal generation of the form of life in this particular place: "where witchcraft unfolds from dwelling and life, Christianity enfolds witchcraft to afford dwelling and life" (Myhre, this volume 178). The difference between Catholics and Pentecostals in this area lies in their respective ways of tapping into this circuity of dwelling and life. Whereas Catholics envelop witchcraft and turn it around through their ceremonies, Pentecostals, as well as politicians and the state, wish to detach witchcraft from life-processes altogether because it is regarded as an evil interference.

The second theme of this book, although related to these issues of equality, envy, consumption, and corruption, is more tied to forms of governance and what we have termed spiritual politics. Rijk van Dijk (2001) writes from Ghana that the rise of "independent Christianity," particularly in the form of the prophetic healing churches, initially implied a syncretization of religious discourse and practice. Many of the churches initially incorporated important elements of local cosmologies, healing practices, and styles of leadership (2001, p. 101), but more recent Pentecostal churches have taken a step further. They cleared out the traditional healing practices and recreated the occult realm as a clean slate to be filled with new creatures and healing technologies (2001, p. 101). No longer syncretic, no longer apologetic for African traditions, they redefined both Christianity's agenda and the spiritual world into a universalist place where "[n]o one doubted the reality of witchcraft" (2001, p. 107). This also demonstrates what Birgit Meyer (1999, p. xvii) maintains—that breaking with the forces of the past may also re-invigorate them:

> I came to understand in the course of my stay, demonization by no means implies that the former gods and spirits will disappear out of people's lives. As servants of Satan they are still regarded as real powers that have to be dealt with in a concrete way … Put differently, the image of Satan offers a discourse with which to approach these powers as "Christian" demons.

There appears to be tremendous potential in this change, to make religious values all-encompassing of social life. When church and spiritual traditions are no longer separate, and when the realm of the otherworldly flows into the streets and neighborhoods and into people's daily lives, Pentecostals come to see the whole of society as their responsibility and as a site for transformation. This touches on a key issue concerning the importance of the Pentecostalist transformation, which overcomes regional distinctions between Africa and Melanesia. As noted above, sorcery and witchcraft form their own language of power and governance, and Pentecostalist confrontations of this power follow the universalist assumption that this form of governance is unified as *evil*. This is in a sense the invention that Pentecostal Christianity brings to the field: its Manichaeism and its confrontational line of action. What we see playing out is an experiment with the notion that an alternative politics is necessary: that is, a spiritual politics that not only measures wealth and material development, but that is constantly maintaining and reinforcing a spiritual order through ritual activity. We have seen how Pentecostals in Guatemala City target the main sites of political corruption and gang violence (O'Neill 2010), and this also comes through clearly in Hackman's account of Cape Town (2015), where the city is a field for competing modes of governance in a politics of space. Hackman observes:

> Detailed spiritual maps were essential. Christians needed to know what specific types of demons were present in an area and where they were located because prayers had to be "strategic" and "targeted" to have the most impact. (2015, p. 110)

She goes further, to note,

> they used spiritual mapping to police ambiguous boundaries and "protect" the city's moral health and future. (2015, p. 113)

The same occurs in the most remote corners of Melanesia. Jorgensen mentions a spiritual mapping exercise called "Night vision goggles" among the Telefolmin of PNG (2005, p. 447) that was explicitly about the Pentecostal technology of spotting and mapping spiritual and moral deficiencies. In another campaign in 1999 called *Prea Banis* (prayer fence), the whole PNG nation was purified of evil spirits by an airplane and a navy patrol boat that circumnavigated the country's boundaries (2005, p. 449). A successor of this was Operation Joshua, which took place in Telefolmin using a template for a spiritualized geographical space, a cartographic imagery, and a view of a military-like operation of spiritual cleansing (2005, p. 451), wherein the Telefolmin spirit house, as an ancient center for Ok ritual activities, along with its ancestral relics, became a selected strategic target and was burnt down. The movement also practiced the activity of "discernment"—"like watching television" (2005, p. 454)—to reveal sorcerers as well as hidden spiritual or satanic substances. Jorgensen draws on the work of Meyer (1999) and Robbins (2004) to state that Pentecostal Christianity is alternating between world-breaking and world-making. By choosing the Telefolmin ancestral house as a site for spiritual warfare, Operation Joshua restored the centrality of Telefolmin ritual knowledge, but by destroying the home of the ancestral cult. In this way, Telefolmin could recapture their centrality in the universe—placing it back on the spiritual map, so to speak.

Thus, it is not necessarily the past that is at issue, but rather the main regimes of social control. When society is governed by ritual forms, shamans, oracles, or kinship-based leadership, this is targeted as demonic by the Pentecostals. In different settings modern technologies, capitalist companies, or government policies may be the new targets (see Pype, this volume). A case in point here is Eriksen's (2009b, p. 192) example from Vanuatu, where a Pentecostal women's group targeted the electricity company as a source of evil and a threat to the Christian nation. Across Melanesia, recent years have seen the demonization of museums and ancestral cultural heritage, but also demonization of foreign missionaries and state agencies. During the presidential election in Vanuatu in 2009, Pentecostal pastors joined hands to protect the city of Port Vila from malign forces. Their spiritual campaign consisted of sending out "spiritual warriors" to selected places that marked the outer boundaries of the city, where they prayed day and night during the last days of the election so that the nation should not suffer under these malign forces. In Chap. 8 of the present volume, Eriksen and Rio outline the contours of a Melanesian city that has become thoroughly Pentecostalized in the sense that everyday life follows certain routines—attending church meetings on an almost daily basis, for example—but also because there is a routine awareness of how workplaces, the city's roads and markets, the spaces of leisure, and people's homes are being challenged by moral ruptures. The outcome of this at the household level is that they are now physically fenced in and protected from foreign malevolent influences, symbolizing the constant spiritual struggle that goes on inside. Not only do congregations go on spiritual warfare crusades, but people also frequently meet with Pentecostal healers and set up spiritual protection against the "demons" that they perceive to be looking in on them. In such a situation where the person, the household, and the nation are sites of invasive forces, spiritual mapping and detailed modes of governance are potent. This is world-breaking, in the sense that such activities cut social life into manageable and compartmental domains, with clear boundaries between person and person, between yards and houses, and between communities.

This form of urban spiritual campaign is also closely linked to the spiritual cleansing that Tom Bratrud in Chap. 9 describes on one of the outer islands of Vanuatu. During an intensive period in 2014, the entire Christian congregation of the small island of Ahamb in Vanuatu came out of their church building and besieged every corner of their island in order to drive out demons and evil spirits. It culminated in a witch hunt, where people of the congregation ganged up on accused witches, and in the end killed them by hanging them in the community hall. All this activity relates to Joel Robbins's (2009) point that Pentecostalism is marked by an intense preoccupation with ritual—to the degree that ritual cleansing overflows church boundaries and becomes concerned with all social life. It approaches social life out in the streets, in people's homes, in the market place, in forests and meadows, in parliament and, especially, in sites of nocturnal enjoyment such as nightclubs and bars. For places like Port Vila or Telefolmin, Kinshasa or Luanda, this means that Pentecostalism is omnipresent: its activities are about cleaning, dividing, dissecting, observing, and healing. It performs pervasive rituals for transforming and separating good from evil, clean from unclean, and seeks to create people who are protected from bad spiritual influences. Spiritual warfare is a form of ritual practice wherein the person, the neighborhood, or even the nation is continually defended and protected against alien invasion. This also means that Pentecostalism tends to overflow the boundaries between different forms of Christianity and between religion and everyday practice and forms of life (see Eriksen et al., n.d.).

This observation is further elaborated upon in Chap. 10 of this volume, where Barbara Andersen focuses on how nursing education in PNG influences the way sorcery and witchcraft are conceived in relation to health. Andersen does not connect this to Pentecostalism as a religious doctrine but demonstrates how the Pentecostal faith and participation in it becomes an alternative space of belonging for the nurses, who live away from home in order to work in health institutions in rural areas. In their mediation between largely autonomous rural communities and an increasingly distanced state, their Pentecostal vision transcends place-boundedness: hence, they are also able to transcend local understandings of sorcery and witchcraft. Their intense talk about sorcery and witchcraft among themselves is "socially productive," in Robbins's sense (2009), in the way that they confine and compartmentalize the dark forces of their narration about the "local way of life" (*pasin*, in Tok Pisin).

Koen Stroeken in Chap. 11 describes the influence of Pentecostal indigenous African churches in the realm of health and healing in Tanzania. His research background in traditional healing brings him to perceive Pentecostalism to be particularly influential in terms of certain cosmological and social practices. Like Myhre, Stroeken deals with the logic of the break that Pentecostals make with witchcraft. Whereas Myhre located this as a break with the circuity of life forces, Stroeken points to the Pentecostal tendency to collapse what were previously multiple frames of existence and cosmology. Complementary to Myhre's point that the "occult economy" as an anthropological concept has become detached from culturally specific frames and personal experiences, Stroeken maintains that the Pentecostal movement as a global, universal frame also had to stop shifting between experiential frames. As for the PNG nurses in Andersen's chapter, the occult is reduced here to a unitarian form of framing—that of a "local way of life" as seen from the outside. Stroeken describes how, for instance, healer and witch are part of the same frame for Pentecostals, since they treat magic, bewitchment, divination, ritual sacrifice, and spirit possession as belonging to one domain. Therefore, they also tend so see themselves as potentially always threatened by an external peril—where the peril is one unified form of evil—since they are not inside witchcraft but outside it, if we think in terms of Myhre's concept of dwelling. Even though peril is inherently inside the person and inside society, it is still Other and alien. This is what Stroeken calls a "nuclearization of the lifeworld"—which involves compartmentalizing, externalizing, and marginalizing what used to be integral to social life. Importantly, it also involves keeping this realm *close but separate*. Here, then, we have returned to Newell's observation of "Pentecostal witchcraft" (2007) as a domain of life that is both a primary concern and a constant danger.

Concluding Comments

In the chapters that follow we observe that Pentecostalism puts in place a particular form of governance or social ordering. Whereas state forms of governance, such as policing or schooling, stop short of powers to regulate the social life of households or the inner person—except through direct attack, violence, and destruction—the often rhizomatic forms of Pentecostal spiritual campaigns gain direct access. Pentecostals are concerned with creating new moral orders in a concrete way—through reforming neighborhoods and persons and addressing a public space directly though technologies such as "spiritual warfare."

A further hypothesis might also be suggested—that Pentecostalism, in these moral governance campaigns, runs up against other forms of governance, and that the ensuing friction creates a lot of the social energy and heat that we see in the Pentecostal churches. In direct competition with the governance of traditional leadership, market orders, ritual orders, and state orders—but above all, with what we might call "witchcraft orders"—it is demanded that these competitors submit to the Pentecostal moral order. Pentecostals understand that witchcraft represents a form of governance of its own in the way it invades people's lives, directing them to be watchful and suspicious, ordering them to share generously with others, prohibiting them from moving freely, and in creating anxiety in society, making people see their relations in new ways, causing, for example, illness, weakness, or loss of consciousness. Pentecostals see it as a counterforce to dwelling and the circuity of life, to draw on Myhre, and they pursue witchcraft in the domain of dwelling in order to banish it, cast it out, and destroy it. Witchcraft seeks out life forces and vital substances and it strikes down relations of intimacy, to the extent that Pentecostalism sets itself up in that same realm in social life—by, in a sense, following witchcraft into its domain of intimacy and social relations. Pentecostalism thereby becomes a form of presence in social life that populates anew the space of witchcraft. In MacCarthy's case from the Trobriand Islands (Chap. 6, this volume), they directly drive out the witch from within the woman's body and let Jesus inhabit that potent space. This is simultaneously a way of taking hold of the person and making her into a different person: a productive versus a destructive person; an arduous and laborious person; a person aware and conscious of, and perceptive about, the future of the community and her family. Pentecostal witchcraft in this case is a new regime of witchcraft that overturns the social life of the Trobriands as we know it as a classic case in anthropology. We will let that serve here as a concluding example of the world-breaking and world-making capacities of the regime of Pentecostalism in the African and Melanesian cases outlined below.

Notes

1. The epigraph to this chapter is drawn from (Arnold 1997, p. 13).
2. This attack had similarities to a "*chute na santa*" (kicking the saint) episode that had taken place in Brazil in the 1990s, in which a Pentecostal preacher destroyed a Catholic statue on a live television broadcast (Giumbelli 2003).
3. See Eriksen and Andrew (2010) on Port Vila, and Maggio (2013) on Honiara.

References

Akyeampong, Emmanuel. 2000. Africans in the Diaspora: The Diaspora and Africa. *African Affairs* 99 (395): 183–215.

Arnold, Clinton E. 1997. *Three Crucial Questions About Spiritual Warfare*. Grand Rapids, MI: Baker Publishing Group.

Ashforth, Adam. 2005. *Witchcraft, Violence and Democracy in South Africa*. Chicago: University of Chicago Press.

Badstuebner, Jennifer. 2003. "Drinking the hot blood of humans: Witchcraft confessions in a South African Pentecostal Church". *Anthropology and Humanism* 28 (1): 8–22.

Barker, J. 1990. "Encounters with evil: Christianity and the response to sorcery among the Maisin of Papua New Guinea." *Oceania* 61 (2): 139–155.

———. 2000. "Africa in the World: A History of extraversion." *African Affairs* 99: 217–267.

Beam, Joe. 1998. *Seeing the Unseen: A Handbook for Spiritual Warfare*. New York: Howard Publishers.

Brodwin, Paul. 2003. "Pentecostalism in translation: Religion and the production of community in the Haitian Diaspora." *American Ethnologist* 30 (1): 85–101.

Coleman, Simon. 2006. "Studying 'global' pentecostalism: Tensions, representations and opportunities." *PentecoStudies* 5 (1): 1–17.

Comaroff, Jean, and John, Comaroff. 1999. "Occult Economies and the Violence of Abstraction: Notes from the South African Postcolony". *American Ethnologist* 26 (2): 279–303.

Dalton, Doug. 2007."When is It moral to be a sorcerer?" In *The Anthropology of Morality in Melanesia and Beyond*, ed. J. Barker, 39–59. London: Ashgate.

Englund, Harri. 2003. "Christian independency and global membership: Pentecostal extraversions in malawi." *Journal of Religion in Africa* 33 (1): 83–111.

Englund, Harri, and James Leach. 2000. "Ethnography and the meta-narratives of modernity." *Current Anthropology* 41 (2): 225–239.

Eriksen, Annelin. 2009a."Healing the nation: In search of unity through the Holy Spirit in Vanuatu."*Social Analysis* 53: 67–81.

———. 2009b."'New life': Pentecostalism as social critique in Vanuatu."*Ethnos* 74 (2): 175–198.

Eriksen, A., M. MacCarthy and R. Blanes. n.d. *Going to Pentecost.* Forthcoming jointly authored monograph.

Eriksen, Annelin and Rose Andrew. 2010. "Churches in Port Vila." Report to the Vanuatu Cultural Centre. Accessible online at: http://www.google.no/url?sa=t&rct=j&q=&esrc=s&frm=1&source=web&cd=1&ved=0ahUKEwjJm9mC_JnKAhVKknIKHSx_AUoQFggbMAA&url=http%3A%2F%2Fgenpent.b.uib.no%2Ffiles%2F2012%2F11%2FMaggio-2013-Pentecostal-Churches-in-Honiara.pdf&usg=AFQjCNE5aPmyUFkqPn_qALZXJONQWX-t-Q.

Eves, Richard. 2000. "Sorcery's the curse: Modernity, envy and the flow of sociality in a Melanesian society."*Journal of the Royal Anthropological Institute (New Series)* 6: 453–468.

———. 2010. "In God's hands: Pentecostal Christianity, morality, and illness in a Melanesian society."*Journal of the Royal Anthropological Institute (New Series)* 16: 496–514.

Eves, Richard, Nicole Haley, R. J. May, John Cox, Philip Gibbs, Francesca Merlan et al. 2014. *Purging Parliament: A new Christian Politics in Papua New Guinea? SSGM* (Discussion Paper 2014/1). Canberra: State, Society and Governance in Melanesia Program, Australian National University. Accessible online at: http://ips.cap.anu.edu.au/sites/default/files/SSGM-DP-2014-1-Eves-et-al-ONLINE.pdf.

Ferguson, James. 1999. "Global disconnect: Abjection and the aftermath of modernism." In *Expectations of Modernity: Myths and Meanings of Urban Life on the Zambian Copperbelt*, ed. James Ferguson, 234–254. Berkeley: University of California Press.

Forsyth, Miranda, and Richard Eves. 2015. *Talking It Through: Responses to Sorcery and Witchcraft Beliefs and Practices in Melanesia.* Canberra: Australian National University Press.

Geschiere, P. 1997. *The Modernity of Witchcraft: Politics and the Occult in Postcolonial Africa.* Charlottesville: University of Virginia Press.

Geschiere, P. 2013. *Witchcraft, Intimacy and Trust: Africa in Comparison.* Chicago: Chicago University Press.

Gibbs, Phillip. 2012."Engendered violence and witch-killing in Simbu." In *Engendering Violence in Papua New Guinea*, ed. M. Jolly, C. Stewart, and C. Brewer, 107–135. Canberra: ANU E Press.

Giumbelli, Emerson. 2003. "O 'chute na santa': Blasfêmia e pluralismo religioso no Brasil". In *Religião e Espaço Público,* ed. Birman, Patrícia, 169–199. São Paulo: Attar editorial.

Haley, Nicole. 2010."Witchcraft, torture and HIV." In *Civic Insecurity: Law, Order and HIV in Papua New Guinea*, ed. V. Luker, and S. Dinnen, 219–235. Canberra: ANU E Press.

Harris, Hermione. 2006. *Yoruba in Diaspora: An African Church in London.* New York: Palgrave Macmillan.

Haynes, Naomi. 2012."Pentecostalism and the morality of money: Prosperity, inequality, and religious sociality on the Zambian Copperbelt."*Journal of the Royal Anthropological Institute* 18 (1): 124–139.

Hackman, Melissa. 2015. "A sinful landscape: Moral and sexual geographies in cape town, South Africa."*Social Analysis* 59 (3): 105–125.

Jacobs, Donald R. 2012. "Out of Africa: Evangelism and spiritual warfare", ed. C. P. Wagner. 279–289.

Jorgensen, Dan. 2005. "Third wave evangelism and the politics of the global in Papua New Guinea: Spiritual warfare and the recreation of place in Telefolmin." *Oceania* 75 (4): 444–461.

———. 2014. "Preying on those close to home." *Australian Journal of Anthropology* 25: 267–286.

Kelly, Raymond. 1993. *Constructing Inequality: The Fabrication of a Hierarchy of Virtue Among the Etoro.* Ann Arbor: University of Michigan Press.

Knauft, Bruce M. 1985. *Good Company and Violence: Sorcery and Social Action in a Lowland New Guinea Society.* Berkeley: University of California Press.

Krause, Kristine. 2008. "Transnational therapy networks among Ghanaians in London." *Journal of Ethnic and Migration Studies* 34 (2): 235–251.

Lambek, Michael, and Andrew Strathern (eds.). 1998. *Bodies and Persons: Comparative Perspectives from Africa and Melanesia.* Cambridge: Cambridge University Press.

Lattas, Andrew. 1993. "Sorcery and colonialism: Illness, dreams and death as political languages in West New Britain." *Man* 28: 51–77.

Lattas, Andrew, and Knut Rio. 2011. (eds.). The Arts of Government: Crime, Christianity and Policing in Melanesia. *Oceania* 81 (1): 1–109.

Lindenbaum, Shirley. 1981. "Images of the sorcerer in Papua New Guinea." *Social Analysis* 8: 119–128.

Lipuma, Edward. 1998. "Modernity and forms of personhood in Melanesia." In *Bodies and Persons,* ed. A. Strathern, and M. Lambek, 53–80. Cambridge: Cambridge University Press.

Louwerse, John. 2012. "Power evangelism in pioneer Mission", ed. C. P. Wagner. 259–273.

MacCarthy, Michelle. n.d. "Doing away with *Doba*? Women's Wealth and Shifting Values in Trobriand Mortuary Distributions". Paper currently under peer review.

Macdonald, Fraser. 2015. "Lucifer is behind me: The diabolisation of Oksapmin witchcraft as negative cosmological integration." *Asia Pacific Journal of Anthropology* 16 (5): 464–480.

Maggio, Rodolfo. 2013. Pentecostal Churches in Honiara. http://www.google.no/url?sa=t&rct=j&q=&esrc=s&frm=1&source=web&cd=1&ved=0ahUKEwjJm9mC_JnKAhVKknIKHSx_AUoQFggbMAA&url=http%3A%2F%2Fgenpent.b.uib.no%2Ffiles%2F2012%2F11%2FMaggio-2013-Pentecostal-Churches-in-Honiara.pdf&usg=AFQjCNE5aPmyUFkqPn_qALZXJON-QWX-t-Q.

Malinowski, Bronislav. 1926. *Crime and Custom in Savage Society*. London: Kegan Paul.

Marshall, Ruth. 2009. *Political Spiritualities: The Pentecostal Revolution in Nigeria*. Chicago: University of Chicago Press.

———. 2014. "Christianity, anthropology, politics." *Current Anthropology* 55 (10): 344–356.

Marwick, Max. 1970. "Witchcraft as Social Strain-Gauge". In *Witchcraft and Sorcery*, ed. Marwick, 280– 296. London: Penguin Books.

Maskens, Maïté. 2013. *Cheminer avec Dieu: Pentecôtismes et migrations à Bruxelles*. Brussels: Éditions de l'Université de Bruxelles.

Mbembe, Achille. 2001. *On the Postcolony*. Berkeley: University of California Press.

Meyer, Birgit. 1998. The Power of money: Politics, occult forces and Pentecostalism in Ghana. *African Studies Review* 41 (3): 15–37.

———. 1999. *Translating the Devil: Religion and Modernity Among the Ewe in Ghana*. Edinburgh: Edinburgh University Press for the International African Institute.

Murphy, (ed.). 2003. *The Handbook of Spiritual Warfare*. Nashville: Thomas Nelson.

———. 2012. "We are At War." In *Supernatural Forces in Spiritual Warfare: Wrestling with Dark Angels*, ed. C.P. Wagner, 53–75. Shippensburg: Destiny Image Publishers.

Myhre, Knut C. 2013. Introduction Cutting and Connecting: 'Afrinesian' Perspectives on Networks, Relationality and Exchange. *Social Analysis* 57 (3): 1–24.

Newell, Sasha. 2007. "Pentecostal witchcraft: Neoliberal possession and demonic discourse in Ivoirian Pentecostal Churches." *Journal of Religion in Africa* 37 (4): 461–490.

Newland, Lynda. 2004. "Turning the Spirits into Witchcraft: Pentecostalism in Fijian Villages". *Oceania* 75 (1): 1–18.

O'Neill, Kevin L. 2010. *City of God: Christian Citizenship in Postwar Guatemala*. Berkeley: University of California Press.

Parish, Jane. 2003. "Anti-witchcraft shrines among the Akan: Possession and the gathering of knowledge." *African Studies Review* 46 (3): 17–34.

Pennoyer, F. D. 2012. "In Dark Dungeons of Collective Captivity", ed. Wagner. 229–249.

Rio, Knut. 2011. "Policing the holy nation: The state and righteous violence in Vanuatu." *Oceania* 81 (1): 51–72.

———. 2014. "A Shared Intentional Space of Witch-Hunt and Sacrifice". *Ethnos* 79 (3): 320–341.

Robbins, Joel. 2004. *Becoming sinners: Christianity and moral torment in a Papua New Guinea society*. Berkeley: University of California Press.

———. 2007. "Morality, politics and the Melanesian big Man." In *The Anthropology of Morality in Melanesia and Beyond*, ed. J. Barker, 25–39. London: Ashgate.

———. 2009. "Pentecostal networks and the spirit of globalization: On the social productivity of ritual forms." *Social Analysis* 53 (1): 55–66.

———. 2012. "On Enchanting Science and Disenchanting Nature: Spiritual Warfare in North America and Papua New Guinea." In Nature, Science, and Religion: Intersections Shaping Society and the Environment, ed. Catherine M. Tucker, 45–64. Santa Fe, NM: School for Advanced Research Press.

Roitman, Janet. 2005. *Fiscal Disobedience: An Anthropology of Economic Regulation*. Princeton: Princeton University Press.

Silverman, Eric K. 2015. "Commentary: Modernism, Jews, and Frazier." *Oceania* 85 (3): 359–375.

Smith, D.J. 2001. "The arrow of god: Pentecostalism, inequality, and the supernatural in Southeastern Nigeria." *Africa* 71 (4): 587–613.

Stephen, Michele (ed.). 1987. *Sorcerer and Witch in Melanesia*. Melbourne: Melbourne University Press.

———. 1996. "The Mekeo 'man of sorrow': Sorcery and the Individuation of the Self." *American Ethnologist* 23 (1): 83–101.

Strathern, Marilyn. 1991. *Partial Connections*. Savage, MD: Rowman and Littlefield.

———. 1991b. "One man and many men." In *Big Men and Great Men*, ed. M. Godelier, and M. Strathern, 197–214. Cambridge: Cambridge University Press.

Turner, Victor. 1964. "Witchcraft and sorcery: Taxonomy versus dynamics." *Africa* 34: 314–325.

Trnka, Susanna. 2011. "Re-mythologizing the state: public security, 'the Jesus strategy', and the Fiji police." *Oceania* 81 (1): 72–88.

Van Dijk, Rijk. 2001. "Witchcraft and skepticism by proxy." In *Magical Interpretations, Material Realities*, ed. H.L. Moore, and T. Sanders, 97–118. London: Routledge.

———. 2004. "Negotiating marriage: Questions of morality and legitimacy in the ghanaian Pentecostal diaspora." *Journal of Religion in Africa* 34 (4): 438–467.

———. 1997. "From camp to encompassment: Discourses of transsubjectivity in the Ghanaian Pentecostal diaspora." *Journal of Religion in Africa* 27 (2): 139–159.

Viveiros de Castro, Eduardo. 2004. "Perspectival anthropology and the method of controlled equivocation." *Tipiti* 2 (1): 2–20.

Wagner, C.P. (ed.). 2012. *Supernatural Forces in Spiritual Warfare: Wrestling with Dark Angels*. Shippensburg: Destiny Image Publishers.

Weiss, Brad. 2009. *Street Dreams and Hiphop Barbershops: Global Fantasy and Popular Practice in Urban Tanzania*. Bloomington: Indiana University Press.

West, Harry. 2005. *Kupilikula: Governance and the Invisible Realm in Mozambique*. Chicago: Chicago University Press.

Zelenietz, Marty, and Shirley Lindebaum, (ed.). 1981. *Sorcery and Social Change in Melanesia. Social Analysis* 8: 1–136.

Zurenuoc, Theodore. 2013. "Building the foundation and directing the future of Papua New Guinea," *Post-Courier* newspaper 17th December, 2013. Reprinted online at: http://www.pngblogs.com/2013/12/building-foundation-and-directing.html.

Authors' Biography

Knut Rio is Professor of Social Anthropology at the University of Bergen, Norway, and is responsible for the ethnographic collections at the Bergen University Museum. He has worked on Melanesian ethnography since 1995, with fieldwork in Vanuatu. His work on social ontology, production, ceremonial exchange, witchcraft and art in Vanuatu has resulted in journal publications and the monograph *The Power of Perspective: Social Ontology and Agency on Ambrym Island, Vanuatu* (2007). He has also co-edited *Hierarchy. Persistence and Transformation in Social formations* (with Olaf Smedal, 2009), *Made in Oceania. Social Movements, Cultural Heritage and the State in the Pacific* (with Edvard Hviding, 2011), and *The Arts of Government: Crime, Christianity and Policing in Melanesia* (with Andrew Lattas, 2011).

Michelle MacCarthy is an Assistant Professor in the Department of Anthropology at Saint Mary's University in Halifax, Canada. She was previously a Postdoctoral Fellow in the Department of Social Anthropology at the University of Bergen (where she undertook the research and writing of the chapter in this book), and where she was a contributor to Annelin Eriksen's

Norwegian Research Council–funded project on gender and Pentecostalism in Africa and Melanesia. She completed her PhD at the University of Auckland in 2012. Her monograph, entitled Making the Modern Primitive: Cultural Tourism in the Trobriand Islands (2016), examines tropes of primitivity and authenticity and mechanisms of cultural commoditization. She recently co-edited (with Annelin Eriksen) a special issue of The Australian Journal of Anthropology on Gender and Pentecostalism in Melanesia (August 2016).

Ruy Blanes is a Ramon y Cajal Fellow at the Spanish Research Council (CSiC). Previously he has been a researcher at the universities of Bergen (Norway) and Lisbon (Portugal), as well as visiting fellow at the University of Leiden (Netherlands) and the London School of Economics and Political Science. He has worked on the anthropology of religion, identity, politics, mobility and temporality. His current research site is Angola, where he explores the topics of religion, mobility (diasporas, transnationalism, the Atlantic), politics (leadership, charisma, repression, resistance), temporalities (historicity, memory, heritage, expectations) and knowledge. He has published articles in several international journals and edited volumes on the corporeality in religious contexts (Berghahn, 2011, with Anna Fedele) on spirits and the agency of intangibles (Univ. Chicago Press, with Diana Espírito Santo), and on 'Prophetic Trajectories' (Berghahn). He is also board member the APA (Portuguese Anthropological Association) and co-Editor of the journal *Advances in Research: Religion and Society,* edited by Berghahn.

CHAPTER 2

German Pentecostal Witches and Communists: The Violence of Purity and Sameness

Bjørn Enge Bertelsen

Introduction

"They have been sent to kill and eat us!" my long-time interlocutor 'José' said. "What do you mean 'they have been sent?'", I asked, somewhat bewildered.[1] This was 2008 and we were discussing the recent problem of lions in the area that had, allegedly, preyed on and eaten a number of people around Chimoio, Manica Province, Mozambique. "The Germans! They have created and sent these lions to kill and eat us! Don't you remember the case of the eucalyptus plantation? They have done this before!". José was referring to a long-term preoccupation with Pentecostal pastors from Germany—as well as the presence in the past of left-wing, communist activists from *Humana from People to People*—an organization involved in development projects, also identified as German. Both these types of 'Germans'—whom I will call here

B.E. Bertelsen (✉)
University of Bergen, Bergen, Norway

K. Rio et al. (eds.), *Pentecostalism and Witchcraft*, Contemporary Anthropology of Religion, DOI 10.1007/978-3-319-56068-7_2

Pentecostal Germans and Humana Germans—are widely believed to be witches with fully developed lycanthropy. Both groups of Germans are said to violently express the urge to kill and harm, as well as demonstrating a cannibal hunger for human flesh and the life-energy of others.[2]

This chapter examines these connections, which were made repeatedly over a number of years by my interlocutors. Two claims are made here: first, that the phantasmagoric characteristics that condense around utopian and radical endeavors—such as Pentecostalism and communism—foment an idea of having already transgressed the everyday and visible worlds. That is, the radically different horizons offered by Pentecostal and Humana German witches revealed their intimate knowledge of forces of cosmological re-formulation and bodily, spiritual and societal transformation—in visions of the coming of Christ, or in the ideals of a future communist community. Moreover, for my interlocutors, it gradually became clear that the knowledge of bodily, spiritual and societal transformation that was possessed by Pentecostal and Humana Germans, also implied that they were well versed in practices of predation and, hence, violence and destruction. As will be explored below, the two groups of Germans believed to have been witches matched a contemporary version of cannibalistic and destructive inclinations associated exclusively with sorcery and witchcraft or *uroi* (see also Bertelsen 2009b, 2014, 2016a).

Second, both Pentecostal and Humana Germans proselytized with vigor, militancy and messianic drive these ideals of sameness, equality and communion, which created tensions among members of the community. These tensions were not simply tied to the future-oriented, benign (but differing) worlds offered by both groups—although these visions resonated locally with historical experiments with populist, messianic Afro-socialism following independence (in 1975) from Portuguese colonialism (Isaacman 1978; Sachs and Welch 1990), as well as with a long history of Christian charismatic churches and cults in the region (Bourdillon 1977; Maxwell 2006; Schoffeleers 1992; Sundkler 1964 [1948]). Rather, such tensions also strongly reflected racial, bureaucratic, pecuniary and ecclesiastical hierarchies that remained painfully present and which were unsuccessfully encompassed by the values of egalitarianism, equality, unity and various prosperous futurities. This context engendered a powerful notion of an 'other same', such as a witch—in this case, one with a cannibalistic inclination.

Witchcraft in Postcolonial Mozambique

A former Portuguese colony, Mozambique gained independence in 1975 following a long and bloody war of liberation that itself ended a violent and brutal colonial order (Newitt 1995). Following independence, the liberation movement Frelimo (*Frente de Libertação de Moçambique*) embarked on a socialist path of development, attempting to revolutionize the justice and production sectors and the domain of government, which drew on its own particular rendition of Afro-Marxism (Saul 1985). These experiments in socialism were not fully realized, however, as a civil war ensued from 1976 to 1992. Frelimo, by then in government, was pitted against Renamo (*Resistência Nacional Moçambicana*), a guerrilla group funded largely by racist Rhodesia, Apartheid South Africa and the West, but which enjoyed widespread popular peasant support (Geffray 1990). The civil war was characterized by extreme violence, mass kidnapping and forced labor (Bertelsen 2016a).

The civil war ended in 1992, and the post-war period has been characterized by multiple interventions by numerous international development organizations, which have effectively created a constant 'state of structural adjustment' (Obarrio 2014). Propelled by Mozambique's rapid economic growth (Castel-Branco 2014), the post-war era has also seen new forms of socio-economic stratification with an increasing gap between poor and wealthy citizens (Mozambique News reports and clippings 2016). Although predominantly a period of peace, the post-1992 era has nevertheless been characterized by endemic political tension between the government and Renamo. The last decades have also seen spates of lynchings in rural and urban areas, repeated instances of violence by police agents, recurring urban uprisings, and a widespread and growing mistrust of the state and its forces, as these are seen to protect corrupt and greedy networks of politicians and businessmen (Bertelsen 2009a, b, 2010, 2011, 2016a, b).

Crucially, these *longue durée* trajectories of predation, wealth accumulation and violence have unfolded alongside perceptions of witchcraft and sorcery. Here, with reference to a case study, I will present some general characteristics. In Honde, a rural to peri-urban locale close to Chimoio in central Mozambqiue, where I have been undertaking fieldwork since 1999, a senior man whom I will call 'Rui' is widely considered to be a witch (*muroi*) engaging in *uroi*—a term encompassing domains of both sorcery and witchcraft, as these are commonly distinguished in anthropology (see Evans-Pritchard 1976 [1937]). A married man in his sixties, with seven children, Rui is a comparatively successful peasant in terms of generating a small income from the sale of agricultural produce (especially tomatoes) at the markets in Chimoio. The suspicion of him being a *muroi* has been conveyed to me directly and indirectly on numerous occasions by neighbours, kin and even members of his own household. A specific event in around 2000 decided people on the issue, and was recounted repeatedly. Meat was found hanging from the roof beam of his house—and the meat was believed to be of human origin and a result of his nocturnal, predatory forays. Thus, Rui is widely recognized to have as his vice (*vicio*) the consumption of human meat, which is also indicated by him attending funerals to satisfy his *kurha nhama io munho*—his lust for human flesh.[3]

Rui was also believed to have undertaken other dark forms of *uroi*. Specifically, he was said to have engaged the forces of the lion (a potent animal) in the form of a *mhondoro*—a spirit lion.[4] These abilities were appropriated with the help of a *n'anga* (a traditional healer) in a ritual during which Rui consumed a piece of lion hide. His eating of the skin generates an authority in his body that is physically experienced as a sense of fear in his presence—akin to what people would experience when confronted by a lion or a *mhondoro*.[5]

In conversation, some confirmed that he showed other signs of being a *muroi*: significantly, he often eats alone. This description is an important constituent of what might be termed a speech genre (Bakhtin 1986) of *uroi*: a constantly evolving, dynamic and embracive body of expressions and notions, this speech genre includes a number of partly covert ways to allude to someone being a *muroi*—especially as it evidences greed and anti-social behaviour in the presence of (non-*muroi*) kin and family (see also Huhn 2016; West 2007).[6]

Beyond eating alone, a more visible, tangible and distinguishing characteristic is the rich yield from Rui's *machamba* (rain-fed garden) and *matoro* (irrigated garden). This produce provides him with a comparatively high income from cash crops such as tomatoes (*matemate*). As widely documented in other contexts in Southern Africa, a conspicuously successful crop yield is frequently related to engaging in forms of magic or other illicit behaviour. As Gluckman (1963 [1956]: 96) noted half a century ago, "exceptional achievement is bought at the cost of one's fellows. The man who is too successful is suspected of being a witch and himself is suspicious of the witchcraft of his envious fellows."[7] In the speech genre of *uroi* in Honde (as well as in Chimoio), several methods are envisaged by which crop yields may be increased. One powerful measure is the covert drugging of others in order to force them to undertake labour on a *machamba* during the night in a practice called *kurima no zwiphoko*. Another measure uses powerful *mutombo* (medicine or drugs) to make maize, water–melon, sweet potatoes, beans or other crops increase in size, grow more quickly, evade the gaze of thieves, and avoid pests.[8]

Clearly, then, what informs the notion of *uroi* are *both* the classical aspects of witchcraft—an internalized craving that may be inherited and sometimes unconsciously enacted—*and* sorcery—that is, conscious actions undertaken to become empowered through, for instance, eating lion skin. The composite figure of *uroi*, melding together these classical conceptions of witchcraft and sorcery, thereby reflects broader Southern African trends, as well as historical developments internal to what I have elsewhere called 'the traditional field' (Bertelsen 2016a). However, *uroi* has also been pentecostalized during recent decades, particularly through a re-definition of *uroi* as the work of Satan, who is supported by local spirits enlisted as the Devil's lesser demons. Reflecting a global Pentecostal translation of sorcery into demonology (see Chap. 1), the increasing satanification of cosmologies of protection (in the shape of ancestral and other spirits) and predation (zombification and other forms of *uroi*) has meant that Pentecostal pastors and so-called *profete* (who heal through the use of the Holy Spirit), increasingly shape the phantasmagoric spaces of sociality and cosmology (Van de Kamp 2016; Pfeiffer 2005).[9]

For Rui, this has also meant that his *uroi* is seen to epitomize Satanic evil—especially among his Pentecostal co-villagers. Nominally a Catholic himself, Rui views Pentecostal churches with suspicion, believing them to be money-making devices for pastors, which is a common accusation across Africa (see Haynes 2012; Meyer 2002, 2007). In this case, matters escalated and came to a head at an event in 2005. Commanding respect and authority in Honde, despite being viewed as a *muroi*, Rui organized some co-villagers to meet a local Pentecostal pastor and his aides down by the river—feigning to want to join the church. After the meeting, Rui organized his fellow villagers to beat the pastor with sticks, accusing him of being a thief and stealing people's money. Following this event, Rui was perceived even more strongly to be under the spell of Satanic evil—an accusation supported by accounts of also other acts evidencing *uroi*. In summary, and as indicated by what Rui is believed to have been involved in, *uroi* as a phantasmagoric space has been expanded by the impact of Pentecostalism during recent decades—both in Chimoio and Honde, and elsewhere in Mozambique.

Hunting and Eating Children—the *Uroi* of Churches and Camps

In Mozambique's post-war market-oriented context, sorcerous methods of acquiring saleable goods are believed to be common, as in Rui's case. Moreover, post-war Mozambique was inundated with ambitious development schemes, organizations and churches. In one sense these influxes were not new: Manica province has witnessed extensive trade and missionary presence since at least the 1500s. The area has also suffered a number of violent and extractive political, military, economic and administrative regimes, involving European, Arabic and other non-Mozambican agents (Allina 2012; Bhila 1982). However, from the 1990s onwards these factors have multiplied and intensified nationally (Obarrio 2014), and the situation in Honde is no exception. Here, development work and missionary activity—including various forms of Pentecostalism—operate alongside one another. Crucially, in the early to mid-1990s a eucalyptus project was initiated to provide Honde inhabitants with a source of revenue through the sale of timber for house construction and wood for cooking stoves. The project was initiated by Humana People to People, a radical Left-leaning organization, often accused of having a cult-like nature. They appropriated a large and attractive area of land between Honde and Chimoio, supported by the local municipality.[10]

From the outset, however, the plantation proved problematic—not least because the area had an important local history prior to the development project. Holding traditional graveyards as well as sites of massacres that had taken place during the civil war, local people were critical of it becoming part of a silviculture project. Contrary to how many other foreign development agents behaved—aloof and mostly passing through by car—my Honde interlocutors repeatedly described how the blond tall 'Germans' (*alemãoes*) insisted on being in close proximity to local people; in fact, they lived at the local school.[11] Probably wishing to establish collective, local 'ownership' of the now transformed land, the Humana

Germans organized night-long vigils at which the eucalyptus project was discussed and contextualized within a global political context (see also Walker 2012). At these events, food was always served and the Humana Germans ate similar foodstuffs to people in Honde and emphasized the importance of shared, communal meals. They tended to profess with some intensity the ideals of equality, solidarity and a common humanity (see also Huhn 2016).

At around the same time, a Pentecostal church, known as *Igreja da Nova Vida* (Church of the New Life) or, simply, *Nova Vida* (New Life), was established close to the camp of the Humana Germans, as well as to the eucalyptus plantation. According to my Honde interlocutors, this church was also directly involved in and supportive of the eucalyptus project. Often visited by blonde 'Germans', according to my interlocutors, the church recruited aggressively and drew local people into their compound for sermons, for construction work building walls around the church and for growing vegetables, which they sold at the markets—an attractive feature for cash-strapped local people. The Pentecostal Germans held their main activities during all-night sermons and prayers: they addressed redemption, viciously attacked the widespread work of Satan, exorcized evil spirits from attendees and professed the communion of the church belonging and, mirroring the Humana Germans, the radical equality of humans (see also Englund 2003).

From the numerous accounts I gathered in Chimoio and Honde from 2000 until 2016, both the Humana Germans and the Pentecostal Germans were active in attempting to reshape the local sociocultural order and its cosmological horizons: through prayer sessions at the church or night vigils in the camp, the sinful paths and traits of the peasant majority were addressed, including jealousy, laziness, selfishness, individualism, greed and cruelty. Recounting these attacks on people's behavior during prayers and vigils, an elderly man, 'Rogério,' explained in a conversation with me in 2010:

> *Eh pah*! These Germans were heavy (*pesados*)! There was no playing around – they wanted everything we did to finish. Whether you went to the camp or the church ... it was the same: 'You have to change! We are all together! Honde must be a place for all working together, as one'. They were strong, strong, strong. All was working well for them, for us. We were together.

Thus, despite initial resentment, the eucalyptus plantation grew and the Humana Germans' camp gradually turned into permanent housing. Similarly, the church's presence consolidated and expanded with the affluence of its pastors; this influence materialized in terms of money, as well as in such items as cars owned by the church. As reflected in Rogério's statements, both the camp and the church seemed successful in drawing together many people from Honde and beyond into their domain.

However, in 1995, according to interlocutors, a dramatic event occurred. In a concerted attack at dusk, Germans from both camp and church drove around in cars and '*fizeram merda*' ('did shit'), as some phrased it. Specifically, the Humana and Pentecostal Germans attacked the area around Honde by driving vehicles to which they had attached sharp bamboo poles. They drove the cars on paths and dirt roads, purposefully aiming at children and throwing their victimg into the cars after they had been hit. Ending the attacks abruptly, after returning to their camp and to the walled church, they proceeded to prepare, cook and eat these children. Interlocutors readily shared details from the assault and I was shown by several men the exact locations in which the incidents had occurred. I interviewed a young man (in 2008) who had barely survived the raid and had done so by hiding in the forest. I also spoke to an elderly lady who had lost a son in the 'German witch' attack. Several people claimed that a child's remains were found outside the church. Running through the narrations were descriptions of the Germans as *muroi*, who during these events had grossly exaggerated features: sharp nails, shrill voices, long teeth and excessive amounts of body hair. Together with the nature of the raid, these grotesque features were said to have revealed them to be *muroi*.

In shock following these events, the Honde villagers began to imagine sorcerous activities going on within the church walls—or in the houses of the Humana camp. Rumours spread that there had been further attempts to kidnap children, which informed local suggestions that *uroi* and cannibalism were continuing. This imagery was sustained by Honde residents selling the Germans snakes, chameleons and cats at exorbitant prices. Allegedly preparing these typical sorcerous forms of meats in a stew, the Humana Germans attempted to coerce local people into sharing these meals with them—most rejected it or ran away. The prayers and night vigils at both church and camp, however, still attracted people from Honde: they concentrated, as before, on messages of conversion to create new realities for a Pentecostal—or communist—future.

However, towards the end of the 1990s, the church was suddenly abandoned, the Humana Germans left and the eucalyptus development project failed. Some, in interviews in 2016, gave accounts of a final five children who were lured into cars before the 'Germans' took off, never to return. This might have been the end of the German witches in Honde—but it was not.

German Witches as a Recurring Destructive Force

In May 2008, a *mhondoro dwozutumua*, a form of a lion that devours and destroys, ravaged a community that neighbours Honde, attacking three women who were walking along a path during the day. The animal or animals—people disagreed about whether it was a group or a single animal—killed the women, biting off their heads and dragging their bodies into the forest (*mato*) to devour them. In what ensued, after the details had been established locally,[12] popular speculation revolved around the past and present contested political and social issues, seeking to locate an originary cause. A typical conversation ran something like the following, which I had with a young man, 'Romeo'. As with many others, Romeo was certain about the non-local origins of the lions:

R: The lions were sent. That is what they say.

B: Who sent them?

R: They were sent by a country. They say it is Germany. The lions are here to create confusion (*confusão*).

B: Why Germany?

R: To kill and create trouble. Don't you remember the case of eucalyptus trees and the way the Germans hunted our children? It is the same thing. They send bandits and they send lions and leopards.

B: But are the lions made [i.e. man-made]?

R: They say they were raised in a park or perhaps outside the country. And there they were left with nothing to eat for two days. Then they were dropped off close to Gondola [a town near Chimoio].

B: Is it not possible to make a ceremony or protect oneself against these?

R: Elder brother (*Mano*) Bjorn, if it had been a natural lion (*leão natural*), then you could perform a ceremony to protect. But with this type that is made, you cannot. This type is called *mhondoro dwozutumua*. It is made to bite, to kill, this one. The traditional type of ***mhondoro dwozutumua*** is to guard and roar only, not bite and maim like this. This type we have here is not new, but it is different from the traditional lion. This one is very bad for the gardens (*machambas*) here. No-one wants to go. And the community police will not go either.

B: Why do you not arm yourselves?

R: Yes! But the government cannot do it—they have no power. You need special arms to do it. Renamo say that if it had been them in power, this could not have been possible. Renamo is more traditional. They could end this problem. But Frelimo are related to the bandits and only want to fill their bellies.

There is a clear preoccupation here with relations between aid and transgression.[13] In these popular conceptions, 'Germany' and 'Germans' are central to key accounts of the abduction, killing and consumption of children in Honde and beyond. 'Germany' and 'Germans' denote complex practices of a predatory consumption of human flesh, which enables the perpetrators to acquire the life force and to 'appropriate the energy' (Colson 2000: 340; see also Huhn 2016) of others through sorcerous transgression. Further, Germany and Germans were evoked later the same year when a particularly brutal and violent wave of robberies and break-ins terrorized poor areas around Chimoio. Catching some of the alleged thieves and lynching them, people generally agreed that they had been sent by Germany to create problems—equating thieves with witches, as is common in, for instance, Mozambique (Bertelsen 2009a; Jacobs and Schuetze 2011), South Africa (Niehaus 2001; Pelgrim 2003) and in Africa more generally.

Cannibalism, Christianity and Colonialism: Partial Connections

How are we to understand these beliefs in long-term and recurring cannibalistic and predatory behaviors emanating from this composite German witchcraft complex? A common means of unraveling cases of foreign and/or white alleged cannibalistic behavior in African contexts is to re-contextualize it within the impact of Christianity more broadly. For one, Heike Behrend (2011) demonstrates a number of historical and sociocultural dynamics underpinning witch-hunts undertaken by charismatic offshoots of the Catholic Church in Uganda. Behrend shows that the teaching of the Eucharist in the Tooro Kingdom in Western Uganda, and in particular the central image of transcendentalism—eating the flesh and drinking the blood of Christ—was disseminated to those who had risen in the hierarchy of local converts. Thus, the Eucharist as a cannibalistic act being revealed only to a few meant that connections were made among cannibalism, Christianity and the arrival of Catholic missionaries in the area. However, other developments that cast into disarray basic life—death sequences were also underway in East Africa from the eighteenth century onwards—not least the arrival of doctors, medical missionaries, and skull, bone and trophy hunters. In the name of science and the advancement of humankind, the doctors and missionaries carried out painful and often lethal tests on more or less willing patients: they extracted body fluids and removed body parts. Over the same period, limbs, skulls and entire corpses were collected from battlefields, or exhumed, often nocturnally, from grave sites and missionary graveyards. This behavior was carried out in the name of 'collecting'. Behrend (2011: 186) explains,

> Explorers in Africa such as the German naturalist Georg Schweinfurth, for example, collected decapitated heads 'from the enemy' after a fierce fight and cooked them in a big pot to remove the flesh. He wrote, 'doing this business I thought of myself as the personified Nemesis' (543). Nemesis is the Greek goddess of retaliation and justice; thus Schweinfurth, by identifying with her, imagined himself doing justice by taking revenge on supposed cannibals in doing what he thought cannibals did; cook their enemies in big pots.

This crucial dimension of tapping into, extracting from, or reconfiguring African bodies—living and dead, parts and wholes—created a sinister yet nebulous mimesis between motley crews of Europeans (missionaries, doctors and body snatching explorers) and the complex local sociocultural order in which cannibalism, as integral to witchcraft, existed as a real possibility. Behrend (2011: 186) notes: "It is as if the African cannibal cooking his victim in a big pot is, above all, an inverted description of European practices in Africa, a mirroring of their own practices in the Other".

This confluence of presences—Christian and non-Christian—and how these reflected bodily and corporal dimensions, was identifiable across the Portuguese colonies, such as Mozambique: missionaries were concerned with resurrection, as they were throughout the empire. In addition, as Roque (2010) has shown, skull collection was integral to various aspects (missionary, military, medical and anthropological) of imperial expansion between 1870 and 1930. Crucially, he also suggests that ritual violence is regularly was undertaken by colonial forces and local aides, such as in Timor-Leste where "… decapitated heads could add to the vitality of colonial empires at the same time as indigenous headhunting intensified and prospered" (Roque 2010: 17). Further, in a study of race and the Portuguese empire, Matos (2013) explains that Portuguese physical/biological anthropologists were from the 1800s integral to colonial expansion and undertook several expeditions and missions to Mozambique where the collection of skulls was intended to underpin theories of racial superiority and, broadly, legitimize colonial rule and campaigns of pacification.

The German Witches: Utopian Horizons, Violent Egalitarianism and Predation

As Behrend has lucidly shown (2011), and as is evident across Lusophone colonial and postcolonial worlds, local understandings of 'the German witch' reflect colonial pan-African dimensions of cannibalism and Christianity. However, the main concern in what follows is to explore an important dimension that is often eclipsed in analyses such as Behrend's, namely, the similarities at various analytical levels between the Pentecostal Germans and the Humana Germans. This analysis extends Behrend's argument to encompass, first, movements that were not Christian; second, it underlines the utopian, egalitarian characteristics of both. The aim is to go some way towards explaining the consistency in histories of cannibal lusts, predatory hunts and kidnappings that over a period of several decades continued to inform fears of both communists and Christian charismatics in Honde.

My point of departure is that the egalitarian ethos of sameness and togetherness seems central to both Humana and Pentecostal Germans. This reflects what both Thomas Strong (Chap. 3) and Englund and Leach (2000) identify as hypermodern or fundamentalist modern notions of regeneration, renewal and severance (in relation to traditions and to ties to kin) of the Pentecostal modernist orientation (see also

Van de Kamp 2016), which are also evident in Humana speeches. Humana also relies on meta-narratives of a coming modernity—one that will eradicate both hierarchies of exploitation and capitalist usurpers of money and life. Significantly, however, this focus on the range of evils attacked by Pentecostal and Humana Germans has tended to propel them into the phantasmagoric space of *uroi*. The manner in which the Germans became entangled in notions of *uroi* they thought to be external and impervious to resembles a process minutely described by Rio and Eriksen (2013) in relation to early missionaries in Vanuatu. Here, the missionaries became encompassed by and integral to the very forces of evil and sorcery they sought to combat. In a similar fashion and through their ferocious attacks on various forms of evil, the Germans in Honde generated a powerful notion of the 'other same'—that is, of themselves as witches.

Of course, it is also possible to explore, as others have done, how the German presence as farmers in this region benefitted from the brutal Portuguese colonial regime of forced labor, which over time sedimented into an image of the Germans as bloodsuckers, metaphorically speaking—that is, as drawing the life force out of Africans. This kind of view has been maintained over the decades following independence, and exists now as a stereotypical image of exploitation that draws upon powerful conceptions of *uroi*. Given the centuries of colonial violence and extractive rule in the area—as shown, for instance, in Lubkemann (2008) and Allina (2012)—there is good reason to link present witchcraft accusations and experiences with the long shadow of a violent colonial past. Furthermore, African experiences of enslavement, as well as imagery around zombification, are often understood in terms of histories of capture, the slave trade and forced labour as, for instance, Nicolas Argenti (2007: 93–120) has argued in research on the Cameroonian Grasslands, or as Zimba et al. (2006) suggest is a general pattern in East African oral culture. Finally, of course, there is also a long history in Africa (and elsewhere) of seeing colonial officers and other white men in general as witches, sorcerers and cannibals as, for instance, Luise White (1997, 2000) has suggested.

Intriguingly, 'Germany' and 'Germans' carry a particular history in postcolonial Mozambique, because a number of children were sent to the German Democratic Republic (GDR) in the 1980s in the name of education and socialist solidarity (Slobodian 2015). When the children were separated from their families, schools and local communities, this often seems to have left the impression that they were being snatched away. When returning after the Cold War, often with a socialist stance, to a politically and economically transformed Mozambique, the young *magermane*—'ma' being a generic collective term and 'germane' denoting the country—are regarded as having become Other. They have their own language (German), which they speak when they meet each other, and they have become estranged, to many Mozambicans (Müller 2014).

Despite being regarded as 'Other', however, *magermane* are rarely accused of witchcraft; thus, the confluence of Pentecostal and Humana witches/cannibals must lead us to look elsewhere than to instances of past violence or to reverberations from GDR—Mozambique connections—moral accusations from the past propelled into and materializing in the present, as it were. As indicated above in the ethnographic material, there is a constancy over time in communists and Pentecostals coalescing into a witchcraft complex called Germany. This would suggest that we need to open up the analysis of Pentecostals, Communists and *uroi* to other forces that are perceived to operate in destructive and predatory ways.

As has already been established in general terms by Kapferer (2002), and in specific regions such as Melanesia (Rio 2010, 2014), witchcraft may be viewed as a phantasmagoric space with realm-opening capacities. From this perspective, witchcraft is analytically constituted as an intrinsic and generative part of reality that transforms, exacts and instantiates—not necessarily reflecting tangible historical or contemporary processes. A crucial component of this aspect of reality, in a Deleuzian sense (Deleuze and Guattari 2002 [1980]), is its frequently volatile and unpredictable nature: it transforms itself as an open possibility, breaking into and breaking open the mundane in often spectacular ways. This profoundly open nature of witchcraft as part of a cosmological horizon is simultaneously characterizing what one may call the domain of the 'traditional' or 'customary' in Honde and Chimoio. These domains are irreducible to stable sets of sociocultural values, institutions and practices onto which modernity is inscribed; they must be analyzed as continuously evolving domains in their own right (Englund and Leach 2000; see also Rio 2010).

Taking seriously this dynamic view of the open-endedness of traditional cosmology and the phantasmagoric space of witchcraft means that it might be extended to engulf and transform the fantastic nature of egalitarian possibilities and revolutionary futures that both Humana and Pentecostal witches preach. Moreover, the radical egalitarianism of Pentecostalism and communism—as they were conveyed in Honde—reflected a long trajectory in European pre- and post-Enlightenment thought: Cohn (2004 [1957]: 187ff) argues, for example, that Greek and Roman cosmologies fueled Christian millenarian politics and cast long shadows into the present. However, irrespective of their European roots, for people in Honde the phantasmagoric possibilities that condensed around their respective utopian and radical endeavors of Pentecostalism and communism necessarily translated as always already having transgressed the confines of the everyday worlds. Differently put, the radical horizons of orientation that were propagated directly by these German witches implied having dipped into forces of not only cosmological creation—in visions of the coming of Christ, or in communist ideals for the future; they also implied, for my interlocutors, that they were knowledgeable about practices of predation (see also West 2005 on witchcraft in Northern Mozambique). This dynamic bears some similarity to what Newell (2007) proposes, based on the research in Cote d'Ivoire: there, the Pentecostal church attacks on witchcraft, constituting its threat as real, meant that the church itself increasingly became encompassed by witchcraft themselves. In Honde, the phantasmagoric space of *uroi* was similarly appropriated by the Pentecostal Germans and, ultimately, they were consumed by it (see, again, Rio and Eriksen 2013 for a comparative case from Vanuatu).

The intensity of these religious and political encounters is significant, as Pentecostals and communists alike zealously professed equality and communion—facets that were advocated for and proselytized about—and which increasingly created tensions that fed the dynamic and volatile space of witchcraft. Despite the call to unity and equality, various forms of hierarchies—racial, bureaucratic, ecclesiastical, economic—were revealed, which gradually eclipsed the professed values of egalitarianism.

Accounts of the transformation of the Humana Germans in the camp and the Pentacostelists in the church into predatory beings still haunts the peri-urban landscapes of Chimoio and rural Honde in 2016. In January of that year, having first asked me (again) whether I was German, an elderly man who lived next to where this church had once stood (there seems to be a different church there now), reflected:

> These were times when the war had ended. Everything was moving [changing]. The eucalyptus [forest] started. The Germans came and told

> us we all needed to be together, to confront Satan, to fight him! We went there. It was good. We were one and the church was strong! But then they became different. And then came the attacks on our children. Eating our children! We were not the same. This created a lot of problems.

As also suggested in the Introduction to this volume, what we see here through the attacks is the emergence of the powerful and volatile notion of the 'other same' as a witch—in this case, a witch with a cannibalistic inclination. The man's realization that 'we were not the same' further reflects that the egalitarian ethos of forging a common humanity, supported by communion and collective vigils and prayers, was undercut by a notion of sorcerous predation. This is in keeping with Geschiere's (2013: 191) observation that the threat of witchcraft in an increasingly Pentecostalized version of it means that the domains of the intimate and the same comprise the space in which witchcraft makes itself present (see also Badstuebner 2003). Several additional aspects of the case from Honde underline such a reading.

First, both missionaries and communists accumulate bodies in the camp and in the church. This accumulation of bodies as a practice of corporeal power is inherently ambivalent, signifying authority, might and resources. Increasingly, however, it was being understood as predation—key aspects of which are a siphoning off of resources and a tapping into vital cycles of production and reproduction. Such nefarious forms of accumulation are also assumed in relation to maize mill owners, who are regarded as accessing the productive and regenerative capacity of women, and maize mills are thus seen as key sites of witchcraft (Bertelsen 2014). Generally, accumulating bodies and corpses, in parts or whole, is a central feature of witchcraft, which also relate to the kidnapping and devouring of children by white missionaries (Kaspin 1993), or to cases such as the 'Petro-naira' boom in Nigeria in the 1970s, where the national currency was believed to be predicated upon the theft of children and the extraction from or transformation of them into monetary wealth (Barber 1982). In Mozambique, others have shown that the power and predation inherent in witchcraft translates into cannibal desires—and this perception has led to violent confrontation in several places (Israel 2009). For instance, Serra (2003) observed that during an outbreak of cholera in Northern Mozambique in the 2000s, health workers were attacked while distributing chlorine to disinfect wells and to use in the collection of the bodies of the deceased; some were even killed by outraged local people who perceived that the morgue-bound bodies were to be consumed by cannibals. More recently and in Northern Mozambique, in an analysis of poverty and death, Trentini (2016) maps a perception of a sorcerous and nocturnal war directed against children—often being led by foreigners, state agents, witches or spirits. Similarly, Igreja (2014) documents a complex case in the 2000s, involving cannibal rumours, violence, criminal proceedings and jail sentences for alleged baby-eating witches in nearby Gorongosa.

Second, as both the Humana and Pentecostal witches established themselves within or close to existing settlements, erecting walls around the church and building permanent houses, this actualized the idea of the potential for a better self and society. In a sense similar to how the world of witches was an already accomplished future and better world in the case from PNG analyzed by Thomas Strong (Chap. 3), the emerging permanence of these sites became a materialization of a better world and a foretelling of a utopian future with increased wealth. Moreover, it may have been seen as an intensified and enhanced doubling of existing rural life. This was strengthened by the newcomers' actions in forging new collectivities, as well as other forms of doubling, where the Humana Germans and the Pentecostal Germans mirrored each other in emphasising shared meals and communion. The ethos of production—agriculture, the eucalyptus plantation and water wells—was disseminated in doctrinal settings aimed at the spirit and body of the people of Honde. There were also appeals, of course, to becoming 'new men,' to becoming pure and part of a common, united humanity (see also Rio and Eriksen 2014). This vision, particularly in relation to the Humana Germans, was probably informed by memories of Mozambique's postcolonial socialist politics. In the countryside, this involved the formation of collective farms, the tentative eradication of traditional rituals and ceremonies, and the instalment of a new form of socialist, nominally egalitarian, leadership by committee—the *Grupos Dinamizadores*, or GDs. These revolutionary transformations were often vehemently contested and were an important aspect of the mobilization to civil war against the state (Bertelsen 2016a; Geffray 1990; Igreja 2008). What is interesting here, however, is that these GDs were sometimes popularly seen as having cannibalistic leanings and in Mozambican Portuguese a member could be been to be a so-called *chupasangue* (blood-sucker): "a supernatural vampire-like figure, the *chupasangue*, who sucked people's blood and abducted them" (Obarrio 2014: 125). Thus, the true representatives of the people in the form of the GDs were believed to have covert agendas—the 'same' being more 'other' than equal—and this was increasingly the case as the blood and life force of others were consumed by them.

Bearing in mind this political history of violent (and some would argue predatory) state formation in the name of a future egalitarian socialist republic, it is likely that people recognized—and were wary of—the similar rhetoric used by the Humana Germans. What my interlocutors stated was that conversations concerning revolution and creating human unity for the future contained a rhetoric with strong political-millenarian or utopian leanings. This corresponds to a large extent with the idioms and ideas expressed in the current Humana Charter:

> WE, who are not secret drinkers in cradles of comfort while watching the world turn itself into a ball of fire, unite in hearts and in words and in deeds with all mankind.
>
> WE, who hereby salute today and salute tomorrow with a courageous clarion call from the yellow trumpet of the future, hoist our banner high over the flags.
>
> The dehumanized human being, the dehumanized society must meet The Solidary Humanism. Man standing shoulder to shoulder with all mankind.[14]

Unfortunately for the Humana Germans, they were in the end perceived to be 'secret drinkers in cradles of comfort'—following the logic of the discernment of evil that is so important to Pentecostal discourse and identification (Igreja 2015): They held nocturnal feasts of witches' food and were regarded as predating on children. The utopian vision of their clarion call for an egalitarian present and future was therefore undercut by assumptions about their acts of witchcraft.

As with Rui, who revealed himself to be a witch, the German witches also erupted violently from the egalitarian ethos of sameness: the 'other same' was believed to be demonic. Tied to the notion that witches travel long distances but are often, at the same time, intimates and kin, the intimacies of the camps and the churches created enduring problematic and violent connections between Honde and the site of witches—Germany. Given the witches' orientation towards, and propensity for, devouring children and adults to eat meat, this problematic relation erupts or actualises from time to time, as in the 2008 case of the *mhondoro dwozutumua*, or as with the Germany-generated thieving witches haunting peri-urban Chimoio. A specifically German witchcraft complex continues to haunt the region, then, and notably, as Jorgensen suggests in relation to a case in Papua New Guinea, witchcraft frequently has these kinds of "non-indigenous sources" (2014: 267).

Conclusion

Like Rui, Honde's German witches were seemingly successful. And between them, the German witches were promulgating a sense of shared purpose and values of spiritual communion and egalitarian order. However, again like Rui, they were revealed to be predatory creatures—'same others'—whose real intentions only appeared gradually, culminating in the dramatic events of predation outlined at the start of this chapter. In other words, the utopian egalitarianism was believed to have covert hierarchies of predation—fueled by a mutually reinforcing propagation of egalitarian futures by Pentecostal and Humana witches. These dynamics unfolded in a cosmological space of constant creation and recreation and among the phantasmagorics of witchcraft—the ambiguous character of which was crucial in revealing to local people the nature of what was unfolding.

While these particular radical egalitarian futures have thus been foreclosed, the specter of vengeance continues to be exacted on Honde and Chimoio through the presence of murderous and predatory thieving witches, or the lions that were bred to be savage. These events remind people of the dangers of the 'same other', whose proffered bright futures in terms of material wealth have been energized by the labor and corporealities of people in Honde. This produces social asymmetry in the place of communion and equality, thereby strengthening, once more, a Manichean understanding of good and evil, insider and outsider.

In conclusion, then, a general observation may be offered: When we in various ways make comparisons involving Pentecostalism, witchcraft, and the particular sites in which we work, the phenomena of especially Pentecostalism and witchcraft should be removed from their disciplinary confinements and regarded in a less insular way. One way to do this has been undertaken here, in showing how the confluence and mutual intensification of two forces of radical egalitarianism in Honde may point to the analytical value of re-conceiving Pentecostalism and witchcraft in relation to other political and non-political future-oriented entities and orientations, such as communism.

Notes

1. The research for this chapter was partly carried out in relation and supported by the ERC Advanced Grant project "Egalitarianism: Forms, Processes, Comparisons" (project code 340673) running from 2014 to 2019 and led by Bruce Kapferer at the University of Bergen. Research and fieldwork has also been supported by the project "Gender and Pentecostalism: *A comparative analysis of Gender in Pentecostal Christianity with focus on Africa and Melanesia*" led by Annelin Eriksen. Thanks are extended to both Bruce Kapferer and Annelin Eriksen. In addition, I would like to thank Ruy Llera Blanes, Michelle MacCarthy and Knut M. Rio both for inviting me to a panel at the American Anthropological Association's annual conference in 2014, where an early version of the paper was presented, as well as doing excellent editorial work on this volume. Thanks are also extended to Aletta Biersack and Adam Ashforth who commented on my AAA paper at that time. I would also like to thank, in particular, Jason Sumich, Paolo Israel, Ørnulf Gulbrandsen, Daria Trentini and Morten Nielsen who have all commented on earlier versions of the text. Last but not least: *Maitabassa maningue* to my long-term interlocutors in Chimoio, Honde and Gondola, Mozambique.
2. The terms 'cannibal' and 'cannibalism' are contested—within anthropology and without. In part, this relates to material and functional explanations of (alleged) acts of cannibalism, spearheaded by Marvin Harris (1978), whose work related it to human evolution, population growth and the development of state systems. This perspective has been much criticized, and rightly so (see Arens 1978; Lindenbaum 2004; Huhn 2016). These long-standing debates are beyond the scope of the present work, but I approach the cannibal-related acts of witchcraft in Honde as reflecting deep-seated, historically rooted cosmological horizons of predation and power (see also Whitehead 2000, 2011). I will therefore use the term 'cannibalism,' instead of the more technical 'anthropophagy,' as the former more aptly retains the sense of moral outrage and despair expressed by my interlocutors than the latter somewhat sanitized term. But see Huhn (2016) for a different analysis of relations among food taboos, sorcery and avoidance of anthropophagy in Northern Mozambique.
3. For a fuller account of Rui's sorcerous proclivities, see Bertelsen (2016a), Chap. 5.

4. Similarly, West (2007: 76) notes that the throat meat of a slain lion is used for nefarious purposes.
5. See also Huhn (2016) for a compelling comparative case from Northern Mozambique of a transformation of a corpse into a sorcerous 'human-lion', as she terms it. Upon seeing visible changes to the corpse, including the development of hide, the mourners undertook several steps to dismember, open and crack the body, succeeding only after several days in blocking the emergence of a 'human-lion'.
6. However, consuming food alone does not unambiguously index anti-social behaviour: in popular corruption discourses in several African countries, 'eat' covers the physical act of consuming food as well as a person engaging in corruption (see also Argenti 2007: 88f; Bayart 1993). Paradoxically, then, eating with others signifies specific anti-social, colluding and predatory forms of communities of corrupt consumption, if I may call it that. This latter form refers more to nocturnal necrophagous feasts of a society of *muroi*—rather than families sharing their meals among themselves or with visitors (see also Geschiere 1995).
7. Transgressive acts to increase agricultural yields have a long history across Africa. Hilda Kuper's (Kuper 1963: 66) reference to two main types of 'murders for doctoring' were 'agricultural fertility' and 'personal aggrandisement'. Burbridge (1925: 26) also notes, and condemns, this: "Perhaps in no instance does the sinister influence of this man [the 'witch-doctor'] appear in darker colours than in the conditions annexed to the use of this agricultural charm *divisi*. These conditions, sometimes incestuous, sometimes murderous, always inhuman and unnatural, were eagerly complied with by the superstitious idler, not witting that by the sweat of his brow he must eat his bread. In sloth, he sat with his friendly benefactor by his side pulling the right string to set the mechanical forces free which were to fill his grain-bin."
8. Enslaving others to work in a garden was documented by H. A. Junod (1962 [1912]: 514f). On this form of enslavement or 'zombification', see also Beidelmann (1963: 66) and Ellis and Haar (2004: 123). On sacrifices, such as the killing of relatives and the use of their body parts, and on illicit medicine or drugs to augment yields, see Marwick (1965: 80) and Gelfand (1964: 71–72). Agricultural or economic productivity is sometimes also conceived of in terms of reflecting incestuous relations, which are often understood in relation to the language of sorcery; see Jacobson-Widding (1990: 54) and Aschwanden (1982 [1976]: 101f).
9. There has been much discussion about Pentecostalism and its effects on sociocultural, gendered and economic realities in African as well as Melanesian contexts: Joel Robbins (2004), Matthew Engelke (2010) and Birgit Meyer (2004) have influenced much of this debate. This

area is beyond my brief here, but as Premawardhana (2016) suggests, it is important to recognize non-Pentecostal and/or global as well as local cosmologies of rupture and discontinuity when assessing the relative impact of Pentecostalism. Here, I assess the impact of the Humana Germans, as well as Mozambique's past experiments with socialism. For a theological reflection on missionizing in Mozambique, and the challenge of African socio-cultural dynamics and Pentecostal churches, see Meyers (2016).

10. On an international level, Humana People to People is controversial; its charismatic leader, Mogens Amdi Petersen, was arrested (and then released) in Miami in 2002, accused of siphoning off large amounts of money for personal use (Wakefield 2002). More recently, investigative journalists have also been highly critical of the organisation, sometimes known as ADPP (BBC 2016), from the Mozambique subsidiary *Ajuda de Desenvolvimento de Povo para Povo/ADPP* (Development Aid from People to People). Globally, it is also known as Gaia, Planet Aid and Tvind.
11. The identities of both the Humana and the Pentecostal Germans have been difficult to ascertain. However, there are clear indications (from their names, photographs I have seen, and memorabilia left behind) that many were Northern Europeans, including at least two Danes and, probably, some holding German citizenship. Ascertaining their nationality is not crucial, however, as 'German' and 'Germany' in this particular context have come to encompass sorcerous capacities of externality rather than correspond to bureaucratic notions of citizenship, language or national territory.
12. I made several attempts to locate the families or households of the three women, and to establish their names. I searched for news in the Beira-based regional newspaper *Diario de Moçambique*, and spoke to a wide network of informants in Chimoio to try to establish additional facts concerning the case, which happened a few days before my arrival. Only a few non-Honde-based informants supported the story while others doubted it. However, the unanimity that characterized the fear of the *mhondoro dwozutumwa* in Honde supports the use of this example. Moreover, the veracity of the attack as a social fact was confirmed during fieldwork in 2016.
13. Several other significant dimensions are evident here—including the politics of state formation and the domain of the traditional. While this is beyond my brief here, see Bertelsen (2016a).
14. Taken from Humana—People to People's charter 1, First Part, available at http://www.humana.org/English/english-charter-2, accessed 10 December 2016.

References

Allina, Eric. 2012. *Slavery by Any Other Name: African Life Under Company Rule in Colonial Mozambique*. Charlottesville: University of Virginia Press.

Arens, William. 1978. *The Man-Eating Myth: Anthropology and Anthrophagy*. New York: Oxford University Press.

Argenti, Nicolas. 2007. *Intestines of the State: Youth, Violence, and Belated Histories in the Cameroon Grassfields*. Chicago: University of Chicago Press.

Aschwanden, Herbert. 1982 [1976]. *Symbols of Life: An Analysis of the Consciousness of the Karanga*. Gweru: Mambo Press.

Badstuebner, Jennifer. 2003. 'Drinking the Hot Blood of Humans': Witchcraft Confessions in a South African Pentecostal Church. *Anthropology and Humanism* 28 (1): 9–22.

Bakhtin, M.M. 1986. *Speech Genres and Other Essays*. Austin, TX: University of Texas Press.

Barber, Karin. 1982. Popular Reactions to the Petro-Naira. *Journal of Modern African Studies* 20 (3): 431–450.

Bayart, Jean-François. 1993. *The State in Africa: The Politics of the Belly*. London: Longman.

BBC. 2016. Teachers Group: The Cult-like Group Linked to a Charity that Gets UK Aid. Published at http://www.bbc.com/news/magazine-36940384. Accessed Nov 04, 2016.

Behrend, Heike. 2011. *Resurrecting Cannibals: The Catholic Church, Witch-Hunts and the Production of Pagans in Western Uganda*. Suffolk: James Currey.

Beidelmann, T.O. 1963. Witchcraft in Ukaguru. In *Witchcraft and Sorcery in East Africa*, eds. J. Middleton and E.H. Winter, 57–98. London: Routledge and Kegan Paul.

Bertelsen, Bjørn Enge. 2009a. Multiple Sovereignties and Summary Justice in Mozambique: A Critique of Some Legal Anthropological Terms. *Social Analysis* 53 (3): 123–147.

———. 2009b. Sorcery and Death Squads: Transformations of State, Sovereignty, and Violence in Postcolonial Mozambique. In *Crisis of the State: War and Social Upheaval*, eds. B. Kapferer and B.E. Bertelsen, 210–240. New York: Berghahn Books.

———. 2010. Securitisation of the Social and State Transformation from Iraq to Mozambique. In *Security and Development*, eds. J.-A. McNeish and J.H.S. Lie, 84–98. Oxford: Berghahn Books.

———. 2011. 'Entering the Red Sands': The Corporality of Punishment and Imprisonment in Chimoio. *Mozambique. Journal of Southern African Studies* 37 (3): 611–626.

———. 2014. Maize Mill Sorcery: Cosmologies of Substance, Production and Accumulation Engaged in Central Mozambique. In *Framing Cosmologies: The Anthropology of Worlds*, eds. M. Holbraad and A. Abramson, 199–220. Manchester: Manchester University Press.

———. 2016a. *Violent Becomings: State Formation, Sociality, and Power in Mozambique*. New York: Berghahn Books.

———. 2016b. Effervescence and Ephemerality: Popular Urban Uprisings in Mozambique. *Ethnos* 81 (1): 25–52.

Bhila, Hoyni H. 1982. *Trade and Politics in a Shona Kingdom: The Manyika and their African and Portuguese Neighbours, 1575–1902*. Harlow: Longman.

Bourdillon, Michael. 1977. *Christianity South of the Zambezi*, vol. 2. Gwelo: Mambo Press.

Burbridge, A. 1925. The Witch Doctor's Power: A Study of Its Source and Scope. *Southern Rhodesia Native Affairs Department Annual (NADA)* 3: 22–31.

Castel-Branco, Carlos Nuno. 2014. Growth, Capital Accumulation and Economic Porosity in Mozambique: Social Losses, Private Gains. *Review of African Political Economy* 41 (1): 26–48.

Cohn, Norman. 2004 [1957]. *The Pursuit of the Millennium: Revolutionary Millenarians and Mystical Anarchists of the Middle Ages*. London: Pimlico.

Colson, Elizabeth. 2000. The Father as Witch. *Africa* 70 (3): 333–358.

Deleuze, Gilles, and Félix Guattari. 2002 [1980]. *A Thousand Plateaus: Capitalism and Schizophrenia*. London: Continuum.

de Matos, Patrícia Ferraz. 2013. *The Colours of the Empire: Racialized Representations During Portuguese Colonialism*. New York: Berghahn Books.

Ellis, Stephen, and Gerrie ter Haar. 2004. *Worlds of Power: Religious Thought and Political Practice in Africa*. Oxford: Oxford University Press.

Engelke, Matthew. 2010. Past Pentecostalism: Notes on Rupture, Realignment, and Everyday Life in Pentecostal and African Independent Churches. *Africa* 80 (2): 177–199.

Englund, Harri. 2003. Christian Independency and Global Membership: Pentecostal Extraversions in Malawi. *Journal of Religion in Africa* 33 (1): 83–111.

Englund, Harri, and James Leach. 2000. Ethnography and the Meta-narratives of Modernity. *Current Anthropology* 41 (2): 225–248.

Evans-Pritchard, E.E. 1976 [1937]. *Witchcraft, Oracles, and Magic Among the Azande*. Oxford: Oxford University Press.

Geffray, Christian. 1990. *La cause des armes au Mozambique: Anthropologie d'une guerre civile*. Paris: Karthala.

Gelfand, Michael. 1964. *Witch Doctor: Traditional Medicine Man of Rhodesia*. London: Harvill Press.

Geschiere, Peter. 1995. *Sorcellerie et politique en Afrique: La viande des autres*. Paris: Éditions Karthala.

———. 2013. *Witchcraft, Intimacy and Trust*. Chicago: Chicago University Press.

Gluckman, Max. 1963 [1956]. *Custom and Conflict in Africa*. Oxford: Basil Blackwell.

Harris, Marvin. 1978. *Cannibals and Kings: The Origins of Cultures*. London: William Collins.

Haynes, Naomi. 2012. Pentecostalism and the Morality of Money: Prosperity, Inequality, and Religious Sociality on the Zambian Copperbelt. *Journal of the Royal Anthropological Institute* 18: 123–139.

Huhn, Arianna. 2016. What is Human? Anthropomorphic Anthropophagy in Northwest Mozambique. In *Cooking Cultures: Convergent Histories of Food and Feeling*, ed. I. Banarjee-Dube, 177–198. Cambridge: Cambridge University Press.

Igreja, Victor. 2008. Memories as Weapons: The Politics of Peace and Silence in Post-civil War Mozambique. *Journal of Southern African Studies* 34 (3): 539–556.

———. 2014. Memories of Violence, Cultural Transformations of Cannibals, and Indigenous State-Building in Post-conflict Mozambique. *Comparative Studies in Society and History* 56 (3): 774–802.

———. 2015. Intersections of Sensorial Perception and Imagination in Divination Practices in Post-war Mozambique. *Anthropological Quarterly* 88 (3): 693–724.

Isaacman, Allen F. 1978. *A Luta Continua: Creating a New Society in Mozambique*. Binghampton, NY: Fernand Braudel Center.

Israel, Paolo. 2009. The War of Lions: Witch-Hunts, Occult Idioms and Post-Socialism in Northern Mozambique. *Journal of Southern African Studies* 35 (1): 155–174.

Jacobs, Carolien, and Christy Schuetze. 2011. 'Justice with Our Own Hands': Lynching, Poverty, Witchcraft, and the State in Mozambique. In *Globalizing Lynching History: Vigilantism and Extralegal Punishment from an International Perspective*, eds. M. Berg and S. Wendt, 225–241. New York: Palgrave Macmillan.

Jacobson-Widding, Anita. 1990. The Fertility of Incest. In *The Creative Communion: African Folk Models of Fertility and the Regeneration of Life*, eds. A. Jacobson-Widding and W.V. Beek, 47–73. Uppsala: Uppsala University.

Jorgensen, Dan. 2014. Preying on Those Close to Home: Witchcraft Violence in a Papuan New Guinea Village. *Australian Journal of Anthropology* 25: 267–286.

Junod, Henri Alexandre. 1962 [1912]. *The Life of a South African Tribe*, Vol. 1. Social Life. New York: University Books.

Kapferer, Bruce. 2002. Outside All Reason: Magic, Sorcery and Epistemology in Anthropology. *Social Analysis* 46 (3): 1–30.

Kaspin, Deborah. 1993. Chewa Visions and Revisions of Power: Transformations of the Nyau Dance in Central Malawi. In *Modernity and Its Malcontents: Ritual and Power in Postcolonial Africa*, eds. J. Comaroff and J. Comaroff, 34–57. Chicago: University of Chicago Press.

Kuper, Hilda. 1963. *The Swazi: A South African Kingdom*. New York: Holt, Rinehart and Winston.

Lindenbaum, Shirley. 2004. Thinking About Cannibalism. *Annual Review of Anthropology* 33: 475–498.

Lubkemann, Stephen. 2008. *Culture in Chaos: An Anthropology of the Social Condition of War*. Chicago: University of Chicago Press.

Marwick, Max G. 1965. *Sorcery in Its Social Setting: A Study of the Northern Rhodesian Cewa*. Manchester: Manchester University Press.

Maxwell, David. 2006. *African Gifts of the Spirit: Pentecostalism and the Rise of a Zimbabwean Transnational Religious Movement*. Oxford, OH: James Currey, Weaver Press and Ohio University Press.

Meyer, Birgit. 2002. Pentecostalism, Prosperity and Popular Cinema in Ghana. *Culture and Religion* 3 (1): 67–87.

———. 2004. Christianity in Africa: From African Independent to Pentecostal-Charismatic Churches. *Annual Review of Anthropology* 33: 447–474.

———. 2007. Pentecostalism and Neo-Liberal Capitalism: Faith, Prosperity and Vision in African Pentecostal-Charismatic Churches. *Journal for the Study of Religion* 20 (2): 5–28.

Meyers, Megan. 2016. Contextualization is Complicated: A Case Study of Contextualized. Worship Arts in Mozambique. *Missiology: An International Review*: 1–12. doi:10.0091829616639323.

Mozambique News Reports and Clippings. 2016. "Survey Shows Inequality Doubled in Six Years". Mozambique News Reports and Clippings, 306, 7 January 2016. Accessible at http://www.open.ac.uk/technology/mozambique/sites/www.open.ac.uk.technology.mozambique/files/files/Mozambique_306-4Jan2016_Big-Inequality-Increase_%2B_other-reserarch%20.pdf, downloaded 20 January 2016.

Müller, Tanja. 2014. *Legacies of Socialist Solidarity: East Germany in Mozambique*. Lanham, MD: Lexington.

Newell, Sasha. 2007. Pentecostal Witchcraft: Neoliberal Possession and Demonic Discourse in Ivoirian Pentecostal Churches. *Journal of Religion in Africa* 37: 461–490.

Newitt, Malyn. 1995. *A History of Mozambique*. London: Hurst.

Niehaus, Isak. 2001. *Witchcraft, Power and Politics: Exploring the Occult in the South African Lowveld*. London: Pluto Press.

Obarrio, Juan. 2014. *The Spirit of the Laws in Mozambique*. Chicago: Chicago University Press.

Pelgrim, Riekje. 2003. *Witchcraft and Policing: South Africa's Police Service Attitudes Towards Witchcraft-Related Crime in the Northern Province*. Leiden: African Studies Centre.

Pfeiffer, James. 2005. Commodity Fetichismo the Holy Spirit, and the Turn to Pentecostal and African Independent Churches in Central Mozambique. *Culture, Medicine and Psychiatry* 29 (3): 255–283.

Premawardhana, Devaka. 2016. Egress and Regress: Pentecostal Precursors and Parallels in Northern Mozambique. *Ethnos*: 1–19. doi:10.1080/00141844.2016.1140216.

Rio, Knut M. 2010. Handling Sorcery in a State System of Law: Magic, Violence and Kastom. *Oceania* 80: 182–197.

———. 2014. A Shared Intentional Space of Witch-Hunt and Sacrifice. *Ethnos* 79 (3): 320–341.

Rio, Knut M., and Annelin Eriksen. 2013. Missionaries, Healing and Sorcery in Melanesia: A Scottish Evangelist in Ambrym Island. Vanuatu. *History and Anthropology* 24 (3): 398–418.

———. 2014. A New Man: The Cosmological Horizons of Development, Curses, and Personhood in Vanuatu. In *Framing Cosmologies: The Anthropology of Worlds*, eds. M. Holbraad and A. Abramson, 55–76. Manchester: Manchester University Press.

Robbins, Joel. 2004. *Becoming Sinners: Christianity and Moral Torment in a Papua New Guinea Society*. Berkeley, CA: University of California Press.

Roque, Ricardo Nuno Afonso. 2010. *Headhunting and Colonialism: Anthropology and the Circulation of Human Skulls in the Portuguese Empire, 1870–1930*. Houndmills: Palgrave Macmillan.

Sachs, Albie, and Gita Honwana Welch. 1990. *Liberating the Law: Creating Popular Justice in Mozambique*. London: Zed Books.

Saul, John S. 1985. *A Difficult Road: The Transition to Socialism in Mozambique*. New York: Monthly Review Press.

Schoffeleers, J. Matthews. 1992. *River of Blood: The Genesis of a Martyr Cult in Southern Malawi, c. A.D. 1600*. Madison, WS: University of Wisconsin Press.

Serra, Carlos. 2003. *Cólera e catarse: Infra-estruturas sociais de um mito nas zonas costeiras de Nampula (1998/2002)*. Maputo: Imprensa Universitária.

Slobodian, Quinn (ed.). 2015. *Comrades of Color: East Germany in the Cold War*. New York: Berghahn Books.

Sundkler, Bengt G. M. 1964 [1948]. *Bantu Prophets in South Africa*. London, New York and Toronto: Oxford University Press for the International Africa Institute.

Trentini, Daria. 2016. 'The Night War of Nampula': Vulnerable Children, Social Change and Spiritual Insecurity in Northern Mozambique. *Africa* 86 (3): 528–551.

Van de Kamp, Linda. 2016. *Violent Conversion: Brazilian Pentecostalism and Urban Women in Mozambique*. Suffolk, NY: Boydell and Brewer.

Wakefield, R. 2002. Trouble from Denmark. *Miami Times*, 21 May 2002. http://www.miaminewtimes.com/2002-03-21/news/trouble-from-denmark/. Accessed June 19, 2017.

Walker, Michael Madison. 2012. A Spatio-Temporal Mosaic of Land Use and Access in Central Mozambique. *Journal of Southern African Studies* 38 (3): 699–715.

West, Harry G. 2005. *Kupilikula: Governance and the Invisible Realm in Mozambique*. Chicago: University of Chicago Press.

———. 2007. *Ethnographic Sorcery*. Chicago: University of Chicago Press.

White, Luise. 1997. Cars Out of Place: Vampires, Technology, and Labor in East and Central Africa. In *Tensions of Empire: Colonial Cultures in a Bourgeois World*, ed. F. Cooper and A.L. Stoler, 436–460. Berkeley, CA: University of California Press.

———. 2000. *Speaking with Vampires: Rumor and History in Colonial Africa*. Berkeley: California University Press.

Whitehead, Neil L. 2000. Hans Staden and the Cultural Politics of Cannibalism. *Hispanic American Historical Review* 80 (4): 721–751.

———. 2011. The Cannibal War Machine. *Counterpunch* (Weekend edition July 1–3).

Zimba, Benigna de Jesus Lurdina Mateus Lisboa, Edward A. Alpers, and Allen F. Isaacman. 2006. *Slave Routes and Oral Tradition in Southeastern Africa*. Maputo: Filsom Entertainment, Lda.

Author Biography

Bjørn Enge Bertelsen is Professor at the Department of Social Anthropology at the University of Bergen. He has researched issues such as state formation, cosmology, violence and rural-urban connections in Mozambique since 1998. Bertelsen has authored the monograph *Violent Becomings: State Formation, Sociality and Power in Mozambique* (2016), as well as co-edited Crisis of the State: War and Social Upheaval (with Bruce Kapferer, 2009), *Navigating Colonial Orders: Norwegian Entrepreneurship in Africa and Oceania, ca. 1850–1950* (with Kirsten Alsaker Kjerland, 2015), *Violent Reverberations: Global Modalities of Trauma* (with Vigdis Broch-Due, 2016), and *Critical Anthropological Engagements in Human Alterity and Difference* (with Synnøve Bendixsen, 2016).

CHAPTER 3

Becoming Witches: Sight, Sin, and Social Change in the Eastern Highlands of Papua New Guinea

Thomas Strong

Introduction

The Bible talk was about the fourth chapter of Genesis. A story every Christian knows. The brothers Cain and Abel made offerings to God. The elder, Cain, was a farmer and he offered some of his crops. Abel was a shepherd and offered a lamb. But God was displeased with Cain's sacrifice, provoking anger and humiliation. Cain killed his brother in jealousy. Retelling a classic story, the pastor asked us: why had God rejected Cain's gift?

We were in the United Pentecostal Church in Dudumia village in the upper Asaro valley of Papua New Guinea's eastern highlands. The United Pentecostal Church is one of the several Pentecostal congregations in the area, alongside Revival Centres International and the PNG Revival Church. As with Pentecostal services everywhere, that Sunday morning was meant to feel unscripted, characterized by spontaneity and inspiration rather than formal routine. Congregants were drawn

T. Strong (✉)
Maynooth University, Maynooth, Ireland

K. Rio et al. (eds.), *Pentecostalism and Witchcraft*, Contemporary Anthropology of Religion, DOI 10.1007/978-3-319-56068-7_3

from the various villages of the upper Asaro; some had walked for an hour or more to attend. Men wore their best trousers and shoes, if they had them; women wore colorful blouses and laplaps. The social space beneath the corrugated tin roof was divided by a notional aisle dividing the cement floor into separate sections for men and women. In the front of the church, behind the altar, appeared two images: the logo of the United Pentecostal Church International—a grid of the latitudinal and longitudinal lines of the globe circled by the words "The Whole Gospel to the Whole World," with the address for the Church's headquarters in Hazelwood, Missouri underneath—and a poster with photographs of the American couples assigned to oversee the Church's missions around the world. We were in a high mountain valley in New Guinea contemplating themes of global, universal significance.

The man who held the podium that day wanted to know: why did God look unfavorably upon Cain?

> God wanted them to show themselves, their hearts, to him *(olsem bel bilong tupela, tupela soim em*). Because there was some bad feeling there, there in Cain's body. Some bad feeling toward his brother. There were some 'motives' (in English) there. So this offering Cain made to God, it didn't sit well with God (*em i no go tru long bigpela*). The offer wasn't straight. However, the sacrifice of Abel was good. God accepted his offering because God looked ...

And here he paused. "God doesn't just see your body when he observes you. When God looks at you what does he see? What does Samuel 16:7 say? What does he see?" The congregation replied: "Spirit." The sermon continued:

> Your spirit! He sees your heart (*bel*)! If I look at you, I just see your face. But God, he gazes (*glasim*) inside. How much you love him, how much you love him. Do you love him half-heartedly? God weighs you up (*skelim*) as he observes you. Are you hiding something behind your back? Or in some other corner of your person (*hap kona*)? God, he knows. People hide things, but in the eye of God you are so clear. What does Hebrews 4:13 say? Everything is open to him and he sees.

Each Christian life is like an offering to the Lord, he continued: "A sacrifice." But each person must offer himself to the Lord as a whole person and with a pure heart; one should not hold back any part of the self. Referring to Isaiah 6:4–8, he proclaimed:

> You must be cleansed by the fire of the Holy Spirit. We must place ourselves on the fire of the Lord and he must purify (*kukim*) us: each part of us. Our whole body. Our hair, our mouths, everything. Without this there is no heaven. You must remove these bad ways from yourself. What must you do?
>
> Congregation: Defeat sin.
>
> Whoever wronged you, or did something bad to you, or stole from you, or wronged your family—you can't hold on to this 'backside thinking' or this 'bad feeling' (*tingting nogut*) about them. Because then to God you would be giving a bad offering. Cain harbored bad feelings about his brother, jealousy or envy, and so he gave what kind of offering? A spoiled one. We can't hide. Our minds (*tingting*), our hearts (*bel*), they must always be open and entirely free. We must defeat sin. As it says in 1 John 3:15: If you resent your brother (*bel nogut*), what do you do to him?
>
> Congregation: Kill him.
>
> If I resent my own brother Stephen, I kill him! I may not physically kill him, but in spirit, I murder him. This is hidden sin. It's 'secret' sin, 'unseen' (in English) sin, right? We can't see it with our eyes: other people can't see this. Only you. And God.

In the upper Asaro valley, people live in fear of what is hidden in each other and indeed in themselves. Though the Bible story relates that Cain killed Abel after God's rejection of his sacrifice, the sermon located Cain's failing earlier in the tale: in the hidden resentment that rendered his sacrifice ruined, poisoned. This poison, the pastor warned, must be removed from people offering their souls to God. But the sermon contained another meaning that I only realized afterward—a warning about witchcraft (*gwumu, sanguma*).

Gwumu witches see inside persons, their victims, but conceal themselves from sight. The invisibility of witches makes possible an occult realm existing in parallel to everyday life, another "side," endangering people's vitality, growth, and relationships. Evangelical and Pentecostal sermons often focus on these dynamics of in/visibility. Christian piety, for example, is evinced as a shine on the body that deflects the covetous and hungry gaze of witches. Congregation members are said to be covered by the blood of Christ; only those who attend church will enjoy the protection that God's grace affords. In 2014, a Baptist preacher described witchcraft to me as a "wildfire" in the valley, threatening the patrimony of both clan and country, dimming peoples' hopes for future development, and robbing the country of the little wealth it had. Frequently during my fieldwork, my informants told me that the very land they lived on was "cursed." Christian discourse, and especially Pentecostal emphasis on "evil spirits" (*spirit nogut*), simultaneously speaks to and elicits fears of this "curse" of witches, and offers a solution: redemption through the church.

This chapter explores relationships among constructs of sin and sight, the "heathen" and the hidden, in the PNG highlands. Beginning in 1998 and continuing with several return visits through 2014, I conducted fieldwork with people who perceive themselves as plagued both by witchcraft and by the attempts of youth to "mobilize" (*mobilais*) against suspected witches through violent and sometimes deadly witch hunts (Jorgensen 2014). My analytical focus on sight is motivated by two connections. The first pertains specifically to how people talk about witchcraft. Much of the discourse on witchcraft revolves around dynamics of "in/visibility." Witches remain hidden, yet evidence of their presence is everywhere: in sickness and death, in poverty and lack of development, in portentous world events and an overall feeling that the end times, the apocalypse, is upon us. Though themselves mainly invisible, witches are gifted with special powers of sight, provoking them to covet the vitality and value they spy in other persons and enabling a perspective that discloses a modern world only they can see. Witchcraft discourse, then, dwells on problems of vision and value, gazing and greediness, even as it evokes an *invisible* world of material bounty obtained through malicious influence. These paradoxes of perception articulate witchcraft idioms with those characteristic of Pentecostal and charismatic Christianity that speak of individual redemption and piety in terms of the shielding white light of God's grace.

The second connection motivating a focus on the sense of sight relates to its importance in local concepts of power, order, and moral comportment. Deliberate acts of concealment and revelation are associated with power, especially in its distinctive Melanesian manifestations as vitality (growth) and value (wealth) in persons (Strathern 2013). At the same time, materializations of such power, in beauty and bounty, may engender feelings of resentment and jealousy in witnesses. Such incipient inequalities are troubling to people committed to an axiomatic Melanesian moral ethos of egalitarianism. Wealth exchange (e.g., Strathern 1975; Munn 1992) has been analyzed as both manifesting and mediating a Melanesian cultural tension between equality and competition, between autonomy and relationality (Read 1955). Today, this tension is catalyzed by an economic scene of growing inequality between persons and between places, as, for example, the inequality felt between those who inhabit towns and live on money and those thought to be left behind in villages and gardens. Thus, if the sociality of sight has been an important analytic in the ethnography of Melanesia, it becomes especially salient in a discussion of witchcraft and Christianity in Papua New Guinea today. Below, I first situate the upper Asaro ethnographically, before proceeding to a discussion of sin, sight, and sociality as these are informed by Melanesian cultural dynamics. Highlighting the theme of sight allows us to pinpoint areas of articulation between Pentecostal Christianity and the powers of contemporary witchcraft.

Who Is Blocking the Road to Development?

The Dano-speakers (Strange 1965) of the upper Asaro live in nucleated villages composed largely of small round grass houses. Villages are most often constituted by an exogamous, patrilineal clan, and social structural segmentation—as between clan, subclan, and the units of which they are comprised such as lineages—is usually isomorphic with residential patterns; lineage members tend to cluster within villages. Affinal, matrilateral, and sororal ties create an important matrix of "kindred" (*kandere*) extending beyond the agnatic clan, creating relational resources and obligations that always exist in tandem and in tension with the dominant patrilineal order. The relation between clan and kindred is the principle focus of the ceremonial exchange practices accompanying events such as birth, puberty, marriage, and death.

The valley floor, which rises from about 1800 m, is overlain with a patchwork quilt of abundant, well-tended gardens, as well as the remains of large multihectare plantations that were established prior to independence but have since been abandoned and mostly reclaimed by smallholder coffee growers (Strong 2006; Downs 1986). People supplement the staple crop sweet potato with many other crops (taro, corn, beans, peanut, oranges, avocado, coffee, and so on), and fresh vegetable marketing is today a lucrative source of income (Benediktsson 2002). People also consume store-bought goods like cooking oil, rice, or ramen noodles that they usually acquire in Goroka town, the provincial capital, about an hour away on the back of a flatbed truck. Pigs and cooked pork are the most prestigious wealth items in ceremonial exchanges, though those exchanges also always involve state currency often ritually displayed on bamboo poles sometimes referred to as "money trees." Parents spend their days tending to gardens while their children attend local schools, and in the evenings, generator-powered "video houses" provide entertainment for villagers, who may also recharge their mobile phones in them.

Lutheran, Seventh Day Adventist, and Catholic missions began successfully to convert people in the upper Asaro to varieties of Christian practice around 1950, arriving in the immediate vicinity of my field site in the 1960s. People today are enthusiastically Christian, and attend Evangelical Brotherhood, Revival Centres International, Assemblies of God, SDA, Mormon, Four Square, Salvation Army, Pentecostal, Baptist, and Catholic churches.

Since I began fieldwork, Papua New Guinea has witnessed precipitous social change. The commodities boom of the 2000s, especially in the Pacific Rim, impacted PNG dramatically. Foreign investment in the country has risen, mainly in the area of natural resource extraction. A massive Exxon Mobil-operated liquid natural gas project in the Southern Highlands began piping petroleum out of fields in the southwest highlands in 2014. Some of my informants have found employment in these fields, and though dreams of natural resource wealth figure significantly in how people imagine the future for themselves and their country (Golub 2014; Jacka 2015), grassroots economic benefits of such large scale projects are rarely seen (Kirsch 2014). The project, "PNG LNG," literally doubled the GDP of the country in 2015, the 40th anniversary of national independence. Many people interpreted this event in Biblical terms: PNG would finally emerge from its 40-year "trial" of independence to become a resource-rich leader of Pacific Islands nations.

The State has grown almost entirely dependent on natural resource extraction and exploitation for revenue (Kirsch 2014; Lattas and Rio 2011). Newly rich Papua New Guineans, whether politicians, public servants, businessmen, or those heir to a tribal (petrochemical) patrimony, are dramatically driving up real estate prices, and prices of Coca-Cola and frozen chickens, in the major towns. The 'Real Estate' section of the Post-Courier, a News Corporation-owned concern, features advertisements for gated estates in Cairns and Brisbane, from which Virgin Australia now operates two daily departures to Port Moresby.

This boom, already now historical with the global collapse of petroleum prices, created both pathways of opportunity and potholes of deprivation, as does the hopping and skipping of global capital everywhere (Ferguson 2006). While resource-rich areas benefit from new roads and other infrastructure, the people of the upper Asaro believe they have been "left behind," or worse, are "reversing back" and losing even the services once associated with the colonial plantation economy. Two nostalgias can be identified in frustrated commentary on this situation: one for lost vitality—as when people say that the ancient ancestors were physically much stronger and bigger than people are now (Strong 2007)—and another for the ostensibly more productive colonial social order and the development it brought to the valley in the twentieth century. As people search for reasons why the blessings of modernity have been persistently withheld from those in the village, nefarious, invisible witches are increasingly blamed for "blocking" the road to development and material wealth.

If witchcraft is a problem many Papua New Guineans see themselves sharing in common, in national and elite discourse on mystical violence locally distinctive types of witchcraft and sorcery are sometimes confused. Arguably deriving from the imposition of a generic category—"the spiritual"—upon a diverse set of ideas and actions, NGO and legal discourse refers most frequently simply to "sorcery" and "sorcery-related killings" or "SRK." Yet often there are locally salient distinctions between *sorcery* as an instrumental technique for harming others, often used by people who *also* acquire techniques of healing and divination, and *witchcraft* as an innate or unlearned propensity to carry out invisible violence. Evans-Pritchard's old (1937) dichotomy accurately captures an important distinction salient in many parts of PNG, but especially in the Eastern Highlands: the sorcerer may be feared and stigmatized by his dabbling in the diabolical, but he may also be respected (cf. Lindenbaum 1979; Godelier 1986)—whereas the witch is always regarded as purely malevolent (Stephen 1987a, b). My ethnographic focus here is on ideas about witchcraft specifically characteristic of the central PNG highlands, and in particular what has become known as *kumo* witchcraft (I follow the Dano orthography of Newman (1964, 1965) in rendering this word as *gwumu*).

Even as diverse ideas about witchcraft and sorcery are found across the country, PNG national culture is increasingly occupied by a common set of Christian ideas and symbols, especially those of evangelical, charismatic, or Pentecostal varieties. These ideas and symbols are strongly characterized by a theology of "spiritual warfare" found in Pentecostal and charismatic Christian teaching (Jorgensen 2014; Schram 2014; Robbins 2004b; Wesch 2007). This framework envisions recent PNG history as a rupture with a tradition that must be repudiated as demonic: symbols and ideas associated with traditional or customary pasts become associated with Satan, who must be overcome in a manichean struggle between forces of 'good' (Christianity) and 'evil' (tradition; compare especially Meyer 1999). This process of resignification sits uncomfortably alongside discourse that *eulogizes* the loss of the cultural practices of which Pentecostal Christianity demands repudiation, creating scenes of sharp contestation between an ethos of nostalgia for traditional pasts and an aspirational ethos of hope for a different future. Perhaps the most emblematic example of the tensions generated by an ascendant equation of PNG nationality with Christianity came in 2013 when the Speaker of Parliament attempted to purify and sanctify Port Moresby's Parliament House by destroying special carvings originally intended to emblematize PNG pride in its customs, but now seen by some Christians as retaining the presence of the demonic (the traditional) in the very seat of national power (Schram 2014, see also Introduction, this volume). Christian repudiation of the symbolism of traditional culture also occurs in provinces and in villages (Tuzin 1997). In the Eastern Highlands Province, for example, the traditional figure of *nokondi* on the provincial emblem and flag has long been suspected to inhibit the province's development because of its association with traditional beliefs, that is, with the demonic. *Nokondi* is a spiritual mischief-maker found across the eastern highlands (Lindenbaum 2002), and people in the Eastern Highlands frequently decorate themselves as *nokondi*-like figures for regional cultural festivals. Yet people speculate that *nokondi's* presence in the official iconography of the provincial government has exerted a malicious influence over the region. During a National Prayer Day event in Goroka in 2013, Prime Minister Peter O'Neil joined Governor Julie Soso in honoring the "Covenant of the People of Papua New Guinea with the People of Israel" (see Newland and Brown 2015). Afterwards, approving talk circulated that Soso had officially decreed that *nokondi* was to be removed from all provincial insignia. This attempted erasure of a symbol simultaneously thought to signify "tradition" and to manifest the demonic was reminiscent of events occurring decades earlier, when most villages in the eastern highlands were subject to the public exposure and destruction of secret or esoteric ritual artifacts (such as sacred flutes) as part of missionary programs of "collective conversion" of villagers (Smith 1979).

This framework, which reinterprets symbols of indigenous religion as signs of a Christian struggle between good and evil, layers moral value over historical rupture (Robbins 2004a, b). Symbols of the (traditional) past are taken to represent and realize an evil that must be overcome, whereas Christian symbols point to future redemption (Bashkow 2000a; see also Eriksen and Rio, this volume). Thus, a further aspect of this national Christian culture is eschatological discourse that forms the dominant mode of contemporary historical interpretation both on the national scene and in villages, as people read news and events for signs portending the inevitable return of Christ. In the Asaro region then, the "curse" of witches overtaking village and valley is consistently interpreted as indicating that PNG and the world more broadly have entered into the "bad times," *taim nogut*—the apocalypse.

Although my recent fieldwork focus was on the Evangelical Brotherhood Church (EBC) and United Pentecostal Church, I mainly attended a local Baptist congregation in 1998, 2000–2001, and 2003. Each of these denominations has distinctive doctrinal precepts and ritual practices. The EBC has a decades-long history in the valley and is associated with a Swiss mission and an important health center and aid post about an hour walk from the village in which I do fieldwork. Pentecostal churches are much newer arrivals on the scene. Older Lutheran, Catholic, Baptist, and Seventh Day Adventist congregations are important institutions in the valley and the eastern highlands more generally. But the arrival of new churches occasions considerable interdenominational criticism, contestation, and conflict, particularly between the adherents of the mainline older congregations and those of the newer charismatic variety (Handman 2014; Jebens 2005). Lutheranism, in particular, is associated with older generations and even with the *tumbuna* (ancestors) comprising the first generation to have converted to Christianity in the years following World War II. Indeed, youth today often reject older congregations as remnants of a traditional social order needing reform; the historical rupture that Christian conversion creates between "old" and "new," figured in this discourse as a generational conflict, is recreated in the present as a contest between styles of Christian devotion. For example, male evangelical youth sometimes entertain diabolical fantasies about satanic rituals and infant sacrifices occurring beneath the largest Catholic churches in the eastern highlands.

Nevertheless, some common Christian themes inflect local talk of all kinds, such as how recent history is interpreted or specific village misfortunes are understood. Particularly in connection with witchcraft, a generalized Christian culture is the most important lens through which people view their circumstances. A potent image sums up this culture: the image of the blood of Christ covering the devout and protecting them from the invasive gaze of jealous witches.

"The Witches Are Professionalizing"

Ideas about witchcraft in the upper Asaro valley dwell on problems of visibility and violence, dilemmas of sight and sociality, in many ways. Here is Virikare, a young man who grew up in Port Moresby but who for the last few years has lived in the village:

> My brothers have shown me the list of witches. Some of the family members I have stayed with, they are a witch family. But … I don't say to myself: "Ah, This is a witch family, I'm afraid, I'll run away." Because in fact all the time there will be witches: so who would I stay with? Who is a good man with whom I would stay? They are all witches. So I just bow my head and go around. I'm hungry, I go to the house and eat. I don't worry too much … I know God is watching, and if they want to do something bad to me, or something good to me, I don't mind. It's true that the village is full of witches.
>
> T: So you heard that in Moresby too?
>
> In Moresby, they told me all about it. It's a big story. When my brother came down to Moresby to be a security guard, he said: don't go back to the village. It's full of witches. But I grew up in Moresby, and I was tired of it. … So I wanted to come here to see the life in the village, the situation — and then return to the city. It's true, the village is full of witches. Really, no one is innocent. Even babies — when they give the babies milk, they give them witchcraft (*sanguma*). When the babies grow, they are taken to the cave at Owia stone … They go to the stone, and file their teeth and when they see that they are sharp, then they know that the child is ready. They can eat people now … kill people … destroy people. From

the time they are babies they are prepared .... Now many of the little children — they are witches. But you can't tell ....

Our leaders too are witches. So when it comes to killing the witches, the leaders defend them. Say one witch attacks some other person. So the young men think about attacking or killing this witch. They think of ... capturing it and putting it inside a house. They will tell this witch: "Call out the names of all the witches." They will threaten the witch with a knife, use a hot wire and shoot the witches arms and legs with it, or whatever. The witch will suffer and feel pain, the witch will confess or 'talk out.' He will confess: "this man is a witch, this woman is a witch, this child is a witch." Or the witch can call out the name of a whole family, "they are all witches from mother to father to child." He will call out the other names, saying "them also, and them also." But some of the leaders in league with witches, they will be afraid... that a witch will reveal themselves also as witches. Because the leader didn't stop the young men from attacking the witch, so the witch will say this leader too is a witch. So the leader will try his best to defend the accused person. So our leaders too, they are witches! Plenty of times when the youth 'mobilize' in order to attack the witches, they'll say: "don't kill the witches! Let them be and just exile them." And when the young men hear this kind of talk, they'll say: "... You defend the witches, it means you are a witch also." Even if you are a 'good man,' they'll attack you.

They don't like the older men to control the village. Our mothers and fathers, they are "before line," they hold the way of the ancestors, such as witchcraft, "custom." Our new generation, we are born in the time of modern technology, the time of "computerized systems" .... This witchcraft practice, we don't know about it....If you oppose them, the youth, then you are a witch. So now, we young men we don't control the village. But now these young are saying, "we are tired of the old leaders — the traditional (*bifo*) leaders... they will defend the witches, we young men will run this village." We need to get rid of these witches. They destroy our business and curse our gardens. The children aren't growing well either — the witches are preying on them. That's what the witches do. ... Their hidden thinking, their gut thinking, they don't want the good people to remain. They want it just to be a world of witches. So they are killing the good people. So this is the thinking of the young men — they are tired of the older generation of leaders.

The lives of witches have changed. They've *developed. They've* developed. Their society has developed. Like America or Australia. On the "spirit side," ... they are capable of all this. They have airplanes... cars... ships.

> Now here we are, you and me, and we look at this house we are sitting in, and it's made of grass and bush. But ... in the eye of the witches, this village is something else altogether... a very nice place. There are buildings, and big stores, that kind of thing. They've already developed, on the spirit side. And we "normal" people, we look at this village and it isn't very good. It's bush. But for them, this village is good, it's a city. So when you talk about witches, they are everywhere.

Virikare's monologue vividly captures ways in which the discourse of witchcraft expresses interlinked concerns for people in the upper Asaro: the repudiation of tradition, intergenerational tensions, unequal relations between village and city, a hoped-for social transformation (development) that seems ever out of reach, and above all the idea that the village is cursed by witches, but also by conflict about what to do about them.

The basic premise of witchcraft in the upper Asaro is not unlike that found elsewhere in the world: some people are thought to be inhabited by a concealed or invisible spirit called *gwumu* in the local language and *sanguma* or *spirit nogut* (evil spirit) in the national *lingua franca*, Tok Pisin. These beings are sometimes referred to as "Satan's angels," evil spirits ruled by the angel cast out of heaven. Some say that these demons were first brought to the world through the medium of pigs, an interpretation of Mark 5:13, where Jesus exorcizes demons by first sending them into the body of pigs. These beings, when manifest as witchcraft, reside in the gut or under the armpit of person; they most often dwell in the uterus, lending discourse about witches a decidedly gendered aspect, though men may also be accused and possibly killed after an accusation. *Gwumu* are often thought to be passed from person to person, sometimes unwittingly in market transactions via the sale of betel nut or via the intermediary of pigs (as when sweet potatoes purchased from witches are fed to pigs, who then transmit witch substance to those who consume them). But transmission especially occurs as a kind of inheritance, as Virikare mentions, so that the children and relatives of witches are themselves often suspected of harboring *gwumu*, because witchcraft may be passed along through the commensality and care associated with kinship relations. Indeed, the children of accused witches are stigmatized and whole families struggle under a spoiled reputation or "bad name."

People describe *gwumu* as an agency hiding inside the body of another: it may be referred to as a "doll" for example, and an additional idiom I recorded referred to these familiars as "little sisters." Though *gwumu* are held to be concealed in the interior of persons, they may nevertheless sometimes be seen as apparitions, especially when they have left the body of a person to hunt. In 2013, I recorded many types of apparition that witches were said to manifest as they travel about, such as lions, goats, bears, or wild dogs. Most commonly, however, people say that *gwumu* take the form of small, quick, highly mobile creatures—bats, rats, birds, moths, grasshoppers, butterflies, cicadas, and other insects. During coercive witchcraft confessions, butterflies and bats are said to cluster close-by; coming into contact with one of these creatures threatens infection and sparks fear. A bat flying overhead at night may hush conversation around a fire, and a startling nighttime encounter with any animal might elicit a rumor about a nearby witch. Talk of witches sometimes prompts talk of other sinister beings at large. In 2000–2003, rumors of a *drakula* spread through the valley: a Tolai woman from elsewhere in PNG was said to have learned the secrets of *drakula* during her education in Australia. Gossip about witches and demons today freely incorporates imagery derived from Hollywood movies and when I inquired whether white people have witches (cf. Schram 2010; see also Pype, this volume), the answer usually referred to the vampires represented in Hollywood films. The emphasis on "blood sucking" in the idea of vampires has begun to inflect local Asaro constructs of witchcraft, as when young men emphasize the sharpened teeth of child witches. Indeed, one of my informants claimed that witchcraft has come from white people—though, as indicated by Virikare, most people would say that it is an indigenous ancestral inheritance.

Witches are figures of unmitigated hunger or greed. At night, they feed on the internal organs of persons or pigs, eating livers, hearts, lungs, and brains. They may feed on the recently deceased so participants in funerary proceedings are therefore suspicious of persons who loiter near grave sites. An intense and covetous gaze is a further sign of nefarious intent, as witches can see *into* the bodies of their victims.

In fact, the presence of *gwumu* inside persons fundamentally changes their perception of the world, allowing them to peer beyond conventional appearances or external reality. They may see *through* the skin to the human vitality embodied in organs and blood, stimulating hunger. And they may see *through* conventional appearances to the "spirit side" beneath: an invisible world inhabited by witches, but *already* developed. "You see a village," Virikare told me, "they see a city." Significant features of the scene of village life both disguise and reveal aspects of the "spirit side." People might point to a large tree: "there is the witch's office building." That particular tree, a dying eucalyptus, is believed to be inhabited by witches because lights (fireflies) are seen in it at night; the rhythmic buzzing of cicadas that live in it are building alarms. In this "office building," the witches have a blackboard where they deliberate on who to kill, and witches can mark the exact time of death of people. Two large trees located across each other on the main road leading to one village high up the valley are known as the "witches' gate," a kind of monumental arch "on the spirit side." A stone may be a bus stop for the witch's transports. On the spirit side of the village, there is also a leisure club and a disco.

Moreover, across the central highlands, it is well known that Mount Elimbari is the "parliament of the witches," suggesting that the world of the witches has a proper, modern, even bureaucratic government. Witches are said to keep books, to meet regularly keeping lists of future victims. Their society also observes norms of reciprocity and exchange characteristic of a proper moral sociality. While witches only kill their own kin, they are said to trade these victims between each other (cf. Newell 2007).

In this invisible modern world, witches are "professionalizing," people told me. They are "increasing their standard," improving their techniques and attending school and university. As "normal" people figure out ways to track witches, witches develop new ways to evade detection, to bewitch people more efficiently, quickly, and without leaving a mark or any evidence—for example, with one shot from the "witches' guns."

On the spirit side, witches also hold occupations that for villagers most represent a "changed" (*senis*)—modern—society. One informant said: "On the outside you may see a *pipia man*, a rubbish man, a man with no wealth and no social standing. But 'on the inside' this individual may be a salaried employee." One woman who was killed in 2012 was thought to be an "air hostess," on the spirit side, because of the flair for the style she exhibited in her everyday dress. Two men were said to be "lawyers" in the world of witches because in everyday village life they "talk a lot." Witches have their own police men, their own members of parliament, and so on.

Witches, in short, are already the people that Papua New Guineans would like to become. Against a background of rotting grass houses and unruly youth, witches inhabit a wealthy and ordered modernity. If they are feared and condemned, *they are also figures of desire,* for they embody the style of life that people seek for themselves. The kind of acquisitive and individualistic subjectivity the witch symbolizes is appealing to people, while also instilling fear. The mixture of desire and repulsion that witches provoke condenses the manifold moral quandaries that modernity generates into a potent and contradictory figure: the modern citizen-subject who is also a monster committing unspeakable acts of mystical violence.

Apprehending the Witch

Although witches inhabit an invisible world, the presence of witchcraft is ascertained through analysis of images and events both everyday and misfortunate. Men known as *glasman* in pidgin or *lusuve* in the local language, are people best thought of as seers, people who can divine the sources of illness or misfortune. *Lusuve* say that in recent years their influence is being pushed aside, especially due to evangelical and Pentecostal sermons condemning them. Today, far more important in the unfolding of witchcraft accusations are spirit mediums, people possessed by the ghosts of witch's victims who may reveal their mystical assailants during trance-like episodes. It seems significant that both mediums I have spoken to attend Pentecostal churches. Thus, traditional modes of divination and sacred authority are being displaced by newer Christian ideas. Nevertheless, *lusuve* and spirit mediums may intervene in particular instances of misfortune, especially when sickness and death are involved. In such circumstances, people inspect the social environment for signs of bad feeling. Crucially, in the Asaro valley, witches are thought to prey *only* upon their own kin (cf. Geschiere 2013). So when looking for hidden resentment, people look to their kin first. Did the deceased give money to some kin but not others? Was a pig consumed that wasn't shared? Every accusation I have encountered revolves around the breaking of the ethos of reciprocity among kin.

Ultimately, however, misfortune itself is held to be the sign—the index (cf. Blanes, this volume)—of witchcraft. So the apperception of witchcraft in the world does not necessarily require the intervention of a medium or a diviner, and the ideas described here are drawn mostly from everyday conversations I had with people outside the context of any *particular* accusation. People speak frequently of the "curse" of witches. They point to their own apparent inability to develop socioeconomically and secure the promises of modernity as evidence that witches are stealing from them. Moreover, forms of premillennial dispensationalism script local misfortunes and worries into apocalyptic narratives about the end of times. Local affairs evoke momentous developments on the world stage, so that, for example, the arrival of a new mobile phone tower in the mountains above the village is taken to represent the advent of a One World Government, an important notion in this type of thinking, since the tower is held to be controlled from within the new World Trade Center building in New York City.

The curse of witchcraft consists in what witches do and the kinds of harms they produce. Witches consume vitality resulting in sickness and death. But they also steal value: people blame witches for failed business enterprises or the breakdown of a truck. Several people told me how witches "eat" the "value" (*valu*) of money, so that while an individual may think he or she has accumulated a certain amount of money, its value will be consumed by witches, and after spending the money a person will be left with nothing. Witches leave behind only "shadow" (*sado*) money. Because the village is cursed by witchcraft, only those that go to town can succeed in business. As indicated in Virikare's comments, relations between "village" and "city" are a fundamental dimension of witchcraft discourse, as symbols of contrasting social orders, one associated with subsistence and the demands of reciprocity and the other with development and individualism. Finally, during election seasons, unsuccessful candidates accuse witches of stealing their votes.

So people speak frequently of mutations in life, labor, and law when they describe the effects of witchcraft on their communities: witches consume vitality, value, and votes. They insinuate themselves into the major forms of contemporary social reproduction: family, economy, and government. This image of a distorted modernity, in which the promises of social change are visible but out of reach, tempting but not tangible, bears comparing to anthropological accounts elsewhere in the world that analyze the relationship between unseen forces and visible wealth (Comaroff and Comaroff 1993; Ferguson 2006; Geschiere 1997). Newell's (2007) notion of "Pentecostal witchcraft" conjures a hybrid phenomenon—simultaneously traditional and modern—responding to these contemporary conditions of desire and transformation, and their attendant inequalities and conflicts. Both Pentecostal worship and ideas about witchcraft engage with problems of money and morality, power and politics, individual redemption and social obligation, in a world where futures are uncertain and where people feel buffeted by unfair fates. Insofar as it blames demonic forces for the scattershot distributions of good fortune, Pentecostal discourse imagines its congregants as locked in a "spiritual battle," warding off or exorcizing the agencies that thwart progress. Whether this battle requires them to repudiate the past or to abstain from an emerging future (Pype, this volume), the agonism itself joins people ever more closely to the thing that troubles them. Indeed, in the next section, I show how Pentecostal witchcraft—a synthetic and complementary realm of malicious evils (witches) and protective pathways (churches)—demands that people search *themselves* for signs of the sin that turns into witchcraft. As MacCarthy describes for the Trobriands (this volume), witchcraft is a force hidden in the self, but made visible in the harms and depredations visited upon others. If "Pentecostal witchcraft," then, names the hybrid cultural imaginary of spiritual warfare, we might call "Pentecostal witches" those persons who newly imagine themselves as the subjects, indeed the very sites, of that battle. This imaginary figures a changing world, placing local struggles on a global scene, and inviting people to view their own personal conflicts and relations within a framework of universal, even mythical significance, as when a sermon finds in mundane feelings of resentment between siblings the seed of murderous malevolence with world historical consequence. In so doing, this imaginary queries the kind of people Pentecostals see themselves becoming.

Hidden Sin: Cain and Abel as Parable

In the Bible talk on Cain and Abel with which I opened this chapter, God was able to look past the body to the disposition of the spirit that animates people: there God saw that Cain was acting duplicitously and deceptively. The sermon argued that the presence of this hidden feeling in Cain explains both God's disfavor at his offering, and Cain's later murder of Abel. Pentecostal Christians distinctively emphasize "the spiritual" and the direct manifestation of the presence of the Holy Spirit. The Holy Spirit is visible most especially in the movement of the body in ways held to reveal its presence. This manifestation of the spiritual makes visible a *wanbel* (reconciled, agreed, peaceful) state indicating the alignment of the individual Christian subject (worshipper) with God (Street 2010; cf. Kelly-Hanku et al. 2014). Thus, Pentecostals often describe two types of Christian—"spirit Christian" (the truly devout) and "body Christians" (those too concerned about material things, those who do not truly "believe" or have "faith")—a sort of interdenominational pejorative that condemns doctrinal emphasis on outward ritual rather than inner belief (Keane 2007). The outer body should ideally reveal an inner "spirit body," as, for example, through the kinds of ecstatic experience often associated with Pentecostal religious fervor.

In contrast, sin is understood as *hidden* in the body. Sermons that focus on sin as hidden thinking or emotions are interpreted by people listening as themselves a form of veiled speech referring to a problem of great consequence in communities: witchcraft. Through notions of hidden resentment or unseen discord, this Christian discourse associates sin with the *gwumu* witchcraft I have described. Following the sermon on Cain and Abel, church members told me that the visiting preacher was referring to witchcraft by using a local metapragmatic category of talk called *tok bokis* (literally, "box talk," but usually referred to as "veiled speech") or *gramiyi harekeneve* ("hidden talk") in Dano. Ideas about hidden sin are extremely common in Pentecostal services and discourse, and the idioms in which hidden sin is described are frequently *also* associated with witchcraft. Sin is often described in the local language as hidden in the *bilum* ("netbag") of the self, where the word *bilum* (*ro* in Dano) also means uterus, the location in the body where *gwumu* lives. This is a gendered, but flexible, discourse, as some accusations are also made against men. Nevertheless, Sunday morning altar calls seemed to me to be directed mainly at women congregants; speakers might even turn toward the side of the church where women sit when discussing hidden sin.

Thus people increasingly understand Christian discourse about sin to be *about witchcraft*. As I realized this, the very common Pentecostal themes of interior "spirit" bodies, hidden bad feelings, and so on gained new resonance: these were themselves "hidden" speech referring to the witchcraft concealed in the congregation (cf. Newell 2007: 472).

Two dimensions of the Cain and Abel parable stand out in regard to it as a parable of witchcraft. First, the story involves both material exchange and resentment, and almost all explanations of specific witchcraft incidents involve resentment, envy, or jealousy in relation to reciprocal obligations. Notably, it is the hiddenness of witches that allows them to elude demands for sharing wealth, and therefore enables them to accumulate. Second, the story involves bad feeling between *siblings*, and witches in the upper Asaro attack only their own close kin.

The message of many other sermons and commentary I recorded turned on these themes of interior/exterior, hidden/revealed, in emphasizing that God's grace alone affords protection from the invasive gaze of witches. Here is how one congregant described this phenomenon:

> There is no safe place, only in the church will you find help. *Em banis tru.*
>
> You must hide underneath the blood of Christ. (*Bai yu hait insait long blut bilong Jisas.*) Jesus shed his blood on the cross, and this blood has all the strength for protecting us.
>
> There is no other road. Only Jesus will protect (*banisim*) us.
>
> When witches confess, they say things like: "When we encounter people who follow Jesus, when we would like to get close to them, there is a light! A strong light! It reflects against our vision, and we can't get close to them."
>
> We church-goers have asked the witches (*sanguma*), the people with demons (*spirit nogut*). And those people say: "we want to harm you, to consume your meat, to take out your heart, your brain, your body... but there is a white cloth (*laplap*) that covers you, either a white shroud (*laplap*), or blood, red blood, it covers you. And it makes it hard for us to see you. ... Those who don't go to church — that's our highway! It's easy to go inside and eat. We can look inside you, in any corner (*insait long wanem hap*) — if you ate sweet potato. We can see that! Suppose you ate chicken, we can see that too there. If you ate pig and came, we could see that too. That's the power of the witch."
>
> They wouldn't know except that they have this demon (*spirit nogut*) that sees. They can see into your very gut. If you ate sweet potato, or rice, they see it.
>
> But the witches ruin *our* vision so that we can't see them. When they walk around, talking to each other, they can close your eyes. This spirit of theirs, it clouds your eyesight. This is some kind of *power* they have. It's some kind of *power.* It's the power of Satan.

Here two important Christian idioms resonate. First, Christian piety manifests as "light" or "shine" in the body and person of the devout. Pious Christians, those who especially exhibit the presence of the Holy Spirit, are so bright they are like "mirrors": they *reflect back* the invasive gaze of the witch. Second, and similarly, people discuss the blood of Christ as offering protection from witches. While often used as a metaphor, where the blood of Christ symbolizes redemption from sin, it is often described by my informants in quite material and bodily terms as a veiling shroud that prevents witches from seeing inside a person. Rather than the interior of bodies, the witches will instead see only the blood of Christ. One might say that the blood of Christ on the exterior of the body is actually the interior of the Christian body being made exterior, a body being turned inside-out (Strathern 1979). All of these ideas evoke powerful Melanesian constructs linking power and persuasion to what can and cannot be seen, how people make themselves visible to one another, and how that visibility implicates people in moral relationships to each other.

Conclusion: On Sight and Sociality, the Sinful and the Spiritual

Ethnographic discourse on Melanesia often associates ideas about vision and dynamics of display with concepts of growth, social efficacy, and the moral relationship that obtains between objects and observers, persons and perspectives. An important dimension of this analysis pertains to the qualities Melanesians attribute to the sense of sight itself, to seeing as a particular kind of act, and to the effects that seeing can have on a witnessing subject. Bashkow refers to these dynamics as an "interpersonal economy of sight." Witnessing inequalities in attractiveness, wealth, or health, provokes feelings of either pity or poverty depending on perspective. To rectify this imbalance, the morally appropriate response is the exchange of a gift that reestablishes mutual respect and recognition: "Until … the feeling of imbalance is counteracted, the perception of imbalance has the potential to assume a negative form, jealousy, that may lead to destructive actions" (Bashkow 2006: 123).

In the upper Asaro, for example, resplendently decorated dancers sometimes must give gifts to those who witness them, gifts known as *ho* or sun, an idiom that emphasizes brightness as a quality of health and wealth that is experienced as a ray that pierces the being of the subject who sees it.

In a context where to be seen is to be drawn into an interpersonal economy of sight, growth or transformation is achieved through concealment or secrecy, lest desiring others demand transactions that diminish such growth. Opacity, concealment, enclosure, and secrecy are all linked to ideas about growth, whether we speak of vibrant vital energies of the high mountain forest, thickly concealed with vegetation (Biersack 1982), or if we are thinking of the deliberate secrecy or opacity associated with many ritual activities in Melanesia, including especially forms of male initiation that grew young boys into strong men by removing them from the sight of their mothers and others, as was the case in the upper Asaro and its male cult (Read 1952).

Dialectics of sight and sociality, display and domination, exhibition and egalitarianism, are key qualities of the happening of social life in Melanesia. Yet this ethnographic literature on the social effects of tactics of concealment and display has focused largely on the motivations and intentions of social actors, on their personal and political purposes. The problem of witchcraft, however, involves dynamics of the concealed or unseen in contexts where people might wish to see but cannot. In the discourse of witchcraft, we find ideas about those who deceive without being perceived, and people who feel watched but cannot witness. Witchcraft in an important sense is about the disruption of the interpersonal economy of sight.

During my interviews with lawyers, police, and legal experts in Port Moresby and Goroka in 2013 and 2014, witchcraft was often said to be a "spiritual problem." When asked to describe what they mean by "the spiritual," people refer to things which cannot be seen—the invisible (cf. Blanes, this volume). Witchcraft is believed to be an especially troubling phenomenon because it is both everywhere and unseen. For those in PNG's law and justice sector, then, it is a problem precisely because it cannot leave evidence in its wake, making it impossible to prosecute, and contributing to the sense that witchcraft is increasing. A further connotation of what is meant by "spiritual" refers to the spirits or souls of persons and the corruption therein. Law and justice sector discourse characterizing witchcraft as a "spiritual problem," then, is also a discourse that locates the best means of addressing witchcraft in those institutions that address the souls of persons: churches. Most PNG police, scholars and others with whom I have worked would agree that the solution to PNG's problem of witchcraft is ministry. Ministry alone is thought to be capable of redeeming the community. But the irony of "Pentecostal witchcraft" reemerges, for the ministry that might solve the social problem of witchcraft can only do so by finding it over and again in its congregations.

Witches inhabit a hidden world of material wealth by clouding the vision of the kin with whom they might otherwise feel obligated to share that prosperity. If this form of hiddenness is morally condemned, indeed is the very symbol of evil, Christian ideas offer redemption as itself a protecting shroud of piety—blocking the supernatural sight of witches with the white light and red blood of Jesus. To protect oneself from the poisonous envy of the prying eyes of kin, one must expose oneself entirely to the eye of God. The Pentecostal subject exchanges the perspective of kinship, associated with mutual aid and reciprocity, for the perspective of God and the Holy Spirit, associated with purity and individual salvation (Robbins 2004a). Thus purified by the fire of the Holy Spirit, the pious Christian subject becomes a kind of mirror of or for God, aligning the internal spirit body with the outward body visible to others, shining bright.

These ideas themselves reflect each other insofar as they emphasize the power of concealment itself. Power is to be found in the evasion of the affects and obligations of others, especially kin. But viewed through the convex lens of morality, these ideas about sight, sociality, and sin invert the values they appear to reproduce. Whereas ideas about witchcraft proclaim jealousy to be an insidious and harmful feeling within kin relations, their covert effect is to assure that kin be attentive to each other—to recognize each other through the material transactions thought to manifest obligation and visible harmony. The overt Pentecostal vision of redemption requires that such thoughts in the self be purged, but their covert message is that by purging oneself of negative feelings *toward* others, one gains protection against those very feelings *in* others through the alignment of the individual self with God (Schram 2010). The covert morality of witchcraft requires wealth to be shared. The morality of Pentecostalism offers liberation from these obligations. This is a fitting moral vision in a context where people badly desire for themselves the material benefits of a modernity that continues to elude, to hide, from them.

The discourse of "Pentecostal witchcraft" affirms a world threatened by witchcraft, and it does so in a *personal* way. In addressing congregants as people harboring bad feelings toward their kin, it insists that they view themselves as subjects of this temptation. Purging bad feeling yields a kind of piety that allows people to conceal themselves from the envious gaze of others. That is to say, they make themselves invisible to witches, appropriating the very power of concealment that witches are thought to monopolize. The Pentecostal church and the world of witchcraft are thus reciprocal visions of the power entailed in disrupting the interpersonal economy of sight. Moreover, accepting the Pentecostal dispensation means acknowledging the sin in oneself in order to achieve redemption. But since sin is another name for witchcraft, becoming Pentecostal means first acknowledging the witch you already are.

References

Bashkow, Ira. 2000. "Confusion, Native Skepticism, and Recurring Questions About the Year: 'Soft' Beliefs and Preparations for the Millennium in the Arapesh Region, Papua New Guinea." *Ethnohistory* 47 (1): 133–169.

Bashkow, Ira. 2006. *The Meaning of Whitemen*. Chicago: University of Chicago Press.

Benediktsson, Karl. 2002. *Harvesting Development: The Construction of Fresh Food Markets in Papua New Guinea*. Ann Arbor: University of Michigan Press.

Biersack, Aletta. 1982. "Ginger Gardens for the Ginger Woman: Rites and Passages in a Melanesian Society." *Man* (*N.S.*) 17: 239–258.

Comaroff, Jean, and John Comaroff. 1993. *Modernity and Its Malcontents: Ritual and Power in Postcolonial Africa*. Chicago: University of Chicago Press.

Downs, Ian. 1986. *The Last Mountain: A Life in Papua New Guinea*. St. Lucia: University of Queensland Press.

Evans-Pritchard, E. E. 1937. *Witchcraft, Oracles and Magic among the Azande*. Oxford: Clarenden Press.

Ferguson, James. 2006. *Global Shadows: Africa in the Neoliberal World Order*. Durham: Duke University Press.

Geschiere, Peter. 1997. *The Modernity of Witchcraft: Politics and the Occult in Postcolonial Africa*. Charlottesville: University Press of Virginia.

Geschiere, Peter. 2013. *Witchcraft, Intimacy, and Trust: Africa in Comparison*. Chicago: University of Chicago Press.

Godelier, Maurice. 1986. *The Making of Great Men: Male Domination and Power Among the New Guinea Baruya*. Cambridge: Cambridge University Press.

Golub, Alex. 2014. *Leviathans at the Gold Mine: Creating Indigenous and Corporate Actors in Papua New Guinea*. Durham: Duke University Press.

Handman, Courtney. 2014. *Critical Christianity: Translation and Denominational Conflict in Papua New Guinea*. Berkeley: University of California Press.

Jebens, Holger. 2005. *Pathways to Heaven: Contesting Mainline and Fundamentalist Christianity in Papua New Guinea*. London: Berghahn Books.

Keane, Webb. 2007. *Christian Moderns: Freedom and Fetish in the Mission Encounter*. Berkeley: University of California Press.

Kelly-Hanku, Angela, et al. 2014. "'We call it a virus but I want to say it's the devil inside': Redemption, moral reform and relationships with God among people living with HIV in Papua New Guinea." *Social Science and Medicine* 119: 106–113.

Jacka, Jerry. 2015. *Alchemy in the Rain Forest: Politics, Ecology, and Resilience in a New Guinea Mining Area*. Durham: Duke University Press.

Jorgensen, Dan. 2014. "Preying on those close to home: Witchcraft violence in a Papua New Guinea village." *The Australian Journal of Anthropology* 25 (3): 267–286.

Kirsch, Stuart. 2014. *Mining Capitalism: The Relationship between Corporations and Their Critics*. Berkeley: University of California Press.

Lattas, Andrew, and Knut Rio. 2011. "Securing Modernity: Towards and Ethnography of Power in Contemporary Melanesia." *Oceania* 81 (1): 1–19.

Lindenbaum, Shirley. 1979. *Kuru Sorcery: Disease and Danger in the New Guinea Highlands*. Palo Alto: Mayfield Publishing.

Lindenbaum, Shirley. 2002. "Fore Narratives Through Time: How a Bush Spirit Became a Robber, Was Sent to Jail, Emerged as the Symbol of the Eastern Highlands Province, and Never Left Home." *Current Anthropology* 43 (S4): S63–S73.

Meyer, Birgit. 1999. *Translating the Devil: Religion and Modernity among the Ewe in Ghana*. Edinburgh: Edinburgh University Press.

Munn, Nancy. 1992 [1986]. *The Fame of Gawa*. Durham: Duke University Press.

Newell, Sasha. 2007. "Pentecostal Witchcraft: Neoliberal Possession and Demonic Discourse in Ivoirian Pentecostal Churches." *Journal of Religion in Africa* 37 (4): 461–490.

Newland, Lynda, and Terry Brown. 2015. "Introduction: Descent from Israel and Jewish Identities in the Pacific, Past and Present." *Oceania* 85 (3): 251–255.

Newman, Philip. 1964. "Religious Belief and Ritual in a New Guinea Society." *American Anthropologist* 66: 257–271.

Newman, Philip. 1965. *Knowing the Gururumba*. New York: Holt, Rinehart and Winston.

Read, Kenneth. 1952. "Nama Cult of the Central Highlands, New Guinea." *Oceania* 23: 1–25.

Read, Kenneth. 1955. "Morality and the Concept of the Person among the Gahuku-Gama." *Oceania* 25: 233–282.

Robbins, Joel. 2004a. *Becoming sinners: Christianity and moral torment in a Papua New Guinea society*. Berkeley: University of California Press.

Robbins, Joel. 2004b. "The globalization of Pentecostal and Charismatic Christianity." *Annual Review of Anthropology* 33: 117–143.

Schram, Ryan. 2010. "Witches' Wealth: Witchcraft, confession, and Christianity in Auhelawa, Papua New Guinea." *Journal of the Royal Anthropological Institute* 16 (4): 726–742.

Schram, Ryan. 2014. A New Government Breaks With The Past in The Papua New Guinea Parliament's "Haus Tambaran." *Material World*, February. http://www.materialworldblog.com/2014/02/a-new-government-breaks-with-the-past-in-the-papua-new-guinea-parliaments-haus-tambaran/.

Smith, R. M. 1979. "Christ, Keysser and Culture: Lutheran Evangelistic Policy and Practice in the Highlands of Papua New Guinea." *Canberra Anthropology* 2 (1): 78–97.

Stephen, Michelle. 1987a. "Contrasting images of power." In *Sorcerer and Witch in Melanesia*, ed. Michelle Stephen, 249–304. New Brunswick: Rutgers University Press.

Stephen, Michelle. 1987b. "Introduction." In *Sorcerer and Witch in Melanesia*, ed. Michelle Stephen, 1–14. New Brunswick: Rutgers University Press.

Strange, Gladys. 1965. "Nominal Elements in Upper Asaro." *Anthropological Linguistics* 7 (5): 71–79.

Strathern, Andrew. 1975. *The Rope of Moka: Big-Men and Ceremonial Exchange in Mount Hagen New Guinea*. Cambridge: Cambridge University Press.

Strathern, Marilyn. 1979. "The Self in Self-Decoration." *Oceania* 49 (4): 241–257.

Strathern, Marilyn. 2013. *Learning to See in Melanesia*. Manchester: HAU Society for Ethnographic Theory.

Street, Alice. 2010. "Belief as relational action: Christianity and cultural change in Papua New Guinea." *Journal of the Royal Anthropological Institute* 16 (2): 260–278.

Strong, Thomas. 2006. "Land and Life: Some Terrains of Sovereignty in the Papua New Guinea Highlands." *Suomen Antropologi* 31 (3–4): 37–52.

Strong, Thomas. 2007. "'Dying Culture' and Decaying Bodies." In *Embodying Modernity and Post-Modernity in Melanesia*, ed. Sandra Bamford, 105–123. Durham: Carolina Academic Press.

Tuzin, Donald. 1997. *The Cassowary's Revenge: The Life and Death of Masculinity in a New Guinea Society*. Chicago: University of Chicago Press.

Wesch, Michael. 2007. "A Witch Hunt in New Guinea: Anthropology on Trial." *Anthropology and Humanism* 32 (1): 4–17.

Author Biography

Thomas Strong is a lecturer in the Department of Anthropology at Maynooth University in Ireland. He was educated at Reed College (BA) and Princeton University (Ph.D.). He is currently completing a monograph on witchcraft, violence, and modernity in highland Papua New Guinea, where he first began fieldwork in 1998.

CHAPTER 4

The Ndoki Index: Sorcery, Economy, and Invisible Operations in the Angolan Urban Sphere

Ruy Blanes

Introduction

In Angola, the contemporary religious sphere has observed dramatic transformations in recent years. One effect of such transformations is the emergence of sorcery (*nodki*, in local language) accusations as a 'social problem', with complex and often violent outcomes for those involved. In this article, I explore some possibilities that contextualize this emergence from the point of view of Christian (Pentecostal, Evangelical, and Prophetic) believers.[1] I argue that the different configurations and effects identified in sorcery produce what could be called an 'index' with financial consequences, very much analogous to the kind of work operated by the Dow Jones index in financial markets in Wall Street and across the world. The '*ndoki* index' will thus appear as an ideological construct that is able to describe and regulate the 'spiritual market' in both capitalistic and noncapitalistic modalities. To do so, I begin with a description of the epistemology of sorcery in Angola, and then describe how it appears in the contemporary urban religious sphere of Luanda. I will argue that the

R. Blanes (✉)
Consejo Superior de Investigaciones Científicas, Madrid, Spain

K. Rio et al. (eds.), *Pentecostalism and Witchcraft*, Contemporary Anthropology of Religion, DOI 10.1007/978-3-319-56068-7_4

emergence of sorcery is contiguous to the urban experience and participates in its moral and economic dimensions.

Invisible Notes Concerning *Ndoki*

Whenever I am debating contemporary Angolan politics with my friends in Luanda, the part that I find more interesting is that the conversation somehow yet inevitably ends up in a discussion on sorcery and its effects.[2] This association of witchcraft and politics, as we know, is not specific to Angola, but is rather a theme that pervades African social life (see, e.g., Englund 1996; Geschiere 1995; Comaroff and Comaroff 1999; Moore and Sanders 2001; Ashforth 2005; Marshall 2009). Thus what seems interesting is the recurrence and social pervasiveness of this politization of witchcraft throughout time and with an intriguing superficial sense of continental continuity in what comes to such perceptions. In this text, in complement to these points of view, I propose to explore their ramifications, such as the outpouring of sorcery into other dimensions of social life—namely morality and economy—in the urban settings of Angola.

In Luanda specifically, considering the significant place of the Bakongo ethnicity in its current social, cultural, and demographic configuration, sorcery is often identified with the kikongo name *ndoki* (or *kindoki*), vulgarly translated as *feitiçaria* (in Portuguese) or sorcery.[3] As I have argued elsewhere (e.g., Sarró et al. 2008; Blanes 2014), the Bakongo play a highly relevant yet problematic role in the contemporary history of Angola. On the one hand, they were pivotal in the Angolan liberation wars (1961–1974), hosting the guerrilla and military movements that would then proceed to become the political protagonists of Angolan independency (see, e.g., Rocha 2003). They were also instrumental in the development of transnational commercial networks and the introduction of trade goods into Luanda, and in the dramatic urban development of the capital observed since the 1970s (see, e.g., Lukombo 2011; Pereira 2015). On the other, they remain associated to ideas of 'foreignness' and 'backward-ness' (traditionalism) that are antithetical to the sociopolitical project of the ruling political elite (MPLA), based on the enforcement of centralized national integrity and modernistic, iconoclastic ideas of progress (Schubert 2014). This is related to what is widely perceived as the Bakongo's dubious political allegiance—connected to the memory of the ancient Kingdom of Kongo[4]—and the centrality of 'tradition' in their social, religious, economic, and political configurations, where *ndoki* plays a central role. Within this framework, there are active narrative and semantic configurations that associate this ethnicity with informality, illegality and, ultimately, sorcery.

But what is, after all, *ndoki*, and how is it perceived from within the specific context of urban, post-war Angola?[5] A commonsensical understanding would refer simply to 'evil spirits', their presence and/or effect. But there are more overarching narratives. My Bakongo friends in Luanda—Christian and non-Christian alike—usually frame it as a system of knowledge that is closely connected to certain aspects of 'tradition', in the sense that it refers to knowledge transmitted within the *kanda* or lineage (Cuvelier 1934; Van Wing 1959; Thornton 2001), from uncle to nephew, concerning the 'agency of things and places'; it is an 'ancestral property' connected to the 'spirit' of such things and places. According to local traditional epistemologies, there is a recurrent association of *ndoki* with the idea of ingestion, as something that is introduced inside the body. Eoghan Ballard (2005) notes that historically this has been negatively linked (by Catholic authors, unsurprisingly) to acts and processes of 'poisoning'. This seems to complement what J. Van Wing, the Belgian missionary and folklorist noted, when he tied it to the image of 'clanic blood'—*liens du sang*, blood connections (1959: 359–360). So there is in such theories an implicit logic of bodily 'internalization' of witchcraft that is simultaneously its concealment from the public gaze while remaining pervasive in the social sphere as a narrative of suspicion. Here, the conflation of 'substance' and 'power' in the body becomes politically active (Graeber 2005). This becomes evident in the way notions of secrecy come to envelope the discourse of *ndoki*, ultimately rendering it as an 'invisible agency', but also ensuring its endurance and persistence, as I describe below. In other words, if *ndoki* were not a secret, it would no longer be *ndoki*. As Gabriele Bortolami (2012: 297) describes, this sense of secrecy and mystery was also in itself a factor of prestige within the traditional social structure, namely for those who could somehow access or master such wisdom. However, the prestige does not eliminate suspicion (Graeber 2005: 418). For instance, figures such as the *nganga* ('witch doctor') not only refer to a ritual/spiritual specialization or expertise, but also to political agency (Bortolami 2012).[6]

In this respect, a central aspect of this agency is the notion of deferred or remote effect. In other words, it usually involves what Knut Rio (2002) describes, in the case of Vanuatu in Melanesia, as an 'absent third person', an element that remotely intermediates between the cause and effect of sorcery through the establishment of a triadic relationship. From this perspective, if one becomes aware of the effects of *ndoki* (illness, death, and bad luck), the cause (or causer) will most likely remain invisible or anonymous unless it is revealed by an intermediary with the appropriate knowledge and power. But in any case, the focus always becomes the relationship, the space of connection that conveys meaning and possibilities of action for the actors involved in the process.

But one thing is the knowledge or theory of *ndoki*, and the other its practical unfolding. From this perspective, there is also 'good' and 'bad' *ndoki*, which leads to a subsequent distinction between sorcery (*feitiçaria*) and fetishism (*feiticismo*), both concepts harboring different levels of moral configuration. At this point, we argue, the urban space of cities such as Luanda introduces the moralizing element into the equation, becoming the third element that totalizes the experience of *ndoki* and makes it constitutive of the social relationships (Rio 2002: 130).

A case in point is the current 'epidemic' (as it is usually framed in the local media) of child sorcery accusations in Luanda, related to both an idea of a corrupted use of *ndoki* knowledge and a heightened sense of insecurity and paranoia in the particularly harsh context of the city's neighborhoods. As Luena Pereira describes in her ethnography of the Bakongo *regressados*[7] in the Palanca neighborhood of Luanda, child sorcery accusations, although not new in local history, have been object of the 'social construction of a problem' (2008: 31) that involves traditional authorities, the state and concurrent institutions, and local media, within a progressive narrative that invokes the destructuration of the traditional familial model, the consequences of war, the perils of urban life and economic crisis (see also Pereira 2016; Soares 2016). This has reinforced the historical production, on behalf of both colonial Portuguese and postcolonial Angolan political and religious authorities, of *ndoki* as an inherently negative phenomenon, one that illustrates the kind of past that needs to be erased, be it for the sake of a 'modern' colonial empire or for a 'developed' postcolonial nation (on this see, e.g., Milando 2008). Simultaneously, it reveals the agency of moralized political discourse in its configuration (on this see Brinkman 2003).

Mario,[8] a good friend of mine from Luanda, told me once how he interfered in a case of accusation of child sorcerers in the neighborhood of Palanca, using his authority as an elder and spiritual savant to solve one such case. He attended an interrogation session, where they were asking children what they had dreamed about, in order to decide if they were sorcerers or not. Mario contested this process, arguing (in a somewhat Freudian fashion) that it was very normal for children to dream about people they know, since it was part of the process of infantile socialization.

Mario thus managed to abort what would have eventually made yet another media headline. In the newspapers, every now and then we hear gruesome stories about *feitiçaria* that end up in a moralizing epilogue about how it represents a 'backward Angola' that has no place in the new, modern country. One particularly striking case became a running joke in Luanda, back in 2011: the national television channel, TPA, ran a story about a woman who had given birth, after a 21-month pregnancy, to a turtle. In the news piece broadcasted in the television, André Manuel, a traditional healer she had resorted to, could not hide his amazement: "*this is sorcery. I have treated many people and never seen this before in my life*". The undertone of ridicule and abjection in the news piece was evident, and several people I talked to shared and commented on this story as an example of how far people can go down the road of irrationality in what concerns sorcery and its effects.

Likewise, child sorcery accusations also become part of the same discourse of abjection. In one such example, in early 2008, several news pieces circulated in the local media concerning how members of a Catholic congregation rescued several children in the Palanca who had been beaten and abandoned by their parents, accused of sorcery. One of the Catholic nuns involved in the rescue, sister Rita, declared to the local media that what was beneath such phenomena was "*social disorder and extreme poverty, and the main victims are the children*" (*Ecclesia*, 30 January 2008).

However, Mario was not recalling the episode he intervened in to argue how 'wrong' these accusations were from a moral perspective, but rather from a methodological one. For him, there were traditional structures and procedures within the Bakongo tradition that secured the collective regulation of such phenomena. From this perspective, as Bortolami (2012) and Milando (2013) describe in the case of rural northern Angola, *ndoki* acted in principle as a regulator of collective interaction. However, in Luanda, due to the dramatic societal change experienced by the Bakongo, such procedures were no longer being respected. 'Tradition' had somehow been corrupted by the process of extreme urbanization.

This example shows us how, through the distinction of positive and negative *ndoki*, and of *ndoki* in theory and in practice, a process of moralization emerges. As I will explain below, this is the result of plural and competing understandings of *ndoki* on behalf of different religious (mostly Christian) and political agents. But it is also the outcome of what has been described in the field as process of commodification in the stricter Marxian sense, of insertion of *ndoki* within a capitalist, money-driven system that is proper of urban life (see also Pype, this volume). Both processes are, undeniably, interconnected.

On Capitalist Sorcery

As I tried to argue above, perhaps the most defining characteristic of *ndoki* practice is its invisibility, or the fact that it exists insofar as it is concealed from public sight and therefore public knowledge. It only becomes manifest through what Philippe Pignarre and Isabelle Stengers, in their book on the *sorcellerie capitaliste* (2004) called 'the power of the event'(2004: 11),[9] or in abstract, the agency of fabricating effects. From this perspective, one could argue that sorcery theories and practices such as *ndoki* work with a 'cloaking device', an imagined technology[10] by which objects, agents, or actions are necessarily invisible or concealed, although its consequences are not necessarily so. In fact, as I suggested above, despite its inherent secretive condition, it is fundamental that *ndoki*'s effects become visible in order for it to 'be' *ndoki*.[11] Such consequences and mechanisms of 'turning visible', I argue, involve a process of capitalization.

Taking this argument further, as a realm of knowledge that is an art of producing effects, *ndoki* can be seen as resembling other forms of sorcery. I am obviously thinking, from Pignarre and Stengers' suggestion concerning capitalism as the ultimate form of creating relations and effects. This obviously resonates with the Comaroffs' notion of 'occult economies' (1999), where they uncover the 'big business' (ibid.: 286) behind the postcolonial enchantments—or, in other words, how sorcery is a means to material ends produced within the millennial capitalism context (see also Myhre, this volume). Similarly, Harry West (2005), looking at the case of Mozambique, acutely described how the invisible realm is appended to processes of postcolonial governance in neoliberal reform contexts, explaining how, transcending the analytical prism of encapsulating sorcery (*uwavi*) with the past (see also Geschiere 1997), we can detect its agency as a contemporary social technology that orders, secures, explains, and empowers. Within this particular framework, *uwavi* works as a counter-critique of the neoliberal reform project of the Mozambican state, and reveals an alternative understanding of economy in the Mueda Planalto where West conducted his fieldwork. I am particularly interested in this last point: understanding sorcery as an economy in itself, and not just an expression of, or reaction to, a millennial capitalism (on this, see Austen 1993).

Here, we can perhaps relate to the notion of the 'market as God', as Harvey Cox (1999) eloquently suggested in his discussion of a 'business theology'—ideas conveyed by economics gurus about the self-regulatory capacity of the financial market, and ultimately the inherent justice of the capitalist system, precisely due to its detachment from the effect of individual, subjective behavior. This, Cox argues, is parallel to religious utopian eschatology, and inherits the history of an equally religious ascension of The Market (as Polanyi would have it) into a state of 'Olympic supremacy' (ibid.: 20). This ascension, to be fair, is at the core of Max Weber's argument on the 'spirit of capitalism', the transformation of a household *oikonomia* (Agamben 2011) into a public financial *emporium* (Booth 1994). Thus economy becomes part of a theology, imbued with a spiritual component. Within this framework, 'Capital' becomes prophecy and millennium.[12]

From this perspective, this association with capitalism is not just a recursive strategy on my behalf. In fact, it refers to a subsequent narrative that pervades interactions in Luanda such as those described above: the idea that the current transformation of *ndoki* as a 'social problem', displayed in the public sphere and involving different sectors of civil society in Angola, is the outcome of its display within an urban environment, with the subsequent dramas that it entails: disconnection, individualism, hyperconsumption, accumulation, etc. In other words, many religious folk I encounter in Luanda argue that, in contrast with the idea of immobility or stability of rural life, there is a process of social and spiritual corruption associated with urban life, which produces a metadiscourse concerning tradition, social change, and the power of spirits (see Bortolami 2012). Some, in fact, trace the 'arrival' of *ndoki* to Luanda from the rural areas to the 1960s, with the beginning of the war in the northern provinces of Angola and the subsequent social upheaval, which in turn coincided with the process of the Angolan capital's urban growth and economic development. This process of corruption refers to the conflict that emerges from the disconnection, in the urban sphere, with traditional forms of social, familial, and territorial organization, by which the *regra tradicional*, the traditional rule, that binds knowledge, relationality, and place, is broken.[13]

The overarching association of witchcraft with problems of modernity (Geschiere 1997; Eves 2000), development (Moore and Sanders 2001), and morality (Ruel 1965; Austen 1993; Englund 1996) has been extensively debated and is obviously pertinent in this discussion. But another underlying narrative in discourses pertaining to witchcraft is its association with wealth, accumulation, and other financial operations. Here the association of money and morality is obvious (Parry and Bloch 1989), but we can also speculate around the idea of other, economic activities that are not so morally charged. Jane Parish (2001) has described this in her depiction of witchcraft among the Akan in Ghana, where the emergence of a market of anti-witchcraft shrines and talismans is a response to tourists seeking an 'authentic Africa' (2001: 133). But there is also a necessary point about the vicissitudes of urban life, the perceptions of danger and insecurity that often invoke the emergence of *ndoki*.

Here, I understand the recurrent references I hear in Luanda about the idea of 'insurance' (*assegurado*)—i.e., the need to ensure spiritual protection in order to achieve success and prevent the effects of *inveja* (envy)—as part of a wider perception of spiritual agency that incorporates, detects, and delineates, but is not exhausted in, the idea of morality. One example was given to me by the *mais velho* (elder) Malungo, who built the first multi-story building in the Palanca neighborhood—now used as a mechanical garage, hostel for Chinese workers, and headquarters of the Union des Traditions Kongo (UTK)—back in the early 1980s. The construction was recurrently attacked and sabotaged, object of *ndoki*, and thus took ages before it was 'finalized' (the building still looks unfinished and somewhat ghostly). All this because the neighbors did not agree with such a display of wealth on behalf of one of their own. Malungo never explicitly told me so, but I quickly assumed that this was only possible after obtaining some kind of 'guarantee' at a spiritual level.

A similar story was told concerning a neighbor who, back in the 1970s, attempted to build the first supermarket in the neighborhood. The supermarket was constantly attacked due to its symbolic and visual association to an idea of accumulation and storage that was antithetical to Bakongo logics of circulation and redistribution. But unlike Malungo, the neighbor gave up on his idea and left the Palanca.

From this perspective, *ndoki* is necessarily a response to questions of spiritual and material insecurity (Ashforth 1998; Rio 2010), but it is also part of what Filip de Boeck (2011) called a 'spectral topography', a way of inhabiting the city through its processualities and evanescences. Insurance, as any broker would tell you, can cover misfortune, but it can also create conditions for a protected future. This balance between action and prevention within the spectral topography thus becomes part of the index and regulatory mechanisms displayed through *ndoki*. And with the example of Mavungo's house, we can also see a constant balancing between mechanisms of individual accumulation and, per contra, social regulation towards redistribution. *Ndoki* can thus be seen as a regulatory mechanism that responds and simultaneously anticipates and creates.

It is at this point where I see a parallel with financial markets and indexes, such as the Dow Jones Industrial Average (Dow, in short). In Wall Street and elsewhere, the Dow acts simultaneously as a necessarily morality-free reflection *and* definition of economic activity (financial exchange, speculation),[14] configured through an idea of 'standard', i.e., a measure of reference. Based on a statistic analysis of the trading activity of a major set of companies in the USA, the Dow 'objectively' creates a reference that sets the standard for daily stock exchange and economic transaction. This objectivity is attained by the alleged 'freedom' of numbers, whose material existence would, a priori, not depend upon what Noam Yuran (2014) called an 'economy of desire'. However, as the same author notes, this assumption is based on a 'professional blindness' that is oblivious to how money and its circulation relies on expectation and trust, on performance and repertoire (Guyer 2004), and ultimately on values and relationships (Hart 2010; Graeber 2011; Moya 2015), beyond the idea of an inherent, self-contained rationality (Godelier 1972). The Dow, from this perspective, has its own, long, socialized history of fraud, suspicion, and scandal.[15]

Likewise, in Luanda *ndoki* appears with a similar quality, as an operation that produces a commentary of social (urban) life and simultaneously effects upon it. The same conclusion emerges from the opposite perspective: the Dow, as a mathematical operation that, through an analytical device, produces a signal to the financial markets, thus effecting upon its subsequent behavior, reveals a sorcery quality; likewise, *ndoki* becomes an index, a moral marker that participates in the religious agents' spiritual and political mappings of the city, pushing individuals into processes of prevention, insurance, or accusation. Again, as many of my interlocutors stressed, the use of *ndoki* in the urban space is related to problems of reputation and scapegoating, and to the personal ambition of 'becoming big men' or 'big women', proper of an urban lifestyle where the possession of money can entail an increase in individual authority. It also becomes ambiguous and part of a politics of suspicion, as the practice of *ndoki* often becomes confused with its accusation (you never know if the denouncer is, in fact, the sorcerer). A friend from Luanda once told me the following story, which I transcribed in my own notes:

> Once, an elder *comerciante* (tradesman) accused his own children of doing witchcraft against him. A *makanguilu* (communal meeting) was called, and my friend acted as an intermediary, interrogating both sides in order to understand what had happened and what were their motivations. They found out that the children were only trying to find a way to keep their father close to them and not leave for business trips so much. So he managed to 'free' them from the accusation and possibly murder...

This story is telling of how *ndoki* is object of an 'excess of definition', in the sense that it often encompasses more than the actual (or eventual) act of sorcery: it also includes an apparatus of moral and economic statements that envelope it within a wider understanding of spiritual affairs. Here, the role of Christianity plays an active role.

Christian *Ndokis*

Having worked with different churches within the 'charismatic specter' in Luanda,[16] I recognized several discursive continuities and distinctions that offered concomitant and complementary perceptions on *ndoki*, as if trying to delineate different surfaces of a hypothetical object called *ndoki*, discernible only in the three-dimensional stereogram form, when we acquire the necessary technique or technology to 'recognize' it in the otherwise chaotic picture. In doing so, they detect and/or create different patterns and infrastructures within *ndoki*.

One such politics of recognition came from the Catholic Church. Traditionally, since colonial times, the official discourse on behalf of the Catholic leadership signaled *ndoki* as part of a superstition complex, which should be combatted inasmuch as it is the product of backward, wrongful beliefs, and therefore is ultimately inexistent. This configuration of *ndoki* as a virtual or imaginary object can be object of multiple interpretations. Taking a political economy perspective, there has been an evolution in the perception of *ndoki* on behalf of the Catholic Church that is in many ways concomitant of the transition from rural to urban spaces, and from a colonial to a postcolonial state: from its insertion within the colonial apparatus of domination, in which witchcraft appeared as one of the several constructions of moral alterity of the project; to its insertion within the postcolonial construction of an Angolan independent 'modern man' (Blanes 2013; Blanes and Paxe 2015); and finally its post-war insertion within civil and state 'reconstruction' discourses, where witchcraft becomes a problem of social welfare, as I suggest above. From this perspective, the Catholic discourse appears aligned with the secular state's project of nationhood. A good example of this was the creation, in early 2006, of the Inter-Sectorial Committee for the Fight Against Sorcery in Angola (Comité Intersectorial de Luta contra a Feitiçaria em Angola), championed by members of the Catholic and mainline Protestant churches in collaboration with government authorities (see, e.g., *Angonotícias*, January 24, 2006). In 2010, the then leader of Committee, bishop Anastácio Cahango, explained that, upon a request to the committee,

> a group of experts conducted scientific research on the subject of sorcery culture and uncovered the existence of 'merciless traditional and ancestral pirates' who, thanks to the absence of structural measures, (...), 'seduce and entice many towards committing crimes against human life (Jornal de Angola, September 21, 2010; my translation).

A second narrative construction appears within the so-called *Mpeve ya nlongo* movements, which represent, in the Angolan urban setting, what could be described as syncretic movements, in the sense that they convey an explicit process of adaptation of traditional healing practices (*kimbanda*) into a Christian template, and consequent transformation of former healers into pastors and prophets in the urban setting. These churches are usually portrayed as traditionalist, but in fact incorporate highly charismatic and Pentecostal elements (gifts of healing, vision, speaking in tongues, etc.). However, if the old *kimbandeiros* were service providers and could engage in sorcery to solve sorcery, so too are the pastors and prophets, who are specialists who are 'fortunate' enough to be working with the Holy Spirit on their side. From this perspective, among these movements there is a recognition of *ndoki*'s dual (good/bad) nature, and that it can be 'corrected'. One example is the story of a man called Alfredo, a Bakongo involved in political and human rights activism, and who also attends *mpeve ya nlongo* churches, told me:

Alfredo once knew a professor who had knowledge of *ndoki*, and was known in the Malanjinha neighborhood for 'combining psychology and magic'. At a certain point, Alfredo dreamt that this person was attacking him, so he summoned him for a *makanguilu*, but the man refused to participate. Alfredo again dreamed of the man, this time seeing him spreading some dust in his bathroom. A few days later, the professor was eventually seen again and Alfredo and his buddies decided to follow him, finding him spreading some dust in his backyard. When they confronted the professor, he was confused and left in a hurry. Later Alfredo dreamt of him once again, except this time he was tied to an *imdondeiro* (baobab) tree. Again Alfredo summoned the professor for a meeting, but to no avail. Until eventually the man grew seriously ill, with kidney or liver problems. Alfredo, who attended a *Mpeve ya Nlongo* church, then decided to pray for him, and some time later the professor sought him begging for forgiveness, explaining that it was all an act of the devil (something related to an aunt of his who had died)... He asked to be taken as friend again; Alfredo accepted, although his wife wasn't very pleased with his decision. But he stressed that the best way to attack the *feitiço* (sorcery) is to pray to God.

Thus, for Alfredo as for many members of *Mpeve ya Nongo* movements, it is the church that has the Holy Spirit, and the Holy Spirit is the only power that can counteract the negative effects of corrupted uses of *ndoki*.

The third narrative stems from the Pentecostal, charismatic, and *reavivamento* (*revival*) churches, a very strong movement in Angola that nevertheless covers a wide array of phenomena—from the local secessions of international branches (Josafat, etc.) to Congolese-originated *églises du réveil* and to the Brazilian-originated neopentecostal churches, such as the Igreja Universal do Reino de Deus (IURD) or the Igreja Mundial do Poder Deus (IMPD, seceded from the former).[17] From outside these churches, as with the *Mpeve ya Nlongo*, there is the recurring notion that such churches engage with *ndoki* through the perspective of healing practices, which have become commoditized within what is deemed as a neoliberal logic of accumulation of wealth—but does not differ, from the point of view of the believer, from the kind of 'healing service' offered by traditional *kimbandeiros*. From this perspective, as Clara Mafra et al. (2012) have described pertaining the IURD, *ndoki*, and witchcraft in general, has become part of the discourse of this church's 'dialectics of persecution', through which it is recognized as existent, agentive, and powerful, but inherently negative and corrupt, thus occupying a central role in the church's content and demand. The IURD has been particularly successful in the adoption of a 'politics of proximity', working within micro, neighborhood settings, identifying their social and moral particularities and developing a narrative that addresses them within such dialectics (see van de Kamp 2011 for a similar conclusion in Mozambique, and Bratrud, this volume for the case of Vanuatu). Within this policy, sorcery becomes a particular problem that 'explains' micro-social relationships—from nuclear family relationships to love/romanticism, work careers, etc. One can speculate if this is part of the so-called process of modernization and individualization, as has been argued pertaining the Pentecostal personhood complex. But for this discussion, I prefer to look at it from within the urban issue, as something specific to urban culture. From this perspective, sorcery becomes part of a public space used by Pentecostal churches within their attempts to establish their own theo-political messages of community enforcement (see also Andersen, this volume) in a highly competitive, plural religious setting. Within this framework, sorcery and deliverance play a fundamental role.

One example of this strategy comes from an event that took place on October 27, 2013, during my fieldwork in Luanda. The Catholic Church was celebrating the closure of the Year of Faith (*Ano da Fé*) with a multitudinous event in the church of São Domingos in Luanda. A similar event was taking place in the pilgrimage site of Muxima, situated 130 kilometers southeast of Luanda. The sanctuary of Our Lady of Muxima is today perhaps the most iconic Catholic landmark, considering its spontaneous emergence as a pilgrimage site in the last decades. Today, it is sought by Angolan Catholics from all around the country.

On that particular day, the sanctuary was attacked by a group of youngsters, who attempted to destroy the statue of the Virgin Mary that presided the chapel. They were able to cause some damage, and only made it out alive from the compound due to the ready intervention of the police, who prevented a public lynching. Soon later, it was disclosed that these youngsters belonged to the Igreja Profética Arca de Noé (Prophetic Church Noah's Ark), a Pentecostal movement that promoted an iconoclastic anti-idolism against the Catholic Church by accusing the statue in itself of being a product of sorcery[18] (compare similar processes of iconoclasm with Strong, this volume). They claimed to have received the prophetic message to do so in the Muxima.

Similarly, another particularly notorious and 'extreme' version of this kind of appropriations of sorcery takes place in a church located in the Hoji Ya Henda neighborhood, known as Combat Spirituel (the French name deriving from the fact that it is a movement originated in the DRC, and indicating that its public is mostly composed of *regressados*). This church is led by two pastors that are a married couple. As a Bakongo friend of mine explained, their success is based on their strong emphasis on demonology and the organization of 'spiritual crusades' (*cruzadas espirituais*) that engage in deliverance. Through a 'confessional regime' (Badstuebner 2003), believers in this church are required to 'leave everything behind', including their material possessions, in order to be released from the effects of *ndoki*. According to several comments I collected from people from other churches, the point of abandoning your money and possessions (and handing them to the pastors) in order to be healed was central. The heightened expression of such a logic takes place in their well-known extreme fasting sessions (so long that many people are reported to have died in them). Through this operation of bodily and material dispossession promoted by the Combat Spirituel, we see a kind of appropriation of the traditional conception of *ndoki* as an object inside the body, complemented by the fact that the believer who wants to be released must 'become invisible', in the sense of abandoning his material possessions and entering the church compound. Interestingly, I was never 'allowed' by my Angolan friends to visit the church.

The interesting point here is that, more than seeing *ndoki* as an agent of corruption, Pentecostal churches seem to insert it within a logic of production of alterity, of 'cosmological strangeness' (Kwon 2008: 29; see also Bertelsen, this volume), through a Manichean reasoning (whereby *ndoki* is a necessary and convenient corruption) that also emphasizes the economic transaction, similar to what the traditional *kimbandeiros* performed (so there is more a continuity than a rupture, from this perspective). But here, the economic paradigm is inverted: instead of the traditional redistribution, there is a logic of dispossession versus accumulation.

Thus, we can speculate about the material and symbolic role of money in the process. Heonik Kwon (2007) talks about 'dollarized ghost money' to describe how, in Vietnam, mourning rituals became affected by changing political and economic relations in the country.

If traditionally the ritual burning of money signaled the transformation of one economic order to the other (from the living to the dead), with the introduction of foreign currencies in the process made it an explicit 'moral economy'. Similarly, the 'capitalization' of *ndoki* in urban Angola rendered it a Dow Jones in its own terms, operating in the market of the Angolan religious public sphere (Pereira 2016) and affecting the ritual and ideological configurations of the Pentecostal churches. Within this setting, however, Pentecostal churches do not merely engage in the production of prediction and indexicality, but themselves become its objects—for instance, in the recurring accusations that circulate of such churches being hubs of extortion, money laundering, and illicit accumulation.

Conclusion: *Ndoki* and Dow Jones

My speculative proposal of seeing sorcery as an index stems from my previous interrogations on the 'agency of intangibles' (Blanes and Espírito Santo 2013). In that book, we discussed traces and effects of invisible and intangible objects in social life. Here I argue that, beyond the recognition of objects per se, those intangible effects often become shifting and fluctuating 'stock market indexes', objects of measurement of value. Thus, an index is created—not necessarily a mathematical construct like in Wall Street, but a multifarious ideological construct that is able to describe and regulate the 'spiritual market' in modes that may or may not include capitalist modes of economic activity. Therefore, the index necessarily shifts according to who is performing the measurement, and ultimately produces as much regulation as it does deregulation, considering Pentecostalism's particular and continuous moral demand on the person and community, as is noted by Eriksen and Rio (this volume) in the case of Vanuatu.

Thus the point here is that, as an art of invisible agency, *ndoki* becomes object of what Alfred Gell called, via Peirce, 'abductive reasoning', or inference. One recognizes the agency and identifies the effects, and thus finds the best plausible explanation for the connection between two events. So in conclusion, this kind of reasoning produces an index, which varies according to the agents who produce it: catholic, prophetic, Pentecostal. But this index emerges as a moral index precisely because it is perceived as describing *and* affecting economic but also political and spiritual activity.

In what concerns Pentecostals in particular, we appreciate how many churches under this umbrella term engage in different approaches to the index, from processes of service-providing to the public production of symbolic action and, finally, extreme dispossession. Therefore, two concurring tendencies can be observed: the externalizing and connectivity (see Pype this volume) of *ndoki* through its publicization; and the internalizing of *ndoki* through acts of disconnection and dispossession. From this perspective, the traditional argument of capitalist accumulation does not fully encompass what is observed.

Notes

1. As we will see throughout the text, I am using a deinstitutionalized conception of 'Pentecostalism' as more of a spectrum of movements, places, and activities in which the holy Spirit plays a central role. In this respect, I will be referring to different manifestations, traditionally categorized as Neopentecostal, Charismatic, Prophetic, and Evangelical, as well as to other, locally conceived trends.
2. I will henceforth use the word sorcery instead of witchcraft, following the operative empirical distinction between such concepts in the working language of Angola, Portuguese, where there is a distinction between a witch (*bruxo*) and a sorcerer (*feiticeiro*).
3. As part of the Bantu family, the Bakongo (literally, 'the Kongo' in its plural form) are, along with the Ambundu and Ovimbundu, one of the major ethnic groups in Angola, populating the north-western territory from Luanda to the border with the DR Congo. Historically, they formed part of the ancient Kingdom of Kongo—which was subsequently divided, throughout the nineteenth and twentieth centuries, into Portuguese, Belgian, and French colonial administrations—and find themselves divided today between Angola, RD Congo, and Congo-Brazzaville. Although sharing a common language known as kikongo, the Bakongo of these three countries speak in different dialects within the same linguistic family, as well as lingala (a lingua franca). For a classic study of the Bakongo, see e.g., Van Wing (1959).
4. As Ramon Sarró (e.g., 2009; Sarró et al. 2008) has noted, the memory of the Kingdom, one of the greatest existing African kingdoms before its slow demise at the hands of the European colonial forces, is still politically very relevant, and conflicts with the postcolonial mapping of this region of Africa, posing questions of identity and national integrity.

5. It is important to note at this stage that the notion of *ndoki* is also a relevant trope within Afro-American religions, albeit with a different meaning than in places like Angola (see e.g., Ballard 2005).
6. In fact, as Fátima Viegas and Jorge Varanda (2015) note, in Angola the understanding of *nganga* conflates, both in kikongo and kimbundo (language of the Ambundu), ideas of healer, diviner, and sorcerer (see also Calvão 2013 and Bahu 2014).
7. 'Returnees', i.e., former Angolan Bakongo expatriates in the DR Congo who returned, over the past decades, to Angola.
8. All real names of my interlocutors in Luanda have been replaced for anonymity purposes.
9. In their case they are thinking about the events in Seattle in 1999.
10. I am referring to technologies devised in sci-fi productions, although obviously there are other, factual technologies that can be seen under the same framework of turning objects invisible: optical camouflage, stealth technology, etc.
11. Strong (this volume) and MacCarthy (this volume) also detect this centrality of sight or lack thereof in the witchcraft praxis in Melanesia.
12. That is, at least until the publication of Thomas Piketty's *Capital in the Twenty-First Century* (2014).
13. Bakongo 'tradition' invokes perceptions of clanic (*mvila*) and lineage (*kanda*) logics (often referred to as *ngenda* or 'code') linked to particular territorialities (see, e.g., Van Wing 1959).
14. By this I mean that the index is a number that is an indicator or interpreter of a given reality, through a set of calculations, but it also and simultaneously affects and defines that same reality by effecting upon the financial agents, creating expectation and trust or mistrust.
15. In the same vein of social structuring of economy (Bourdieu 2000), see, e.g., the work of Daniel Lopes (Lopes and Marques 2011; Lopes 2013) for a debate on credit and social relationships.
16. Since my first visits to Luanda in 2006 and 2007, I have visited numerous Christian and non-Christian churches, from prophetic, Pentecostal, and traditionalist backgrounds. My main focus, however, has been the Tokoist Church (Blanes 2014).
17. Fátima Viegas (2008; Viegas and Varanda 2015) also uses the concept of 'neotraditional movements' to describe the spectrum of movements that encompass and intersect the categories I am using in this text—from evangelical to Pentecostal, traditional, prophetic, etc.
18. A relevantly analogous event can be found in the famous episode of the "*chute na santa*" (kicking the saint) promoted by a Brazilian pentecostal pastor as a symbolic critique to the Catholic church's idolism (see Giumbelli and Birman 2003).

References

Agamben, Giorgio. 2011. *The Kingdom and the Glory*. For a Theological Genealogy of Economy and Government. Stanford CA: Stanford University Press.

Ashforth, A. 1998. 'Reflections on Spiritual Insecurity in a Modern African City (Soweto)'. *African Studies Review* 41 (3): 39–67.

———. 2005. *Witchcraft, Violence and Democracy in South Africa*. Chicago: University of Chicago Press.

Austen, R. 1993. 'The Moral Economy of Witchcraft: An essay in Comparative History'. In *Modernity and Its Malcontents: Ritual and Power in Postcolonial Africa*, ed. J. Comaroff, and J. Comaroff, 89–110. Chicago: University of Chicago Press.

Badstuebner, J. 2003. 'Drinking the Hot Blood of Humans: Witchcraft Confessions in a South African Pentecostal church'. *Anthropology and Humanism* 28 (1): 8–22.

Bahu, Helder. 2014. '*'Os Profetas e a Cura pela Fé. Um Estudo Antropológico da Igreja Jesus Cristo Salvador do Lubango''*. ISCTE-IUL, Lisbon: PhD diss. Anthropology.

Ballard, E. 2005. 'Ndoki Bueno Ndoki Malo. Historic and contemporary Kongo religion in the African diaspora'. PhD Thesis, University of Pennsylvania.

Blanes, R. 2013. 'Extraordinary Times. Charismatic Repertoires in Contemporary African Prophetism'. In *The Anthropology of Religious Charisma*,ed. Lindholm Charles, Ecstasies and Institutions, 147–168. New York: Palgrave Macmillan.

———. 2014. *A Prophetic Trajector. Ideologies of Time, Place and Belonging in an Angolan Religious Movement*. Oxford & New York: Berghahn.

Blanes, R., and D. Espírito Santo (eds.). 2013. *The Social Life of Spirits*. Chicago: University of Chicago Press.

Blanes, R., and A. Paxe. 2015. 'Atheist Political Cultures in Independent Angola'. *Social Analysis* 59 (2): 62–80.

Booth, William. 1994. 'Household and Market: On the Origins of Moral Economic Philosophy'. *The Review of Politics* 56 (2): 207–235.

Bortolami, Gabriele. 2012. *'I Bakongo. Società, tradizioni e cambiamento in Angola'*. PhD diss.: Cultural Anthropology, Università degli Studi di Sassari.

Bourdieu, P. 2000. *Les Structures Sociales de l'Économie*. Paris: Seuil.

Brinkman, Inge. 2003. 'War, Witches and Traitors: Cases from the MPLA's Eastern Front in Angola (1966–1975)'. *Journal of African History* 44 (2): 303–325.

Calvão, Filipe. 2013. *'The Rough and the Cut: Nature, Value and the Fetish in Angola's Diamond Mines'*. PhD diss: Anthropology, University of Chicago.

Comaroff, J., and J. Comaroff. 1999. 'Occult Economies and the Violence of Abstraction: Notes from the South African Postcolony'. *American Ethnologist* 26 (2): 279–303.

Cuvelier, J. 1934. *Nkutama a mvila za makanda*. Brussels: Impr. Mission Catholique.

De Boeck, P. 2011. 'Inhabiting Ocular Ground: Kinshasa's Future in the Light of Congo's Spectral Urban Politics'. *Cultural Anthropology* 26 (2): 263–286.

Englund, H. 1996. 'Witchcraft, Modernity and the Person: The Morality of Accumulation in Central Malawi'. *Critique of Anthropology* 16 (3): 257–279.

Eves, R. 2000. 'Sorcery's the Curse: Modernity, Envy and the Flow of Sociality in a Melanesian Society'. *JRAI* (N.S.) 6:453–468.

Geschiere, P. 1995. *Sorcellerie et Politique en Afrique: La Viande des Autres*. Paris: Karthala.

Geschiere, P. 1997. *The Modernity of Witchcraft*. Politics and the occult in post-colonial Africa. Charlottesville & London: University Press of Virginia.

Giumbelli, E., and P. Birman. 2003. *O "chute na santa": blasfêmia e pluralismo religioso no Brasil*. São Paulo: ATTAR.

Godelier, Maurice. 1972. *Rationality and Irrationality in Economics*. New York and London: Monthly Review Press.

Graeber, David. 2005. 'Fetishism as Social Creativity. Or, Fetishes are Gods in the Process of Construction'. *Anthropological Theory* 5 (4): 407–438.

———. 2011. *Debt. The First 5,000 Years*. Brooklyn NY: Melville House Publishing.

Hart, Keith. 2010. 'Building the Human Economy Together'. In *Hart, Keith, Jean-Louis Lacille & Antonio David Cattani*, ed. The Human, 1–20. Economy. A Citizen's Guide. Cambridge: Polity Press.

Harvey, Cox. 1999. 'The Market as God. Living in the New Dispensation'. *The Atlantic Monthly* March 1999:18–23.

Kwon, Heonik. 2007. 'The Dollarization of Vietnamese Ghost Money'. *Journal of the Royal Anthropological Institute* (N.S.) 13: 73–90.

———. 2008. 'The Ghosts of War and the Spirit of Cosmopolitanism'. *History of Religions* 48 (1): 22–42.

Lopes, D. 2013. 'Metamorphoses of credit: Pastiche production and the ordering of mass payment behaviour.' *Economy and Society* 42 (1): 26–50.

Lopes, D., and R. Marques. 2011. 'How credit institutions look at society: Economics, sociology, and the problem of social reflexivity reconsidered.' *European Societies* 13 (4): 509–533.

Lukombo, João. 2011. 'Crescimento da População em Angola: Um olhar sobre a situação e dinâmica populacional da cidade de Luanda'. *Revista de Estudos Demográficos* 49: 53–68.

Mafra, C., C. Swatowiski, and C. Sampaio. 2012. 'O Projeto Pastoral de Edir Macedo, Uma igreja benevolente para individuos ambiciosos'. *Revista Brasileira de Ciências Sociais* 27 (78): 81–96.

Marshall, R. 2009. *Political Spiritualities. The Pentecostal revolution in Nigeria*. Chicago: University of Chicago Press.

Milando, João. 2008. 'Actores Invisíveis do Desenvolvimento em África: O Kindoki na racionalização dos comportamentos no meio rural de Cabinda (Angola)', Working Paper, Centro de Estudos Africanos, Lisbon.

Milando, J. 2013. *Desenvolvimento e Resiliência Social em África: Dinâmicas Rurais de Cabinda-Angola*. Luanda: Mayamba.

Moore, H., and T. Sanders (eds.). 2001. *Magical Interpretations, Material Realities. Modernity, witchcraft and the occult in postcolonial Africa*. London & New York: Routledge.

Moya, Ismaël. 2015. 'Unavowed Value. *Economy, Comparison, and Hierarchy in Dakar', Hau: Journal of Ethnographic Theory* 5 (1): 151–172.

Parish, J. 2001. 'Black Market, Free Market: anti-witchcraft shrines and fetishes among the Akan'. In *Magical Interpretations, Material Realities. Modernity, witchcraft and the occult in postcolonial Africa*, ed. H. Moore, and T. Sanders, 118–135. London: Routledge.

Parry, J., and M. Bloch (eds.). 1989. *Money and the Morality of Exchange*. Cambridge: Cambridge University Press.

Pereira, L. 2008. 'Crianças Feiticeiras: reconfigurando família, igrejas e estado no pós-guerra angolano'. *Religião e Sociedade* 28 (2): 30–55.

———. 2015. *Os Bakongo de Angola: etnicidade, religião e parentesco num bairro de Luanda*. Rio de Janeiro: Contra Capa.

———. 2016. 'Feitiçaria e Esfera Pública: Estado e Cultura no Pós-guerra Angolano', *Sankofa* IX (XVI). http://www.revistas.usp.br/sankofa/article/view/110351. Accessed online on Jan 2016.

Pignarre, P., and I. Stengers. 2004. *La Sorcellerie Capitaliste*. La Découverte: Pratiques de désenvoutement. Paris.

Piketty, Thomas. 2014. *Capital in the Twenty-First Century*. Cambridge MA & London: Belknap Press.

Rio, K. 2002. 'The Sorcerer as an Absented Third Person: Formations of Fear and Anger in Vanuatu'. *Social Analysis* 46 (3): 129–154.

———. 2010. Handling Sorcery in a State System of Law: Magic. *Violence and Kastom in Vanuatu*. *Oceania* 80 (2): 182–197.

Rocha, Edmundo. 2003. *Angola: contribuição ao estudo da génese do nacionalismo moderno angolano (período 1950–1964), testemunho e estudo documental*. Lisbon: Dinalivro.

Ruel, M. 1965. 'Witchcraft, morality and doubt.' *Odù: Journal of Yoruba and Related Studies* 2 (1): 3–27.

Sarró, R., R. Blanes, and F. Viegas. 2008. 'La Guerre en temps de Paix. *Ethnicité et Angolanité dans l'Église Kimbanguiste de Luanda'*, *Politique Africaine* 110: 4–101.

Schubert, Jon. 2014. *'Working the System: Affect, Amnesia and the Aesthetics of Power in the New Angola'*. PhD diss.: African Studies, University of Edinburgh.

Soares, Pedro. 2016. 'Um estudo etnográfico sobre o acolhimento e reintegração social de crianças acusadas de feitiçaria em Angola'. MA Thesis, Department of Anthropology, ISCTE-IUL, Lisbon.

Thornton, J. 2001. 'The Origins and Early History of the Kingdom of Kongo, c. 1350–1550'. *International Journal of African Historical Studies* 34 (1): 89–120.

Van de Kamp, L. 2011. 'Converting the Spirit Spouse: The Violent Transformation of the Pentecostal Female Body in Maputo Mozambique'. *Ethnos* 76 (4): 510–533.

Van Wing, J. 1959. *Études Bakongo. Sociologie – Religion et Magie*. Paris: Desclée de Brower.

Viegas, Fátima. 2008. 'As Igrejas Neotradicionais Africanas na Cura e Reintegração Social (1992-2002): un estudo de caso em Luanda'. *Revista Angolana de Sociologia* 1: 143–158.

Viegas, Fátima, and Jorge Varanda. 2015. 'Saberes e Práticas de Cura nas Igrejas Neotradicionais em Luanda: Carismas, Participação e Trajectórias das Mulheres'. *Etnográfica* 19 (1): 189–224.

West, H. 2005. *Kupiliklula. Governance and the Invisible Realm in Mozambique*. Chicago: University of Chicago Press.

Yuran, Noam. 2014. *What Money Wants*. An Economy of Desire. Stanford CA: Stanford University Press.

Author Biography

Ruy Blanes is a postdoctoral researcher on the Gender and Pentecostalism project. He has been postdoctoral researcher at the Institute of Social Sciences and he is a Ramon y Cajal Fellow at the Spanish National Research Council (CSIC). Previously, he has been a researcher at the universities of Bergen (Norway) and Lisbon (Portugal), as well as a visiting fellow at the University of Leiden (Netherlands) and the London School of Economics and Political Science. He has worked on the anthropology of religion, identity, politics, mobility and temporality. His current research site is Angola, where he explores the topics of religion, mobility (diasporas, transnationalism, the Atlantic), politics (leadership, charisma, repression, resistance, activism, utopias), temporalities (historicity, memory, heritage, expectations) and knowledge. He has published articles in several international journals and edited volumes at Berghahn, Brill and University of Chicago Press, among others. He is the author of *A Prophetic Trajectory* (2014, Berghahn). He is also co-editor of the journal *Advances in Research: Religion and Society*.

CHAPTER 5

Branhamist *Kindoki*: Ethnographic Notes on Connectivity, Technology, and Urban Witchcraft in Contemporary Kinshasa

Katrien Pype

Introduction

This chapter is concerned with the variety of expressions of witchcraft[1] (*kindoki* in Lingala, *sorcellerie*) in contemporary Kinshasa. The analytical lens will focus on the dialectics among the urban, technology, and Pentecostal imaginations of the occult. For Kinshasa's inhabitants, *kindoki* references a wide variety of skills, practices, actions, and conditions, the origins, sources, causes, and roots of which are located in a mystical, hidden, second world (see also Blanes, this volume). *Kindoki* can be innate, immaterial, material, consciously or unconsciously acquired, and can be expelled through discursive or physical operations. *Magie*, or the use of tools to influence reality, is a particular type of *kindoki*. Different types of *magie* exist among Kinshasa's Pentecostal Christians, ranging from *fétishes* (*nkisi*, or power objects) used by diviners, magicians, and

K. Pype (✉)
KU University of Leuven, Leuven, Belgium

K. Rio et al. (eds.), *Pentecostalism and Witchcraft*, Contemporary Anthropology of Religion, DOI 10.1007/978-3-319-56068-7_5

their clients, and constituting the tools of an ancestral type of magic, to Western-based forms of *magie*. Many Kinois hold that *magie* as such originated in the West but was brought to Congo by colonists and missionaries (Pype 2012: 50–51). Here, the secret societies of Freemasons and Rosicrucians, reputed for extending their tentacles into academic, military, and political circles, are identified as the major spaces where this kind of *magie* is performed. New Age spiritualism and popular culture representations of *kindoki* (such as the Harry Potter films or the American TV series *Buffy the Vampire Slayer* and *Bewitched*) are also very popular in Kinshasa, and one can expect that these media products have expanded Kinshasa's Christians' imaginings of *kindoki*.

In a Christian context, any type of *kindoki* is held to be diabolical and is opposed to the miraculous healing powers of the Holy Spirit (*Molimo Mosanto*). This is the basic explanation of how Kinshasa's Pentecostal-charismatic Christians understand *kindoki*. However, there is much uncertainty as to what tools and objects are useful in *kindoki* practices, and how they actually transmit occult powers.

I will mainly focus on Branhamist Christianity, one of the many variants of Pentecostal-charismatic Christianity (hereafter PCC) in Kinshasa.[2] Outsiders call followers of the American prophet William Marion Branham (1909–1965)[3] *Branhamistes*, though most of these reject the appellation as it suggests that they venerate a human being instead of the Christian God. In previous research, I have mainly worked with the so-called Awakening churches (*églises du réveil*), and from the beginning of my field research in Kinshasa (begun in 2003), Kinois have spoken about a rift within the Branhamist Christian community. Indeed, the contemporary "Branhamist Christian scene" in Kinshasa is diverse, and, while many dividing lines must be drawn among Kinshasa's many Branhamist Christian communities (according to the pastor's ethnicity for instance),[4] for most Kinois (inhabitants of Kinshasa) the Branhamist Christian community is mainly split into two camps, separated by their different approaches towards modern communication technologies.[5] Branhamist Christianity in Kinshasa thus includes churches that diabolize all electronic technologies outright, while other Branhamist Christians advocate a more pragmatic point of view and even set up their own media ministries. This material allows me to contribute to the ever-expanding scholarship on witchcraft in postcolonial societies by linking themes of the urban with the technological. Overall, the main question I intend to address here is how Pentecostal communities' novel forms of urban witchcraft are imagined, addressed, and "lived with". As the following vignette illustrates, technology (and in particular information and communication technologies – ICT) occupies a major role within debates about *kindoki* among Branhamist Christians.

Kinshasa, 19 August 2014. I visited Fabrice, a young man of 22, at one of Kinshasa's largest markets, *the Freedom Market* (*Marché de la Liberté*). For more than 6 months, Fabrice had been employed in selling smartphones (Lingala *tshombo*) and accessories. That day, as was generally the case, clients constantly interrupted our conversation. The following encounter stood out in my fieldnotes:

A mother and a teenage girl arrived at the counter. In a very self-assured manner, the mother shouts "Nani azoteka (who sells here)?" Fabrice asks my permission to suspend our conversation and turns towards the prospective clients. The young girl was promised a smartphone because she succeeded in the state exam (*exétat*). To my surprise, I hear Fabrice advising against purchasing a smartphone. He embarks on the "dangers" (*ya mabe*, "bad things") that girls are exposed to "when surfing on the net, chatting with strangers, and seeing images that do not suit their age". During Fabrice's anti-sales pitch, I notice that the young girl is growing increasingly nervous. After some time, and having apparently become really annoyed, she interrupts Fabrice and tells her mother not to listen to him. "We can buy the smartphone somewhere else," she states. Fabrice, who fears losing a client, quickly changes his game and showcases a few smartphones on sale.

After Fabrice finally sells a second-hand smartphone to the mother, he returns to me. When I confront him about his strange marketing strategies, Fabrice mentions his religious identity. In his church, Shekinah Tabernacle, youth are only allowed to use smartphones from 22 years of age. I had known Fabrice for over a few months by then, and I was visiting him because I knew he was "born and grew up in the Message" (*akoli na Message)*. The idiom, "to have grown up in the Message," suggests that Fabrice's parents were already followers of Branham before he was born.[6] Along with many Branhamist Christians, Fabrice claims that radios, television sets, and telephones can set *kindoki* in motion if improperly used. "Children have little idea of the occult possibilities of mobile phones and the Internet," he argues, and therefore prohibiting the usage of these tools is a measure of protection against the potentially devilish outcomes of the medium.

Accompanied by a friend from his church, Fabrice visited me in my house that same evening, and our conversation came to be dominated by the two friends' reflections on Branhamist Christians' take on *kindoki.* They had brought a pamphlet (*brochure*), *La Télévision selon William Marrion Branham*, published in French in Kinshasa. The document contained a transcription of William Branham's teachings on television. Very spontaneously, and in a fashion very familiar to me because of previous research among proselytizers, this visit turned into a teaching session, during which Fabrice and his friend, in turn, read out excerpts from the pamphlet and then rephrased the main ideas in their own words or illustrated them with personal anecdotes.

The pamphlet's overall implication was that a television set is a tool that the Devil has used to enter into domestic spaces and thus turn American souls away from the Christian God (*Nzambe ya Cristu*). Set in late 1950s or early 1960s US, and speaking exclusively about American society, the text emphasizes how makeup and miniskirts, worn by media celebrities and showcased in commercials, diverted the minds of American spectators away from the good and the moral. Fabrice and his friend agreed, and, referring to contemporary Kinois society, added that time spent watching television is the time a Christian should ideally spend in church. The young men emphasized the importance of *hearing* the word of the Bible 'live', thus echoing Branham's warnings that many televangelists also counter the work of the Divine (*Musantu*).

Referring to a US source in order to explain *kindoki* and the spiritual battle unsettles taken-for-granted assumptions about "Pentecostal witchcraft" on the African continent. Fabrice and his friend did not mention the classic ingredients of African Pentecostal witchcraft such as "tradition" (*biloko ya bakoko*), "the village" (*mboka*), "*féticheurs*", "the elderly" or *nkisi* (power objects used by witch doctors); rather they used analogies with American society to explain Kinshasa's spiritual insecurity. And technology was central: television was the theme of the pamphlet, while smartphones and the Internet dominated our conversations.

Technology figures prominently not only in my fieldnotes about my interactions with Fabrice but also in most of the contemporary witchcraft stories documented in ethnographies of African cities. Key elements of modernity such as the car, the airplane, and pharmaceutical drugs are integrated in the quest for success and power (Geschiere 1997; Meyer 1998; De Boeck 2005; Bonhomme 2012; Englund 2007). These objects are identified as carriers, tools, or vehicles used by *bandoki* (Sg. *ndoki,* witches, and sorcerers). Geschiere (1997, 2013: 5–6) understands the embedment of objects of electronic modernity within the occult imagination as a manifestation of globalization: witchcraft adapts to changing living conditions. In the contemporary global age, where new types of physical and virtual mobility expand people's social worlds,[7] the tentacles of witchcraft stretch as well, just as the tools and objects associated with occult practices constantly change. For Meyer (1998), diabolizing commodities such as pens, cars, makeup, and other objects that can be purchased on the market, combined with promoting the Christian prayer as a necessary and most efficient ritual to divest these objects of their diabolic powers, represent symbolic strategies Pentecostal Christians deploy to tame these exogenous goods and allow African subjects to participate in the global economy despite global structural inequalities (see also Introduction this volume). In this chapter, I propose to move beyond a symbolic and pragmatic analysis of the consumption of a global commodities culture. I take the urban rather than the global as a scale of reference and ask what the animization of ICT goods reveals about what it means to live in an African city today. ICT, *kindoki*, and urban sociality triangulate in contemporary Kinshasa. I will argue that the increased possibilities of connectivity, i.e. the possibility of establishing new social relations, expanding one's social network, and connecting to invisible realms of knowledge, are the very elements that induce fear among most Branhamist Christians in Kinshasa, leading Pentecostal Christians to immoralize ICT. This allows me to make two claims: first, I claim that the study of witchcraft should pay greater attention to connectivity as a crucial mode of social personhood. And second, I formulate the notion of "the witchcraft complex" in order to do justice to the heterogeneity of the material and affective dimensions of witchcraft.

The article is structured as follows: first, I explore the role of technology in the Kinois imagination of the occult as well as the embedment of ICT (mobile phones, cellular companies, and mobile communication) in social networking and the formation of "the Christian subject". Second, I explore Branhamist Christians' understandings of scientific knowledge and the ways in which knowledge and information connect humans to invisible worlds. This will be complemented with an analysis of the variations regarding *kindoki* among Branhamist and other Pentecostal Christians. Here, I propose to approach the imagination of *kindoki* as a "complex". In the conclusion, I bring the discussion back to the urban. Material is derived from ethnographic fieldwork in Kinshasa. Since 2003, I have been working with evangelizers from Awakening Churches (Pype 2006, 2011, 2012). Since 2011, I have begun conducting research among Kimbanguist (Pype 2014a) and Branhamist Christian communities.

Witchcraft, Technology and the African City

The dialectical relationship between witchcraft and the city has fascinated many Africanist anthropologists. The changing role of the city in the experience of the occult is poignantly addressed in Geschiere's most recent work on witchcraft, intimacy, and trust (2013), which draws on almost 50 years of ethnographic research on the imagination of witchcraft in Cameroon. In the beginning of his research, in the 1960s and 1970s, Geschiere found that Maka Cameroonians believed themselves to be safe from witchcraft in the city; moving to the city, moving away from *djambe,* or "witchcraft from the village", constituted a sufficient strategy for escaping the dangers of witchcraft. However, urban centres were increasingly affected by the spiritual powers of witches. Trying to establish a physical distance between the city and the village very soon proved useless because of the "increasing mobility attributed to [the occult] forces and thus the increasing scope of the witchcraft of the house". *Djambe* also played out in the city, thus generating "translocal forms of witchcraft". By the early 1990s, *urban* forms of witchcraft, such as *ekong* or *famla,* appeared and were eventually "imported from the city to the village" (Geschiere 2013: 45). Geschiere analyses these transformations through the lens of muted interactions between the village and the city following modernization, urbanization, and the cash economy.

The ethnography of Congolese witchcraft also offers interesting insights into how urban life can generate new forms of occult practices. Based on a return visit she made to the Lele of the Kasai region in 1987, after initial fieldwork started in the mid-twentieth century, Mary Douglas (1999) provides a compelling overview of the transformations of witchcraft-related[8] practices such as accusations, cleansing rituals, and protection strategies among the Lele. For Douglas, intergenerational tensions had drastically altered the dialectics between city-dwellers and villagers, structuring changes in the imagination of evil. Lele elderly remained in their villages, while younger generations had moved away to towns, where they became relatively successful in trade and other professions. As the elderly imagined city-dwelling Lele to be wealthy, sorcery became an important mediator in the articulation of responsibilities between the generations. Douglas expected city Lele to define the village as a space of witchcraft, but, much to her surprise, she quickly learned that the urban Lele were accused of witchcraft by their village relatives. Similar to what Geschiere documented for Cameroon, in the Lele context, the city became imagined as a space full of occult activity. Though Douglas did not explore the ways in which Lele villagers discussed urban occult conniving further, De Boeck's ethnographic work in Kinshasa (2005) provides a lengthy discussion of the novel forms of *kindoki* generated in the urban context. He characterizes the emergence of child witchcraft as the outcome of changing structures of power and authority *in* the city itself. With children increasingly becoming important economic actors, and gerontocracy losing its power and control over their urban offspring, younger generations are readily identified as *ndoki*.

In the case of Kinshasa's child witches, the transfer of occult powers still remains within the "house" (Geschiere 2013), that is to say, within intimate spheres of belonging (chiefly, the extended family). In a more recent transformation of *kindoki*, urban others (mainly neighbours) are readily identified as potential witches whose victims do not belong to their consanguine or affinal networks. To a certain extent we can claim that these co-residents are still part of people's intimate lifeworlds. Yet, other forms of witchcraft, occurring outside the space of (fictional) kinship, have been documented in urban Africa as well. One such example is the case of the penis snatchers. As Bonhomme (2012: 212) reminds us, penis snatching "occur[s] in public settings, but never in the intimacy of the home." Crowded spaces such as markets, minivan taxis, streets, and open squares are the locales of these incidents. Unsurprisingly, they are also spaces where the urban public, filled with "intimate strangers" (Nyamjoh and Brudvig 2014), assembles. Urban anonymity proves to be a fecund breeding ground for new forms of occult powers. Other new types include bewitchment through satanic text messages, unidentified phone calls, and the reception of anonymous gifts. As will become clear in the remainder of this chapter, ICT increase the possibility of encountering anonymous others and enable invisible, unknown, and "strange" powers to circulate.

Technology and "African Witchcraft"

Although, as Geschiere (2013: 10) observes, in academic writing, "[w]itchcraft often presents itself as the very opposite of science, as the archetypes of everything that is secret and opposed to transparency", various forms of Pentecostal Christianity, Branhamist Christianity included, emphasize the commonalities between science and witchcraft. William Branham fulminated powerfully against education and science. One of his many quotes on the subject is: "Knowledge, science, education, is the greatest hindrance that God ever had. It is of the devil."[9] Branham's suspicion of the diabolical origins of science coincides strikingly with Pentecostal popular discourse in Africa about intellectual leaders, scientific experiments, and technological innovations. In his pamphlet, *Delivered from the Powers of Darkness*, the programmatic text of the 1990s' Pentecostal imagination in urban Africa, Emmanuel Eni explicitly formulates the connection between science and the occult. At the bottom of the sea, where Mami Wata reigns, Eni places a scientific laboratory "where scientists and psychiatrists have joined forces to design 'flashy cars', the 'latest weapons', 'cloth, perfumes and assorted types of cosmetics', 'electronics, computers and alarms'" (Eni 1988: 18 in Meyer 1998: 765). In Luanda (Blanes this volume), *ndoki* are "cloaking devices", that render objects, agents or actions invisible or conceal them. He makes a striking parallel with "technologies devised in sci-fi productions" (Blanes this volume, footnote 23). For the Melanesian context, and in particular the eastern highlands of PNG, Andersen (this volume) shows the commensurability of medical training (in the case of nurses) and beliefs in occult action. As illustrated in Taylor's (2016: 7–8) research on mobile phones and power dynamics in Vanuatu, esoteric forms of agency are assumed to be facilitated by the handsets, to the extent that Vanuatu women turn their mobile phones off during the night out of fear that magical attacks can occur through these. Curses as well remain powerful even when transmitted over cellular technologies. Strong's (this volume) research participants in PNG also mentioned modern technology, or "computerised systems" as a "particular type of witchcraft", which is opposing generations against one another because of the youth's assumed possession of required skills to work with these modern technologies. In Kinshasa too, technology and science play a central role in the imagination of and discourse about the occult.

First, among Kinois, distinctions between so-called African and Western *kindoki* are explained according to differences in technology. In Kinois parlance, engine and electricity powered technologies are defined as the "witchcraft of white men" (*kindoki ya mindele*). Examples include motorcars, airplanes, kitchen robots, mobile phones, and the computer. "African witchcraft" (*kindoki ya biso*, 'our witchcraft'), by contrast, refers to the occult practices that witches and so-called traditional healers activate. Scholars of witchcraft in Accra (Kwabena Asamoah-Gyadu 2007), Abidjan (Newell 2007), and Cameroon (Geschiere 2013) mention the same division. This distinction does not necessarily attribute spiritual powers to these objects; rather the concept of witchcraft here suggests "knowledge", "techne", and craftsmanship. The concept of *nganga* can encompass witches (*ndoki*), but can also refer to a (medical) "doctor", a "professor" (or teacher), an engineer or a scientist. The *nganga* qualities of those involved in modern science refer to the occult world from which these experts draw their knowledge, insights, and mastery. While a *ndoki* usually is attributed evil *intentions,* which set in motion (destructive) *kindoki*, these other kinds of *nganga* have connected their souls to the occult in order to heal, invent, and explain. Ashforth (2005: 146) writes similarly, for South Africa, that "'African science' [secret African knowledge and skills] in everyday talk occupies a place alongside the miracles of Scripture and the magic of what is usually referred to as Western or White science in its ability to transform the world in mysterious ways."

Second, electric and motor-driven technologies appear in the confessions of former witches in southern and central Africa (Comaroff and Comaroff 1993, 1999; De Boeck 2005; Geschiere 1997). Following the time-space compression brought about by the technologies of globalization (with electronic media at the forefront), and the uneven distribution of wealth and riches, analogue and digital media are interpreted as technologies for mediating access to occult powers, which in turn produce an increase in capital, as well as greater mystification of the circulation of money and consumer goods. This has been explained as a way of incorporating western modernity, which remains out of reach for many. Situating these tools as key drivers of occult worlds and activities represent symbolic actions that position these same tools in the immoral domain, and are thus symbolic ways of downplaying their attractiveness (see also Strong this volume).

Third, electric and motor-driven technologies are also regarded as crucial tools in setting *kindoki* into motion and/or transferring spiritual powers. In Kinshasa (Pype 2012, 2014a, fc.), members of the Awakening Churches regard the television, the radio, and the mobile phone as objects that mediate spiritual powers (divine and demonic). As do other religious groups, Kinshasa's Pentecostals insert technology into contemporary debates about urban (im)morality and personhood. According to many Kinois, *les anti-valeurs règnent à Kin[shasa]* ("anti-values reign in Kin"). The concept of *anti-valeurs* refers to asocial actions like corruption, immodesty, and looseness, and are connected to the quality of one's personal relationships, be they with the nuclear and extended family, friends, neighbours, and business partners. Various authorities (parents, husbands, pastors, political leaders, etc.) who stress "*anti-valeurs*" in Kinois society want to limit the "potentially liberating and revolutionary" fantasies that electronic technologies carry with them by voicing concerns about the "right" usage of technology. This is not to say that Kinshasa's Pentecostals have an entirely negative view of technology or only see its asocial consequences. Rather, most Pentecostal Christians will agree that ICT, and the mobile phone, in particular, occupies a central role in communication with friends and relatives elsewhere in the country and in the diaspora, in the transfer of money for living costs and education, and in the maintenance of amicable and romantic relations. In addition, many Pentecostals also read Bible verses on their smartphones and participate in prayer chats. Yet, these approved ways of handling electronic communication technologies are not topics of public debates and moral anxieties as they are expressed in Kinshasa's (semi-) public spheres. Moral anxieties about ICT-related *kindoki* dominate public discourse in Kinshasa's Pentecostal worlds (see Pype fc.).

The heterodox Branhamist Christian discourse suggests a unique conception of *kindoki* and technology in which evil spirits seem to be absent. The following is a condensed version of Fabrice's explanation of Branhamist Christian principles concerning the dangers of television:

> Brother Branham has instructed us that the devil put television sets in households, in order to reach viewers' souls. [...] Branham also shows that Christians will suffer with their eyes. People who watch too much television, those who sit in front of the TV set all day, will need glasses. They will not be able to rub their eyes to see better. Rather, the devil has taken television. He knows that the television set will ruin people's eyes, and that they will be looking for drugs to heal their eyes. The Bible says that the [Holy] Spirit will come in a time of corruption; at a time when people will be crazy ... we are living this now... there is so much destruction in the minds of children. They suffer from a mental deficiency. It is because the devil has put the TV set in your home. But we want to see Jesus. People stay in their houses and watch television. They do not go to church anymore. God has made us long for Him. But the devil has put the TV set in front of them, ... the pleasure that the TV set offers forbids people from meeting up with other Christians in the church.

Fabrice's explanation strikingly omits the interference of spirits. The sole actor is the devil, who works through technology. No human agents are inserted as mediators, nor does the common trope of the gift—as a social act that transmits occult powers—appear in the story. This understanding of ***kindoki***, which we can take as the official Branhamist Christian explanation of ***kindoki*** through television, is somewhat different from Awakening Churches' explanations of how media is positioned in spiritual warfare. For the latter, viewing experiences (emotional unrest, social discord, etc.) are said to be indicative of either divine or demonic powers, which audiovisual footage transmits. Born-Again Christians refer to the Spirit of Hatred (*molimo ya likunya*), Jealousy (*molimu ya zuwa*), Sexual Deviation (*molimo ya kindumba*), etc. which are transmitted through images of Harry Potter, wrestling shows, science fiction, and music video clips of worldly and folkloric music. Shouting out Jesus's name and changing the channel to a Christian TV station are strategies that Pentecostals of the Awakening Churches deem powerful enough to counter the footage's negative influence (Pype 2012).

Many Branhamist Christians, such as Fabrice, his parents, his pastor, and his friend, eschew television. While Fabrice does have a TV set at home, his family does not watch any television stations. Rather, they use the set together with a DVD player to watch DVDs and videotapes of sermons delivered by *Brother* Branham. Fabrice is more lenient towards the telephone—an object about which *Brother* Branham did not preach. Still, usage is monitored closely, and, according to Fabrice, the same logic that shapes ideas about the devil's hand in the television set are at play with the smartphone. "Good usage" is perceived as crucial. Yet, not everybody knows what this "good usage" entails, nor are there ready-made instructions about this. Confusion regarding the possibilities of new technologies thus renders these objects suspicious in a religious scheme.

Urban Connectivities

Pentecostal anxieties about "proper" use of technology such as television, radio, and the smartphone draw our attention to the role of connection, or ties, among individuals, between the individual and the larger world, and the consequences for one's spiritual well-being. This takes us into the domain of urban sociality. Therefore, quite apart from consumption, connectivity should have a more prominent place in the analysis of witchcraft in Africa. Various technological artefacts (satellites, antennae, television and radio sets, and the mobile phone) have become prime objects in the social and moral imagination of contemporary Kinshasa and have inspired a new vocabulary for speaking about social, economic, and spiritual personhood. In popular parlance, the ideal for a city-dweller is to be *branché* (to be well connected), meaning to be able to move around in various social worlds and have a well-established network. This network made up of people who can help one find a job, a partner, money, and solutions for ad hoc problems, is called *le réseau*, just like the telephone infrastructure of network operators. The *réseau* constitutes the most important social space of belonging in an urban context, where kinship ties are weaker and usually described in terms of responsibilities and duties (Pype 2012: 65). *Contacts* are individuals with whom one has (weak or strong) ties, which can be mobilized when needed. Other idiomatic expressions that illustrate how ICT shapes reflections of social identity are: *kozala na baunité* (having plenty of phone credit) refers to being physically big, which is a token of material and social success; *kozala lowbatt* (low battery) means barely having enough money; a *carte sim blanche* (a SIM card without a phone number attached to it; something you acquire when your mobile phone is stolen and that helps you to maintain your old phone number) refers to a girl who has plenty of boyfriends but no steady lover. In Christian discourse, the SIM card references the soul, and *déverouiller la carte sim* (as into unlock a locked smartphone) means delivering someone from *kindoki*.

If we return to the vignette with Fabrice above, we see that he considers the smartphone dangerous because of the new connections girls can potentially make through phone conversations. Fabrice reminded me about two particular types of mobile phone usage. The first one is the practice of masking, in which callers' names, conversation histories, and received and sent text messages are hidden or deleted, yet retained in the shared histories of anticipated or actual sexual partners. These strategies counter the public ideals of monogamy, fidelity, and honesty. The second set of practices could be glossed as "securitizing practices". Allowing or forbidding someone to use a mobile phone, controlling the contacts they make through mobile communication, and gifting airtime are practices that aim at securing the social connections of others. Both practices participate in wider sets of anonymizing and securitizing technologies, including architectural design and rituals that Kinois can mobilize when controlling the social networks of their wives, sisters, and daughters. The connective capacities enabled by the new information and communication technologies lead to new fantasies and practices that can be either morally approved or rejected. These refusals and acceptances vary from one society to another and need to be traced alongside other spaces and transformations. These moral debates about technology among Kinois amplify social transformations in contemporary urban Kinshasa, and particularly the increased mobility of its youth.

The ICT-induced possibilities for penetrating deeper into the social fabric of intimate relations show striking parallels with how *kindoki* itself actually works. The workings of both ICT and *kindoki* are couched in obscure, invisible, and difficult to define powers.[10] This is not unique to the sub-Saharan African context. A text message circulated in Vanuatu stating "Digicel [one of the local telephone companies]—Devil Is Getting In Control of Everyone's Life" (Taylor 2016: 6). Here, a connection is made between cellular technologies, corporate logics, and the occult. Also for most Kinois, there is no doubt that telecom corporations such as Vodacom, Airtel, Tigo, and Africell have ties with occult forces. Around town, one hears many stories about how gaining entrance into these companies is only possible after initiation, which usually involves sexual intercourse (stories about homosexuality, in particular, abound) and the obligatory participation in secret meetings in Freemason temples. Secret societies, like the Freemasons and Rosicrucians, which arrived in DR Congo during colonial times, are said to include not only politicians among their members, but also the heads of Vodacom, Tigo, and the like. In these secret societies, the latter also meet businessmen from other successful corporations, banks in particular. Private groups where industrialists, wealthy entrepreneurs, and politicians meet, such as the Rotary Club, may well have colonial origins, but they are perceived as urban spaces, intimately connected to hidden powers. Magic and the occult reign in these circles, it is commonly argued. Such suspicions about these companies' employees' and stakeholders' involvement in diabolical schemes also further Christians' suspicions about urban sociality in general given that these companies actually provide the basic infrastructure of contemporary ideal personhood, i.e. being well connected (*branché*). Such suspicions of connections between occult, hidden, worlds and flourishing economic initiatives disclose the levelling mechanisms that Geschiere (1997) suggests are at play in witchcraft accusations in general. Here, the levelling takes the form of a moral distancing from those who have gained access to wealth and luxury by being hired at these companies. As previously mentioned, those who are lucky enough to be employed in the offices of these companies are the objects of much suspicion. Usually, their salaries are better and more regular than those earned at other, local, enterprises. A man in his mid-30s hired as an engineer for Tigo earned 1500 US$ per month after 3 years of work, which is far more than any NGO, the state, or another company could pay. Working at the reception of the Airtel central office in the city centre promises a monthly income of 600 US$. These wages and in particular the lifestyles of telecom employees make these firms very attractive to young Kinois, especially those who have passed the secondary school state examination. So, aside from attraction, there is much suspicion, due to the fierce competition for gaining employment at one of the various cellular companies in town.

Mobile phones and mobile conversations are also embedded within the practices of invisible agents. Pentecostal pastors integrate cellular phones within the logic of *kindoki* and warn people that conversations, or accepting handsets or phone credit, can produce ties between them and unchristian others. Outside of church settings too, Kinois interpret certain mobile phone conversations as the performances of occult agents. One example is Kinois' reactions to phone calls I initiated through Skype. The person called would either see "private number" (*numéro privé*) or "unknown number" (*numéro inconnu*) appear on the phone display, or a strange number formation would appear (for instance one informant told me that one of my calls had given the sign "111111111"). People uninformed about how different Internet-mediated telephone conversations might present themselves on their small phone screen might not pick up the phone. The man who saw my caller ID as "111111111" told me he had been afraid that this was a satanic phone call. Thus, in Kinshasa, although less prominently than in other sub-Saharan African countries (like Nigeria, Gabon, and Malawi, see Bonhomme 2012 and Englund 2007), mobile phones are inserted into the occult economy.

Crucial to Pentecostals' take on the dangers of ICT is the importance of responsibility and the necessity of knowing how to take responsibility for one's technologically mediated moral subjectivity. How, in other words, should one act morally in a world of technological objects? As was clear from Fabrice's narrative, it is not so much the actual possession of technological objects (mobile phones, television sets, cameras) that is at stake, but what people choose to do with the technologies. Specifically, the concern is with the relationships that are mediated by these material objects, which can lead to confusion, mistrust, and uncertainty, and which push many Pentecostal Kinois to think about "appropriate" and "inappropriate" ways of interacting with and through ICT.

This emphasis on responsibility contrasts with the more familiar Pentecostal approach to taming electronic commodities or goods coming from the West. Usually, prayer over an object breaks its occult ties (see Meyer 1998). Fabrice did not suggest prayer as a strategy to make the smartphone safer. Rather, the user was supposed to possess sufficient Christian knowledge to handle the technology in a moral way. Therefore, along with "mediation", a currently hot topic in the anthropology of technology, "connectivity" deserves greater theoretical investigation. Both "mediation" and "connectivity" emphasize interaction (social or spiritual) and allow room for agency; yet, while "mediation" emphasizes the in-between, the transfer of communication, power, and value, and at times even suggests the resolution of conflict, "connectivity" attends to the relationships generated, to "accessibility" or "availability", and to the possibility of entering into a relationship with an Other (socially and/or spiritually), whether technologically mediated or not. In Kinois terms, it is "*you* who open the door" (*ofungoli porte*)—a familiar idiom to describe one's receptiveness to the Holy Spirit or to bad spirits. Witches are not just mediators of evil powers; they also connect the souls of their victims to demonic powers. Through *kindoki*, bewitched people have access to new, invisible, realms of identity, success, and power. Witches open the doors between the visible and invisible worlds. Very much like ICT, therefore, witches connect people with other worlds, even as people are not always aware of the consequences of entering therein.

Telling in this regard is the name attributed to the ingredients of the medicine *bugota* used in magic by Sukuma farmers in Tanzania (Stroeken, this volume): *shingila*, entrances. As Stroeken describes, the power of this medicine depends on its relatedness to others parts of culture. "Wherever 'magic' works in the world, the reason is a sense of differential relatedness". Via the medicine, the patient is connected to multiple worlds. This complex state of belonging defies homogenization and total control and is characterized by ambiguity and negotiations. According to Stroeken, who draws on Gluckman's distinction between simplex and complex societies, Pentecostal Christianity cannot accept the multiplexity of people's relationships and tries to reduce the ties between people.

Pentecostal discourses emphasizes one's responsibility in "opening the door" via technology. The ways in which "connectivity" or "accessibility" is debated in contemporary technological cultures are of utmost importance for anthropologists, as this allows us to reflect on issues of personhood, subjectivity, and sociality. This draws attention to the dividuality of personhood (Marriott 1976; LiPuma 1998; Strathern 1988; Pype 2011) and opens up new realms for the study of agency, social (im)mobility, and power (De Bruijn and Van Dijk 2012). While personhood, the self, and interactions with Others (often spiritual others) have been studied within the medical and religious spheres, Pentecostal reflections on communication technologies force us to perceive the ways in which "contact" with Others (social and/or spiritual) can be initiated, mediated, evaluated, broken off, and even repaired. The attribution of moral and/or immoral meanings to the possibilities of "connecting", as analysed here, foregrounds the importance, precisely, of "being accessible" as an essential feature of the social person.

Scientific Knowledge

"Electricity," said Pastor Dominique, a Branhamist Christian pastor, during a formal interview, "can be used for good, that is, to cook, to have light, to use machinery, but it can also lead to death; when you touch electrical wires, it can lead to an accident. The word of God contains only good; technology can be good and bad." The pastor continued that "life" (*bomoyi*) is only captured in the word of God (*liloba ya Nzambe*). The good side of technology is nonetheless always empty (*vide, ya pamba*). This emptiness is the consequence of technology's cosmological position: it is the outcome of the snake's knowledge. In the Garden of Eden, mankind did not need technology; the contemporary material world, however, does require technology.

Pastor Dieudonné, who uses big plasma screens, microphones powered with electricity, and even audiovisual footage and live online streaming (when connecting, for instance, with a Branhamist Christian church in the German city of Krefeld) in preaching, stressed that technology is morally ambiguous. Although, for him, the knowledge that leads to technological innovation is de facto diabolical. When I asked Pastor Dieudonné for clarifications, following a Sunday morning sermon at which his assistant pastor taught that "we should know that all knowledge of these technologies is the consequence of the Snake (*le Serpent, nyoka*)", the pastor explained that "*kindoki* and science are not useful for a child of God (*mwana ya Nzambe*). The knowledge (*mayele*) that has allowed people to make microphones, satellites, and even nuclear energy is diabolical. The only way scientists have obtained this knowledge is through an engagement with death." Pastor Dieudonné earned a *License* degree in physics (equivalent of an M.A.) from the University of Kinshasa (UNIKIN). After working as a teaching assistant at the university for a few years, he abandoned the academic world because he found it increasingly difficult to reconcile his faith with his work as a scientific researcher. For Pentecostal Christians, any knowledge that distracts the Christian from God's path is perceived as anti-Christian. Knowledge in itself is not diabolical or divine, rather the difference lies in the *source* of knowledge. Some knowledge is God-given (*euti epay ya Nzambe*). Most Christians have received this gift of knowledge (*bwanya ya Nzambe*), which allows them to understand the world, to interpret signs of the material world as metonyms of invisible powers and spirits, and act upon it (Pype 2012: 112–115). However, other kinds of knowledge are inspired by the devil (*ya Satani*). To understand whether certain knowledge is "Christian" or not, one should look into its consequences: does it sow death, as, for instance, the atomic bomb? Or does it harm people, as do weapons, for example?

The types of knowledge that do not "come from God" are abstract and irrelevant for daily social life. Pastor Dieudonné explained how he had refused to continue his postgraduate studies at the university. Having finished his *License* degree with a dissertation on metallurgy, he felt uncomfortable with the level of abstraction that studies in physics entail. The mysteries of abstract thinking undoubtedly lead to the devil. According to pastor Dieudonné:

> There were certain demands that I could not perform. Especially things that you cannot grasp with your five senses. We have five senses, but some scientific experiments rely on another sense. As a Christian, my 6th sense is my faith. If I cannot feel, taste, hear, see, or smell something then I need to believe that God is there. But, I know that in those sciences, people do not rely on God.

In this scheme of things, scientific knowledge is the devil's knowledge, the consequence of the alliance between the *Serpent* and Eve. The pastor's words lead us into the domain of scientific innovation, scientific expertise, and the position of the researcher in the religious context. As the body is God-given, the five senses are what people can and should rely on in order to make statements and claims about the human and non-human environment. However, once we enter into the domain of the impalpable, or the immaterial, confusion arises. How is scholarship related to the religious world? Pastor Dieudonné explains faith as "believing without having seen". How do physicians believe/understand/explain scientific musings? While certain phenomena and causalities in the physical domain can be explained through "pragmatics", there is a whole domain of physics that lies beyond the pragmatic. Here, the pastor questions the use of this kind of knowledge.

Just as Kinois Christians (Branhamist Christians included) are suspicious of the knowledge that diviners, magicians, and healers can mobilize, they also question the spiritual qualities of scientific expertise and the origins of scholarly excellence. Rumours abound concerning the occult ties of Kinshasa's scholars and professors. Stickers pasted on professors' cars, the rings or hats they wear, or even the book collections they display in their houses, are read as signals of their adherence to secret societies such as Freemasonry and Rosicrucianism.

Well-known pastors with academic degrees are also met with suspicion, and the slightest word or phrase that could hint at affiliation with mystical societies are exploited by their competitors as signs of alliances with diabolic occult powers. Obviously, these arguments are made in the context of competition over authority and influence, and aim at downgrading the elite status of one's rivals.

Pastor Dieudonné told me that some of his colleagues had refused to continue doctoral research because they had been invited to be initiated into secret societies. Rumours abound about Freemasons operating on university campuses, recruiting students, and passing on knowledge and intelligence to them by way of special initiations.[11] Most Kinois believe that many, if not all, outstanding students procure their intelligence in the occult world. "Naturally" intelligent students are envied by others and may become the targets of madness (*liboma*), a spiritual affliction thrown at them by jealous fellow students and *féticheurs*. In addition, it is taken as common knowledge that many professors of local universities have either a mad son or daughter in their families. These psychological illnesses are interpreted as the outcomes of sacrificial *kindoki* (Pype 2010), in which a father offers his son's/daughter's wisdom or mental health to the devil in order to secure his own academic position.

The suspicion about the dangers of abstract academic and scientific knowledge also informs the movements of Christians on campus.

Pentecostal students regard libraries as spaces of danger. Jeremy, a medical student in his late 20s nearing the completion of his degree, told me that one can leave books on a table in the university library for weeks on end without fearing that someone might steal them. Books could be technologies of initiation into occult societies, not only because of the mysteries they describe and explain but also because of the spirits that accompany them. If one does not know the spiritual identity of the person who has laid the books on the table, opening a book and starting to read puts one at risk of bewitchment through letters and drawings. Jeremy related how one of his friends had given him a new book, an updated version of what they were studying at the university. For one reason or another, Jeremy never managed to actually open the book and start reading. A month later, his friend asked Jeremy what he thought about the book. Jeremy lied and said he liked it very much. His friend said: "You are lying. I see you have not read a single word of the book. If you had, you would have responded differently." This reply triggered Jeremy's curiosity, and that same evening he decided to start reading. However, very quickly, perhaps after 15 min, Jeremy began suffering from a headache and had to go to bed. His mother, who often wakes up in the night when she hears her son going to bed, went into his room and told him that she had dreamt that someone was initiating her son. She warned him to be careful. Jeremy became worried. He understood his mother's warning, the headache, the frequent power cuts, and the fatigue that had continued to plague him as he tried to read the book, as divine interventions to protect him. That book obviously contained occult knowledge, Jeremy thought. And he feared that further reading would tie his soul to the devil. The next day, Jeremy returned the book to its previous owner and told him not to give him anything any more.

These anxieties about book knowledge, and schools and universities as hotbeds of occult activities are not limited to Kinshasa, and neither are they new (Bastian 2001; Tonda 2000; Ndaya 2008). Yet, they are often ignored in the study of Pentecostal witchcraft, which is biased by a tendency to examine the occult origins of customary rituals. Yet, the concerns over the acquisition of "right" and "spiritually safe" knowledge seems crucial among Pentecostals, and, all over Africa, PCC leaders are establishing Pentecostal universities. These offer a Christian environment to students and train them to become leaders in the Christian community, and also, often, in the nation where the university has been planted.[12]

Books have much in common with electronic communication technologies. Just like mobile phones, and radio and television sets, books and other written media are objects with which users (readers/listeners/viewers) engage in a sensual way in order to acquire information. People hold these objects, use their hands to turn pages, make notes, alter frequencies, or carry them around. The book, the smartphone, and the television share an emphasis on the ocular as the main entrance point into the invisible, immaterial, realms of the Real. By means of reading and watching, the recipient's soul becomes connected to images, ideas, and desires that escape total control or delineation.

Connectivity is more than merely expanding one's social network; humans are connected to non-humans, spirits, imaginations, and other temporalities and locations. ICT and books mediate these connections; yet people can choose the worlds into which they want to enter—or not enter. Pastor Dieudonné's choice to abandon academia was motivated by his desire to not be connected to potentially harmful occult realms. In a way, in order to preserve his ties with the Divine, the pastor closed that door; just as Jeremy literally closed his friend's book after supernatural signs informed him about potentially harmful effects to his soul should he continue to read it.

More fundamentally, the ethnographic material draws our attention to the literally *formative* possibilities of information circulation and knowledge acquisition. For Kinois Pentecostals, the Bible, the pamphlets and audiovisual recordings containing sermons, as well as e-prayer groups, digital Bible verses, and online healing connect users' souls to the divine realm and offer strategies for healing, instructing, and blessing. Other forms of information, whether transmitted through paper or electronic media, transform the soul by spiritually killing it, linking it to the devil, and connecting it to a realm of anti-social, potentially disruptive powers. Here as well, we see how mediation and connectivity represent two complementary explanatory modes for the imagination of human entanglements with invisible and visible realms, and with the social and the spiritual.

The Witchcraft Complex

In this last part, I wish to render the analysis of Branhamist Christians' understandings of *kindoki* even more complex. At certain times, especially during evangelization campaigns, Branhamist leaders in Kinshasa articulate a very "classic" Pentecostal approach to *kindoki*, that is one centred around objects of the past (*ya bakoko*). During these sessions, the pastors do not rehearse the dogma of the Branhamist church: that television and other media are bad, and that women should avoid wearing trousers or putting on makeup. They rather lean heavily on the concepts of *fétishes* and *magie*, and on their demoniac natures: a mask, a rope to put around the waist, a bracelet, a *nkisi* statue, or a bundle of herbs that women in the market place under their baskets in order to attract clients.

Juxtaposing this Branhamist understanding of *kindoki* with Fabrice's explanation of *kindoki* illustrates the hybridity of the imagination of the occult within one form of Pentecostal Christianity. During evangelization campaigns, Kinois Branhamist leaders define "African traditions" as demonic. As I argue in my work on the representations of *kindoki* in evangelizing teleserials produced by born-again Christians (Pype 2012: 46), we must approach the presentation of witches, fools, and pastors, and thus of *kindoki* and the occult, as intended constructions. This particular mode of (re-) presentation of witchcraft allows us to see how quoting Bayart (2005: 137), "the *imaginaire* is first of all an interaction"—not only an interaction between past, present, and future, but also "an interaction between social actors" (ibid.). Born-again Christians do not live in a vacuum and do not invent the metaphors and images of *kindoki*. (Re-) presentations of this material diverge from the existing dominant imaginary, which they present in a particular fashion, so as to sustain their own agendas. The discourse articulated in the evangelization campaign also draws our attention to the constructedness of *kindoki*. Messages can be adapted to particular crowds. Most probably, Branhamist pastors emphasized a classic type of Pentecostal witchcraft because they cater to a yet-to-be-converted crowd. In order not to frighten them too much (with the emphasis on the occult dimensions of new technology), they chose to play the familiar type of witchcraft suspicions card.

This observation and interpretation illustrate the heterogeneous aspect of witchcraft among Pentecostal communities. Just as the "Pentecostal" field is not unified, there is also no common Pentecostal definition of witchcraft. Major lines are drawn among Kinois Pentecostal groups in terms of their different approaches to the substance of *kindoki*. While the majority of the PCCs in Kinshasa (especially those belonging to the *Eglise de Reveil du Congo*-Awakening Churches) ascribe an utterly spiritual aspect to *kindoki*, other churches (those said to be closer to the

ATRs) see *kindoki* as material as well. *Kindoki* here references a material substance located in the belly. Vomiting and physical extraction are unsurprisingly some of the more common purifying practices in these ATR churches, while the majority of PCCs claims that speaking out the name of Jesus and the discursive chasing off evil spirits are the only "Christian" practices for healing the afflicted.

Therefore, I propose the concept of "the witchcraft complex" in order to acknowledge the variety of Pentecostal understandings of witchcraft, strategies for cleansing and repairing, and entanglements with local and global scales of reference. A "complex" is at once (a) a composite bringing together many interconnected parts, an assemblage of associated things; (b) a fixed idea or obsessive notion; and (c) as used in psychology,[13] a core pattern of emotions, memories, perceptions, and wishes in the personal unconscious organized around a common theme, such as power or status. The notion of the "complex" thus allows us to acknowledge the juxtaposition of objects and types of materiality that contrast "tradition" and "modernity" in the imagination of evil. Smartphones and *nkisi* statues can appear side by side in testimonies about *kindoki*. Planes, television sets, and Rolex watches are all potentially dangerous, just as the ritualistic paraphernalia of a customary chief. Objects assumed to be "traditional" seem to be quite hybrid as well. In her overview of demonization discourses in Africa, Hackett shows (2003: 62f) that the so-called "typically African" patterns of witchcraft often have trans-local origins. In particular, the demonology can be traced back from West- and East-Africa to the US, South Korea, and Brazil. The "Traditional" is "invented", a transnational blend of images, names, props, and practices (Ibid.).

The second meaning of "complex" does justice to the fixation of PCC on witchcraft and the occult. In the Kinois context, PCC places greater emphasis on deliverance and the spiritual battle than on the gospel of health, wealth, and success. PCC is rejected by other Christian churches precisely because of Pentecostal communities' consistent emphasis on *kindoki*. These same critics of PCC claim that the witchcraft confessions, sermons about how *kindoki* began and how one should protect oneself against witches, actually initiate Christians into the realm of the occult.

The third semantic layer of the notion of "the complex" draws attention to the affective dimensions of *kindoki*. For many types of *kindoki*, fear, jealousy, envy, desire, anger, hatred, and other anti-social emotions are considered to be at once constitutive of witchcraft and the outcome of *kindoki*. A "complex" influences an individual's attitude and behaviour. Fears, suspicions, and uncertainties about occult powers vested in objects or transmitted by others steer the ways people interact with each other and live with objects. These emotions can lead to asocial behaviour. Witches themselves can be said to suffer a "complex", as their actions are also driven by feelings (mostly envy, jealousy, or hatred) and are socially disruptive. In turn, PCC structures emotional regimes in which "good" and "bad" emotions are identified according to their connections to the spiritual and their potential involvement in *kindoki* (Pype 2014b).

Concluding Thoughts: Urban Sociality and *Kindoki*

In concluding, I bring the discussion back to the urban scale. If discourse about *kindoki* is about the present, and if it is an explanatory system for understanding the distress of the present, one could argue that the variety of *kindoki* explanations indexes the spiritual insecurity (see Ashforth 2005) that Kinois society is experiencing. Within the Branhamist discourses on *kindoki* presented in this article, we observe three major shifts away from recent academic interpretations of urban African witchcraft. First, Branhamist *kindoki* is largely impersonal. Both in the evangelization campaign in Lemba and in the interpretations of ICT enhanced *kindoki*, no emotions of jealousy, hatred, and envy or evil intentions are mentioned. The "classic" intermediaries (the maternal uncle who is looking for vengeance; the neighbour who has made a pact with the devil to enrich himself; etc.) are strikingly absent. The city is presented as an environment full of potentially harmful objects. This relates to the role of consumption in the city: everything needs to be purchased, and collecting material goods is a sign of success in the city. The city, with its array of commodities from the ancestors as well as high-tech goods from faraway countries, has become a space filled with contagious magic. Every single object has the ability to transfer occult powers.

Second, the centrality of ICT in recent interpretations of *kindoki* speaks to new forms of expanding one's social network (see above) and also draws our attention to the "technologisation" of urban Kinois life, where ICT goods dominate everyday life (even when there are power cuts). One cannot underestimate the relevance of cellular technologies in everyday life in Kinshasa. The mobile phone as a commodity together with phone credit structure intergenerational (Pype 2017) and sexual relations (Pype fc.); the cellular networks are also important job providers, contributing to the emergence of a middle class in urban Congo; they are major sponsors of Congolese entertainment (music festivals, TV shows, etc.); and, finally, these companies occasionally become political actors, as, for instance, when the internet is shut down due to government orders; when they communicate the results of the state exams (via text messaging), etc. Doubting the morality of ICT means critically observing the dominance of these new capitalist players, as well as devalorizing these technologies' contribution in rapidly expanding and difficult to control forms of urban sociality (see also Blanes this volume).

Third, and probably most striking, is the absence of the gift as a crucial performance in the transmission of spiritual powers, or in the bewitching act. A decade ago, De Boeck (2005) already argued that *kindoki* had left the lineage and had become random, although the gift continued to be an important intermediary act in the spiritual battle. Receiving a biscuit, money, or other commodities from strangers or relatives remains a major way of having one's soul captured and thus being tied to the Devil. Branhamist discourse about *kindoki* does not emphasize the gift.[14] This impersonal variant of witchcraft as well as the variety of *kindoki* described by Branhamist Christians expresses total confusion. Both "the past", or "tradition", as metonymically represented in the *kindoki ya biso*, and "the present", or "modernity" , as manifest in the *kindoki* of modern communication technologies, science and electricity are potentially harmful. The diffuse reactions within the Branhamist Christian scene in Kinshasa (some rejecting new technologies; others embracing them but fully controlling them) show how profound the uncertainties are. Also, the emphasis on personal responsibility (in handling the technologies), or the necessity of possessing the *bwanya ya Nzambe* in order to use the new technologies in spiritually safe ways, hint at the importance of the individual. One's spiritual well-being still depends on social others, but it is the Christian him- or herself who is ultimately accountable for his or her own spiritual health. This suggests an increasing degree of autonomy of the urban citizen. Such discourses show that people depend on *themselves* for survival, and to find jobs and prosper.

Indeed, most Kinois know that they should not expect that relatives, marital partners, or even offspring, will be able to help them in moments of need. Moreover, as the Pentecostal leaders argue, one ought to perhaps mistrust these intimate connections too. By focussing on the possibility of being bewitched by any object whatsoever (be they from the ancestors or the high tech world), Branhamist Christians are reminded time and again that ***kindoki*** is epidemic, that the risk of contagious affliction is real and omnipresent, and that becoming and remaining "a good Christian" depends strongly on "good" connectivity.

Notes

1. See Geschiere (2013: 7–13), who elaborates on the "pitfalls of [the] notion" of witchcraft and sketches the epistemological, ethical, and semantic problems that this category invokes. I am following his suggestion to stick as closely possible to local, emic, categories and unpack their various semantic layers.
2. Branhamist Christian communities frequently organize evangelization campaigns in Kinshasa, and a Branhamist Christian TV station (RTAE, *Radio Télévision Aigle de l'Eternel*) broadcasts old footage of Branham's sermons. A Christian website claims that there are 2,000,000 followers of William Branham in DR Congo. It is unclear how the data were collected. http://www.speroforum.com/a/49578/Protestants-in-DR-Congo-to-partner-with-USbased-ASCI#.Vp1lhhjhAfE consulted November 15 2015.
3. A synonym used in Kinshasa to refer to Brahnamist Christianity as *la religion du Message* (the religion of the Message). The *Message* (*Le Message*), a synonym used for Branhamist Christianity mainly by Branhamist Christians themselves, is shorthand for *Le Message du Temps de la Fin* (Message of the End Times), which summarizes Branham's understanding of the world.
4. While the origins of Branhamist Christianity are located in post-second world war US society, it has taken diverse arrival routes into Kinshasa. William Branham never visited central Africa (he visited South Africa in 1951) but American, German, and African evangelizers, who crusaded in Congo/Zaire, brought Branham's pamphlets with them. Baruti Kasongo claims he first learned about William Branham when receiving a pamphlet from a deacon of the FEPACO-Nzambe Malamu Church (an independent Pentecostal Church set up in 1960s Congo by the Congolese preacher Ayidini Abala Alexandre). Similar *brochures* were distributed in Kinshasa's Assemblies of God communities. During the late 1970s and 1980s, the Branhamist community remained rather confined. In the 1990s, when a general Pentecostal wave hit African urban centres, Branhamist Christianity gained influence in Kinshasa. While the initial phases of Branhamist Christianity in Kinshasa can be traced back

to the efforts of European and African evangelizers, an increasing number of Branhamist Christian prayer groups in Kinshasa have direct links with mother churches elsewhere in DR Congo. A large majority of the Branhamist Christian churches set up in Kinshasa in the last decade have strong ties with churches in Lubumbashi and, especially Mbuyi-Mayi. These two major cities in central Congo are commonly known to be in Luba-territory (an ethnic group). The origin stories of the newer Branhamist Christian churches in Kinshasa very often mention pastors or members of mother churches in Lubumbashi or Mbuyi-Mayi who relocated to Kinshasa, usually not in order to proselytize, but rather for personal (social and/or economic) reasons. Once in Kinshasa, they decided to set up a chapter of their mother church or their own church. Branhamist Christian churches whose genealogy runs through Luba-land, eagerly invite pastors and Branhamist Christian leaders from their home regions to participate in evangelization campaigns.

5. The major Branhamist Christian churches in Kinshasa are *Shekinah Tabernacle* (since 1990), *L'Assemblée Chrétienne de Righini* (since the 1980s), and *Eglise Tabernacle de Gloire*, although there are many more. Probably the best-known Branhamist pastor in Kinshasa is Baruti Kasongo. His church *L'Assemblée Chrétienne de Righini* is also popularly called "Baruti Tabernacle". Pasteur Baruti embraces modern technology and runs a TV station (RTAE) and a website, and frequently travels abroad to evangelize among diasporic Congolese communities (e.g. Dallas, Texas in 2013, Australia in 2015).
6. The American Prophet William Marion Branham (1909–1965) was a prominent figure of the 1940s–1950s US healing revival. While Branhamist Christianity lost relevance in contemporary American society, Branhamist Christianity is thriving in the DR Congo. Branhamist websites from Asia and Africa claim that DR Congo has the largest group of Branhamist Christians (as Branham's followers are popularly called) in the world. Weaver (2000: 153) mentions 25.000 followers in DR Congo, but the numbers have only increased since then. It is unclear how many Branhamist Christians are practicing in Kinshasa nowadays, although it is likely that most Congolese Branhamist Christians live in the capital city.
7. For excellent discussions of the ambiguous reception of the new forms of mobility enabled through mobile phones: for Inahmbane society in Mozambique Archambault (2012), and McIntosh (2010) on Malindi town, Kenya.
8. Douglas does not use any local terms in this article to refer to witchcraft and sorcery. She solely uses the noun "sorcerer" to indicate "witches, demon-possessed persons, or wizards supposed to have secret power

to wreak harm, not like a robber might work, secretly at night, but by occult, supernatural means. Sorcerers are evildoers, and the context here is how believers try to combat them." (Douglas 1999: 177)

9. Branham, 65-0801 M—The God of this Evil Age.
10. I thank Knut Rio for drawing my attention to this.
11. Bastian (2001: 76–81) discusses the same phenomenon ("campus cultism") in Nigeria.
12. Some examples: Pentecost University College in Ghana: http://pentvars.edu.gh/about-us/core-values; Pentecostal University in Uganda: http://upu.ac.ug/—both consulted 8 December 2015. Currently, in Kinshasa, Branhamist and Awakening churches have not yet set up their own educational institutions. The Kimbanguist community, by contrast, does have its own schools and even a university.
13. From the Oxford English Dictionary: "A group of emotionally charged ideas or mental factors, unconsciously associated by the individual with a particular subject, arising from repressed instincts, fears, or desires and often resulting in mental abnormality; freq. with defining word prefixed, as *inferiority*, *Œdipus complex*, etc.; hence *colloq*., in vague use, a fixed mental tendency or obsession."
14. Meyer (1998: 752fl) remarks in a footnote that classic Pentecostal churches in rural and urban Ghana animate commodities, while recent waves of Pentecostalism since the 1980s which are popular among urban elites emphasize the gift in the demonization of objects and "appear to be less concerned with dangers imbued in commodities."

References

Archambault, J.-S. 2012. Travelling While Sitting Down: Mobile Phones, Mobility and the Communication Landscape in Inhambane, Mozambique. *Africa: Journal of the International Africa Institute* 82 (3): 393–412.

Ashforth, A. 2005. *Witchcraft, Violence and Democracy in South Africa*. Chicago: Chicago University Press.

Bastian, M. 2001. Vulture men, campus cultists and teenaged witches: modern magics in Nigerian popular media. In *Magical Interpretations, Material Realities. Modernity, Witchcraft and the Occult in Postcolonial Africa*, edited by H Moore and T. Sanders, 71–96. London: Routledge.

Bayart, J.-F. 2005 [1996]. *L'Illusion Identitaire*. Paris: Fayard. Translated: The Illusion of Cultural Identity. London: Hurst and University of Chicago Press.

Bonhomme, J. 2012. The Dangers of Anonymity: Witchcraft, Rumor and Modernity in Africa. *Hau: Journal of Ethnographic Theory* 2 (2) http://www.haujournal.org/index.php/hau/article/view/hau2.2.012/1025.

Comaroff, J., and J.L. Comaroff (eds.). 1993. *Modernity and its Malcontents: Ritual and Power in Postcolonial Africa*. Chicago: University of Chicago Press.

Comaroff, J., and J.L. Comaroff. 1999. Occult Economies and the Violence of Abstraction: Notes from the South African Postcolony. *American Ethnologist* 26 (2): 279–303.

De Boeck, F. 2005. The Divine Seed: Children, Gift and Witchcraft in the Democratic Republic of Congo. In *Makers and Breakers: Children and Youth in Postcolonial Africa*, ed. A. Honwana, and F. De Boeck, 188–214. Oxford: James Currey.

De Bruijn, M., and R. Van Dijk (eds.). 2012. *The Social Life of Connectivity in Africa*. Basingstoke: Palgrave/Macmillan.

Douglas, M. 1999. Sorcery Accusations Unleashed: The Lele Revisited, 1987. *Africa* 69 (2): 177–193.

Eni, Emmanuel. 1988. Delivered from the Powers of Darkness. http://www.divinerevelations.info/dreams_and_visions/dilivered_from_the_powers_of_darkness_by_emmanuel_eni.htm. Retrieved 16 June 2017.

Geschiere, P. 1997. *The Modernity of Witchcraft: Politics and the Occult in Postcolonial Africa*. Charlottesville: University of Virginia Press.

Geschiere, P. 2013. *Witchcraft, Intimacy, and Trust: Africa in Comparison*. Chicago: Chicago University Press.

Englund, H. 2007. Witchcraft and the Limits of Mass Mediation in Malawi. *Journal of the Royal Anthropological Institute* 13 (2): 295–311.

Hackett, R.I.J. 2003. Discourses of Demonization in Africa and Beyond. *Diogenes* 50 (3): 61–75.

Kwabena Asamoah-Gyadu, J. 2007. Broken Calabashes and Covenants of Fruitfulness: Cursing Barrenness in Contemporary African Christianity, *Journal of Religion in Africa* 37 (4): 437–460.

LiPuma, E. 1998. Modernity and Modern Forms of Personhood in Melanesia. In *Bodies and Persons: Comparative Perspectives from Africa and Melanesia*, eds. M. Lambek, and A. Strathern, 53–79. Cambridge: Cambridge University Press.

Marriott, M. 1976. Hindu Transactions: Diversity Without Dualism. In *Transaction and Meaning: Directions in the Anthropology of Exchange and Symbolic Behavior*, ed. B. Kapferer, 109–142. Philadelphia: Institute for the Study of Human Issues.

McIntosh, J. 2010. Mobile Phones and Mipoho's Prophecy: The powers and Dangers of Flying Language. *American Ethnologist* 37 (2): 337–353.

Meyer, Birgit. 1998. Commodities and the Power of Prayer: Pentecostalist Attitudes Towards Consumption in Contemporary Ghana. *Development and Change* 29 (4): 751–769.

Ndaya Tshiteku, J. 2008. *'Prendre le bic.' Le Combat Spirituel congolais et les transformations sociales.* PhD Dissertation, Leiden: Centre d'Etudes Africaines.

Newell, S. 2007. Pentecostal Witchcraft: Neoliberal Possession and Demonic Discourse in Ivoirian Pentecostal Churches, *Journal of Religion in Africa* 37 (4): 461–490.

Nyamnjoh, F.B., and I. Brudvig. 2014. Conviviality and Negotiations with Belonging in Urban Africa. In *Routledge Handbook of Global Citizenship Studies*, eds. E.F. Isin, and P. Nyers. London: Routledge.

Pype, K. 2010. Of Fools and False Pastors. Tricksters in Kinshasa's TV Fiction. *Visual Anthropology* 23 (2): 115–135.

Pype, K. 2011. Confession-cum-Deliverance. In/Dividuality of the Subject Among Kinshasa's Born-Again Christians. *Journal of Religion in Africa* 41 (3): 280–310.

Pype, K. 2012. *The Making of the Pentecostal Melodrama: Religion, Media, and Gender in Kinshasa.* Oxford and New York: Berghahn Books.

Pype, K. fc. Blackberry Girls and Jesus' Brides Pentecostal-Charismatic Christianity and the (Im-)Moralization of Urban Femininities in Contemporary Kinshasa. *Journal of Religion in Africa.*

Pype, K. 2014a. Media as Technologies of Enchantment. Initial Comparisons Between Kimbanguist and Pentecostal Media Pedagogies. In *Simon Kimbangu. Le Prophete de la Liberation de l'Homme Noir.* Tome II. eds. E. Mbokolo, and D. Kivilu Sabakinu. Kinshasa: L'Harmattan RDC. 135–158.

Pype, K. 2014b. The Heart of Man: Mass Mediated Representations of Emotions, The Subject and Subjectivities. In *New Media and Religious Transformations in Africa*, eds. R. Hackett, and B. Soares. Bloomington IN: Indiana University Press.

Pype 2017. Brokers of Belonging. Elders and Intermediaries in Kinshasa's Mobile Phone Culture. In *From Media Audiences to Users. Everyday Media in Africa*, eds. Mano, Winston, and Wendy Willems. Chapter 4. London: Routledge.

Strathern, M. 1988. *The Gender of the Gift: Problems with Women and Problems with Society in Melanesia.* Berkeley: University of California Press.

Taylor, J.P. 2016. Drinking Money and Pulling Women: Mobile Phone Talk, Gender, and Agency in Vanuatu. *Anthropological Forum* 26 (1): 1–16.

Tonda, J. 2000. Capital sorcier et travail de Dieu. *Politique africaine* 79 (October): 48–65.

Author Biography

Katrien Pype is an anthropologist who has been studying Pentecostal Christianity and media cultures in Kinshasa since 2003. Based on extended ethnographic fieldwork, Pype tries to understand how ICT and religion produce new forms of life and generate new aesthetics. Her work has been published in leading academic journals such as *Journal of the Royal Anthropological Institute, Ethnos, Journal of Modern African Studies* and many others. Her monograph, *The Making of the Pentecostal Melodrama. Religion, Media and Gender in Kinshasa* (2012, Berghahn Books), explores the production of evangelizing TV serials.

CHAPTER 6

Jesus Lives in Me: Pentecostal Conversions, Witchcraft Confessions, and Gendered Power in the Trobriand Islands

Michelle MacCarthy

Introduction

In August 2013, I attended a Revival Crusade in the Trobriand village of Omarakana. Pastors from various Pentecostal and evangelical churches had been invited from southern Kiriwina and the outer islands to preach, testify, and perform alter calls to engage the holy spirit and effect conversions for those ready to be born again. While these male pastors who were generally the figures leading prayers and alter calls were charismatic and compelling, what interested me most of all were the conversations I had on the periphery of these proceedings, mostly with women from the southern Kiriwina village of Sinaketa. Several of these women, including a pastor's wife named Esther, told me that they were witches, but that they had now been *kalobusivau* (born again) in the Pentecostal faith, and had renounced their past misdeeds. After living for nearly two years on the island, I had had it firmly instilled in me that no one, ever, would openly

M. MacCarthy (✉)
Department of Anthropology, Saint Mary's University, Halifax, Canada

K. Rio et al. (eds.), *Pentecostalism and Witchcraft*, Contemporary Anthropology of Religion, DOI 10.1007/978-3-319-56068-7_6

admit to being, or having been, a witch. Accusations might be made in hushed tones amongst close kin or friends, but never spoken publically, and there are no public or violent reprisals against known witches, unlike in other parts of PNG and Melanesia. How was it that Pentecostal Christianity had made it possible not only to proclaim to both friends and strangers that one is, or has been, a witch, and what does this mean for women's agency and power? How are these various forms of power embodied, and as embodied power, how can a witch denounce that which is physically a part of herself? What is the particular power of Revival Christianity that can disembody the embodied? These questions pressed me to think about gender, Pentecostal Christianity, and witchcraft in my own case study, and to understand these phenomena in a comparative perspective.

Witchcraft and Sorcery in Comparison: The Massim and Beyond

Massim witchcraft and sorcery are of course well-documented and amply represented in the anthropological corpus. Malinowski had much to say on the topic of magic in both its malevolent and beneficent forms, and his work was shortly followed upon by Reo Fortune in his classic treatise, *Sorcerers of Dobu* (1932). Since then, Stanley Tambiah, Susanne Kuehling, Martha Macintyre, Mark Mosko, and Nancy Munn, among others, have had much to add to our understanding of magic, sorcery, and witchcraft as they are variably practiced and understood in this anthropologically rich region. PNG, and Melanesia as a whole, are known to host a variety of occult forms, and has often been contrasted with Africa in this respect; for example, Marwick made the distinction in 1964 between Africa's "witches" as insiders and Melanesia's "sorcerers" as outsiders (1964), a dichotomy that has since, not surprisingly, been shown to be far too neat to reflect reality. Geschiere (2013) has also taken up this comparison, as we do in this set of papers.

In the Trobriands, a variety of occult forms is locally recognized. The vernacular term *meguwa* is usually translated as magic, a generic term that denotes any kind of manipulation of phenomena to effect a desired outcome, positive or negative, though it most generally refers to benevolent (or at least, not evil) forms of magic such as love magic, beauty magic, healing magic, garden magic, or weather magic (though these may also have more specific terms). These are for the most part (with the exception of weather magic) democratic, unspecialized forms of magic, which do not require elite or chiefly status, particular specialization, or unique qualities to perform. Usually effected through spells, charms, the observance of taboos, and so on, the incantations and associated actions can be learned, usually taught by an elder relative and usually requiring some form of payment. Those whose skill in performing particular kinds of magic are well-known are sometimes solicited for help in performing magic on someone else's behalf, and again this normally requires some kind of payment in the form of valuable wealth items like pigs, shell valuables, stone axe blades, clay pots, and/or cash.

Trobrianders also distinguish between *bwagau* and *yoyowa*, two forms of supernatural and largely negative magical power which they consistently translate into English as sorcery and witchcraft respectively. *Bwagau* and *yoyowa* create a great deal of fear, unrest, and suspicion, especially in the context of sickness or death, as these are inevitably construed as the result of malevolent action (usually due to jealousy, anger, or resentment) on the part of a sorcerer or witch. Local conceptions of the supernatural power of witches, on the one hand, and sorcerers, on the other, largely fall in line with Evans-Pritchard's classic descriptions (1937). That is to say, "a witch performs no rite, utters no spell, and possesses no medicines. An act of witchcraft is a psychic act...sorcerers may do...ill by performing magic rites with bad medicines", which, in the Trobriands case, often means natural or chemical poisons (Evans-Pritchard 1937: 1). Furthermore, as we shall see from the ethnographic case of the Trobriands, witchcraft is considered (as it is for the Azande) to be in and of the body (Evans-Pritchard 1937: 3). Witchcraft resides as a sort of substance, or perhaps essence, in the body, and yet acts of witchcraft are performed while the witch is *dis*embodied; a Trobriand witch performs evil acts as a spirit which leaves the physical body of the witch while she sleeps; while the spirit is absent, the body is at great risk, as any disturbance to the sleeping shell will mean sickness or even death to the witch. Conversely, sorcerers perform their malevolent acts by physically moving around at night, under cover of darkness, to perform rites, give bespelled or even poisoned comestible items to victims, and particularly strong sorcery is often related to chiefly rank.

Malinowski (1929) describes the differences between *bwagau* on the one hand, and *yoyowa* or *mulukwausi*[1] on the other:

> Although by far the most important of them all, the *bwaga'u* is only one among the beings who can cause disease and death. The often-mentioned flying-witches, who come always from the Southern half of the island, or from the East, from the islands of Kitava, Iwa, Gawa, or Murua, are even

> more deadly. All very rapid and violent diseases, more especially such as show no direct, perceptible symptoms, are attributed to the *mulukwausi*, as they are called. Invisible, they fly through the air, and perch on trees, house-tops, and other high places. From there, they pounce upon a man or woman and remove and hide "the inside," that is, the lungs, heart and guts, or the brains and tongue. Such a victim will die within a day or two, unless another witch, called for the purpose and well paid, goes in search of and restores the missing "inside." (Malinowski 1929: 76)

Malevolent Places, Bodies, and Metaphysics

As Malinowski alludes, there is a certain geographical division between the domains of sorcerers and witches, though these are by no means mutually exclusive. In the northern regions of Kiriwina Island, sorcerers dominate. This is, not coincidentally I think, the ancestral homeland of the highest-ranking of the Trobriand matriclans, including the Tabalu clan, to which the Paramount Chief of the islands must belong. The long-standing seat of chiefly power, Omarakana Village, is where the Trobriand Paramount Chief resides and is also home to stones that only he can manipulate to bring rains or drought as he sees fit. In the south, as well as in the smaller outer islands of the Trobriand group—the areas to which the chiefs and leaders of the northern district travel by *kula* canoe to exchange valuables, often across dangerous seas—is where witches predominate. My own fieldwork was mostly carried out in the village of Yalumgwa, in the north, the domain of sorcerers. While I was sometimes told that my adoptive father had to be careful to avoid being poisoned by sorcerers, as his own father was purported to be, I was not led to believe that I had anything to fear. Mata's father had been sorcelled because of his own ambition; he had built a yam house, though he was not himself a chief, and this was seen by the rightful chiefs of the village as subordinate and a challenge to their authority, according to my adoptive mother. Mata kept his own ambitions far less lofty, to avoid a similar fate. And if sorcerers were something to be aware of, they were inevitably amongst us, and we simply had to manage the risk. Whenever I traveled to the south or the outer islands, however—that is, to the domain of witches, the "other" of potentially evil supernatural forces (or perhaps the "other same", as suggested in the introduction to this volume)—my adoptive mother gave me lengthy lectures about how to behave, to ensure that I did not inadvertently upset a witch, and bring sickness or death to me or to the family who cared for me. Should a woman there compliment me on my clothing, string bag, jewelry, or anything else, I was not to hesitate, but to give it away immediately. Even such a small thing as failing to give a betel nut to a witch could potentially result in retribution. There were plenty of stories to be recalled and retold about the sorts of things witches could do and had done. While to be sure, there were a few witches living in our own villages, it was *those* witches, in *those* villages, who were truly to be feared. Witches in this context are *both* inside (relatives, in neighboring villages) ***and*** outside (not-exactly-us-but-those-people). They are the outside threat that is also intimate and internal, as argued in the introduction to this volume.

There is also a gendered distinction. While men can be witches and women can be sorcerers, these are symbolically gendered categories. In practice, the majority of sorcerers are men, and witches predominantly (but by no means exclusively) women, though my Trobriand interlocutors were adamant that the gendered categories were not absolute. This may be an example of what Sanders (2008: 161) refers to as a performance of gender, in which gendered ideals are performed or enacted irrespective of men's and women's sexed bodies. To return again to Malinowski, he states it thus:

> The magic of illness and health, which can poison life or restore its natural sweetness, and which holds death as it were for its last card, can be made by men and women alike; but its character changes entirely with the sex of the practitioner. Man and woman each have their own sorcery, carried on by means of different rites and formulae, acting in a different manner in the victim's body and surrounded by an altogether different atmosphere of belief. (1929: 45)

Fortune also paints a stark contrast in gendered forms of supernatural power, though he (like Malinowski) clearly makes gendered divisions absolute and tied to sexed bodies:

> Witchcraft is the woman's prerogative, sorcery the man's. A witch does all of her work in spirit form while her body sleeps, but only at the bidding of the fully conscious and fully awake woman and as the result of her spells, it is said. Not only is all that we term accident as opposed to sickness ascribed exclusively to witchcraft, but a particular way of causing illness and death is the monopoly of women. This method is that of spirit abstraction from the victim. The man, as sorcerer, has the monopoly of causing sickness and death by using spells on the personal leavings of the victim. (Fortune 1963: 150)

This is perhaps more a product of the era in which it was written and the more dichotomous, less nuanced view of gender prevalent at the time of Fortune's research, rather than a reflection of the emic point of view of who can and does practice witchcraft and sorcery.

Equivalence and Influence

Despite hierarchies of chiefs, headmen, and ranked sub-clans, individuals are accorded significant autonomy in all social relationships (Weiner 1976: 212). Weiner stresses that in the Trobriands,

> [T]here exists a strong ethic of *equivalence*, despite rank and other status differentiations. People are not free to command each other. They cannot effect their will over another person. But Trobrianders believe that it is possible to influence the disposition of others. Such influence, however, has limitations, and the process is notoriously fallible. (Weiner 1976: 212; italics in original)

Such influence is achieved through two primary means: gifts and the use of magic. The latter might further be subdivided into the kinds of benevolent magic or *meguwa* as described above, and the two malevolent forms of supernatural power, *bwagau* (sorcery) and *yoyowa* (witchcraft). Gifts and their reciprocation are the basis of all functional relationships in the Trobriands; between kin, affines, friends, lovers, marriage partners, business partners, and so on. Indeed, many are the Trobrianders who complain, especially in a place where money is scarce and hard to come by, about the heavy burdens of exchange obligations. Witches, in many ways, reinforce the moral obligation to share what one has. *Pogi* (in the vernacular) or *jelas* (in Tok Pisin), meaning jealousy or envy is the usual cause of a witch's wrath, so giving freely and thus meeting and exceeding all expectations for exchange obligations (with close and further kin and with those from outside one's own community and family) is the only surefire way to protect oneself from becoming ill or unwell at the hands of a witch's actions (see also Strong, Pype, and Stroeken's contributions to this volume). Indeed, the primary reason given why a witch would cause trouble and bring illness or death to someone is always considered to be that she is, for one reason or another, jealous, envious, or covetous. The relationship between *jelas* and witchcraft and/or sorcery is well established in this contemporary Melanesian context (Bratrud, this volume; Rio 2010; Eves and Forsyth 2015; Taylor 2015). Related to this is the point that envy is an idiom of egalitarianism. Nancy Munn (1986) has similarly argued that Gawan society is characterized by an egalitarian ethos, as does Lepowski based on her fieldwork in Vanatinai (1993). The witch is simultaneously a personification of dominion and radical superordination that negates equalization and balance in intersubjective relations; and at the same time, she emerges punitively in contexts where an imbalance appears to violate this ethic of egalitarianism (Munn 1986: 233). The witch, Munn tells us, "operates to enforce the principle that any increment accruing to one or more persons over and above what others have is subject to another's claim" (1986: 233). She suggests that the contradiction can be reconciled by understanding Gawans' experience with individualistic egalitarianism in their society as domination, a domination personified in the witch. Munn also identifies the intrinsic hiddenness of another's views/intentions/thoughts: "we do not know his/her mind" (*Gala tanukwalisi matona/minana lananamsa*). Pretense and deception (*katudewa*) are always possibilities, and this is particularly potent when the underlying threat of deception includes violence or illness wrought by witchcraft or sorcery. This holds as true for Kiriwina and in the discourses of my interlocutors as Munn describes for Gawa in the 1970s. The extent to which such a looming threat actually affects equivalence or redistribution is debated, however; Taylor (2015: 48), for example, argues that the jealousy of witchcraft only reinforces existing political and socio-economic inequalities, perhaps exacerbating rather than mitigating them.

Power is a significant concept here, and should not be glossed over. As Zelenietz (1981: 5) pointed out, the use of sorcery and witchcraft are expressions of a desire to control both one's own fate and the destiny of others. But it is not only available to those in socially recognized positions of authority, such as chiefs. Those in the margins may also exercise this form of power, and Zelenietz suggests that "sorcery and witchcraft assume their most terrifying aspects when used by peripheral members of society to assert control over destiny, to redress what they perceive as wrongs or imbalances in society" (1981: 5). This is perhaps the case with acts of sorcery carried out by children or adolescents, or witchcraft by women of commoner status (compare also the role of children with the gift of discernment, as described by Bratrud in this volume). This notion of sorcery being most fearsome when carried out by marginal or dispossessed individuals as a means of challenging the existing social order is well established in the African literature (see, for example, Badstuebner 2003; Comaroff and Comaroff 1993; Moore and Sanders 2001; Nadel 1952), but perhaps less explicitly so in Melanesia.

What Makes a Witch a Witch and a Sorcerer a Sorcerer?

It should be noted that even within Melanesia, as well as in comparative African contexts, the distinction between what I here describe as sorcery and witchcraft are not so distinct. Indeed, in some cases, these terms seem to be used interchangeably, as they do not seem to fit the "classic" definitions. However, as mentioned at the outset of this paper, in the Trobriands case there is surprising accordance with Evans-Pritchards' descriptions, according to the ways in which my interlocutors described each of these forms of malevolent power. In both the comparative literature I cite here, and in the other contributions to this volume, it is important to distinguish just what is meant by the selection of and use of one or the other of these terms.

Stephen (1987) attempts also to distinguish witches from sorcerers, based on a variety of ethnographic examples from various societies in PNG. She shows a great diversity in manifestations of both sorcery and witchcraft, again demonstrating that the insider/outsider binary is insufficient to capture the complexity of ethnographic reality. She rather asserts that the key difference between the two is in the social roles their practitioners hold: sorcerers use destructive mystical power to gain social influence, while witches are outcasts whose actions lead to social ruin (Stephen 1987: 288). However, she acknowledges that the southern Massim, including the Trobriand Islands and Dobu, are exceptions to her argument, thereby leading her to suggest that Trobriand witches are better described as female sorcerers (1987: 286). While this certainly helps to make her distinctions more applicable, there are difficulties with her argument. She suggests that:

> Melanesian societies usually draw sharp distinctions between male and female roles and spheres of action; it is thus only to be expected that female sorcery will differ from male sorcery. Given the general association in Melanesia of masculinity with order and control, it is appropriate that female sorcery should be less deliberate and less fully controlled than male

> powers, and that it will be symbolized by the destructive aspects of femininity. (Stephen 1987: 286)

Her assertion of a "sharp distinction" between gender roles and actions becomes less compelling in the face of the insistence of Trobrianders that witchcraft is, in fact, *not* the exclusive domain of women; they point to male witches, and they are no more socially outcast than female witches (though, so far as I know, they are not chiefs or leaders in their communities). What is more, the argument that sorcerers are powerful members of society also does not hold for the Trobriand case, where people complain that today, even young people are practicing sorcery. That said, it is most often powerful men (chiefs and other leaders) who have a reputation for the most fearsome sorcery.

The Trobriand witches I spoke to at the Revival meeting were neither prominent figures nor were they dispossessed or marginalized. They were, like most other Trobriand women, mothers, wives, daughters, and aunties; diligent gardeners; and faithful members of their church congregation. Indeed, on the last count, they were more devout than many. They had traveled from significant distances to attend the rally, both for their own spiritual development, and to support their husbands (many of the women were in fact married to church leaders). It is significant, I think, that the Pentecostal and Pentecostal-like churches in the Trobriands are notably different from the so-called "mainline" or long-established churches there—namely, Catholic, un-revived United, and Seventh Day Adventist churches—especially in their inclusion of women as lay preachers, song leaders, and musicians (usually playing the tambourine) in church services; in the "mainline" churches, women generally have little voice outside of their designated Women's Fellowship meetings once a week. Women like Esther and her friends not only often have the opportunity to lead or speak for portions of a church service or Revival meeting (though this one was still dominated by male speakers), but they also conduct "open-air" singalongs and services in the government station of Losuia[2]. Their devotion and adherence to a life filled with the Holy Spirit and their stress on the importance of their spiritual rebirth was, at least in part, framed as a contrast to their identification as reformed witches. This contrast served to reinforce the psychological and material importance of being born again, and the spiritual challenges they faced as a result of the egregious acts they had committed before finding their place in the faith.

Fear and Loathing: The Trobriand Witch and Pentecostal Redemption

People described to me the fearful visage of the witch, leering down from the rooftop. She has bulging eyes, a huge, gaping mouth with dagger-like teeth, and snot streaming from her elongated nose. Her ears are also disproportionately large, and she has long white hair. When her victim screams upon sighting her, she will place a "picture" of the coveted item which has aroused her jealousy in the victim's stomach, as people described it to me. This item, out of its proper place, invades the body and causes illness. Alternatively, the witch might "bite" the victim, creating a painful open sore. Biomedicine cannot heal these kinds of sicknesses, Trobrianders contend; they can only be treated with counter-magic.

The southern village of Sinaketa has long had a reputation for the power of its witches, but today this village is also a stronghold of Pentecostal worship in the Trobriands, which arrived in Kiriwina about 25 years ago, following a 100 years of missionization by Methodists and Catholics. While there is still a United Church in Sinaketa, as with many other United Churches the arrival of a Pentecostal denomination, in this case the CRC Church (Christian Revival Crusade), not only sees people converting to the new faith to worship in the CRC congregation, but also instigates a "Pentecostalization" or Revival movement within longer established churches. Some women in Sinaketa, and especially those who have been born again in the Pentecostal faith, confess that they are witches, in itself a departure from the customary taboo on such a public acknowledgment. However, they claim that as born again Christians, they have to pray away the evil that resides within them and would otherwise compel them to behave immorally. Women speak of how *both* witchcraft and Pentecostal forms of Christian belief reside *olumolela*, or "inside", usually described as situated *olopola*, in the stomach. This topic isn't necessarily spoken about in the context of highly public testimonials, but can just as easily occur in casual conversations, as I found out when chatting to some women from Sinaketa on the periphery of the dramatic and charismatic preaching of the Crusade. This is not a case like Badstuebner (2003) describes in South Africa, in which women use "risky agency" to negotiate gender violence and dislocation; nor is it like Pype's (2011) description of public confessions accompanied by spiritual cleansing rituals in Kinshasa.

In fact, the women acted surprisingly blasé about their conversions, using them only to illustrate just how significant they felt their spiritual rebirth to be.

Esther is the wife of a CRC pastor in the southern village of Sinaketa. I met Esther and some of her friends at the island-wide Pentecostal "Revival" crusade I mentioned in the opening of this paper. As I sat in the grass with this group of women, they spoke about their conversions to the Pentecostal faith. I was shocked when Esther told me she was a witch. With no hesitation, she told me how her father, who was also a witch, had instructed her when she was small. She was taught not to use certain objects which signify a woman's expected domesticity, like brooms and coconut husks, as these were *tabu*[3] to witches. She explained how her double would leave her own body as she slept, how her eyes and ears would grow large and grotesque, how she brought sickness and death to those who she felt had wronged her. She would then return to her own sleeping body to reinhabit it, fully aware of the things she had done, but would resume her business in the village the following day without the slightest ill conscience for what she had done. However, when the CRC church came to Sinaketa, and people joined it in high numbers, Esther told me that she saw people "living well" in the church. She came to know the power in prayers of confession, and she was born again: *besatuta navau yegu*, she told me—now, I am a new woman. *Jesu isisu olumwolela*—Jesus lives in me, she insisted, such that the hidden spirit or power of the *yoyowa* is overpowered. With the deliverance, as she put it, gained through prayer and confession of past misdeeds, she "felt free". While it was an ongoing battle to ensure that she did not revert to her old ways, the power of her faith was strong. She said that this was a bit easier for her than for many of the other reformed witches in Sinaketa, however, because she had learned how to be a witch from her father. That is to say, it was given from a member of another matriline, and thus is not her *tukwa*, which could perhaps be translated as "ancestral heritage".

"True" witches, then, have a much harder time to replace the *tukwa*, an essential part of their physical being, with the power of Jesus. The acts of *yoyowa* are frequent topics of discussion in the village. My adoptive parents pointed out, as we sat chatting on the veranda one evening, that these women in the south, even when they claim to *tapwaroru* (pray, attend church, live a Christian life), they still can't help being witches because it comes from their clan members.

When a witch commits an evil act, she is not really responsible for it. Witches do bad things *pela ositukwa*—because it is their ancestral heritage, and because this power is a part of them, a part of their very substance.

A woman I will call Kadubulula explained to me how this is the case. Kadubulula is from one of several southern villages known to be home to many witches. My close interlocutors told me that she was a well-known witch, and she had not been born again. She nominally worshiped in the United Church, but she was still a practicing *yoyowa*, and thus it might be tricky to talk to her. I could not, nor would she, make any reference to the fact that she is a witch; the interview was organized on the pretext that because she was from a village known to host many of them, she would know a thing or two about witches. We would have to conduct the interview while most people were off in the gardens, or Kadubulula might feel shy to talk about these things. If one can have an aura of *yoyowa*, this woman certainly had it. She described for me how a *yoyowa* will pass the knowledge she holds to her daughter (and, indeed, the *tukwa* usually passes from mother to daughter). While the girl is still very small, perhaps just old enough to walk, the two will go together deep into the bush. There, they will both remove their clothes, and the mother will crouch down and open her mouth "as big as a door", as Kadubulula put it. The mother will swallow her daughter, and the young girl will reemerge through her mother's anus. From this moment, the girl will have all of the knowledge as well as the essential substance, so to speak, of the *yoyowa*, though she will continue to train and to further develop her powers.

When a woman is a *yoyowa* because it is her *tukwa,* it becomes harder for her to fully separate herself from this power, which she carries inside her, in her belly: the seat of emotions and understanding, memory, and the storehouse of magic (Tambiah 1983: 179). As Tambiah (1983: 175) points out, women not only reproduce the *dala* or matrilieage through giving birth, but are seen to transmit the *dala* identity or essence "which she carries *inside* her as part of her very constitution". The process of passing on *tukwa*, again following Tambiah, might be seen as an inversion of the (no longer salient) Trobriand belief that conception occurs when a spirit or *baloma* from a woman's deceased ancestor enters her body through her head (Malinowski 1929: 173, 175) and later emerges from her vagina, again being born physically imbued with the essence of the matriclan. There are other inversions; as

Munn (1986: 219) notes, "[Witches] violate ordinary bodily spacetime in flying, a capacity that conveys a radical expansion of spaciotemporal control". They also shapeshift; for example, taking on the shape of a flying fox, a shark, or a falling star. And despite being passed primarily within a matrilineage, members of that same matrilineage are also the rightful targets of a given witch's attacks, according to my Trobriand interlocutors (see also Strong, this volume). The intimate connection between witches and their victims has also, of course, been observed by Geschiere (2013). What is more, witches feed on corpses (compare the body-snatching in Myhre, this volume). In this way, "rather than giving food to others to eat, the witch converts others into food, thus destroying the self-other relation." In this way, as Munn observes, she destroys relationality (1986: 227). In the African context, witchcraft has been described by Geischere as a betrayal of kinship (2003: 47), which just as well applies in the cases described here in the Milne Bay region of Papua New Guinea.

The embodied capacity of *yoyowa*, and the belly or stomach as its locus, is symbolized in other ways, too. Munn (1986: 221) observed that witches in Gawa are seen as hungry and greedy, and it is greed or jealousy (emotions which also resides in the belly) that generally compels witches to commit acts of violence against a victim. Again, from Munn:

> Gawans say that when witches see that another person has something the witches themselves lack, they hate (*-kamiriwey*) that person and desire these things for themselves. The witch is jealous (*-pogi*); the stomach becomes angry (*-kapasala nuwu-ra*); the mind is made bad (*-yageiga nano-ra*), or the forehead made heavy (*mwaw daba-ra*) from seeing that others have more than oneself. (221)

Here, we can see echoes of the claim made in the introduction of this book that "envy in a fundamental way articulates the crucial claim to equality that is fundamental to both consumerism and to the relation between persons and God" (p. 22), as well as fundamental to Trobriand sociality. Perhaps Pentecostalism is in a way a more productive (in the emic view) means of accessing what Englund calls the radical promise of equality inherent in such a practice of Christian fellowship than the destructive, consumptive, and threatening power of the witch (Englund 2003).

Conclusions

When a self-confessed witch is born again into a Revival church, there is a fundamental shift. Now, instead of the power and knowledge of *witchcraft* residing inside the body, that "space", so to speak, should be filled up by Jesus and the power of the holy spirit. This means relinquishing the power that comes with being a witch—the power to intimidate, and to exact revenge. Now, women such as Esther have only the power of prayer to affect the results they hope for. And, instead of being both the product of, and a potential threat to, one's extended kin network and especially one's own matriclan, now one's responsibilities are to the church community and to one's own nuclear family. As I have described elsewhere, the move to Revival forms of Christianity in many respects reorients the focus from spatially and temporally wide-ranging kin obligations to, instead, the household level, especially in the context of redistributive mortuary feasts (MacCarthy, In press). In the Pentecostal context, the *dala* or matrilineal kin, and the obligations for material reciprocity and redistribution entailed in maintaining those relationships, lose importance.

For witches, transcending the body (i.e., by flying at night in disembodied form) is key to their power. In the Pentecostal Christian context, as Eriksen has argued (Eriksen 2016), the ideal is conversely containment of the woman's body. In her study of Pentecostal women in Port Vila, Eriksen notes constraints of mobility and the need to always cover oneself—with clothing, inside the house or the church, etc.—behavioral changes that are seen as necessary in an urban Christian context. While women's physical movement in the Trobriands is not so constrained, the idea of containing femininity within the body offers a potentially useful analytical framework. No more can the spirit leave the body to parody femininity by wreaking havoc on the village; no more should the physical features expand grotesquely, with the exaggerated facial features that are said to characterize the witch; no more should mothers ingest their daughters and pass them through their own bodies, to be expelled pregnant with the skills and power of the *yoyowa*. Instead, good Pentecostal women should dress conservatively, do physical work to feed and care for their children and husbands, implying exactly the broom and the coconut husk so taboo to witches, pray and worship inside the church, and submit to the authority of God.

If witchcraft is inherently anti-social, by corrupting kinship obligations and inverting or subverting social rules, and transgressing the body in dangerous ways, then Pentecostal Christianity perhaps offers a new paradigm which reigns in kinship obligations, creates new social rules, and contains femininity within the body. As Schram (2010) has argued for neighboring Normanby Island, Christianity reshapes cultural conceptions of personhood, space, and time, and provides an epistemic frame in which witchcraft is always perceived as a survival of the past in the present (Schram 2010: 727). In the Trobriands, Pentecostal Christian discourse advocates breaking with the past (Meyer 1998). Pastors preach in Trobriand services about how culture or the old ways (*gulagula*) can be destructive and turn people away from God. They stress the need to give up many aspects of "traditional" Trobriand practice and belief in which unfettered female power is displayed; for example, performing Trobriand dances in traditional dress (wherein women expose their bodies in sexually suggestive performances), and the distribution of so-called "women's wealth", the banana leaf bundles women manufacture and distribute in the wake of the death of a kinsperson, and which are deemed "useless" and "unproductive" in Pentecostal discourses, as I have written about elsewhere (MacCarthy, In press). In such discourses, acts of witchcraft or sorcery are unequivocally evil and must be countered. Others (e.g., Geschiere 2013) have noted that Pentecostalism stresses a stark distinction between good and evil, though many of my informants, from all denominations, point to ambiguities and ambivalences. Nonetheless, to be properly Christian is to be modern, to follow Biblical teachings, and to turn away from past practices that are seen to contradict the word of God. Following the claims of many scholars, especially in Africa, that witchcraft is a thoroughly modern phenomenon (Geschiere 1997), it is also in the Trobriands recast inside a modernist discourse where witchcraft comes to stands for old, pre- and anti-Christian and unproductive behavior. For women like Esther, denouncing the evil living inside her belly can only be done if Jesus moves into that same space, such that good might overpower evil, and modernity and its associates (prosperity, development, enlightenment) might overcome tradition and the so-called "darkness" it instantiates in local discourses, and wherein *tapwaroru* stands as antidote and antithesis of witchcraft and sorcery. Indeed, the physical body is literally transformed in the process of being born again, replacing the dark powers gained from the previous "rebirth" when a young woman receives her *tukwa* from her mother. With Jesus filling up the space formerly inhabited by dark powers, perhaps these reformed witches can now find "deliverance" in a new community of openness, collective prayer and worship, and a focus on the nuclear family and church congregation—a new social space for women based on their shared transformation and a voice within the Pentecostal sphere which was hitherto limited to dark, solitary, destructive, and anti-social activities. The reformed witch comes to represent then a "new woman", as Esther described herself, not only on level of personal moral and spiritual transformation, but also as a reflection of a village, community, island, and even nation that needs to be reborn in order to move forward in a world where development seems to be lagging and poverty and sickness are still pervasive.

Notes

1. Malinowski often refers to *mulukwausi,* which he uses to refer to the disembodied second self of the *yoyowa* or witch, but my informants just used *yoyowa* to refer to both forms; indeed, as a verb, *yoyowa* means "to fly".
2. These events usually include a group of women numbering perhaps 10–20, who dress in matching calico clothes and travel together to the government station of Losuia with a portable PA system to preach, sing, play music, and perform short skits. On the day I joined them, in August 2013, it was a "combined fellowship" group from Pentecostal congregations from across Kiriwina, but with a good number coming from the village of Sinaketa.
3. The term *tabu* has generated much anthropological debate (Weiner 1976: 39). It means founding members of each matriclan, ancestors in general, grandparent, grandchild, father's sister, father's sister's daughter and other female relatives on one's father's side, and finally, it can also mean "taboo" or forbidden, as Esther used the term in this case.

References

Badstuebner, Jennifer. 2003. "Drinking the Hot Blood of Humans": Witchcraft Confessions in a South African Pentecostal Church. *Anthropology and Humanism* 28 (1): 8–22.

Comaroff, Jean, and John L. Comaroff, eds. 1993. *Modernity and Its Malcontents: Ritual and Power in Postcolonial Africa.* Chicago: University of Chicago Press.

Englund, Harri. 2003. 'Christian Independency and Global Membership: Pentecostal Extraversions in Malawi'. *Journal of Religion in Africa* 33 (1): 83–111.

Eriksen, Annelin. 2016. "The Virtuous Woman and the Holy Nation: Femininity in the Context of Pentecostal Christianity in Vanuatu". *The Australian Journal of Anthropology* 27 (2): 260–275.

Evans-Pritchard, E.E. 1937. *Witchcraft, Oracles and Magic Among the Azande.* Oxford: Clarendon Press.

Eves, Richard, and Miranda Forsyth. 2015. "Developing Insecurity: Sorcery, Witchcraft and Melanesian Economic Development". Vol. SSGM Discussion Paper 2015/7. Canberra: Australian National University.

Fortune, Reo. 1932. *Sorcerers of Dobu: The Social Anthropology of the Dobu Islanders of the Western Pacific*. London: G. Routledge & Sons.

Fortune, Reo. 1963. *Sorcerers of Dobu: The social anthropology of the Dobu Islanders of the Western Pacific*. New York : E.P. Dutton & Co.

Geschiere, Peter. 1997. *The Modernity of Witchcraft. Politics and the Occult in Postcolonial Africa*. Charlottesville: University of Virginia Press.

Geschiere, Peter. 2013. *Witchcraft, Intimacy and Trust: Africa in Comparison*. Chicago: University of Chicago Press.

Lepowski, Maria. 1993. *Fruit of the Motherland: Gender in an Egalitarian Society*. New York: Columbia University Press.

MacCarthy, Michelle. In press. "Doing Away with Doba? Women's Wealth and Shifting Values in Trobriand Mortuary Distributions". In *Sinuous Objects: Revaluing Women's Wealth in the Contemporary Pacific*, ed. A.-K. Hermkens and K. Lepani. Canberra: ANU Press.

Malinowski, Bronislaw. 1929. *The Sexual Life of Savages in North-Western Melanesia*. London: Routledge & Kegan Paul.

Marwick, Max. 1964. "Witchcraft as a Social Strain-gauge". *Australian Journal of Science* 26: 263–268.

Meyer, Birgit. 1998. "Make a Complete Break with the Past'. Memory and Post-Colonial Modernity in Ghanaian Pentecostalist Discourse". *Journal of Religion in Africa* 28 (3): 316–349.

Moore, Henrietta, and Todd Sanders, eds. 2001. *Magical Interpretations, Material Realities: Modernity, Witchcraft and the Occult in Postcolonial Africa*. London: Routledge.

Munn, Nancy. 1986. *The fame of Gawa: A symbolic study of value transformation in a Massim (Papua New Guinea) society*. Cambridge: Cambridge University Press.

Nadel, S.F. 1952. "Witchcraft in Four African Societies: An Essay in Comparison". *American Anthropologist* 54 (1): 18–29.

Pype, Katrien. 2011. "Confession cum Deliverance:In/Dividuality of the Subject Among Kinshasa's Born-Again Christians". *Journal of Religion in Africa* 41 (3): 280–310.

Rio, Knut. 2010. "Handling Sorcery in a State System of Law: Magic, Violence and Kastom in Vanuatu". *Oceania* 80 (2): 182–197.

Sanders, Todd. 2008. *Beyond Bodies: Rain-making and Sense-making in Tanzania*. Toronto: University of Toronto Press.

Schram, Ryan. 2010. "Witches' Wealth: Witchcraft, Confession, and Christianity in Auhelawa, Papua New Guinea". *Journal of the Royal Anthropological Institute* 16 (4): 726–742.

Stephen, Michele. 1987. "Contrasting Images of Power". In *Sorcerer and Witch in Melanesia*, ed. M. Stephen, 249–304. Melbourne: Melbourne University Press.

Tambiah, Stanley J. 1983. "On flying Witches and Flying Canoes: The Coding of Male and Female values". In *The Kula: New Perspectives on Massim Exchange*, eds. J.W. Leach, and E.R. Leach. Cambridge: Cambridge University Press.

Taylor, John P. 2015. "Sorcery and the Moral Economy of Agency: An Ethnographic Account". *Oceania* 85 (1): 38–50.

Weiner, Annette. 1976. *Women of Value, Men of Renown: New perspectives in Trobriand exchange*. Austin: University of Texas Press.

Zelenietz, Marty. 1981. "Sorcery and Social Change: An Introduction". *Social Analysis* 8: 3–14.

Author Biography

Michelle MacCarthy is an Assistant Professor in the Department of Anthropology at Saint Mary's University in Halifax, Canada. She was previously a Postdoctoral Fellow in the Department of Social Anthropology at the University of Bergen (where she undertook the research and writing of the chapter in this book), and where she was a contributor to Annelin Eriksen's Norwegian Research Council–funded project on gender and Pentecostalism in Africa and Melanesia. She completed her PhD at the University of Auckland in 2012. Her monograph, entitled Making the Modern Primitive: Cultural Tourism in the Trobriand Islands (2016), examines tropes of primitivity and authenticity and mechanisms of cultural commoditization. She recently co-edited (with Annelin Eriksen) a special issue of The Australian Journal of Anthropology on Gender and Pentecostalism in Melanesia (August 2016).

CHAPTER 7

The Power of a Severed Arm: Life, Witchcraft, and Christianity in Kilimanjaro

Knut Christian Myhre

Not-being made its appearance in the world as an alternative embodied in being itself; and thereby being itself first assumes an emphatic sense: intrinsically qualified by the threat of its negative it must affirm itself, and existence affirmed its existence as concern. So constitutive for life is the possibility of not-being that its very being is essentially a hovering over this abyss, a skirting of its brink: thus being itself has become a constant possibility rather than a given state, ever anew to be laid hold of in opposition to its ever-present contrary, not-being, which will inevitably engulf it in the end.
Hans Jonas, *The Phenomenon of Life: Toward a Philosophical Biology* (1966: 4).

Introduction

One morning in October 2008, I was sitting in the living room of a school teacher in Rombo District on the eastern slopes of Mount Kilimanjaro in northern Tanzania. A TV in the room showed a Sky News broadcast, where a story concerning Tanzania suddenly appeared. The segment consisted of images from an unidentified village that accompanied a voice reporting on the murder of a person suffering from albinism. I noted the story, even though it was in some respects old and familiar news. Tales of such murders had appeared in the national media during

K.C. Myhre (✉)
University of Oslo, Oslo, Norway

K. Rio et al. (eds.), *Pentecostalism and Witchcraft*, Contemporary Anthropology of Religion, DOI 10.1007/978-3-319-56068-7_7

earlier fieldworks, and had occasionally been a topic of conversation among the rural Chagga-speaking people with whom I lived. Previously, they had described such murders as a practice pertaining to distant areas of central Tanzania, but by 2008 they had become a more pressing concern. Now, stories swirled of albinos attacked or kidnapped in areas closer to Moshi town, which sparked fears that the perpetrators would come to Rombo, and impelled calls for people to protect the region's albinos. These fears reached their peak one Sunday morning, when the Catholic priest announced in church that a girl had gone missing from a nearby village. Amidst gasps from the congregation, he said the girl was last seen entering a car containing several persons, who had approached children on the main road that circles the mountain. Suddenly, we were all alert to strange cars with strange people making strange propositions.

The newscast I saw in the teacher's living room was not an isolated incident that year. In early April 2008, BBC News reported that the President of Tanzania, Jakaya Kikwete had "...ordered a crackdown on witch-doctors who use body parts from albinos in magic potions to bring people good luck or fortune".[1] The order came after 19 such murders had occurred the previous year. Appearing on TV, Kikwete said: "I am told that people kill albinos and chop their body parts, including fingers, believing they can get rich when mining or fishing". His order had little effect, however, as BBC reported in July that 25 albinos had been murdered only since March that year. It reiterated that, "Albinos are targeted for body parts that are used in witchcraft, and killings continue despite government efforts to stamp out the grisly practice".[2] A week later, an additional victim was reported, whose right foot and genitalia had been removed, in an attack that also left the victim's albino wife injured.[3] It said that an investigation by a BBC correspondent had "...revealed that witchdoctors are behind the killings. They use albino organs such as hair, arms, legs and blood to make potions which they claim make people wealthy." On the brighter side, it said that 173 witch-doctors had been arrested since the president "...ordered a crack-down of all those involved in these ritualistic killings for riches."

Some of these claims and numbers resurfaced in a resolution passed by the European Parliament in September 2008 to condemn the murders of albinos and "the speculative trade in their body parts." The resolution referred to unspecified NGO and media reports of such murders, which the Tanzanian government had confirmed. It stated that the events were especially prevalent in Mwanza, Shinyanga, and Mara

Regions of the Lake Victoria zone, which "...are not only notorious for the killing of albinos but also for the killing of people believed to be witches or wizards."[4] The European Parliament welcomed and supported the steps made by the Tanzanian president, his cabinet, and the parliament, but called for further efforts from the national government, local authorities, and civil society. However, the resolution had no more impact than Kikwete's order. Thus around the time, I saw the newscast in the teacher's living room, the British newspaper *The Guardian* reported that the number of killings had reached 30.[5] Moreover, it said that the last three murders had happened shortly after the Tanzania Albino Society organized a demonstration against the murders in Dar es Salaam. One victim was the 10-year-old girl Esther Charles, whose murder and mutilation by a gang who "...wanted to sell her body parts to witch doctors" was reported from Shilela, Shinyanga in western Tanzania by Sky News.[6] The story added that Tanzanian police had reported multiple incidents the previous year of people exhuming the bodies of children to remove organs, like genitals and eyes, to produce remedies used in rituals. It furthermore claimed that such murders were not only prevalent in Tanzania but also reported from Kenya and Burundi, where the authorities provided increased protection for albinos. It even relayed that, "Some reports say albino skin is prized in the Democratic Republic of Congo, another troubled African nation where superstition is high".

From Occult Economies to Modes of Being

A salient feature of these reports and resolutions is the way they seamlessly shift from the murder of albinos to claims regarding witchcraft, magic, and rituals that are performed by witch-doctors and wizards. Their conceptual range resembles and recalls the conflation that Terence Ranger (2007) detects in media accounts, law-and-order responses, and academic representations that lump a plethora of practices under the rubric of 'the occult' and create a chimera of a singular sinister culture enveloping Africa. Accordingly, one BBC report asserted that "Sorcery and the occult maintain a strong foothold in this part of the world, especially in the remote rural areas around the fishing and mining regions of Mwanza, on the shores of Lake Victoria."[7] Similarly, the report on Esther Charles' murder leapt from one incident in a Tanzanian village to a general claim regarding practices and perceptions that effortlessly extended to encompass neighboring countries.

This conceptual reach and geographical embrace are afforded by the recurring emphasis on trade in body parts, along with the claim that these are used to ensure wealth and success. Such assertions invoke the economy as the salient context for the murders, which is accentuated by the suggestion that there is a demand for the body parts that those involved supply and satisfy. The reports thus conjure and lock into the 'occult economies', which Jean and John Comaroff (1999) expose at the root of a range of phenomena that include witchcraft, trade in body-parts, and zombie production, as well as pyramid schemes and other scams. According to them, "'Occult economy' may be taken, at its most general, to connote the deployment of magical means for material ends or, more expansively, the conjuring of wealth by resort to inherently mysterious techniques, techniques whose principles of operation are neither transparent nor explicable in conventional terms" (Comaroff and Comaroff 1999: 297). Their definition accords with Kikwete's claim that the albino murders involve a belief that the deployment of body parts will affect people's economic pursuits, and conforms to the assertion by Shilela Councillor Joseph Manyara that, "It is utterly stupid for some people to believe that albinos have magic powers and their parts can make them rich."[8]

The compound character of the Comaroffs' concept suggests a relationship of equivalence between two terms, but its effect is, in fact, a contrast that assigns priority to the material over the magical. The Comaroffs thus argue that "What counts as magic varies across time and place and context, although it is always set apart from habitual, normative forms of production" (Comaroff and Comaroff 1999: 297). Magic is a historically and geographically variant phenomenon, but it has an invariant yet unspecified relationship to production. Analysis consists in the specification of this relationship, which dictates that the economic provides the ground and context for the occult. Accordingly, the Comaroffs claim "…to trace the causal determinations of the occult economy in postapartheid South Africa across generations and genders, villages and provinces and regions, and a nation-state in transition - not to mention the labile vectors of a post-Fordist, millennial economy" (Comaroff and Comaroff 1999: 294). It is the relationship of causal determination that lends the occult the character of a mysterious mode of production or a perverted form of trade, whose interpretation involves the exposition of how one gives form to the other. The Comaroffs therefore argue that, "Our primary concern here is to examine how-as well as by whom, why, and with what implications-occult practices have come to be *imagined* in rural South Africa" (Comaroff and Comaroff 1999: 297, original emphasis). The conception develops the longstanding idea that witchcraft and related phenomena are metaphoric forms that provide a language for speaking about one thing in terms of something else (West 2007: 24), and extends the notion that they are responses or reactions to social and economic change (Myhre 2009: 119), which combine in the claim that they are critical commentaries on new forms of wealth and commodification (Niehaus 2005). It moreover advances an abiding approach to money and commodity forms as operators of historical change, whose capacity to mediate and represent creates "...isomorphic patterns of economies, symbols and metaphors" (Gilbert 2005: 365).

However, the secretary general of the Tanzania Albino Society suggested a different dynamic, as he told *The Guardian* that, "Our biggest fear right now is the fear of living. If you leave work at night as an albino, you are unsure of reaching home safely. When you sleep, you are unsure of waking up in one piece." Skirting economic processes and imaginative forms, Zihada Msembo claimed that the albino murders involved a fear of life and what may occur in it. Invoking various activities, he articulated a concern that merely going about life may entail death. His claim resonates with the epigraph above, as it suggests that the murders and what they evoke pertain to life and the intrinsic possibility of its negation. It shifts the gaze from questions of economics and representation toward issues pertaining to modes of being and not-being, and the ways in which life becomes and is affirmed in the face of its denial. In this light, the events and experiences pertaining to the albino murders *regard* life and *concern* existence, as the former hold up the capacities the latter entail and embody. The perspective locks into Jeanne Favret-Saada's (2015 [2009]: 102) conception of witchcraft as a matter of 'being affected' that reorders lives and transforms subjects, whose existence is staked in the process. It moreover summons Bruce Kapferer's (2002: 22ff) notion that magic and sorcery open a field of forces or potentialities that reorient people's existence and relationship to the world. It evokes Malcolm Ruel's (1965: 3) idea that witchcraft concerns the potential abilities of persons in relations with others, and recalls Marilyn Strathern's (1988: 273ff) account of the partible person, who detaches and transacts parts of him- or herself to render and transform relationships that constitute his or her being. The circulation of body parts is obviously acute in the albino murders, which raises the question of whether they primarily concern the form and being of persons, rather than matters of economics and forms of representation.

In this article, I pursue this question through an exploration of two events and accounts concerning witchcraft practices that occurred or were invoked during my fieldworks in Rombo District.[9] The purpose of holding these incidents and stories together is not to lump them under one rubric, but to explore the intensities they contain and entail. In particular, I investigate how the events and accounts pertain to the Chagga notion of 'life-force' or 'bodily power' (*horu*) that is transformed and transferred through 'dwelling' (*ikaa*), where its movements and refractions constitute 'life' (*moo*). The events and accounts hence involve and regard practices that concern and affirm life. Importantly, life here assumes the form of a transformational process, which entails the ever-present potential that subjects can convert into objects, and objects may mutate into persons. It is this potential that the events and accounts concern. Furthermore, it means that the events and accounts surpass the attention for life and its negation to rather regard life and its transformations. It follows from this that these phenomena not only pertain to being and not-being, but instead concern different modes of being. The effect of their transformational character is that witchcraft and life fold out of and into each other. These processes moreover envelope forms of Christianity, which has been a firm fixture of this area for over a century (Fiedler 1996). More specifically, the events and accounts show how Catholicism and Pentecostalism fold into each other to fold out of witchcraft, and alternately fold out of each other as inversions or reversals of one another. The result is a set of folding movements and moments where life, witchcraft, and forms of Christianity alternately and situationally emerge from and sink back into each other.

The Story of a Severed Arm

In 2001, a story began circulating in the area I was doing fieldwork that the arm of a human being had been found outside the Catholic Church in the neighboring parish. When I arrived at the church a few days later, the priest received me in his office where he proudly confirmed the story. He said the arm had been found in the morning in front of the door of the church, where they were certain it had been discarded in the night by a witch (*mchawi*).[10] Enthusiastically, he said its appearance was due to an initiative by the church for parishioners to give up witchcraft (*uchawi*) and stop visiting healers and diviners (*waganga*).[11] For this, they had called on people to bring and dispose of their witchcraft and healing paraphernalia at the church, where they read a special Mass before burning the gathered objects. The arm had arrived after this event, but they had burned it too so it was not possible to see it. However, he illustrated its appearance by holding up his forearm and curling his fingers into a claw, while pointing out that the one they found was thinner, darker, and smaller in size. It could possibly have stemmed from a monkey, he said, but added they were certain it was the arm of a human being. To justify this, he reiterated what many villagers already had told me and described how a witch digs up the grave of the person that he or she has killed and steals a part of the body. The witch brings the body part to his or her homestead and places it in a cooking-pot (*chungu*) in the cooking-hut attic (*dari*), where the heat and smoke of the hearth (*jiko*) dry it out and preserve it. The limb then withers and blackens to gain the appearance of the arm they found on the doorstep. Occasionally, the witch takes the body part down from the attic and uses it to stir the food that is cooking on the hearth. Doing so averts the blood (*damu*) of the victim from returning to wreak vengeance on the witch for intentionally (*makusudi*) killing another person. The witch is thus able to continue his or her life without suffering the consequences of having taken the life of someone else.

The story of how the witch exhumes a dead body and steals a limb resembles and recalls the reports regarding the albino murders, and is underscored as the priest acknowledged that the witch may retrieve and deploy other parts of the victim's body. Nevertheless, it is no coincidence that an arm featured in this incident. The arm– *koko*– namely plays central roles in crucial activities and their surrounding discourses.[12] Persons with a 'good arm'—*koko kesha*—are for instance favoured for carrying out certain tasks, such as the annual pruning of the banana garden, where excess off-shoots (*ndaka*) are uprooted and the stumps (*matonga*) of harvested banana trees are removed. Its purpose is to enable a smaller number of trees to grow to full stature and produce the largest possible bunches of fruits without being depleted by a surfeit of *ndaka*. The pruning also serves to tweak and tune the composition of the banana garden, as the excess off-shoots are replanted to ensure an even distribution of trees or increase the amount of certain kinds of banana. Superfluous *ndaka* are also gifted to friends, relatives, and neighbours, who request off-shoots to replenish their banana gardens. In either case, replanting is delegated to a person with a good arm, which ensures that the off-shoot will 'seize' or 'stick' (*iira*) in its new location to grow and yield further off-shoots and fruits.

The good arm hence ensures the growth of the banana garden, where a significant part of daily activities consists in harvesting the leaves and stems of the banana trees. These are used as fodder for the livestock, which are exclusively stall-fed due to a shortage of grazing land. The arm features here too, as the homestead's inhabitants slice (*itena*) the leaves and stems for the animals to eat. The role of the arm is accentuated in conversation, where this activity is often neither named nor mentioned, but illustrated by a cutting motion with the arm, where the extended hand manifests the blade of a machete. The arm is moreover used to sweep and gather the manure of the livestock, which is placed at the foot of the trees in the garden to ensure continued growth of fodder and plentiful bananas for the staple food. In fact, people stress that the main purpose of keeping cattle is the provision of manure, which is crucial for the intensive form of horticulture presently practised. However, cows are also treasured for their milk, which is used fresh in morning tea and curdled for inclusion in various foods. Milk is also churned into butter-fat (*msika*) that is used for cooking and applied to make the skin 'shiny' or 'clear' (*uaa*), and hence 'beautiful' (*usha*). The arm is also implied by the term *msika*, which derives from the verb *isika* that is used for the act of shaking a gourd to churn milk into butter. In fact, the supply of milk also relies on a person with a good arm, who is usually asked to lead a cow to another homestead to be impregnated by a bull. Like for the *ndaka*, the semen is more like to 'seize' or 'stick' (*iira*) and result in a calf, when the tether of the cow is held by a *koko kesha*.

The good arm hence ensures growth in both the banana garden and the livestock-pen, which moreover enfold through the provision of fodder and manure by means of the arms of the homestead's inhabitants. Their imbrications mean that *koko* is a pivot that turns vegetative matter into fodder, which animal digestion converts to manure that is spread to fertilise the banana garden. Indeed, the notion of *iira* articulates pivots of different kinds, which turn excess off-shoots into trees that provide fodder and foodstuffs, and transform a heifer or a dry animal into a lactating cow that yields animal offspring and milk for human consumption and application. In both cases, *iira* concerns a critical point that acts as a fulcrum on which further engagements of the arm hinge and turn. The arm thus enables and entails forms of transformations that afford further conversions where the arm is required and plays a role.

In addition to fodder and fertiliser, the arm and its activities yield milk, meat, and bananas, which combine in cooking with eleusine, maize, beans, and other crops that are grown in the plains below the mountain. These different foodstuffs comprise *horu* or 'life-force' to a greater or smaller degree, which is compounded when the substances conjoin in cooking and consumption. The arm features here too, as cooking is conducted over an open hearth (*riko*), where ingredients combine in an aluminum vessel (*sufuria*) or clay cooking-pot (*nungu*), which is stirred with a long-handled wooden spoon (*kilikyo*) that is also used for serving food on plates or in bowls.[13] Using different utensils, the arm hence combines and converts various ingredients and conveys the resultant foods to those who consume them. The significance of the arm for these processes is accentuated in the making of banana beer, where the malted eleusine millet is usually added to the wort by someone with *koko kesha*. The justification is that the good arm ensures that the malt and wort—which both are high in *horu*–'turn' (*iunduka*) to become beer that is fit for consumption.

Along with beer, different foods increase the person's *horu* and raise the heat (*mrike*) of the body, as they boost the amount of blood (*samu*) and its circulation. Prominent here are diverse kinds of 'soft food' (*kelya kiholo*) that variously combine milk, meat, eleusine, fat, blood, and particular kinds of bananas to contribute to the person's capacities, health, and well-being. These foods enable the person to use his or her arms in banana-farming and livestock-keeping, which expend *horu* and deplete blood, yet provide life-force in the form of powerful foodstuffs. As it both provides and requires *horu*, the arm is simultaneously a means for, and an effect of, the conversions and conveyances of life-force that occur through production and consumption. The mutable and movable character of *horu* entails that the ends and means of these activities are mutual transformations that assume different forms but are of the same fundamental character (Myhre 1998: 127).

Meat, milk, beer, and bananas are not only consumed within the confines of the homestead, but also provided as bridewealth prestations that afford and justify reproduction, and enable a man's claim to the children he fathers. The prestations are hence effects of the arms of the groom and his contributing agnates, which his intermediaries (*wakara*) carry to the bride's parents' homestead (Myhre 2014: 511ff). The prestations afford the bride's relocation to the marital homestead, which comes into existence as a place of production and consumption on her arrival.

It is then said of the groom that 'he has a hearth' (*nere riko*), where the produce of the banana garden and the plot in the plain is converted into foods of different kinds. Consequently, the bridewealth prestations enable the couple to deploy their arms in banana-farming and livestock-keeping at the marital homestead, as well as in cooking and consuming the foodstuffs they yield. These foods not only afford further productive engagements, but also facilitate sex and reproduction, where the bride employs her back (*moongo*) in conceiving, birthing, and caring for their children (Myhre 2014: 515ff). Through these activities, the groom transfers *horu* in the form of semen, which contributes to the blood of the bride and their child that she in turn conveys through childbirth. The emphasis is on the bride's back, but the arm features here too, as the groom provides his parturient wife with soft foods that replenish the *horu*, heat, and blood she lost in childbirth, and contribute to her lactation. The husband's arms hence conjoin and contribute to the wife's breasts (*mawele*) with the result that parents make extended and extensive reproductive contributions, which involve and occur through multiple body-parts.

These considerations entail that different bodyparts transform and transfer *horu* in different forms, and hence constitute the body as a circuitry of life-force. Thus, the arms yield foodstuffs that are taken in by the mouth (*dumbu*) to afford activities like sex and reproduction, where *horu* converts and conveys as bodily substances by means of backs, breasts, and genital organs. The reticulated character of these flows and transformations is articulated by the use of *mawele* to mean both women's breasts and men's testicles through which *horu* flows in different forms. Its use moreover concerns how one part of one person's body engages and involves a different part of another person's body to affect his or her being. This occurs in all activities, but is perhaps most striking with the bride's back, which she acquires through the bridewealth prestations and that therefore emerges as an effect of the arms of others (Myhre 2014: 516ff). Moreover, the use of *moongo* to also mean the doorway of the house and the backbone of animals reveals how the circuitry of *horu* extends beyond the human body to enfold other beings that include inanimate objects. Accordingly, there are sexual prohibitions that surround the practices performed by *koko kesha*, which channel and direct the flows of *horu* to ensure that off-shoots and semen stick, and the beer turns around (cf. Myhre 2007: 322ff). In fact, the multiple uses of *koko* entail and concern that vegetative, animal, and human being conjoin through the conversions and conveyances of *horu* that occur through production, reproduction, and consumption. These practices constitute the notion and activity of *ikaa*, which I translate as 'dwelling' and from which the homestead (*kaa*) derives its name (Myhre 2007: 321). They moreover engage and involve substances and entities whose terms derive from the notion of *moo* that translates as 'life'. These include the chyme (*mooshe*) that forms the transformational or intermediary form between fodder and manure, as well as the doorways and backbones (*moongo*) that feature in bridewealth and reproduction. As substances and conduits that convert and convey *horu*, chyme, backbones, and doorways afford life, which in Rombo assumes the form of transfers and transformation of life-force.

In light of the concept of 'occult economies,' it is important to realize that these concepts and practices are neither exempt from nor opposed to monetary and commoditized forms of exchange. Thus, the pruning of the coffee trees is also delegated to a person with a good arm, who moreover is subject to sexual prohibitions to ensure that the trees grow and bear fruits, which are exclusively sold through the regional cooperative or to agents that operate at the behest of multinational concerns. Capitalist exchange hence does not have a detrimental or destructive effect on these phenomena. Instead, the movements of *horu* encompass and include this cash-crop to entail that money itself is an effect of its transfers and transformations. Money is therefore 'life-force' in one particular form, whose transactional and fungible character extends the modes and means of *horu*.

Organs Without Body

These considerations entail that when the witch removes a part of the victim's body, he or she appropriates a means for and effect of the conversions and conveyances of *horu*. The witch thus intervenes in the circuitry of life-force through the victim's body, and interferes in the transfers and transformation that constitute human, animal, and vegetative being. The dynamic is underscored, as the witch places the body part in a cooking-pot and treats it as a foodstuff, or uses it to stir the food on the hearth and handles it as a utensil for converting and preparing comestibles. Similarly, hiding it in the cooking-hut attic treats the body part like the firewood, which is stored to dry out over the hearth, whose fire it eventually feeds. It also handles the body-part like the beer bananas, which are ripened by the heat (*mrike*) and smoke (*musu*) of the hearth to enhance their *horu*. Such bananas darken like the arm described by the priest, but differ from it as they plump up and soften to sometimes nearly liquefy, while the arm shrivelled and shrank as it dried out.

The witch's detachment of body parts moreover recalls the butchering of animals, where shares of meat manifest how people expend *horu* to afford the being of others (Myhre 2013: 119ff). Butchering was in fact invoked by Zihada Msembo, who told *The Guardian* that "They [the albino murderers] are cutting us up like chickens." But where the shares of animal meat compensate the recipients' expenditure of *horu* to afford their continued engagement in dwelling, the witch removes a means for transforming and transferring life-force, and thus inhibits its flows or renders them unproductive. In fact, the use of a body part as a form of foodstuff, firewood, and cooking implement collapses the distinction between means and ends that these transformations and transferals involve and entail, and thereby implodes the world-relations that constitute dwelling and life. This is perhaps most striking in the case of an arm, which no longer yields, pivots, and provides *horu* that is transformed and transferred through other body parts, but instead is acted upon by another arm and treated as a form of *horu*. The witch dismantles the victim and turns one of his or her body parts from a means for converting and conveying *horu* into an entity that is subject to the same processes. He or she thus turns the victim from a subject that transforms and transfers *horu*, into an object that is dissolved back into the currents of life-force. Creating and deploying an organ without body diverts the victim's blood from harming the witch, only at the expense of his or her children who villagers stress will suffer from eating the food that was stirred by means of the body part. Its divertive character was manifest in the dry and thin appearance of the immobile arm that the witch discarded on the doorstep of the church, which contrasts with the mobile and flexible character of a strong and good arm. It moreover differs from the round form and soft consistency of the beer bananas ripened in the attic, whose shape and character people comment on when they are peeled. Such bananas body forth a capacity for transformation and flow, which diverges from the emaciated and inert quality of the arm the witch discarded.

As the witch turns subjects into objects that are deployed to affect the capacity and being of others, its activities concern existence, in the manner suggested by the epigraph above. It is underscored by the fact that these activities engage the means and ends of *horu*, and thus arise as an alternative within the processes of dwelling and life that afford being. Indeed, the activities of the witch owe their form and existence to dwelling and life, as they too involve and consist of transformations. Where life assumes the form of flow and transformation, there is an ever-present possibility that these may be transmuted and diverted. Or, in a world where everything is a conversion of something else, life itself is vulnerable to conveyance. As the person consists of multiple means and ends for transformation and transaction, he or she too is also liable to transformation and exchange. Crucially, this means that witchcraft is not a reaction to an external imposition or phenomenon, but an internal generation of the form of life in this particular place. Witchcraft hence folds out of dwelling and life, at the same time as its activities enfold the relationships that these processes involve. It is an issue pertaining to intimacy and closeness (Geschiere 2013; Myhre 2009: 133) precisely because it unfolds from and redirects the material and practical relationships of dwelling and life that are constitutive of modes of being. In fact, witchcraft constitutes the limit of dwelling and life that is generated by these activities themselves. It is an action upon actions, or a transformation of transformations, that centers on the victim's body but assumes dwelling and life as its horizon.

The Priest and the Witchcraft Snake

The argument above is expanded and deepened by another story from Rombo, which more directly concerns the relationship between witchcraft and Christianity in Rombo. The story pertains to Father Dominic, a Catholic priest from the area who is well known and greatly admired for the development (*maendeleo*) he brought to the parish where the witch discarded the arm in 2001. During his tenure at that parish, Father Dominic not only enabled an extension of the church, but also refurbished the primary school and created a vocational training college. These are located right next to the church, where they create a compound that people point to as a manifestation of Father Dominic's abilities. His achievements were allegedly due to financial assistance he attracted from Catholic parishes in Europe, but this resulted in Father Dominic's transferral to the diocese in Moshi, where people suspect the bishop and clergy wished to retain and enjoy the funds he raised.

People argue that Father Dominic's transformative powers are due to the fact that his mother was a witch, whose powers he destroyed when he was a child. According to a story that is frequently rehearsed, his mother performed her witchcraft by means of a snake that she kept in a cooking-pot in the attic, which bore a human face and responded to her calls and communications. She called the snake by rattling the milk gourds by the hearth, which made it slither down an attic-pole. To perform her witchcraft, she fried the snake on a pot-shard over the hearth and scraped off its burned scales, which she either added to food she served her victim or applied to his or her skin. People describe and mimic how the snake cried like an infant when it was fried, but add that she breastfed the animal and applied *msika* to its skin to comfort it and make it soft and supple.

One day, the mother went to the plains to farm and left her first-born son—Dominic—in charge of the house. She instructed him to cook eleusine porridge as a midday-meal for his siblings, but emphasized that he was not to add milk or *msika* to it. At lunch-time, however, his younger siblings nagged Dominic to do just that to make the porridge tastier. At first he refused, but when he relented and picked up a gourd, it rattled against the others to call the snake down from the attic. Seeing the snake, Dominic grabbed a machete and hacked it to pieces, which he proudly showed their mother on her return. She reacted by running away, while wailing: "They have killed my first-born child" Realizing then that she was a witch, Dominic cut off contact with his mother and devoted himself to become a priest and serve others.

Like the incident involving the witchcraft arm, the case of Father Dominic and his mother concerns conversions and conveyances of life-force by means of different body parts and implements. *Horu* here occurs in the form of eleusine, milk, and *msika*, which are handled by means of cooking-pots, spoons, and gourds, and channeled through the mother's breasts and hands that feed and anoint the snake. In contrast to the case above, these acts do not collapse the means and ends of *horu*, but recombine them in ways that destabilize dwelling and life. Instead of domestic animals being fed by means of arms to obtain foodstuffs that contribute to a woman's lactation, a wild animal is breastfed and smeared with butter-fat, which otherwise nurse children and beautify people. The acts do not involve appropriations of body parts, but their redeployment that concern and affect bodily transformations, where the snake acquires human features and attributes, while the witch obtains the ability to harm others. It creates and involves an animal that undercuts the boundaries between the human and the nonhuman, whose modes of being entail and depend on conversions and conveyances of *horu* in distinct forms. By contrast, it creates a common mode of being, where life-force is relayed in the same forms between humans and animals.

Accordingly, this uncanny animal replaces or substitutes for the first-born child, who occupies a particular position in Rombo. Termed the 'child in front' (*mwana wa mbele*), the first-born son not only bears the name of the father's father, but until recently assumed his position, as he received on his marriage the homestead that his older namesake once occupied (Myhre 2015: 107). The naming and inheritance practices entail that the first-born son literally replaced his father's father, whose relational and geographical position he assumed. In fact, these practices mean that the first-born son reproduces his parents, who in turn provide his replacement. Replacing or substituting the *mwana wa mbele* with a not-quite-human, not-quite-snake thus enfolds or collapses the past and the future to enable the witch's destructive abilities in the present. Like in the case of the severed arm, it means that the witch sacrifices his or her own offspring for the benefit of saving his or her skin. It contrasts with the activities of those who bear children to reproduce their parents and butcher animals to compensate the *horu* of others. Such people act with others in mind, while the witch acts with herself in mind, as she either nurses an animal to simultaneously replace a child and a parent, or decomposes other persons to transpose the effects of taking their lives onto her children. In either case, it collapses the unfolding relationships of the past and the future to create a present moment, where the singular figure of the witch reigns supreme.

The Catholic majority of the area is proud of Father Dominic and tell his story as an epitome of his powers. In killing his mother's snake, he saved her potential or future victims from harm, which included himself and his siblings, who would eventually have suffered the consequences of what she did. He thus acted with an unknown multitude of others in mind, which anticipated his work of bringing development (*maendeleo*) to the congregation and the community at large. Dominic is therefore an anti-witch, who brings development where the witch destroys it (Myhre 2009: 118–119). His power to do so is considered partly the result of eradicating his mother's capabilities of harm, which he turned around for the benefit of others. However, his power is also considered an effect of Christianity, which people say bestow the ability to vanquish witchcraft. People hence tell his story to articulate how Christians can usurp evil and redirect destructive forces for good and constructive purposes. It is this dynamic that lends significance and urgency to the events at the church, when people discard witchcraft objects and remedies obtained from healers and diviners. Such an event is not only an occasion for ridding the community of destructive forces and influences, but a moment where these can be appropriated and turned around for common benefit. Powers that mark the limits of production, reproduction, and consumption are on these occasions folded in and reoriented as forces that enable the extension of dwelling and life in time and space. Thus, where witchcraft unfolds from dwelling and life, Christianity enfolds witchcraft to afford dwelling and life. It is this dynamic and process that draw large crowds to these events, where people come to participate in Mass and take part in efforts to turn the destructive into something constructive. The events nevertheless undergird the concept of witchcraft and people's conviction of its presence and reality in life. Witchcraft is accordingly a recurring topic of the Catholic priests' sermons, where it is castigated as a harmful and sinful practice that people must give up. It is not discredited as an occult illusion, but excoriated as a means and mode for people to relate to each other and the world they inhabit. Like evil, witchcraft is not something that can be overcome or transcended, but an ever-present potential that constitutes the limit of life.

To the area's Pentecostal minority, however, these events and Father Dominic's story show how Catholics dabble in what they call 'matters of the devil' (*mambo ya shetani*). Each case confirms how Catholics engage in witchcraft or visit healers, whom the Pentecostalists consider witches in their own right. To them, these stories and events therefore do not concern the immanent power of religion, but rather how Catholicism is not a true form of Christianity. It is corroborated or reinforced by the way in which Catholics butcher animals for the deceased whom they present with shares of meat, beer, and milk on different occasions. In the eyes of the Pentecostalists and other evangelicals, these acts constitute worship of other deities, in which they refuse to participate. In doing so, they set themselves apart and withdraw from the transfers and transformations of *horu* that these activities involve, which render them suspect as potential witches in the eyes of Catholics. On top of this, Catholics whisper that the Pentecostalists' all-night vigils involve orgies, where they have sex in the dark without being able to identify their partners.

They hence risk consorting sexually with close relatives and thus to engage in incestuous forms of sexuality, which underscores the suspicions that surround their faith and practices.

It is instructive that the Catholics conceive of Pentecostal practices as a warped or inverted form of sex where *horu* flows in destructive ways, while the evangelicals conceive of Catholic practices as an anathema that must be castigated and rejected, even if it entails restricting or avoiding interaction and engagement. Both conceptions trace limits of social life, but in different ways that structure their engagements. To the Catholics, their counterpart is something to be appropriated, encompassed, and turned around, while for the Pentecostalists it is something to be refused, renounced, and denied. Accordingly, Catholics often attempt to accommodate evangelicals, for instance by not stating invocations over animals before they are butchered or cutting their throats instead of suffocating them. They may also refrain from placing shares of meat or pouring milk and beer on the ground for deceased relatives, especially during large ceremonial occasions that require broad participation. Pentecostalists, meanwhile, refuse to eat meat or drink milk if they suspect that these acts were performed, and instead largely engage with the Catholic majority through proselytization and attempts at conversions. One particular Pentecostal pastor can therefore be seen most days, as he is diverted on his way to other activities and held up in animated attempts to convince someone of the wrongs and evils of Catholicism. His steadfast attempts at conversion even include his three brothers, whom he still tries to convert, undeterred by more for than a decade of failure.

Thus, where witchcraft unfolds from dwelling and life, Catholics seek to enfold and turn it around, while the Pentecostalists attempt to banish and expel it. However, the efforts of each appear suspect in the eyes of the other, where it resembles rather than differs from that which they oppose. These connections appear less strange when one remembers that all these phenomena concern life and regard modes of being. In the case of witchcraft, they involve the conversions and conveyances of *horu* that afford human, animal, and vegetative being, while for the Catholics and evangelicals they regard the existence of a sinful being and its potential for eternal life. Where the latter differ is with regards to the means and requirements for the salvation of this being. Joel Robbins (2004: 127) points out that Pentecostal Christianity is structured around the notion of transformation, which commonly involves a rupture or break akin to the refusal to engage in certain activities in Rombo. In fact, one may argue that all of Christianity turns on a concept of transformation, where a transcendent deity assumes a human form, whose death affords eternal life for those who follow him. Moreover, the funeral liturgy of both denominations proclaims that the earthly life of those followers arises from and reverts to ashes and dust, or soil (*udongo*) as it is rendered in Swahili. Transformation is particularly acute in connection with the Eucharist, where the Catholics hold that the priest transubstantiates bread and wine into flesh and blood in front of people's eyes. The Catholics of Rombo are obsessed with the Eucharist, which they consider a necessary component of every act of worship. They therefore lament when a funeral is conducted by lay-clergy, who is not allowed to give the Eucharist, and decry that those who fall foul of the church are punished through the denial of Communion.[14] People are equally concerned with the ability of the priests to create Holy Water (*maji baraka*), which they on occasion bless by the bucketful for people to take home in bottles, where they sprinkle it onto persons, animal, and houses to prevent precisely the harm of witchcraft.

On this basis, one may argue that the two denominations fold out of each other, as they turn on different attempts at dealing with witchcraft. While witchcraft unfolds from dwelling and life, Catholicism and Pentecostalism unfold from each other as two antithetical attempts at reacting and relating to witchcraft. These folding movements and moments corroborate Joel Robbins's (2004: 118) point that Pentecostalism engages local culture in its own terms, which here not only includes conceptions regarding witchcraft, but also encompasses Catholic Christianity, which has been present and active in the area for over a century. They moreover accord with Sasha Newell's (2007) claim that Pentecostalism is encompassed by the witchcraft discourse, even though a large part of its rationale and attraction derives from its endeavor to oppose and reject it. Pentecostalism thus unfolds from witchcraft, yet collapses back into it in its encounter with Catholicism. The result is a set of situational folding movements or transformational moments that draw different limits of a life that itself assumes a transformational form. Indeed, it is the unfolding character of these transformations that allow vernacular conceptions, such as witchcraft, to encompass and include new forms of wealth and Christian denomination, in the manner that has long posed a conundrum for analysts (cf. Geschiere 2013).

Conclusion

The concept of 'occult economies' allows for the exploration of how money, materials, and imaginative constructs circulate and facilitate the extension of social relations through space in such a manner that the local is enfolded in the global (Gilbert 2005: 360). Thus, the Comaroffs claim to center on the plight of young men in the rural north of South Africa, but in fact range widely and effortlessly to encompass a multitude of phenomena. Like the media reports of the albino murders that recycle photos of unidentified persons and places to illustrate different incidents, the Comaroffs endeavor to describe a general experience and therefore hardly name or involve specific persons (Moore 1999: 305). By not locating the phenomena in particular events and relationship they are able to distil the economic from social relations, but only at the risk of partaking in neoclassical economics' own teleology (cf. Gilbert 2005: 359). Indeed, as their analytic has come to circulate along with the phenomena it concerns, the concept itself comes to resemble a commodity that flows beyond its origins of production (cf. Strathern 1985a: 204). It is therefore not only 'occult imaginaries' that circulate, but the concept of 'occult economies' itself. As it is ever-more widely cited and applied, the concept assumes by its own criteria an occult character.

By contrast, the incident of the severed arm and the tale of the witchcraft snake concern how different parts of a person's body convert and convey *horu* in different forms that become constitutive of the capacity and well-being of others. They dwell on how anatomical features and bodily substances are *horu* in different forms that may be detached and deployed for the purpose of particular effects. The events and accounts entail that the witch decomposes the victim into its constitutive relations, which he or she engages to divert and avert the victim's blood and its effect. The witch thus dissolves the victim into the flows of life-force that constitute his or her being, which he or she directs by means of the victim's body parts. Unlike the occult economies, this concept of witchcraft does not float free but unfolds from particular relationships that constitute a mode of life that assumes a specific form.

The media reports moreover reveal that the albino murders involved body parts that form part of these processes and dynamics. Arms and genitalia featured, for instance, which in Rombo convey and convert the life-force that assumes the forms of blood and semen, or the bride wealth that circulates as foodstuffs and people between homesteads

(Myhre 2014). Instead of commodity-like entities that are bought and sold by those who wish to get ahead in economic pursuits, the albino murders concern and involve attempts to appropriate and administer the life-force of others for the sake of one's own personal being. Its urgency in 2008 was possibly linked to the expansion of secondary schooling, where people were required to provide money and materials, as well as contribute labour to build the schools for which they would later have to pay their children's school fees. As these dictates arrived from national and regional authorities and trickled through the local government, the increasing demands and needs for money were experienced as extractions of life-force that pulled people apart. Wary of assigning causal dynamics, I wish to point out that this idea does not weaken the connection between the albino murders, witchcraft, and the economy, but undermines the concept of occult economies where people use 'magical' means or 'mysterious' techniques for material ends. The concept of *horu* entails that these events and practices are neither magical nor mysterious, but material and practical interventions in dwelling and life that affect the modes of being of those involved. They belong to a world where all that exists is *horu* in some form, and hence is a transformation of something else. In such a world, life itself is vulnerable and prone to transformation, which assumes a form where body-parts are used as forms of life-force, deployed as tools for its conversion, or used to nourish an animal counterpart that can be used to harm others. Like in the epigraph above, these engagements emerge as alternatives embodied in life itself, which affirms its existence as a concern for the transfers and transformations of *horu*. Life and dwelling are thus constant possibilities to be seized in opposition to witchcraft, which gives new sense to people's concern and circumspection when sharing and consuming powerful foodstuffs in situations where they may be bewitched (Myhre 2009: 131).

Witchcraft then not only constitutes the end of dwelling and life, but outlines the limit of an anthropology preoccupied with representation. On this account, the concern of witchcraft is with modes of being and not-being, whose intensities these events and experiences evince and convey (cf. Favret-Saada 2015: 104). Accordingly, its character as an action upon action differs from the idea of representation, where one form of action comments on another (Strathern 1985b: 112). Representation is obviously a concern for a discipline that describes and reproduces social life in other forms, but it does not follow that it holds the same interest and urgency for those with whom we work. Indeed, shedding our capacity for extending this idea to the notions and practices we encounter may expand our ability to conceptualize and represent life. Losing this limb, as it were, can effectuate its own mode of transformation, as it allows vernacular actions to act on our practices and redirect our representational powers. Such a move would facilitate a conceptual encounter of the kind promised by 'occult economies', where an equivalence of terms is provided an opportunity for them to modify each other. It requires, however, that we leave behind the presumption that one is a representation of the other, and instead allow ourselves to be bewitched and our hand severed, so that our perspective can be expanded.

Notes

1. BBC News. 2008. Tanzania in witchdoctor crackdown. http://news.bbc.co.uk/2/hi/africa/7327989.stm. Accessed November 10, 2014 (BBC News 2008).
2. BBC News. 2008. Living in fear: Tanzania's albinos. http://news.bbc.co.uk/2/hi/africa/7518049.stm. Accessed November 10, 2014 (BBC News 2008).
3. BBC News 2008. Tanzania's albinos targeted again. http://news.bbc.co.uk/2/hi/africa/7527729.stm. Accessed November 10, 2014 (BBC News 2008).
4. European Parliament. 2008. European Parliament resolution of September 4, 2008 on the killing of albinos in Tanzania. http://www.europarl.europa.eu/sides/getDoc.do?pubRef=-//EP//TEXT+TA+P6-TA-2008-0413+0+DOC+XML+V0//EN&language=EN. Accessed March 19, 2014 (European Parliament 2008).
5. Obulutsa, George. 2008. Albinos live in fear after body part murders. *The Guardian*. http://www.theguardian.com/world/2008/nov/04/tanzania-albinos-murder-witchcraft. Accessed November 10, 2014 (Obulutsa, George 2008).
6. Sky News. 2008. Albino girl killed for witchcraft. http://news.sky.com/story/642546/albino-girl-killed-for-witchcraft. Accessed November 10, 2014 (Sky News 2008).
7. BBC News. 2008. Living in fear: Tanzania's albinos. http://news.bbc.co.uk/2/hi/africa/7518049.stm (BBC News 2008).
8. Sky News. 2008. Albino girl killed for witchcraft. http://news.sky.com/story/642546/albino-girl-killed-for-witchcraft. Accessed November 10, 2014 (Sky News 2008).
9. Fieldwork was conducted between April 2000 and September 2001, October 2006 and February 2007, and August and November 2008,

with shorter visits in October–November 1998, April 2002, April 2003, November–December 2011, and October–November 2012. Support from the University of Oxford, Norwegian Research Council, German Academic Exchange Service, Institute for Comparative Research in Human Culture, Nordic Africa Institute, University of Oslo, and University of Bergen is gratefully acknowledged, as are research permits from the Tanzanian Commission for Science and Technology. I am grateful to Kathleen Jennings and Morten Nielsen for reading earlier versions of this text, as well as input from the volume's editors.

10. Our conversation took place in Swahili, which the Catholic Church uses for both administrative and liturgical purposes. The terms in parentheses in this and the next paragraph are therefore Swahili terms used by the priest, which are cognates of Chagga terms that they are used interchangeably with in the everyday discourse of villagers.
11. Such initiatives are irregular events that occur on the order of the bishop and the diocese, but are organised by the parish. It commonly involves a special Mass that is announced in church several weeks in advance, along with encouragements for people to bring their witchcraft and healing paraphernalia, which they may leave in boxes at the entrance of the church. After Mass, these items are burnt outside the church, while the participants gather in a circle to say prayers and praise god. One such event that I attended in 2006 attracted several hundred at a parish church, where the participants filled several big cardboard boxes with objects that were burned, while lay-preachers led those present in prayers around the bonfire.
12. Like its Swahili cognate *mkono*, the Chagga word *koko* is used to mean both the hand and the arm, depending on the situation and context. I have consistently translated *koko* as 'arm' here, even though the hand also features in most of the activities described.
13. Elsewhere, I describe the use of this spoon for divinatory and ceremonial purposes (Myhre 2006, 2015).
14. More correctly, lay-clergy may assist the ordained priests in handing out Communion wafers during Mass, but are not empowered to effectuate transubstantion, which underscores the centrality of transformation for Catholic Christianity.

References

BBC News. 2008. Living in fear: Tanzania's albinos. http://news.bbc.co.uk/2/hi/africa/7518049.stm. Accessed Nov 10, 2014.

BBC News. 2008. Tanzania's albinos targeted again. http://news.bbc.co.uk/2/hi/africa/7527729.stm. Accessed Nov 10, 2014.

BBC News. 2008. Tanzania in witchdoctor crackdown. http://news.bbc.co.uk/2/hi/africa/7327989.stm. Accessed Nov 10, 2014.

Comaroff, Jean, and John Comaroff. 1999. "Occult Economies and the Violence of Abstraction: Notes from the South African Postcolony". *American Ethnologist* 26 (2): 279–303.

European Parliament. 2008. European Parliament resolution of Sept 4, 2008 on the killing of albinos in Tanzania. http://www.europarl.europa.eu/sides/getDoc.do?pubRef=-//EP//TEXT+TA+P6-TA-2008-0413+0+DOC+XML+V0//EN&language=EN. Accessed March 19, 2014.

Favret-Saada, Jeanne 2015 [2009]. *The Anti-Witch*. Chicago: Hau Books.

Fiedler, Klaus. 1996. *Christianity and African Culture: Conservative German Protestant Missionaries in Tanzania, 1900–1940*. Leiden: E.J. Brill.

Geschiere, Peter. 2013. *Witchcraft, Intimacy, and Trust: Africa in Comparison*. Chicago: University of Chicago Press.

Gilbert, Emily. 2005. "Common Cents: Situating Money in Time and Place". *Economy and Society* 34 (3): 357–388.

Kapferer, Bruce. 2002. "Introduction: Outside All Reason—Magic, Sorcery and Epistemology in Anthropology". *Social Analysis* 46 (3): 1–30.

Moore, Sally Falk. 1999. "Reflections On the Comaroff Lecture". *American Ethnologist* 26 (2): 304–306.

Myhre, Knut Christian. 1998. "The Anthropological Concept of Action and Its Problems: A 'New' Approach Based on Marcel Mauss and Aristotle". *Journal of the Anthropological Society Oxford* 29 (2): 121–134.

———. 2006. "Divination and Experience: Explorations of a Chagga Epistemology". *Journal of the Royal Anthropological Institute* 12 (2): 313–330.

———. 2007. "Family Resemblances, Practical Interrelations, and Material Extensions: Understanding Sexual Prohibitions in Kilimanjaro". *Africa* 77 (3): 307–330.

———. 2009. "Disease and Disruption: Chagga Witchcraft and Relational Fragility". In *Dealing with Uncertainty in Contemporary African Lives*, ed. L. Haram and C. Bawa Yamba. Uppsala: Nordic Africa Institute.

———. 2013. "Membering and Dismembering: The Poetry of Animal Bodies in Kilimanjaro". *Social Analysis* 57 (3): 114–131.

———. 2014. "The Multiple Meanings of *Moongo*: On the Conceptual Character of Doorways and Backbones in Kilimanjaro". *Journal of the Royal Anthropological Institute* 20 (3): 505–525.

———. 2015. "What the Beer Shows: Exploring Ritual and Ontology in Kilimanjaro". *American Ethnologist* 42 (1): 97–115.

Newell, Sasha. 2007. "Pentecostal Witchcraft: Neoliberal Possession and Demonic Discourse in Ivorian Pentecostal Churches". *Journal of Religion in Africa* 37 (4): 461–490.

Niehaus, Isak. 2005. "Witches and Zombies of the South African Lowveld: Discourse, Accusations and Subjective Reality". *Journal of the Royal Anthropological Institute* 11 (1): 191–210.

Obulutsa, George. 2008. Albinos live in fear after body part murders. *The Guardian*. http://www.theguardian.com/world/2008/nov/04/tanzania-albinos-murder-witchcraft. Accessed Nov 10, 2014.

Ranger, Terence. 2007. "Scotland Yard in the Bush: Medicine Murders, Child Witches and the Construction of the Occult". *Africa* 77 (2): 272–283.

Robbins, Joel. 2004. "The Globalization of Pentecostal and Charismatic Christianity". *Annual Review of Anthropology* 33: 117–143.

Ruel, Malcolm. 1965. "Witchcraft, Morality and Doubt". *ODU: University of IFE Journal of African Studies* 2: 3–26.

Sky News. 2008. Albino girl killed for witchcraft. http://news.sky.com/story/642546/albino-girl-killed-for-witchcraft. Accessed Nov 10, 2014.

Strathern, Marilyn. 1985a. "Kinship and Economy: Constitutive Orders of a Provisional Kind". *American Ethnologist* 12 (2): 191–209.

Strathern, Marilyn. 1985b. "Discovering Social Control". *Journal of Law and Society* 12 (2): 111–134.

Strathern, Marilyn. 1988. *The Gender of the Gift: Problems with Women and Problems with Society in Melanesia*. Berkeley: University of California Press.

West, Harry. 2007. *Ethnographic Sorcery*. Chicago: University of Chicago Press.

Author Biography

Knut Christian Myhre is a researcher in the Museum of Cultural History at the University of Oslo. Myhre has long-term research experience from both rural and urban areas of Tanzania, where he has published on a range of topics that include kinship, witchcraft, ritual, exchange, forms of knowledge, and cross-cultural comparison. Myhre has edited *Cutting and Connecting: 'Afrinesian' Perspectives on Networks, Exchange and Relationality* (Berghahn 2016) and published articles in *Africa, American Ethnologist, Anthropological Theory, Journal of the Royal Anthropological Institute*, and *Social Analysis*. Myhre has previously worked at the Norwegian University of Science and Technology (NTNU) and the Nordic Africa Institute and been affiliated with the research project *Egalitarianism: Forms, Processes, Comparisons* at the University of Bergen.

BY

CHAPTER 8

Demons, Devils, and Witches in Pentecostal Port Vila: On Changing Cosmologies of Evil in Melanesia

Annelin Eriksen and Knut Rio

Introduction: Pentecostal Port Vila

Port Vila, the capital of Vanuatu, is a small but growing Melanesian city. In the last decade, an increasing number of migrants from around the archipelago have arrived to take part in the country's growing tourist industry—as taxi-drivers, in hotels or as domestic workers, cleaners, or shop assistants. Many migrants also arrive without work, and spend periods of time just "hanging around" or as "SPR - *sperem pablik rod*"[1] as they are locally phrased, before most of them go back to their island or find some low-income work. The city center itself is dominated by tax-free stores, restaurants, coffee bars, and local handicraft markets, a generally modern sphere of consumerism and wealth that is not really available to most ni-Vanuatu. Few people of Vanuatu origin live in the

A. Eriksen (✉) · K. Rio
University of Bergen, Bergen, Norway

K. Rio et al. (eds.), *Pentecostalism and Witchcraft*, Contemporary Anthropology of Religion, DOI 10.1007/978-3-319-56068-7_8

city center itself. Some of the most centrally based residential neighborhoods and gated communities are almost exclusively settled by white ex-pats, who operate on the managerial levels of the tourist industry, as advisors or NGO-workers. The migrants from the different islands of the country live in semi-formalized neighborhoods at the outskirts of the city center. From the perspective of a village-dweller in the rural areas, these urban settlements are somewhat strange and alien places. This is also often pointed out in urban discourses: *Vila i difren* or *Vila i tanem kastom* ("Port Vila is a different place" or "Port Vila changes traditional life"). As a small city, it is not just a big composite village or a more compact version of a Melanesian place. Whereas in a village context kinship systems, avoidance rules, ceremonial obligations, marriage patterns, and agricultural routines order everyday life, in the urban neighborhoods people from different islands live side by side with different languages, different kinship systems, and marriage principles, and social life is regulated by completely different regimes. The workplaces, the playgrounds, health services and schools, the different settlements and their numerous kava-bars[2] and stores, the many different church communities,[3] all form a new order of life. What matters is not that the city brings people much closer in terms of access to the market, to the state or to modernity, or that people abandon their kinship awareness or relational obligations—but that city life represents a unique situation with other social parameters and values (see also Mitchell 2011). It has other spiritual, moral and ritual bearings. The city of Port Vila can, therefore, be understood as "another world," and we argue that we might see this as a Pentecostal world.

Since 2006 we have done research on Pentecostal churches in Port Vila.[4] In the first phase of this research, we were eager to define what kind of churches were Pentecostal and which were not. More recently, however, we have found that this was not necessarily the most useful way to operate. It has recently dawned on us that it might be more revealing for our understanding of Port Vila if we viewed the whole city as a Pentecostal context (see Eriksen 2009a, b; Eriksen forthcoming). First, because the wave of what we might call charismatic and spiritual influence affects the Catholic, the Presbyterian, and the independent churches as much as it does the self-declared Pentecostal churches. Thus, the practices by which we often identify the Pentecostal faith, such as speaking in tongues, being slain in the spirit, and spiritual healing, are now as much a part of, for instance, the Presbyterian register as they are the Pentecostal (see Bratrud, this volume). Second, and even more importantly, the core ideas and perspectives that emanate from the Pentecostal worldview are not just relevant for a "religious" context. Rather these ideas and practices are structuring everyday life in a total sense. People relate to the presence of the Holy Spirit everywhere; as much in the grocery store where there is a healing room in the back, as in the market where women heal or talk about healing in-between selling fruits and vegetables, or in the schoolyard where secondary school students talk about their experience of trance and encounters with the Holy Spirit. But Pentecostalism has a total presence also for the non-converts who relate to the claims, observations, and stories of spiritual and divine presence. In this chapter, we claim, in accordance with the general argument of this book, that an escalation of witchcraft and sorcery activity is integral to this Pentecostal world (see also Newell 2007). Furthermore, we argue that in order to understand the reason for the escalation, we need to understand the emergence of what we will call a new cosmology of evil. Thus, in this chapter, we present ethnographic glimpses from fieldwork in 2010 and 2014, when we experienced an intensification of cases of witchcraft and sorcery and the issue of spiritual insecurity in Port Vila.

A City in Need of Protection

At the same time as we were going around the city to document the many new charismatic so-called "break-away churches," in the spring of 2010, we also became aware of numerous allegations of mysterious illnesses, magical robberies, and suspicious deaths (see also Rio 2011). This was a period of intense attention to new forms of magic and sorcery, articulated in conversations between people in the streets and settlements, in kava-bars, in churches, and in the media. As much as possible we tried to get close to the events and tried to find people who were involved. We got partial accounts of these happenings, some from the pastors we interviewed, some from old friends, and some from newspapers reports. We do not have space here to fill in the total picture, but we will try to convey a few snapshots of this many-sided situation.

Just after we arrived in January of 2010, we were talking to one of the Pentecostal pastors about politics and the presidential election that had just taken place in the fall of 2009. He was eager to tell us that in the build-up to the election the Port Vila Council of Churches had decided to run a spiritual campaign, in order to "protect the nation" at this critical point. The pastor and his fellow preachers from other churches had surrounded the city with spiritual protection. They set up prayer sites at the geographical points that marked the city's boundaries—one on Ifira Island to the east, one close to the national airport in the north, one on the Bellevue hill to the east and one on Pango Point to the south. This was to ensure that "evil" and "dirt" and "corruption" should not enter into the election, and the league of pastors with their intense prayer and spreading of holy water hence upheld the moral integrity of the city during that election weekend. At the same time, all the people in the various churches around the city also joined in prayer directed toward the city as a circumscribed realm. The people of the churches thus fenced in the city at this liminal moment.

It should be noted that whenever political decisions are being made people in Port Vila suspect that magic is also being used to influence politicians as well as voters. One of the pastors we talked to added that every first Monday of each month, the Prime Minister prayed in his house with two or three chosen pastors from different Pentecostal ministries. They prayed for upcoming sessions of the Parliament if there were unrest, fragmentation, or motions of no confidence; they prayed for the progress of the national economy; they prayed for the success of the building of a new road, or they prayed for better health and less sorcery and evil. These are all things that threaten to harm the benevolent nation by continuously exposing it to the powers of fragmentation and inequality.

Here, we are already touching on what we imply when we refer to Port Vila as a Pentecostal city. It is a space that is held out by its citizens as a special, almost holy realm, and a personified realm that is like a person in need of protection, care, and leadership. It might easily be corrupted by evil, through the influence of overseas businessmen or missionaries, or from ancestral traditions brought in from the outer islands, but also from within the city itself in terms of envy, selfishness, and greed. These corruptive and disruptive influences are the foundation for the "Pentecostal witchcraft" (see Newell 2007), that the many new churches around Port Vila are focused on. They define this realm very widely and populate it with "demons," "spirits," (*devil* in Bislama), "black magic," "poisoning" with herbs, and sorcerous remedies such as *su* (instruments of homicidal sorcery). When there is an illness in a household or in a neighborhood people often speculate if a *su* or other magical remedies such as human ashes or bones of stillborn babies are buried in the ground or hidden behind the house of the victim. The new "healing ministries" specialize in spiritual warfare raids into such neighborhoods to clean them out and to detect such remedies. Our student Hildur Thorarensen, also did fieldwork in Port Vila in the spring of 2010, on the Survival Church in the neighborhood of Freswota. She describes in detail such a spiritual warfare raid in her Master Thesis. A family came to the church asking for help because they were afraid there might be some sort of *nakaimas* (sorcery) in their house. There has been a lot of suspicion of black magic going on in that street, and four persons were said to have died in mysterious ways. The members of the church prepared "spiritual warfare," and one night the congregation walked together to the cursed house, the pastor and his wife, some of the older founders of the church, some of whom were "Prayer Warriors" and one was a "Prophetess," in addition to some choir girls and boys from the Youth Group. They were met by the family, sitting quietly on a mat inside their corrugated iron house. The congregation stopped outside, and the Pastor started giving instruction for the ceremony. Most were to stand in the back singing, some were to pray out loudly. They were now watching for something to react to the singing or praying, a rat, a gecko or an insect, since that would be a 'devil'. Members of the group were to give notice or try to kill it immediately. The Prophetess, the Pastor, and the Prayer Warriors went inside the house and started praying, while the rest of the congregation stood outside and began to sing. Thorarensen writes:

> Suddenly the Prophetess came running out of the house, her eyes are closed and her arms are shaking; a usual sign of her being possessed by the Holy Spirit. The Prayer Warriors and the pastor follow right behind her, still praying loudly, as the prophetess runs away from the house and down a path. After them follows the family, and finally the rest of us, still singing. At this point a girl from the Youth Group whispered to me that the Prophetess has now felt the presence of evil spirits, and that she has begun chasing them. The chase continues up and down narrow paths around the neighboring houses at such an increasing pace that in the end we are all running, and finally uphill towards some banana trees. The Prophetess and the Prayer Warriors start hitting the trees, chopping them down to the ground with their bare hands. Some Prayer Warriors are still praying, and one of them is angrily shouting *"Out, devil! Out"*. (Thorarensen 2011: 91–92)

What Thorarensen describes here was going on in many parts of the city. These local events were about protecting neighborhoods that were marked by evil spirits, either as outside influences or internal corruptions. This particular form of spiritual warfare also defines the general measures taken for protection, being as relevant on the level of the nation and the capital as inside the household and toward the individual.

During our explorations of Pentecostal Port Vila in 2010, we also talked to some of the members of the Melanesian Brotherhood, an action-oriented branch of the Anglican Church that is dedicated to sorting out spiritual, demonic, and sorcery-related problems. They wear black robes as uniforms, and all brothers have a powerful walking stick that is highly respected and widely reputed to perform miracles. The brothers gave us accounts of two episodes that had taken place in the last months. The first one concerned one of their members who had died suddenly after leaving Port Vila for his home island. As part of their spiritual investigation of what they perceived to be a suspicious murder, they had traced his movements during his last days in Port Vila. They were convinced that he had been victim to a sorcery attack in Port Vila, and by following "spiritual leads" around town they were on the track of the killer. Their search became a detailed spiritual mapping, where they found hotspots for evil forces in certain locations of the city and tried to divine these places as part of the investigation. They had formed a complete picture of the deceased person's trajectory toward his death and the various human and spiritual agencies involved in it. They had concluded that their brother was already dead in the Port Vila harbor when he set his foot on the ship that was to take him to his home island. He had only appeared to be still living on board the ship and when going ashore at home two days later–because he was put in a zombie state by the sorcerers who had killed him in Port Vila. As a result of this killing, the Melanesian brothers now considered themselves to be implicated in a spiritual war. They were under attack from a league of sorcerers that they believed wanted to control the city.

Another case that had occupied them in this spiritual war concerned a young man who had become a "vampire" (*fampa* in Bislama). The vampire was first held captive by the chiefs in his neighborhood, and the Melanesian Brothers were called in since they were the only ones who could come close to him and detain him. He had superhuman strength and they had to ritually pacify him, they told us. This was a young man in one of the squatter settlements who had been transformed into a phantasmagoric creature, half man half animal. The brothers had deduced that it had all began because the boy had been smoking a lot of marijuana and living an outgoing and "wild" life. In their reasoning, they pinned down the start of his transformation to one particular night when he had smoked so much marijuana that he had become completely unconscious. The Melanesian Brothers believed that it was at this time that a witchcraft creature had entered his body and that this creature was now controlling him. He was publicly exposed as a vampire when his girlfriend had to go to the hospital because she lost her strength, and the doctors confirmed that she was low on blood. At the hospital, she had told her family that her boyfriend had regularly been sucking blood from her (see also Rio 2011: 57). When reported in newspapers, TV, and gossip, the case caused much alarm and confirmed the widespread worry about the spiritual siege that the city was under. When we talked to the chiefs of the vampire's settlement they also emphasized the special role of the Melanesian Brothers. It was because of them that they had managed to restrain him, to pacify his powers and liberate him from the grasp that the witchcraft creature had over him. After he had been treated by the Brothers, the boy was sent to prison, but he was released after a while since he collaborated with the police and gave up the names of the people who were behind the witchcraft. Again the idea—equally widespread among the Brothers, inside the system of law as well as on the streets of Port Vila—that there was a league of sorcerers that wanted to control the city, and that anyone and everyone would be victim to their superhuman powers.

We experienced that these circumstances were new and surprising for people in Vanuatu. Not only because it was so widely publicized in the news, and since it implicated the Melanesian Brotherhood, the police and courts of law in new alliances around the occult scene, but also because people could not recognize in it any traditional forms of spirit possession, sorcery or witchcraft. On national television, it was said that a "White millionaire" was behind the league of criminals and that he had supplied them with magic that originated in the Western world. It was added that as the boy drank blood from his girlfriend, he would become a white woman. Reportedly, the special tooth that he used for sucking blood had been an instrument from African magic. All sorts of mixed rumors and speculations of this kind arose, and people pointed out to us that it was as if the city was under attack or that their city security had been breached. Despite the intensive measures for protection set up by the churches and healers, unknown occult powers of evil were on the loose inside their own city.

Another case that got our attention at the same time was a court case around police brutality. In 2009, the police had launched a campaign called "Operation Clean-Up," where the aim was to recapture a group of escaped prisoners. One of the captives was probably killed during the man-hunt, although never found, another was killed during interrogations. He suffered "32 different injuries to his head, chest, abdomen, right upper limb, left upper limb, right lower limb, left lower limb, and back" (Daily Post, March 5, 2010). The violence of the operation shocked the urban population as they read about it in the newspapers. Because of this extremely violent death, an Australian coroner was appointed to lead an official enquiry into its circumstances. During his work, it became clear that members of the police sabotaged his work and even threatened him (Dawson 2010: 33). Police officers excused the death by saying that "the deceased was not looking normal, being overly aggressive and under the influence of drugs" and that it was the drugs that had killed him (Dawson 2010: 17).

Generally, it seems to us that in this case, the intense activity of detecting evil in the pentecostalised protection of the city spilled over into the state apparatuses in a very brutal and direct way. We knew from our visits to the healing ministries and new church congregations that these specific members of the police force were eager participants in one of the new international charismatic churches in town. There were thus clear parallels between "Operation clean-up" and Pentecostal crusades, spiritual warfare, and campaigns for a moral cleansing of the city. The people performing the latter were also the chief agents of the former (see also a comparative case from Fiji, Trnka 2011). The newspaper writings as well as the coroner's report revealed the police understanding of the prisoners as "sinners," due to their breach of a moral code around rape, alcohol, and marijuana. This breach of a moral order and thereby the tainting of the city's larger moral integrity provided the energy with which the police found the escaped prisoners, the violent punishment as well as their treatment of the foreign Coroner who was also seen to be invading and trespassing into the moral order of the city. In this latter case, we can see the ways in which also the state becomes part of the totalizing Pentecostal context.

The issue of marijuana ran through many of the cases and much of the talk of the city. We became painfully aware of this in relation to another situation that came up during our stay. A close relative of the family with whom we had stayed during our previous fieldwork back to 1995 was seriously ill. The young man had been working as crew on one of the cargo ships that deliver goods to the outer islands, and his father, himself a member of a small independent church in one of the settlements, told us that for the last few years his son had been smoking a lot of marijuana. This drug, more than alcohol, in these circles of Port Vila, is seen to draw evil forces to a person, as the intoxication leads to unconsciousness and change of mind. Seemingly, this state of mind implies a corruption of the person that is very much a target of Pentecostal warfare in Port Vila. In the case of the young man, it also became clear why. The problem with marijuana is that it blocks one's capacities for communicating with God and the Holy Spirit. A clear mind and alert perception are required to be a good Christian. At one point we were invited to see the sick man and his family on the outskirts of the town. He was lying on the floor, trembling and delirious. His father and mother and other members of the family were sitting around him, praying. They had been doing this continually for a few days, each taking their round so that the prayer could be kept up around the clock. But, as they explained, it couldn't be fully effective, since the boy himself wasn't able to communicate with God because of his delirious state. As in the case of the vampire above, the problem was that the marijuana had taken hold of him and blocked his abilities for communicating with God. It turned out in our later communications with the father that when he said "marijuana," he meant this in a broad sense. It was also a form of sorcery (*posen* in Bislama) that came with the marijuana that had put him in such a delirious state. "It had entered his blood," he said, so that there could be no cure for it. His father speculated that the marijuana lifestyle on board the trading ship had made him an easy target for the sorcery from one of the outer islands. The boy died a couple of days later. At the hospital, they told us that he had cancer in his blood and that he couldn't have been helped by doctors or medicine.

These few glimpses of rumors, concerns, and activities related to witchcraft and sorcery in Port Vila in 2010, reveal the moral warfare that was taking place at all levels of city life. When we argue that Port Vila is a Pentecostal city in a broad sense, we imply not only that the city sees a growth in Pentecostal, or Pentecostal-like congregations, but that concerns and activities which we identify as Pentecostal, such as spiritual warfare and healing, take place at all levels of social life (in the police force, in family life, in prayer circles, in politics, in media, etc.). These activities involve an intense occupation with where evil comes from, cleaning it up, and providing protection from it. Let us now turn closer scrutiny to what this concern with evil is about.

Toward an Anthropology of Evil in Port Vila

In this Pentecostal world the distinction between good and evil, between prayer and sin, between past and present is paramount. It is the world where binaries are center stage. Pentecostalism produces this black and white world. The order that emerges in the neighborhoods of Port Vila displays a very specific historic and cultural dynamic, but it has also much in common with places like Luanda in Angola (see Blanes, this volume) or Kinshasa in The Democratic Republic of Congo (see Pype, this volume), or for that matter Guatemala City (see O'Neill 2010); anywhere in the world where Pentecostals engage in "world-making and world-breaking" (see Jorgensen 2005).

Evil is often understood in a personified form in Christian thinking. Evil takes the form of the devils and demons. Surprisingly little is found in the Bible about the devil, but it is important in the teaching of particularly Protestant thinkers and theologians, as Calvin and Luther (see Meyer 1999; Russell 1986). As has been pointed out by historians of religion, theologians, and anthropologists alike, evil has a specific significance in Christian cosmology. This is true both for its European development (see Russell 1986, 1987) and in missionary activities in for instance Africa (Meyer 1999; Englund 2004) in Oceania (Barker 1990; MacDonald 2015) and elsewhere in the global south. One might say that the concept of the devil creates a phantasmagoric space where crucial world-making processes take place.

In spite of this, there has been little focus and discussion about the role of this conception of evil and of the devil, as Christianity has arrived outside of the areas where it has had its historical origins. However, with the rise of Pentecostalism, ethnographic descriptions of articulations of the devil have emerged. Meyer, working among the Ewe in Ghana (1999), has argued that Pentecostals became successful exactly because they took the devil, the personified form of evil, seriously. Ewe Christians who had heard from established Presbyterian missions that Ewe ancestral spirits were diabolical and proof of the devil's work, were caught in a paradox; if their heathen traditions belonged to the devil, how could one be free from them? Free from one's past and what was understood as the devil's work? With the Pentecostals' focus on deliverance, a new tool

a machine producing Manichean binaries, and the binary between good and evil is the most significant, this fundamentally shapes social life. The nation of Vanuatu, the city of Port Vila, the specific neighborhoods, and household, as well as interiors of persons, are spaces where evil is to be kept at a distance. With tools like discernment, prayer, healing and spiritual warfare, protective boundaries against evil are erected. These boundaries need constant ritual work and maintenance. Thus, there are mainly three aspects of healing; first, seeing (or "discernment" as the healers call it) where evil is located and, second, casting out the demons and banishing them from the perimeters, and, third, erecting and keeping boundaries between the good and the evil. The most effective healers, and those with the most prominent reputation have different versions of what they call the gift of discernment. They have x-ray sight, they can see in dreams, or they receive specific sensations when evil approaches (as a throbbing pain in the forehead or in the palms of the hands). These abilities mark the healers as distinct from others. Most people cannot see, nor feel, where and how the evil will approach. Therefore most people are dependent on the healers for protection.

Also in Port Vila evil takes a personified form. "Demons are all around us," one of the healers told us. When she walks the streets of the city center in Port Vila, she does not see the faces of ordinary people passing by. Rather she sees the grotesque faces of demons. She can see what others cannot, and even the people who are possessed by evil demons might not know it.

The healers are often just known as "women who pray."[5] One of the ways in which one can protect oneself from the demons is through prayer. If one regularly attends prayer meetings, organized by the healers, one can achieve a certain protection. However, very often, people neglect to "trust God," and for instance listen to advise given by well-meaning relatives to drink herbal brews, to wear specific protective items to guard against specific magic or to heal specific symptoms. According to women who pray these remedies open the way fully for demons: these are the very media through which the demons enter the body and, ultimately, the soul.

Sorcery, or *posen* and *nakaimas*, can appear in many different versions, but the healers often detect it as material or territorial technologies which are instantiated consciously by someone to inflict harm on someone else. For instance, this can be a parcel made from specific bones and ashes planted outside a house to inflict harm on those living there. One of the healers we worked with has the gift of X-ray sight, and she can see right through persons or materials. She is also a popular healer for businessmen who are afraid of competitors who might target them with *nakaimas* to drive them out of business. A healer is therefore often asked not only to bless new businesses, and thus protect them, but also, regularly, to "scan" the places for sorcery. The healers adjust their treatment to the specific kind of evil that is in question. If a person is possessed by a demon, the healers need to identify the medium though which the demon has gained access to the patient's body. If the symptoms are different, for instance just trouble at work, in marriage or politics, the cause might not be a demon but *nakaimas*. However, the healers often articulated that the differences or nuances between instruments or causes didn't matter to them. Whether an affliction was caused by ancestral spirits, urban demons, overseas magic or local sorcery items it still had the one and same origin and cure. It was the result of an opening or a crack in the moral constitution of the person–a crack that had allowed the evil forces inside the self – and the crack had to be closed by the Holy Spirit through discernment and prayer. In Port Vila evil is becoming an absolute phenomenon; there are no "grey" areas. There are no forms of sorcery or witchcraft or demons that are only slightly evil. And the question of evil must be located to the integrity of the person affected by it. As an extension of the argument forwarded by Robbins in his article on Pentecostal ritual (2004) we should add that probably the most important factor for explaining the popularity of Pentecostalism must be the role that healing rituals and rituals of discernment play for redefining an entirely new field of "spiritual powers" around the individual person. The cleansing of neighborhoods, cities or nations–where the ritual is taken out of the church building and into the streets, brings about the change that is the Pentecostal revolution. This is what Robbins calls "the Pentecostal promotion of ritual as a mode of sociality" (Robbins 2009: 63). People leave behind the church building and its ritual services and instead cast the everyday as a platform for generalized ritual activity. By ritual, we here imply a form of routinely engagement with forces that lie beyond the observable and tangible, that pertains to the sorting out of invisible forces that have penetrated into persons, things, or relations. The object of the rituals is the discernment of these invisible influences, their cleansing or casting out and the reestablishing of the normality of the situation. In Port Vila everywhere you go you are subject to attacks from these spiritual influences, and so the city is also becoming obsessed with purity on all levels. The sources of evil might be from ancestral spirits from your homeland, it might come from foreign products like the canned food in the Chinese stores, it might enter through your mobile phone or through television or the Internet, or it might arrive in the form of intentional sorcery in the form of magic parcels of sorcerous remedies planted under your porch or in your garden.

What is new in the situation is not that people in Port Vila are under the influence of destructive forces, and, as elsewhere in Melanesia and the rest of the world, people in Vanuatu have probably always taken very seriously the negative influence from other human and non-human beings. What is new in the Pentecostal circumscription of social life in Port Vila is both that people subject all afflictions to a unitary language of Pentecostalist warfare and healing and that they perceive their life, wellbeing, and personhood to be primarily related to protection and a hygiene of spiritual cleanliness. This cleanliness is no longer associated with specific customary taboos, avoidance of certain relatives, nor achieved through measures of generosity and gift-giving. It is no longer possible to keep ancestral spirits at a distance by performing initiations or sacrifices. Instead, the ancestral spirits are now purely penetrative agencies who roam free in the urban setting, in accompaniment with all the other destructive agencies that cause danger to person and community. The Pentecostal way of life is a form of constant warfare, which also results in the direct attacks on the specifically local diversity of spiritual forms. Pentecostalism invests a lot of energy into this local diversity but only in order to attack it and try to overcome it with its own form of universalism. In the recent decade in Vanuatu this has also resulted in violent attacks on accused witches, and sometimes even the murder of witches (see Rio 2011; Bratrud, this volume).

Overturning a Traditional Vocabulary

As noted in the introduction to this volume the vocabulary of sorcery and witchcraft is always written into histories of translation and social change. Similarly, *posen* and *nakaimas* in Port Vila are concepts that reproduce and reinvigorate and sometimes overwrite former usages. They are Bislama words that have absorbed in them especially the life in the city and the danger of being exposed to other people's traditions. They become key words for sorcery and witchcraft which are practiced in different ways around the many islands of Vanuatu. Although the words in Port Vila are now unified around ideas of evil, it is not necessarily so elsewhere in Vanuatu. On the island of Ambrym where we did fieldwork previously, in the 1990s, *abiou* as a local concept was understood and explained in a very different way. Most importantly, the Ambrym concept of *abiou* was not necessarily understood as evil (see Rio 2002; Rio and Eriksen 2013), and as it has also been the case in the rest of Melanesia, sorcery was often a legitimate form of governance and control (see Stephen et al. 1987; Dalton 2007). Although Ambrym has had a long history of Christianity, beginning with the first missionaries in the latter part of the nineteenth century, the binary notion of good and evil had lesser significance for the concept of *abiou*. Catholicism, Presbyterianism, and SDA forms of Christianity had an influence on people's lives and in particular on gender relations and notions of equality (see Eriksen 2005; 2008). Social life was structured on the continuity of kin relations and on the value of connectedness, but not so much around good and evil[6]. In this discourse of *abiou*, it was not easy to determine who the guilty one was since spiritual powers were per definition ambiguous, ephemeral, and hard to determine. The figure of the diviner was determining cures based on relational skills and herbal knowledge and not so much judging either victim or sorcerer on moral grounds. This is in line with many accounts of Melanesia, where we have learned that sorcery and witchcraft were underlying structural conditions of relations and an ever-present potential of social relations (Hocart 1925; Malinowski 1926; Layard 1930; Fortune 1932). Sorcery and witchcraft were heterogeneous and multivocal aspects of ordinary intimate relations (see also Geschiere 2013; Stroeken, this volume). *Abiou* on Ambrym worked in a clearly non-personified form; it was neither caused by a specific, unitary person nor did it attack a unitary victim as much as his or her relational capacities. It was dangerous, something to be aware of and be careful about, but at no point related to the moral qualities of the inner unitary person, classified as "evil" and opposed to "the good". We can thereby say that there is a long stretch, and an ontological rupture, between the world of Ambrym *abiou* and Port Vila *nakaimas* or *demon*.

In Port Vila in its Pentecostal state, evil is becoming personified not only in the sense that the devil, demon, witch or sorcerer is a person who wants to harm you, but also in the sense that the result of evil is the eradication of the person. In other words, the cause of evil is personified but the target of evil is also the inner self. Thus, when the healers work, they need not only to identify the cause of the patients' suffering (the form of corruption, who or what has caused it etc.), but also to restore the person. When a person has experienced becoming possessed by a demon, the healer needs to not only rid the body of the evil, but also to restore the boundaries of the person. One might say that in order for the moral person to appear healed after possession, the person needs to be reconstituted through the reestablishment of the active, conscious self. In cases of *nakaimas* sorcery and demon possession, this is what the healer does; she reestablishes an internal subject in active possession of one's own body and mind (see also MacCarthy, this volume).

Demons threaten the subject by extinguishing the internal self. That is, the demon (also in the form of marijuana) is a force that captures the consciousness of the person and takes over the will, the agency and the outlook on the world. It transforms the person into a desiring and craving figure—wanting what others retain; therefore envy is often the sign of evil. A person possessed by a demon, or a person with access to *nakaimas*, is fueled by envy; for other people's wealth, but also for other people's personhood; for their "inner selves," as one of the healers expressed it. In order to protect oneself against this roaming evil one thus needs to always be conscious of oneself; of whether one's actions are in line with God, or following the words of God. In order to trust God and to pray, however, one needs the intact "inner self"; if not, one cannot be "saved" from evil. In other words, healing demands of the person to be conscious (i.e., "awake"), to be able to engage consciously with God, as we saw above. Thus, the healer addresses a field of relationships that are entirely contained inside the person—in the interplay between being awake and being asleep, conscious and unconscious, alien and authentic, healing and corrupting, and good and evil. It is this binary struggle that gives energy not only to the healing process but to the social dynamics of this Pentecostal context; it is from these binaries that the fundamental social mechanisms emerge and shape the constitution and governance of both the person and the household—and, one might argue, the city and the nation.

Trust in God

So far we have argued that the binary distinction between good and evil is fundamental for social life in Pentecostal Port Vila and for Pentecostal witchcraft in particular. We have also argued that evil takes a personified form and it attacks the integrity of the person, of the neighborhood and the entire city. For instance, one of the healers we worked with (in 2014) had identified a so-called "clever", a man with particular knowledge of herbal medicine, as a person who had inflicted harm on others. She had repeatedly noticed that the neighborhood he was living in had been particularly inflicted with sorcery. She also knew the cause. She knew that this older man, who had for long been respected for his particular knowledge of traditional medicine, now gradually was losing his position. Few people consulted him anymore, as healers who worked with the Holy Spirit had become more popular and more accessible, and as the new churches and the new style of worship had become more widespread. After a particular incident, where she had detected a particularly malignant form of sorcery in this neighborhood (bones of a dead baby buried at the entrance of a house), she decided that he had to be named. There is a lot of evidence here, she told us. Not only has almost all his neighbors been affected by his black magic; some had become sick, others had domestic problems, and some had problems at work. Even more significant as evidence, however, was the fact that his wife had an ulcer on her leg that would not heal. She had heard this from a person who had recently visited the house of the old man and his wife. The wife had been sitting on a chair nearby as the visitor consulted the *kleva*. He had seen that the wife had been hiding a sore under a calico. This was no ordinary sore; it was big, open, and smelly. According to the visitor, the sore revealed a leg that was in the process of decomposing. In itself, this is evidence, the healer pointed out. The sore reveals the presence of evil. The sore is evidence that the so-called "clever" cannot heal her. Furthermore, it is proof of his lack of will to seek real help; to be healed through the Holy Spirit. Lastly, he had good reason to be envious; as he was losing his ground as a knowledgeable man.

There is a pattern to the location of *nakaimas* in Port Vila: If people are poor, miserable, sick or victims of bad luck, they have all the more reason to be envious of others. The feeling of envy attracts evil through demons. Dealing with herbal medicine is proof of the lack of trust in God and thus the proximity to evil. Since God is always good to the righteous he will always give blessing and healing to those who deserve it. Every person is responsible for his or her own commitment to God. It is thus very likely that people who suffer from poverty or illness, like this man and his wife whose wound would not heal, have actually welcomed evil and not committed themselves to God.

Conclusion

There is zealous sorting out of the problem of sorcery and witchcraft taking place in the neighborhoods of Port Vila. Many of the churches are designed for exactly the purpose of healing and exorcism, and they attract followers because people come to know them as "healing ministries." Every church and every congregation have several women who specialize in different forms of healing, exorcism, and discernment. In similar ways to what is going on, say, in South Africa or Nigeria, these churches move into suburbs with what they call "spiritual warfare" and approach, clean out or exorcise whole neighborhoods for signs of witchcraft. In the jungle of evil, the healers can see what others cannot, and help in the process of creating order by discerning between good and evil, and thus between God and the devil. This cosmology of evil rests on a kind of "absolutism," of a clear distinction between black and white, clean and unclean, good and evil. This Manichean form of reasoning also triggers social activities that pursue this logic: the logic of warfare, of "cleaning up" and the erection of protective boundaries. Healers are essential in this work, but they are not the only participants. Rather, this is an effort a whole neighborhood can at times be involved in. Accused witches in these suburbs of Port Vila are held captive in their neighborhood and the righteous people of the community legitimately beat them up over several days, in order to get them to tell the truth and confess. In neighborhood trials, imitating Western court cases, the individual suspected of evil is confronted with intent, motive, and circumstantial evidence (see Rio 2014). The direction the witch hunt takes in this Christian context is ambiguous. For outsiders, it may look like punishment or vengeance, but for relatives of the accused it is about separating the good from the evil so as to restore moral integrity and balance in the person. As such, it is first and foremost an act of order and purity, and in the process, the patient should be relieved of demons whereas witches should be exorcised or killed. Christianity's language of sacrifice thereby places itself into and transforms a social ontology that holds sorcery to be a fundamental underlying, constitutional category of social forces.

Witchcraft and sorcery in Port Vila today is thus fundamentally Christian, more specifically Pentecostal. In the discourses about healing and spiritual warfare one can see worries about a "heathen" past where spirits from "*taem bifoa*" (the past) or from foreign places emerge in new disguises, and one can detect a will for another future, where success, material and spiritual, will remove the fear of evil. Establishing protective borders against evil is crucial for social life in Port Vila. These aspects of the universalism of Pentecostal demonology have been widely described from all corners of the world. But Pentecostal healing ministries are also premised on a basis of local engagement. They are popular movements that take seriously the underlying social predicaments of the congregation but not by turning to historical or social conventions about what these predicaments are. Their popular power rather comes from redefining the spiritual and interhuman realm altogether. Their language of "warfare," "spiritual mapping," and "discernment" reveal their intense activity of renaming and reorganizing the inventories of the spiritual realms. People in Port Vila, coming from various islands of the archipelago as they do, used to differentiate between for instance people with magical skills and people who unconsciously embodied cannibalistic desires, between ancestor spirits who had been safely transported to their origin place after death and those who hadn't, between many different remedies such as stones for producing pigs and other stones that would kill people and destroy crops. It was the work of the diviner to address the multiplicity of signs and to create order and remedy out of the multitude. If you ask people in the Pentecostal churches today they will tell you that all this differentiation was itself part of the problem of evil, as was the idea that people from the different areas of the country used to live according to their own "law". The figure of the diviner, merely through his work of disentangling the multiplicity, is now also seen as instead entangling himself into the evil of the multiplicity. It appeals strongly to them that they can now subject all these differential aspects of their past to a unitary and universal cure.

Notes

1. "*Sperem rod*" means, literally, "spearing the road," indicating youth just walking up and down the street.
2. Kava is an intoxicating drink prepared from the roots of the *Piper Methysticum* plant.
3. Eriksen and Andrew (2010) reports on over 50 new Pentecostal churches in Port Vila.
4. Eriksen and Rio have done fieldwork together in Port Vila during repeated visits in 1999, 2000, 2006, 2010, and 2014.

5. It is mostly women who operate as healers. With a few exceptions of adolescent boys, we never heard of male churchly healers.
6. We are here talking about Ambrym in the mid-1990s. Ambrym today might, and most probably is, part of a slightly different religious landscape, with an increasing presence of Pentecostal churches.

References

Barker, J. 1990. "Encounters with Evil: Christianity and the Response to Sorcery Among the Maisin of Papua New Guinea". *Oceania* 61 (2): 139–155.

Dalton, D. 2007. *"When is it Moral to be a Sorcerer", The Anthropology of Morality in Melanesia and Beyond*, 39–55. Aldershot, England: Ashgate.

Dawson, N.R. 2010 'The Coroner's Report. Inquest into the Cause of Death of John Bule', Post Mortem Case No 29 of 2009. Vanuatu Supreme Court Archives.

Englund, H. 2004. "Cosmopolitanism and the Devil in Malawi". *Ethnos* 69 (3): 293–316.

Eriksen, A. forthcoming "Going to Pentecost. How to Study Pentecostalism, in Melanesia for example" In *Journal of the Royal Anthropological Institute.*

———. 2009a. "'New Life': Pentecostalism as Social Critique in Vanuatu". *Ethnos* 74 (2): 175–198.

———. 2009b. "Healing the Nation: In Search of Unity through the Holy Spirit in Vanuatu." *Social Analysis* 53 (1): 67–81.

———. 2008. *Gender, Christianity and Change, an Analysis of Social Movements in North Ambrym*. Aldershot: Ashgate.

———. 2005. The Gender of the Church: Conflicts and Social Wholes on Ambrym. *Oceania* 75 (3): 284–300.

Eriksen, A. and R. Andrew. 2010. "Churches in Port Vila." Report to the Vanuatu Cultural Centre. http://www.google.no/url?sa=t&rct=j&q=&esrc=s&frm=1&source=web&cd=1&ved=0ahUKEwi_v7eQ_ZnKAhViw3IKHbEsCEEQFggmMAA&url=http%3A%2F%2Fgenpent.b.uib.no%2Ffiles%2F2012%2F11%2FChurches-in-Port-Vila-ferdig.pdf&usg=AFQjCNEwbAAiVrKmcom1dvj_67-HMxuNFQ&bvm=bv.110151844,d.bGQ

Fortune, R.F. 1932. *Sorcerers of Dobu*. London: George Routledge & Sons.

Geschiere, Peter. 2013. *Witchcraft, Intimacy and Trust: Africa in Comparison*. Chicago: Chicago University Press.

Hocart, A.M. 1925. "Medicine and Witchcraft in Eddystone of the Solomons." *The Journal of the Royal Anthropological Institute of Great Britain and Ireland* 55: 229–270.

Jorgensen, D. 2005. "Third Wave Evangelism and the Politics of the Global in Papua New Guinea: Spiritual Warfare and the Recreation of Place in Telefolmin." *Oceania* 75 (4): 444–461.

Layard, J.W. 1930. Malekula: "Flying Tricksters, Ghosts, Gods, and Epileptics". *The Journal of the Royal Anthropological Institute of Great Britain and Ireland* 60: 501–524.

MacDonald, F. 2015. 'Lucifer is Behind Me': The Diabolisation of Oksapmin Witchcraft as Negative Cosmological Integration. *The Asia Pacific Journal of Anthropology* 16 (5): 464–480.

Malinowski, Bronislav. 1926. *Crime and Custom in Primitive Society*. London: Keegan Paul.

Meyer, B. 1999. *Translating the Devil: Religion and Modernity among the Ewe in Ghana*. Edinburgh: Edinburgh University Press.

Mitchell, Jean. 2011. "'Operation Restore Public Hope': Youth and the Magic of Modernity in Vanuatu." *Oceania* 81 (1): 36–51.

Newell, Sasha. 2007. "Pentecostal Witchcraft: Neoliberal Possession and Demonic Discourse in Ivoirian Pentecostal Churches." *Journal of Religion in Africa* 37 (4): 461–490.

O'Neill, K.L. 2010. *City of God: Christian Citizenship in Post-war Guatemala*. University of California Press.

Rio, Knut M. 2002. "The Sorcerer as an Absented Third Person: Formations of Fear and Anger in Vanuatu." *Social Analysis* 46: 129–154.

———. 2011. "Policing the Holy Nation: The State and Righteous Violence in Vanuatu." *Oceania* 81 (1): 51–72.

———. 2014. 'A shared Intentional Space of Witch-Hunt and Sacrifice.' *Ethnos, 79*(3): 320–341.

Rio, Knut, and Annelin Eriksen. 2013. "Missionaries, Healing and Sorcery in Melanesia: A Scottish evangelist in Ambrym Island, Vanuatu." *History and Anthropology* 24 (3): 398–418.

Robbins, J. 2004. *Becoming Sinners: Christianity and Moral Torment in a Papua New Guinea Society*. Berkeley: University of California Press.

Robbins, Joel. 2009. "Pentecostal networks and the spirit of globalization: On the social productivity of ritual forms." *Social Analysis* 53 (1): 55–66.

Russell, J.B. 1986. *Lucifer: The Devil in the Middle Ages*. Ithaca, NY: Cornell University Press.

———. 1987. *The Devil: Perceptions of Evil from Antiquity to Primitive Christianity*. Ithaca, NY: Cornell University Press.

Stephen, Michele (ed.). 1987. *Sorcerer and Witch in Melanesia*. Melbourne: Melbourne University Press.

Thorarensen, Hildur. 2011. "*Heal, Pray, Prosper: Practice and Discourse within a Local Pentecostal Church in Vanuatu.*" M.A. Thesis, University of Bergen.

Trnka, Susanna. 2011. "Re-Mythologizing the State: Public Security, 'the Jesus Strategy', and the Fiji Police." *Oceania* 81: 72–88.

Authors' Biography

Annelin Eriksen is Professor at the Department of Social Anthropology, University of Bergen, where she leads a project on Gender and Pentecostalism. She has worked since 1995 in Vanuatu, first on Ambrym and later also in Port Vila. Her work deals with social and cultural change, Christianity and gender relations. Her publications include *Gender, Christianity and Change in Vanuatu: An Analysis of Social Movements in North Ambrym* (2008), *New Life: Pentecostalism as Social Critique in Vanuatu* (2009) and *Contemporary Religiosities: Emergent Socialities and the Post-Nation State* (co-edited with Bruce Kapferer and Kari Telle; Berghahn, 2010).

Knut Rio is Professor of Social Anthropology at the University of Bergen, Norway, and is responsible for the ethnographic collections at the Bergen University Museum. He has worked on Melanesian ethnography since 1995, with fieldwork in Vanuatu. His work on social ontology, production, ceremonial exchange, witchcraft and art in Vanuatu has resulted in journal publications and the monograph *The Power of Perspective: Social Ontology and Agency on Ambrym Island, Vanuatu* (2007). He has also co-edited *Hierarchy. Persistence and Transformation in Social formations* (with Olaf Smedal, 2009), *Made in Oceania. Social Movements, Cultural Heritage and the State in the Pacific* (with Edvard Hviding, 2011), and *The Arts of Government: Crime, Christianity and Policing in Melanesia* (with Andrew Lattas, 2011).

CHAPTER 9

Spiritual War: Revival, Child Prophesies, and a Battle Over Sorcery in Vanuatu

Tom Bratrud

Introduction

Sasha Newell (2007) argues that Pentecostal churches in Africa draw a growing popularity largely from their ability to combat witchcraft in society (see also Geschiere 1997; Meyer 1992; Pfeiffer et al. 2007). This argument is also relevant when trying to understand the impact of a powerful Christian charismatic revival that hit the tiny Presbyterian island of Ahamb just off the south coast of Malekula Island in Vanuatu in 2014. The revival was part of a larger movement that swept through many of the Presbyterian churches in Malekula that year. Its aim was to bring spiritual awakening to the people of this district and beyond, and encompass some unwanted structures and tendencies in society. As it proceeded, an important goal of the revival became to eradicate sorcery. Sorcery is regarded as a serious threat to people's well-being all over Vanuatu, first and foremost because it is employed to bring about misfortune, sickness, and death. It is also dangerous because it is believed to employ harmful spirits related to Satan. The revival, and especially its confrontation with sorcery through a "spiritual war", as it was termed, will be the focus of this chapter.

T. Bratrud (✉)
University of Oslo, Oslo, Norway

K. Rio et al. (eds.), *Pentecostalism and Witchcraft*, Contemporary Anthropology of Religion, DOI 10.1007/978-3-319-56068-7_9

Christianity has a long history of representing the morally good on Ahamb. The value of "love" is for Ahamb people a most important principle of Christianity and reflects God's commandment about loving your neighbor (at least) as much as yourself and the idea that all humans have the same value, as children of God. Christianity was introduced to Ahamb in the early 1900s and coincided in part with a period of disease and death attributed to sorcery. Accusations of sorcery gave rise to fights and revenge killings, and large parts of the population in Malekula (and elsewhere, see Rio 2002) were exterminated during this period (Deacon 1934; De Lannoy 2004; Miller 1989: 194). The Ahamb church, among the first in Malekula, became significant as it practiced a zero-tolerance policy toward sorcery and offered spiritual resistance to its destructive powers. The newly converted Ahamb Islanders were also offering refugees from conflict-ridden mainland villages a safe place to stay on the small island. Conversion to the new religion was therefore understood as a matter of survival for many. This period in history is still important in people's collective memory and influences contemporary relationships between islanders and the church.

Since it was introduced, Christianity has continued to work as a main framework through which Ahamb people have dealt with different challenges of cosmological (harmful spirits, sorcery) and social character (disputes, violence, arrogance, greed). When core values of being and living together are threatened, and the "evil" is on the rise, so to speak, the church is typically mobilized for the "good" to encompass it. Conflict, selfishness, and sorcery thus appear as conceptual oppositions to the Christian ethos on Ahamb, and provide some structuring conditions for the articulation of the religion's importance.

An argument of this chapter is that when exploring the relationship between sorcery and Christianity generally, and specifically the process of the revival, it appears that the cultivation of "good" and "evil" as opposing forces has an effect where the two forces are mutually vitalized. This can be read in light of Clifford Geertz' (1993) classic model of cultural patterns and sacred symbols having an intrinsic double aspect as "they give meaning to a social and psychological reality both by shaping themselves to it and by shaping it to themselves" (1993: 93). With the prevailing existence of evil, it becomes even more important that the Christian life of good is strong and present to combat this power. But as the "evil" is also a part of Christian discourse as an opposition to the desired "good", this threat needs to be addressed and fought, and the evil is thus constantly reproduced as an idea and phenomenon. Christianity as good and sorcery as evil are in this sense mutually enforcing to one another and can be argued to be reproduced as relevant ideas by the existence and cultivation of the other (see De Boeck 2006; Meyer 1999; Newell 2007; Eriksen and Rio, this volume). We will recognize this in the revival, where a stronger presence of the Holy Spirit resulted in a stronger presence of sorcerers that again demanded an even stronger cultivation of the Holy Spirit.

It is important to note, however, that on Ahamb this mutually reinforcing relationship does not only operate in discourse but is also expressed and experienced quite concretely in peoples' lives. I want to stress that Christianity and sorcery in the Ahamb context should neither be approached merely as a belief or a discourse, nor something that can be easily analyzed as an abstract expression of a sociopolitical condition (see Asad 1982). For these people, sorcery is real and experienced as a concrete threat to their daily lives[1] (see Eriksen and Rio, this volume). Most of their uncertainty is therefore not about whether sorcery exists or not (see Bubandt 2014), but instead who the sorcerers are, how to avoid becoming their victims, if an attack against them may be planned in a given situation, and if so, in what form. This fear affects the structuring of everyday life activities for many (see Rio 2002, 2011; Rodman 1993; Taylor 2015; Tonkinson 1981). This point is important to keep in mind as we will now explore the spiritual war, the revival, and the meaning of sorcery and Christianity for personal lives and society on this island.

The Problem of Sorcery

What I refer to as sorcery in this chapter is a general and embracing concept covering all spells and conscious and deliberate manipulation of objects to achieve the desired outcome (see Evans-Pritchard 1937; Eves 2013; Forsyth and Eves 2015: 4).[2] In the Vanuatu context it is sometimes useful to divide sorcery into two categories: evil or "black" sorcery, where magical powers are used to cause harm to someone, and good sorcery, where magical powers are used for positive purposes, such as healing, weather control, and finding lost items (Forsyth 2006: 1). Sorcery is today generally regarded as dangerous and unwanted, however, for a few main reasons. Because all forms of sorcery employ traditional spirits, engaging with it is seen as defying God's commandment that one shall have no other gods than the Christian God. This point is particularly important for those who argue that these spirits are simply Satan in disguise (see Meyer 1999, 2004). In addition, sorcery is by many regarded as unnecessary today because prayers to God do the same job. Good sorcery is therefore largely replaced by Christian prayer on Ahamb. Moreover, the sorcery that was initially good, such as flying (*suu*) and making oneself invisible (*banban*), is now talked about as being used mainly for bad purposes such as transport and disguise during killing operations. The emic terms that describe sorcery, *baxo* in the Ahamb vernacular and *posen*, *nakaemas*, and *blak magic* in Vanuatu's national language Bislama therefore all carry negative connotations today. The term *posen* is perhaps the most frequently used on Ahamb, and I will refer to this term several times in the chapter.

The cultural values of love and care are important on Ahamb, as they are throughout the Pacific (see Hollan and Throop 2011). While the highly valued practices related to love presuppose relationships and devalue what we may call the "possessive individual" (MacPherson 1962; Martin 2013; Sykes 2007), the sorcerer devalues the social through often unprovoked attacks on other members of the social body. The sorcerer is typically a person who is overcome by envy, anger, and greed, and who might turn against even his own close kin. The sorcerer does not "come out in clear places" (*kam aot long klea ples* in Bislama) but is "hiding himself" (*haedem hem*) from the comings and goings of everyday sociality. While a normal person with nothing to hide takes care to be transparent about his activities, the sorcerer moves silently to conceal his movements. Sorcery is "selfishness carried to its most profane result" (LiPuma 2000: 145).

Hope in Revival

When I returned to Ahamb to do my second fieldwork in early 2014[3] I arrived at a time of much tension in the community. Some serious land disputes had been stirred up, chiefs and other community leaders had meager support, church attendance was low among men and youth, and sorcery was seen as on the rise nationwide. The society was thus considered challenged by a range of moral ruptures. At the same time rumors had started to arrive about a "revival" going on in the Presbyterian churches of South West Bay, a 3 hours' boat ride east of Ahamb. A revival of this kind refers to a spiritual reawakening in people emerging from a strong and direct presence of the Holy Spirit. In a revival, believers are typically confronted with miracles and personal experiences with the divine. This often brings a new and convincing awareness of sin and a desire for repentance and humility. Such processes of individual transformation are believed to be able to change the very fabric of life in society and even change the environment as it may lift curses from the land (Blacket 1997; Griffiths 1977; Robbins 2004; Strachan 1984; Tuzin 1997). Seeing that the revival was having a significant impact in South West Bay, the administrative offices of the Presbyterian Church in Malekula declared that a group of their revivalists should tour to all the 18 church parishes in Malekula to spread the movement. Ahamb church leaders were among the first to request the group hoping that they could help improving the moral tone of their community.

A striking feature of the revival in South West Bay,which was now spreading to Ahamb and other places in Malekula, was that the Holy Spirit was granting powerful spiritual gifts of vision and prophecy to predominantly children and youth. Through their vision, they could "see" what was going on in the spiritual world, and they would on a daily basis receive messages from the Holy Spirit to pass on to their community. The messages usually came as the children were struck with the power of the Holy Spirit and fell down; or were "slain in the spirit"; and in a physically unconscious state were approached by the Holy Spirit itself, Jesus, or angels. The visionaries were also taken on spiritual travels to the Heavens or places in South Malekula if the Spirit had something particular to show them. During the revival, people used the active Bislama verb "to *slen*" to describe being struck by—and slain in the spirit. This term appears in several cases in this chapter, and I use this emic term to describe the incidents rather than the passive English term "to be slain."

In the revival, the children were chosen by the Holy Spirit because they had "soft" hearts that enabled them to more easily "open up" and submit themselves fully to the guidance of the Spirit. Their special role was also founded in Biblical prophecies talking about how the Holy Spirit will appear in the last days of time to pour out its spirit on all people, especially the young, by making them see visions and prophecy (Joel 2:28; Acts 2:17). The message that no one will be able to enter the kingdom of God without making oneself humble like a little child (see Mark 10:15, Matthew 18:3) was also central here and worked as a criticism of the adult men who engaged themselves in politics and disputes rather than the church. The explanation for the children's role was communicated by church leaders as well as the visionaries themselves.

At this point, it is worth remembering that the Malekula revival happened in Presbyterian communities that identify as such, and are thus not Pentecostal in the denominational sense. If we define Pentecostalism as Hefner (2013: 2) as "an affectively expressive, effervescent Christianity that takes literally the wondrous miracles described in the new testament's Acts of the Apostles (2:1–3), and proclaims their availability and importance for believers today," however, we can say that the revival was a Pentecostal movement that "Pentecostalized" (Gooren 2010) many Presbyterian churches this year.

Before I continue to the Ahamb revival and the spiritual war, I will take some space to present the story about the revival's beginning in South West Bay as it was told to me by local church leader Elder Dan who himself participated in these first events.

The Revival Outbreaks in South West Bay

The outbreak of the Malekula revival took place in the village of Lawa in South West Bay in November 2013. The Lawa Sunday School was closing for the semester and about eighty children and some adults, including Elder Dan, were gathered in a small village outside of Lawa to prepare a show for the community. During a service in this village, a child suddenly fell to the ground and started rolling around seemingly unconscious. This happened at the same time as Elder Edward, a local church elder known for his spiritual gifts, called Elder Dan on his mobile phone to tell him that "anointing was about to overflow" and that they had to take the children down to Lawa immediately. In the revival context, anointing referred to a powerful blessing, protection, and empowerment from God. Elder Edward was in Vanuatu's capital of Port Vila when he received his vision about the events at home. He explained it to me later as a video playing before his eyes showing "the Heavens opening up and hundreds of angels traveling up and down between South West Bay and the Heavens."

After the first child in South West Bay had *slen*, more followed as the group now started walking toward Lawa village. When the group reached the church they walked around the church house seven times.[4] During the seventh round, lightning struck. In the words of Elder Dan:

> When the lightning struck the sky opened. The children saw it (through spiritual vision). They all fell down. All the children. They were tossed to the ground because they saw directly into the glory of God. While walking the seventh round they opened the door to the church and ... anointing struck (*jokem* in Bislama) everyone. The anointing flowed inside and many cried and many *slen*. This was the first time people had seen anyone *slen* in the power of the Holy Spirit. They might have seen it in other churches but this was the first time in the Presbyterian Church. This was the first time the Lawa parish experienced the power of the Holy Spirit. Many *slen*. Many cried. People who had cameras took photos and you could see *smok* (fog or smoke) inside the church. Flames of fire[5] too.

Over the next days and weeks, more children and youth in Lawa and all over South West Bay started to *slen* in church, during school, and at home. When waking up they would talk about visions and messages given them by the Holy Spirit. Prior to these events in South West Bay, a group of Presbyterian Church leaders had been praying for a decade for a revival to come to Malekula. Malekula was one of the last areas in Vanuatu to be Christianized, and even though Christianity now held a strong position most places, the island was still feared for its sorcery and worship of traditional spirits. A revival would provide a deep spiritual cleansing of Malekula and complete the Christianization process that had begun more than a century ago.

In response to the events that were now taking place, a special revival program was started up in the Presbyterian Churches of South West Bay with Elder Edward as the leader. It was Elder Edward and 52 youths engaged in the revival who in March 2014 arrived on Ahamb to make the power of the Holy Spirit be felt also there.

Anointing Ahamb Island

On the day of the revivalists' arrival, I was helping to prepare their welcome meal in the community hall. As we were more than enough people for the task, I took a break with Arthur, a senior man who was both a custom expert and retired deacon in the church. Arthur told me he was looking forward to the arrival of the visitors. The young people from South West Bay were not, as those in the older generation, afraid to spell it out if they knew anyone was practicing *posen*, he claimed. He continued:

> Nobody will be able to keep it (your *posen* acts) secret anymore. Some people are nervous (*shek* in Bislama) now, when they hear that the group is coming. It is because they are hiding something. The group from South West Bay has come to help us. Because when we die, we must enter the kingdom of God. That is why those who have *posen* must let go of it. The life of *posen* has become too strong. This means that the life of church must become equally strong to meet that challenge.

Ben, a man in his forties, joined our company and added that we were lucky to have such a group in Malekula who could pinpoint bad things that people were hiding:

> If you go to worship with them and you feel that you cannot breathe or that your body is "not right", it is because you are hiding something that is "not good". It is the Holy Spirit that works in you. You cannot hide anything that is "not good" anymore, whether it is fighting with your wife, having cross with your children, practicing *posen* or something else.

Elder Edward and his revival group stayed for two days and ran two services in a crammed church before their main program on the last night. This was held outside the church and the area was packed with just about everyone in the community and many Ahamb islanders living on mainland Malekula. At the center of the area was an impressive tent-like construction of white and red textiles. It was a 'Tabernacle,' known from the Bible's Old Testament as a portable dwelling place for God. The original Tabernacle was built to specifications revealed by God to Moses on the Mount Sinai, and similarly, the specifications of this Tabernacle had been revealed by God to some of the visionary children from South West Bay prior to the program. As in the original from the Old Testament, God was present with his full power inside this Tabernacle.

The program involved sing-a-longs and prayers to ask the Holy Spirit to come and take place inside the Tabernacle, as well as on Ahamb itself, and in us who were present. The part of the program perhaps filled with most anticipation was the one dealing with sorcery. It was believed that sorcerers would have no choice but to surrender during the program because the visiting visionaries would be able to point them out at once. After a service of singing, Bible readings, preaching, and prayers, Elder Edward spoke: "If anyone accuses you of doing *posen*, if you are a woman or man who has a bad reputation for these things you must go inside the Tabernacle now." The message was clear. If you were a sorcerer this was your chance to get forgiveness and make a pledge to God to quit once and for all. If you went inside but continued practicing *posen* at any time, God would "pay back" and cause you serious sickness or death. If you had a false reputation for sorcery, however, no one would be able to accuse you again as you had made this powerful pledge with God.

There was gravity and anticipation in the air as Elder Edward made the appeal. Two well-known sorcery suspects suddenly came through the crowd and entered the Tabernacle. Then a third man, Kevin, entered. Nobody accused him of sorcery but he was popular for his traditional herbal medicine that is associated with good sorcery. It is believed that if you know the good side of these plants, you are also likely to know the "bad side" that can be used for *posen*. Kevin went inside in order to clear any doubt. Elder Edward then called for others who had done something wrong (*no gud* in Bislama) to come inside. A special appeal went out to those who had stolen the big battery of the community hall's solar system 3 weeks earlier. If they came, they would receive their forgiveness from God and the community. We waited in silence, looking curiously around to see if anyone moved. No one came. Meanwhile, the reputed sorcerers kneeled down inside the Tabernacle. Everyone present was asked to join in prayer for the three men and to ask God to work in their lives.

The concluding part of the program involved a big communal meal that worked as a Holy Communion with food and water prepared inside the Tabernacle. Consuming the Holy meal would wash us with Jesus' blood and make God forgive our sins. As our bodies were spiritually clean, it would be possible for the Holy Spirit to enter into us. When the Spirit resided in our bodies, God's work would finally begin and spiritual gifts would be granted to the people on Ahamb as they had been to the people of South West Bay.

It was late night when everyone had finished their meal and the program came to an end. In the calm and quiet air, Elder Edward announced that the island was now clean. He declared that the Holy Spirit was present on the island, that Jesus had arrived, and that there was no one on Ahamb living in darkness anymore. Now it was up to the Ahamb community to make room for the Spirit to prosper by continuing to pray.

"Fresh news from Heaven"

> *We cannot hide anymore! Where will you hide now? There is no place to hide. If you do anything not good, if you think badly about another man, steal or have* posen, *the children will tell you right away now. Because they can see it.*
>
> Mary and George, middle aged husband and wife on Ahamb

When the South West Bay group had left, Ahamb church leader Elder Cyril took over and started up nightly revival worships in the Presbyterian community church. Elder Cyril was himself oriented toward the spiritual aspects of Christianity, and knew well the work that a revival entailed. It took about a week of worships before the Ahamb children also started to *slen* and convey messages. After a month, the number of children who *slen* was around 10–15, and a total number of about 25 were seeing visions and receiving messages. At the most, around 30 gifted children, youth, and women would *slen* during the revival worships and sometimes in school, in the garden or in their villages. The revival worships did not have a fixed program but were arranged after directions from the Holy Spirit given to the visionaries or to Elder Cyril.

The revival worships were especially popular among women and children, who were present every night. The attendance of men varied, as the services interfered with their popular kava[6] drinking sessions. Kava was thus often criticized in the messages of the Holy Spirit as it kept the men away from the church. The climax of the worships was when the gifted lined up and told their revelations one by one in the microphone. Some had several messages to share while others had one, and they varied in length and detail. Visions often involved parables, where the simplest ones could be seeing one dark and one light house symbolizing those who had faith and a clean heart and those who lived in sin and disbelief (*tu tingting* in Bislama). Elder Cyril who led most of the revival worships emphasized that the messages were "fresh news from Heaven," messages given directly from the Holy Spirit to the children. They did not come from any human being, and therefore we had to take them seriously.

Central to the revival was the need to "prepare one's life" to meet God in this life and in the afterlife. To be aligned with God, it was important to fight the "life of this world" (*laef blong wol ia* in Bislama); the deceptive worldly enjoyments that kept people away from a holy lifestyle. This included everything "not good" such as stealing, adultery, unfaithfulness, envy, anger, swearing, fighting, selfishness, being obsessed with money and material things, kava drinking, not going to church, not participating in community work, doubting God, and practicing sorcery. The actions and values that were encouraged as "good" and representing "the life of Heaven" included humility, generosity, kindness, helping people, moderation, faithfulness, going to church, and a full devotion to God. The revival was, in short, recruiting people to a more pious, empathetic, and ascetic lifestyle. It was warning against the corrupting temptations of this world and directing people's attention to the rewards of the next (Hefner 2013: 20; see also chapters by Blanes and Pype, this volume). The revival was therefore not promoting the form of Pentecostalism known as "prosperity" or "health and wealth" gospel where the message is that it is God's will for believers to be rich, healthy, and successful (see, for example, Coleman 2000; Haynes 2012). The revival rather had as its aim for individuals to achieve a state of inner purity which would further lead to a restructuring of society. Attention to money and material prosperity was seen as an obstacle to this process.

Spiritual War

Happenings two months after the revival was introduced, on an afternoon in late May, reinforced the Ahamb community's impression that the movement was important. News reached my village around lunch time that a group of visionary children had found an active *posen* stone outside the island's community hall. My friend John and I were on our way there to find out more when we met two young men who in dramatic terms told us what had happened. The men had been playing soccer at the nearby field when a group of children passing by suddenly *slen* next to the community hall. When the children woke up, they were crying claiming there was a *posen* stone buried in the area that had to be found and removed. The soccer players had collected spades and dug out a stone after directions from the children. The men were still dressed in their football gear and looked distressed as they told us the story. To conclude one of them said, determined: "Tonight, everyone… (pointing towards the church) …must go to church."

John and I continued toward the community hall where we met a group of people, including a chief, his son, and some children. The chief told us that the stone had the shape of a human face. It was clear that this was no ordinary stone. The Holy Spirit had revealed to the visionaries that the stone was placed there by sorcerers who wanted to bring damage to the community. The stone was infused with *bari*, a particular form of sorcery that can cause laziness, sickness, or even death. The chief's son explained that the effect was evident: "You see, the grass keeps growing here (around the community hall) … and it is only cut on special occasions. The place has become like a ruin … people are tired of doing (communal) work!" Someone commented that there would be prayers in the church until dusk to fight this evil power and that those who did not believe in the visionary children and the revival would finally see that it was true.

As expected, the church was full that night. When I arrived, seven children had already *slen*. After a few rounds of singing and prayers, Elder Cyril announced that a prayer group would be put together in one of the next days to walk around the island and pray against *posen*. If there was more *posen* lying around, it had to be found before it did more damage than it already had done. The 19-year-old girl Lisa who had a strong gift of vision then suddenly rose and said: "The Holy Spirit just revealed to me that we have to go out and search for *posen* already tonight. If not, it might be too late." Lisa continued: "when the Holy Spirit says something we have to do it. We cannot wait." Elder Cyril agreed and announced that we were organizing a group of 12 visionary children and a group of adult men to go with them. "Tonight we will carry out these things," he confirmed in his distinctive firm but gentle manner. The children had, through their spiritual vision, already identified the sorcerers responsible for the *posen* stone found at the community hall. Now, they saw that the sorcerers were furious at them for removing the stone. A few of the visionaries rose during the worship and revealed what they were seeing: that the furious sorcerers were now planning to come and kill the children who were revealing the secrets of their *posen*.

Around 30 people took part in the mission to locate and remove *posen* that night. Led by the visionaries, the group stopped at places where they saw that old or new *posen* was hidden. They placed Bibles on affected trees, paths, and houses before everyone joined in loud communal prayers to neutralize or chase away the evil powers. Using, Bibles and prayer against dangerous spirits was not new on Ahamb, however. The Evangelism group in the church had worked with similar tools for decades in traditional taboo areas and in the houses of suspected sorcery victims. Many of the old evangelists had joined the group that was now pulling out or cutting down plants that the Holy Spirit revealed had evil spirits in them. The group chased away some traditional spirits, and they found the skeleton of a dead cat buried outside the house of a newly deceased sorcery suspect. The dead cat made sense as a special cat bone is believed to be used for *suu*, the sorcery of flying. It is also believed that the sorcerer can enter the body of a dead cat and use it to walk around unnoticed. The location of the dead cat consolidated the suspicion that the man had indeed been a sorcerer and that his death was caused by either failed *posen* that had ricocheted or punishment from God for his crimes as a sorcerer.

When walking home from church that night, those who had taken part in the prayer operation talked about their experiences in dramatic terms. "The Holy Spirit came inside the children ... but the dark powers fought with them making the children shake, shout and cry!", one of the men reported in enthusiastic disbelief. The dramatic scenes that took place were a result of fights between the Holy Spirit, who possessed the children, and the evil spirits that the group encountered on their way.

From that night on the spiritual war would increase in strength and scope. The scenes witnessed during this first prayer mission would be a regular sight both in the church and around the villages over the next months. The visionary children were finding more and more *posen*, and they would see people and places who were suffering from their effects. The faces and names of sorcerers from the whole district appeared before the children as on a screen, as they described it, and they could see who the sorcerers were planning to attack next. As the visionaries revealed this highly secret information, they could see the sorcerers' growing anger and how they were now trying to attack anyone on Ahamb.

Every day during the months of June and July, we could hear loud and desperate cries around the island as the visionary children saw sorcerers coming to attack them. Hordes of people would hasten from different corners of the island to help and join in prayers to push the sorcerers back. Men would come with machetes and cut aggressively around the bush or climb tall trees in search of hiding sorcerers who, according to the visionaries, had been able to transform into a lizard, a rat, or a fruit. With the heightened level of risk that the attacking sorcerers represented, and a collective impression that the visionaries' revelations indeed seemed true, the church became an increasingly important place to seek out for comfort, protection, and fellowship. Men were closing their kava bars (at least temporarily) after orders from the Holy Spirit, a big land dispute that was going to court was postponed indefinitely after an agreement between the parties and the chiefs, and many were calling on the visionary children to hear their latest revelations and to be prayed for.

After two dramatic months of spiritual war, things eventually calmed down as the community's renewed faith and trust in the Holy Spirit enforced the latter's protection of the island. The visionaries would occasionally receive messages about sorcerers planning new attacks, but the community's prayers and commitment to the church were making it hard for the sorcerers to come through and take any action. After some exhausting months, people were slowly regaining confidence and peace through their strengthened cooperation with the Spirit. The horrifying conclusion of the spiritual war, however, was still yet to come.

The Community Meeting. Fear, Life, Death, and a Clash Between World Views

In October, seven months after the Ahamb revival began, a man confessed to having participated in the killing of a four-year-old boy by sorcery. The deceased boy was originally from Ahamb but had moved with his family to a small village on the Malekula mainland. Because the sorcerers had been unsuccessful in targeting anyone on Ahamb itself due to the protection of the Holy Spirit, they had decided to search out an Ahamb-related victim somewhere else. Because the small boy's mainland village was not incorporated in the revival and his family was not very involved in church (and hence did not have God's fullest protection), he had been a relatively easy victim for the sorcerers. The man's confession had come during a revival conference in a mainland village close to Ahamb. Here, he had sought out a prayer group to allegedly ease his growing grief for taking the small boy's life.

A community meeting was set up to hear the man's story. During the meeting, the man put all his cards on the table and revealed horrifying details about his and his friends' lives as sorcerers. Given the severity of the man's confessions, the meeting turned into a public hearing that lasted for almost three weeks. During this time, a total of five men from the district admitted to having been involved in at least four deaths by using sorcery. Two older men, who were long-time sorcery suspects, were by the five men pointed out as leaders of their sorcery group.

During the court hearing, the suspects revealed disturbing stories also about the actions and powers of the two older men. One of them had allegedly caused more than 30 deaths over the past decades, in addition to numerous cases of sickness, ruined businesses, and other types of misfortune. Various sorcery objects belonging to the suspects, including bottles, bones, and stones were also handed over to the congregation and their purpose and use explained by their owners. As the secrets and actions of the suspects were revealed, some furious young men occasionally entered the court to attack the suspects. The community chiefs found it hard to intervene and find a solution to the case.

The normal way of concluding a sorcery hearing on Ahamb has been to accept the suspects' denials and seal the case by a communal prayer where the suspects promise to God and the community that they will never again touch any form of sorcery item. God is then believed to bring sickness or death as punishment to the suspect if he or she breaks the pledge. This time, however, the confessions and stories of the sorcerers were of such a severe character that a little group of men saw no other option than to make an end to it all. The five admitting sorcerers had already surrendered and handed over their sorcery items while the two older men had not. Fearing the risk of having the two sorcery suspects living around their families and children, especially after the humiliation they had gone through in the hearing, the group took over when the official hearing ended and the chiefs had gone home and arranged for the death of the two by hanging. This event would shake both the people of Ahamb and the nation of Vanuatu.

During the hearing, I was myself in the capital Port Vila and registered mixed responses to the event. While there was much official criticism in the media and from the police, a number of people claimed it was good that someone "finally took action" against sorcerers who kept terrorizing innocent people. The police were contacted after the hangings and arrested 23 people who had been involved in the hearing. Many islanders criticized the arrests and the police for not dealing properly with the sorcery cases themselves as crimes but concentrating on the two offenses that were easy to prove physically: the hangings and the burning of one of the deceased men's house. For the critics, however, these actions were merely responses to the pain the two men had caused through their sorcery and a way to prevent them from killing again.

Many argued that the significance of the police in this case was limited because they can only prosecute according to a state legal system that does not properly acknowledge sorcery. Like most other Pacific countries, Vanuatu formally prohibits sorcery practice in its Penal Code. Section 151 provides that "No person shall practice witchcraft or sorcery with intent to cause harm or detriment to any other person." The penalty is imprisonment for two years (Forsyth 2006: 12). Since sorcery operates in the spiritual realm, however, it is impossible to prove that sorcery has taken place before a state court using normal evidentiary principles (see however Rio 2010, where some men from Malekula were sentenced by the magistrates' court). If a sorcery case is investigated in detail and considered in the context of the state legal system with its rules of procedure and evidence, it is therefore highly unlikely to ever result in a successful prosecution (Forsyth 2006: 13).

During the police investigation, some of my interlocutors expressed that it was problematic that Vanuatu state law, which the police were following, is based on the British common law system, or "white man's law" (*loa blong waetman*). This law was introduced during the colonial period and has later been revised by foreign law experts engaged by international aid donors. More than reflecting living conditions in Vanuatu, where sorcery is regarded as a living part of the custom, the law was seen as reflecting life in Europe and Australia where sorcery does not exist. Many Ahamb islanders, therefore, saw the involvement of the police and the state law system as an unavoidable clash of world views. In national media, the police criticized the community for taking the case in their own hands instead of letting the police deal with it (*The Vanuatu Times* November 21–27, 2014). But on Ahamb few people found a reason to involve the police, as they had no proper method of dealing with sorcery. The police would, therefore, have had to let the accused go free, and the community would again run the risk of letting the men attack again.

The gap between a people considering sorcery to be a serious crime and a legislation that does not allow convictions to be attained is a problem in many places in Melanesia. This is one of the burning issues discussed in a new book by Miranda Forsyth and Richard Eves entitled *Talking it Through. Responses to Sorcery and Witchcraft Beliefs and Practices in Melanesia* (2015). In the book's introduction, the Papua New Guinea native Gairo Onagi argues that bridging local belief systems with the law is one of the great challenges in addressing sorcery and witchcraft-related issues in the region today (Onagi 2015). Taking the case from Ahamb and the many incidents of sorcery-related attacks and killings from Papua New Guinea as examples (see Jorgensen 2014), this seems indisputably so.

Concluding Discussion

The 2014 revival left a solid mark in the Ahamb society. The spiritual war, including the court hearing that culminated in the two hangings, was important in that context. For Ahamb people the sorcery in question was indisputably "real" and highly difficult to deal with. After the hangings, relatives in town would report home about ruthless newspaper headlines and Facebook discussions that those who had experienced the spiritual war found unfair. In sorcery cases of this kind, the victims from the perspective of most media, international NGOs and human rights organizations, are those who are accused of being sorcerers and witches and who are subsequently attacked or expelled from their communities. But for Ahamb people in this case, and for the majority of people across Melanesia and other places where sorcery and witchcraft are experienced as real, the problem is first and foremost located in the harm that the sorcerers exercise on persons and their communities (Forsyth and Eves 2015: 2).

When sorcery emerges on Ahamb today, as other places in Melanesia and Africa, it is in relations to conflicts and envy that emerge when someone sees another person having success (Comaroff and Comaroff 1993, 2002; Eves 2000; MacCarthy, this volume; Moore and Sanders 2001; Rio 2002). Activities that promote individual wealth and prestige challenge expectations of sharing and reciprocity and lead to broken relationships and new inequalities. Self-centered actions, therefore, become a threat to relational harmony as well as the status and well-being of those who feel overshadowed by the advancement of others. Even though sorcery brings destruction, it can at least in discourse be understood also as protests and in a sense a reinforcement of "the communal moral of giving and sharing as against the modern tendency to claim rights and keep to oneself" (Rio 2002: 132). Sorcery can thus be interpreted as a double-edged blade (Newell 2007: 463), in that it clarifies the moral importance of collectivity and social bonds, but at the same time demonstrates a harmful individualism when letting personal envy override relational compassion in bringing horror, death, and pain to others.

The relational responsibility that fear of sorcery in a sense helps to uphold also very clearly reinforced through the church on Ahamb.

Ahamb people understand a good person to be someone who has love, concern, and sympathy for others. These are the same values that also characterize a good Christian. The antithesis of the good person, however, is one who is selfish and proud. Such a person is typically talked about as "different" (*difren* in Bislama) and doubts are continuously raised about such a person's Christian moral as he or she seems to acknowledge neither God nor kin in his or her life. Christianity is in this sense taking the role of an all-encompassing system on Ahamb, incorporating the main moral framework for social action as well as the cosmological powers of God that are regarded as stronger than any traditional spirit used in sorcery. Christianity thus acts as an umbrella for the good and what is worth aspiring toward, while sorcery, which brings destruction, is the most potent manifestation of the bad and evil. As with other Pentecostal movements, the revival was particularly clear in marking out this distinction, and brought about a more aggressive confrontation against the evil than had been normal. As I have argued, the opposing role of good and evil seem to some extent to be mutually reinforced and reproduced through the existence and cultivation of the other. For Ahamb people, however, this mutual reinforcement has not merely been discursive but is experienced in social practice: the more of the good (especially success), the greater the chance of an envious person (typically a sorcerer) coming to destroy it. The more evil, the more important it is that the church is strong to encompass it.

This mutual reinforcement resonates with examples from Africa where Pentecostal Christianity has been argued to take on the logic of witchcraft and make the church into part of the witchcraft problem itself, as well as a solution to the problem (De Boeck 2006: 173; Newell 2007). In the Pentecostal churches of the Ivory Coast, for example, Newell reports on the elaborate belief in witchcraft and a simultaneous assertion of the ability of the church to transcend it. But some Ivoirians claim that the church is also a haven for the witches, as it asks people to detach themselves from the "corrupting" influence and obligations of kin and rather focus their attention (and money) on the church (and their leaders). The church is thus promoting activities that resemble the self-centered actions of the witch (Newell 2007: 484; Meyer 1999: 170). Pentecostalism is therefore sometimes equated with witchcraft as it encourages exactly the kind of antisocial behavior that Ivoirians understand as witchcraft. As churches recognize the efficacy and reality of witchcraft as under the category of the evil Satan, while also being caught up in the same web of power and money addressed in local cosmologies of witchcraft, witchcraft discourse is let into the heart of the Pentecostal ritual.

Ahamb people's interpretation of the church's role in sorcery matters seems less ambiguous, however. Christianity here already encompasses the society's moral structure by representing an ideology that for most is regarded as good and right. Sorcery, on the other hand, is understood and experienced as a real force that attacks this moral structure as much as it causes sickness and death.

As several chapters of this volume show, Pentecostal movements, of which the revival can be seen as an example, tend to discipline people into a new form of governance or social order. In the context of the long-term moral "crisis" on Ahamb, a spiritual renewal and stricter mode of governance, based on a rerealization of a more pious and morally pure way of living, was more than welcome for many. My impression from being on Ahamb during the revival was that the movement enabled its supporters to "pre-experience" new and alternative futures against the troubled realities of the present. This happened through children and youth that are globally being connected to hope and change. The revival, therefore, constituted a "generative moment" (Kapferer 2015) that gave rise to hope of a new time in which the island society is again united and truly safe. On Ahamb, where Christianity is to such an extent connected to the good, this was understood to be best achieved if everyone was first reconfigured as morally good Christians. As I have tried to describe in this chapter, many islanders understood the revival, as well as its spiritual war, as offering a most fitting opportunity for precisely this task.

Notes

1. As Miranda Forsyth (2006: 1) points out, Melanesians have not traditionally drawn distinctions between the natural and supernatural worlds. Sorcery or witchcraft has therefore not been a separate category of belief, but rather part of a larger whole of beliefs and knowledge about the world.
2. There are many different forms of sorcery, each with its specific technique. They may involve the manipulation of spirits, using plants with magic properties, or adding poisonous plants and toxic substances (such as battery acid) to food or drinks.

3. My research is based on a total of 19 months (7 months in 2010 and 12 months in 2014) of fieldwork in Vanuatu of which most is conducted on Ahamb.
4. The number seven is in Christianity often seen as a foundation of God's word and the number of "completeness" and "divine perfection." The first use of the number in the Bible relates to the creation week in Genesis.
5. During the revival, fire, fog, and clouds often appeared in visions as representations of the Holy Spirit. The Bible has many references to these symbols. Fire appears as a symbol of God's presence in descriptions of God as "a consuming fire" (Hebrews 12:29), the burning bush (Exodus 3:2), Ezekiel's vision (Ezekiel 1:4) and descriptions of how the people of God were led by a pillar of fire at night during the Exodus (Exodus 13:21). The symbolism of the cloud can be related to the Old Testament, where God leads his people with a cloud or appears to them in a cloud (Exodus 16:10).
6. Kava is an intoxicating drink squeezed from the kava plant (*Piper methysticum*). The drink is enjoyed by men in many social contexts.
7. Vanuatu has two legal systems, the state system and the customary legal system. The Malvatumauri Custom law, administered by chiefs, also acknowledges sorcery (Article 3(4)). It is an ongoing question, however, of how to in practice integrate customary law into the state legal system, and what type of consideration there should be of for example procedural and evidential issues in different cases (see Forsyth 2006: 2–3). The prohibition of sorcery in custom law is therefore not more likely to result in a successful prosecution in a state court.

References

Asad, Talal. 1982. "Anthropological Conceptions of Religion. Relections on Geertz." *Man* 18: 237–259.

Blacket, John. 1997. *Fire in the Outback: The Untold Story of the Aboriginal Revival Movement that Began on Elcho Island in 1979*. Sutherland: Albatross/Lion.

Bubandt, Nils. 2014. *The Empty Seashell*. Itacha: Cornell University Press.

Coleman, Simon. 2000. *The Globalization of Charismatic Christianity. Spreading the Gospel of Prosperity*. Cambridge: Cambridge University Press.

Comaroff, Jean, and John L. Comaroff (eds.). 1993. *Modernity and its Malcontents. Ritual and Power in Postcolonial Africa*. Chicago: Chicago University Press.

Comaroff, Jean, and John L. Comaroff. 2002. "Alien-Nation: Zombies, Immigrants, ad Millennial Capitalism." *South Atlantic Quarterly* 101 (4): 779–805.

De Boeck, Filip, and Marie-Françoise Plissart (photographer). 2006. Kinshasa. Tales of the Invisible City. Ghent: Ludion.

De Lannoy, Jean. 2004. "Through the Vail of Darkness. History in South Malekula, Vanuatu." PhD-thesis, School of Anthropology and Museum Ethnography. Linacre College, University of Oxford.

Deacon, Bernard A. 1934. *Malekula—A Vanishing People in the New Hebrides.* Oosterhout: Anthropological Publications.

Evans-Pritchard, Edward Evan. 1937. *Witchcraft, Oracles and Magic among the Azande.* Oxford: The Clarendon Press.

Eves, Richard. 2000. "Sorcery's the Curse. Modernity, Envy and the Flow of Sociality in a Melanesian Society." *The Journal of the Royal Anthropological Institute* 6 (3): 453–468.

Eves, Richard. 2013. Sorcery and Witchcraft in Papua New Guinea: Problems in Definition. *State Society and Governance in Melanesia Program. The Australian National University* 2013/12.

Forsyth, Miranda. 2006. "Sorcery and the Criminal Law in Vanuatu." *Lawasia Journal* 2006: 1–28.

Forsyth, Miranda, and Richard Eves. 2015. "The Problems and Victims of Sorcery and Witchcraft Practices and Beliefs in Melanesia: An Introduction." In *Talking it Through. Responses to Sorcery and Witchcraft Beliefs and Practices in Melanesia*, ed. Miranda Forsyth and Richard Eves, 1–22. Canberra: Australian National University Press.

Geertz, Clifford. 1993. *The Interpretation of Cultures.* London: Fontana Press.

Geschiere, Peter. 1997. *The Modernity of Witchcraft.* Charlottesville: University Press of Virginia.

Gooren, Henri. 2010. "The Pentecostalization of Religion and Society in Latin America." *Exchange* 39 (4): 355–376.

Griffiths, Alison. 1977. *Fire in the Islands: The Acts of the Holy Spirit in the Solomon Islands.* Wheaton: Harold Shaw Publishers.

Haynes, Naomi. 2012. "Pentecostalism and the Morality of Money. Prosperity, Inequality, and Religious Sociality on the Zambian Copperbelt." *Journal of the Royal Anthropological Institute* 18 (1): 123–139.

Hefner, Robert W. 2013. "Introduction. The Unexpected Modern—Gender, Piety, and Politics in the Global Pentecostal Surge." In *Global Pentecostalism in the 21st Century*, (eds). Robert W. Hefner, 1–36. Bloomington: Indiana University Press.

Hollan, Douglas W., and C. Jason Throop, ed. 2011. *The Anthropology of Empathy. Experiencing the Lives of Others in Pacific Societies.* Oxford: Berghahn Books.

Jorgensen, Dan. 2014. Preying on Those Close to Home. Witchcraft Violence in a Papua New Guinea Village. *The Australian Journal of Anthropology* 25 (3): 267–286.

Kapferer, Bruce. 2015. "Introduction. In the Event—toward an Anthropology of Generic Moments." In *In the Event. Toward an Anthropology of Generic Moments*, ed. Lotte Meinert and Bruce Kapferer, 1–28. Oxford: Berghahn Books.

LiPuma, Edward. 2000. *Encompassing Others. The Magic of Modernity in Melanesia*. Ann Arbor: University of Michigan Press.

MacPherson, Crawford. 1962. *The Political Theory of Possessive Individualism: Hobbes to Locke*. Oxford: Oxford University Press.

Martin, Keir. 2013. *The Death of the Big Men and the Rise of the Big Shots. Custom and Conflict in East New Britain*. Oxford: Berghahn Books.

Meyer, Birgit. 1992. ""If You are a Devil, You are a Witch, and if You are a Witch, You are a Devil": The Integration of "Pagan" Ideas into the Conceptual Universe of Ewe Christians in Southeastern Ghana." In *Power and Prayer*, ed. Mart Bax, and Adrianus Koster, 159–182. Amsterdam: VU University Press.

Meyer, Birgit. 1999. *Translating the Devil. Religion and Modernity among the Ewe in Ghana*. Trenton: Africa World Press.

Meyer, Birgit. 2004. "Christianity in Africa. From African Independent to Pentecostal-Charistmatic Churches." *Annual Review of Anthropology* 33: 447–474.

Miller, J. Graham. 1989. *Live: A History of Church Planting in Vanuatu, Book Six*. Port Vila: The Presbyterian Church of Vanuatu.

Moore, Henrietta L., and Todd Sanders (eds.). 2001. *Magical Interpretations, Material Realities: Modernity, Witchcraft and the Occult in Postcolonial Africa*. New York: Routledge.

Newell, Sasha. 2007. "Pentecostal Witchcraft. Neoliberal Posession and Demonic Discourse in Ivoirian Pentecostal Churches." *Journal of Religion in Africa* 37: 461–490.

Onagi, Gairo. 2015. "Foreword. Sorcery- and Witchcraft-related Killings in Papua New Guinea." In *Talking it Through. Responses to Sorcery and Witchcraft Beliefs and PractIces in Melanesia*, ed. Miranda Forsyth and Richard Eves, Vii–x. Canberra: Australian National University Press.

Pfeiffer, James, Kenneth Gimbel-Sherr, and Orvalho Joaquim Augusto. 2007. "The Holy Spirit in the Household. Pentecostalism, Gender, and Neoliberalism in Mozambique." *American Anthropologist* 88 (4): 688–700.

Rio, Knut M. 2002. "The Sorcerer as an Absented Third Person. Formations of Fear and Anger in Vanuatu." In *Beyond Rationalism. Rethinking Magic, Whitchcraft and Sorcery,* edited by Bruce Kapferer, 129–154. Oxford: Berghahn Books.

Rio, Knut M. 2010. "Handling Sorcery in a State System of Law. Magic, Violence and Kastom in Vanuatu." *Oceania* 80 (2): 183–197.

Rio, Knut M. 2011. "Policing the Holy Nation. The State and Righteous Violence in Vanuatu." *Oceania* 81 (1): 51–72.

Robbins, Joel. 2004. *Becoming Sinners: Christianity and Moral Torment in a Papua New Guinea Society*. Berkeley: University of California Press.

Rodman, William. 1993. "Sorcery and Silencing the Chiefs. Words of the Wind in Postindependence Ambae." *Journal of Anthropological Research* 49 (3): 217–235.

Strachan, George. 1984. *Revival—Its Blessings and Battles. An Account of Experiences in the Solomon Islands*. Lawson: Mission Publications of Australia.

Sykes, Karen. 2007. "Interrogating Individuals. The Theory of Possessive Individualism in the Western Pacific." *Anthropological Forum* 17 (3): 213–224.

Taylor, John P. 2015. "Sorcery and the Moral Economy of Agency. An Ethnographic Account." *Oceania* 85 (1): 38–50.

Tonkinson, Robert. 1981. "Sorcery and Social Change in South East Ambrym, Vanuatu." *Social Analysis* 8: 77–88.

Tuzin, Donald. 1997. *The Cassowary's Revenge: The Life and Death of Masculinity in a New Guinea Society*. Chicago: University of Chicago Press.

Author Biography

Tom Bratrud is a Ph.D. research fellow at the Department of Social Anthropology, University of Oslo. He has conducted fieldwork in Vanuatu in Melanesia for a total of 19 months in 2010 and 2014. His research interests include cosmology, social organization and social change, and he is currently preparing his Ph.D. thesis exploring a powerful Christian revival on the Vanuatu island of Ahamb in Malekula.

CHAPTER 10

Learning to Believe in Papua New Guinea

Barbara Andersen

Introduction

If being educated is an important part of being modern—as it is in Papua New Guinea as well as elsewhere in the postcolonial world—then what is the relationship between belief in witchcraft[1] and educational status? Is higher education, which relativizes "local" or "cultural" ontologies in favor of universal models of reality, necessarily a corrective to "traditional" beliefs?

In this chapter, I will consider how higher education is involved in the reproduction of witchcraft in Papua New Guinea today. While conducting ethnographic research on nursing education in a multicultural and co-educational college in the Eastern Highlands (PNG), I observed the social, religious, and epistemological practices through which students learn to make sense of the uncanny, the occult, and the demonic.[2] While many of these students enter nursing education already convinced of the reality of witchcraft, their experiences as students and public servants did not necessarily change this. Media explanations for the persistence of witchcraft in PNG often note the country's low rates of higher educational achievement and scientific literacy, sometimes offering the suggestion that with knowledge of the true, biomedical causes of illness,

B. Andersen (✉)
Massey University, Auckland, New Zealand

K. Rio et al. (eds.), *Pentecostalism and Witchcraft*, Contemporary Anthropology of Religion, DOI 10.1007/978-3-319-56068-7_10

and death, "personalistic" (Foster 1976) explanations for misfortune will drop their hold on the imagination (Ware 2001). Such explanations ignore the wider social context of higher education, and how being an educated person can make one vulnerable to jealousy, resentment, and violence.

Upper secondary schools, colleges, and universities in PNG are important sites for the socialization of an educated elite that understands itself as distinct from the rest of the country's largely rural population—not simply because of the things they learn and the professional roles they eventually take up, but because of how the experience of education disrupts their connection to place, complicating their relationship with the potentially dangerous forces, human, and otherwise, inhabiting rural spaces. I argue that the financial demands of kin and the perceived threat of retributive violence from clients encourage health workers to see themselves as social outsiders. Students narrate their experience of higher education *itself* as being punctuated by occult violence and Satanic trials, which Pentecostal (and other) church social groups give them the power to resist. Pentecostalism, in this analysis, is less significant for its theological or epistemological stances than for the social function it fulfills: providing alternative forms of belonging that can mitigate the dangers of living between rural and "educated" ways of being. These encounters with diverse forms of evil can be productively mapped onto a Pentecostal universalism that demands direct intervention and resistance: an "insistence on taking control of the forces of life and death with universality as a key technique" (Rio et al. this volume, 7).

As other contributors to this volume have suggested, Pentecostal movements take a strongly practical and active stance against evil. They embrace fully the invisible world and take control of it. They describe the different forms of life and creatures that exist in it, and they offer techniques for taming it and making the invisible visible (Rio et al, this volume). Nursing education encourages a similarly practical approach to the various microscopic threats to human wellbeing, teaching health workers to make them visible and knowable to their clients. If Pentecostalism in Melanesia and Africa is "about cleaning, dividing, dissecting, observing and healing" (Rio et al. this volume, 27), then so too is nursing, a profession whose members frequently describe themselves as instruments of God's healing power. "We treat,

God heals" was the motto of the students at the college where I conducted research.

Robbins (2009) suggests that Pentecostalism is unusually "socially productive" when compared with its mainline competitors. He links this productivity to how it teaches the ritualization of everyday life—techniques and linguistic formulae that any believer can draw on in order to shift the interaction frame from profane to sacred. Thus, "whenever any two or more Pentecostals are co-present, they have everything they need to engage in ritual together" (2009: 60). At nursing college, students were rarely alone and were compelled to share bedrooms, textbooks, equipment, and meals with one another. Prayer and fellowship rituals like those described by Robbins helped mediate the tensions that inevitably emerge in such close quarters. I want to suggest that witchcraft talk is another socially productive technology that helps students narrate—and thereby produce—their experiences of being "outside" or "beyond" village life.

Health Education and the Problem of Tradition

In contemporary Papua New Guinea, health workers are trained, formally and informally, to collapse almost all forms of social inequality into a distinction between homogenous "rural" or "village" people and even more vaguely characterized "educated" or "town" people. The cliché that PNG has an "85% rural majority" has become a motto for the Department of Health, whose letterhead trumpets "Service Delivery to the Rural Majority and the Urban Poor." While there are certainly differences between rural and non-rural communities–experienced primarily in terms of unequal access to economic, social, linguistic, and cultural capital—most health workers know quite well that people can move fluidly between rural and urban spaces, lifestyles, and identities. Some of the nursing students I worked with during my research openly embraced their rural roots; and even those with the most elite backgrounds, who were perhaps second or third generation high school graduates, acknowledged their obligations to relatives in the village. However, the idea that there are "*ples* people" and "educated people" with fundamentally different cultures and lifeways is the central ideological construction through which the health sector reproduces its own authority. A course handout written by one of the instructors at the college describes PNG's nurses as the moral guardians of a spiritually and culturally dispossessed majority who, in the wake of colonialism's destruction of their culture, have also lost their conscience: "Something else must then become a real conscience, or the end result will be lawlessness. ... We must think, discuss, and pray as we work to help people understand their world. If we don't the new ideas we bring could be much worse for them than the old ideas we want to help change."

European nurses in Papua New Guinea during the colonial period thought of themselves as challengers of traditional culture, bravely facing down "native law," "fear of taboos," and the supernatural forces that held such a prominent place in indigenous explanations of illness (Kettle 1979). In the decade leading up to Independence in 1975, Papua New Guineans of both sexes were recruited to replace the European sisters and matrons that had previously held the majority of government nursing positions alongside lower ranked male orderlies and medical assistants. The assumption was (and to a certain extent remains) that these educated nationals would serve as cultural brokers between the newly independent state and the rural majority, understanding, if not actually sharing, indigenous etiologies and healing practices. Over 40 years after Independence, nurses in PNG are indeed exceptionally attentive to "customary beliefs," though perhaps not in the ways that national development planners had hoped. Rather, in the contemporary context, with quality health care largely inaccessible outside of urban areas, nurses are taught to see witchcraft, sorcery, and magic as weapons of the weak, with which rural clients can elicit recognition from neglectful others, including the absentee state and its representatives. Classroom lectures emphasized that students should always treat claims of supernatural illness as real and accountable matters: as teachers explained, "Customary belief, it can affect us, so you must entertain it. Otherwise, they will start a big war in the village and they will take the hospital to court." They taught students that the Nursing Council's professional code of ethics *required* acknowledging the reality of *pasin tumbuna* (ancestral practices). Whether the forces behind these beliefs were ontologically real or not, "If you don't respect the beliefs, the talk will come back to get you, it will hold you." Bjørn Bertelsen, in Chap. 2 of this volume, notes that contemporary witchcraft and "traditional" cosmologies share a "profoundly open nature… irreducible to stable sets of socio-cultural values, institutions and practices" (Bertelsen, this volume, 50). For my informants, the openness, and volatility of customary belief were part of what made it so frightening, and its geographical variability—what people believed and practiced could change from one village to the next—made set lessons on "culture" impractical. What students learned, rather, was to be vigilant and open to the possibility of "strange happenings," especially in remote places where they lacked social ties.

For many students at the nursing college, and particularly for the young women who made up approximately 60% of the student population, participation in Pentecostal fellowship groups helped them to manage feelings of dislocation and vulnerability associated with living away from family. They slept in a poorly guarded dormitory that was subject to break-ins by young men from nearby urban settlements and hamlets and faced constant sexual harassment from so-called street boys—unemployed and presumably uneducated urban youths—whenever they dared to step outside the hospital fence. In this context, church fellowship groups allowed them to leave the hospital compound, to enjoy the pleasures of urban life while also preserving their reputation and safety. Student life was organized along denominational lines, with fellowship and prayer groups of *wanlotu*[3] students providing social and spiritual support to their members. Scholars of Pentecostalism in PNG have argued that these new forms of religious membership are cosmopolitan and outward-looking, linking believers to a global community of Christians and helping to assuage feelings of marginalization and humiliation (Jorgensen 2005; Robbins 1998) . Among the aspiring nurses I worked with, participation in fellowship groups granted them new opportunities for social and physical mobility in an otherwise constrained urban setting. They exchanged digital copies of music produced by Australian megachurch Hillsong and bootlegged DVDs of films about the Illuminati, the End Times, and the Mark of the Beast. They attended multiday revival camps with their *wanlotu* classmates and teachers, traveling to other towns and provinces and establishing social ties that spanned the country. A few even had opportunities to travel to Australia with their church groups—a distant dream for most Papua New Guineans, who despite their geographical proximity are rarely able to legally travel to their former colonial metropole without institutional support.

For many Pentecostal students, nursing college was not the first time they had drawn on their church ties for protection against evil. Their reflections on secondary schooling and dormitory life were replete with stories of supernatural happenings and occult practices.[4] Here I will give just a few brief examples, though I recorded accounts of many more. Janet, remembering her high school dorm in Lae, described how the female relatives of students from Samarai Island[5] would secretly fly pots of food to some of her classmates during the night. Janet insisted that she had always refused to partake in these witch-delivered meals, no matter how hungry she was, finding comfort through prayer instead. Here, the "traditional," place-oriented students have an economic advantage over their "believer" classmates, who in rejecting the proceeds of witchcraft suffer hunger and social isolation.

Priscilla, who had attended Port Moresby National High School, recalled an experience of possession in tenth grade which she described as a test of her faith, a consequence of her own adolescent *bikhet* ('bighead' disobedience) opening her up to demonic powers. She did not remember anything about the event, but her friends reported that her body went rigid and shook. "I said all sorts of things (*kainkain toktok*), but I don't remember. My friends called our church pastor and with my fellowship group he came and prayed over me for hours, holding me down on the bed." Finally, the demon was crushed by the power of the Holy Spirit, and Priscilla was free. Another of Priscilla's classmates, a young man, told me had left his original high school, moving to another province, to escape pressure to participate in "the generation system," a secret society that exists in upper secondary schools across the country and whose members are said to practice black magic (Api 2010; Drawii 2008). Others described cult practices as a serious problem in high schools, which they felt was threatening to students with the strong Christian faith.[6] Participation in church fellowship groups gave students the power to resist the supernatural influences inherent in student social life, whether those influences were traditional (flying Samarai witches), Satanic (demonic possession), or ambiguously modern but magical (the generation system) in provenance. Like the Congolese urban spaces described by Katrien Pype, secondary schools and colleges in PNG are "fecund breeding ground[s] for new forms of occult powers," where culturally and denominationally diverse students get their first lessons in managing spiritual conflicts (Pype, this volume, 121).

While these formative school experiences convinced many students that witchcraft was a real and dangerous force in contemporary life, in the context of nursing education it is important to highlight the position of nurses as middle figures mediating between largely autonomous rural communities and a dysfunctional state. Emplacement and locality—characteristics of the *ples lain* or village people who were their primary clients—were sources of deep ambivalence for nursing students. Aspiring to a cosmopolitan, Christian lifestyle and subjectivity, young nurses were torn between a moral imperative to bring development to their people and a desire to disavow traditional village life, with its potentially satanic ancestral practices and place-based politics. Indeed, participation in Pentecostal church groups helped them to transcend the place-linked forms of sociality associated with traditional PNG life. Church groups were proudly multiethnic, providing an alternative to what students sometimes maligned as the "wantok system"—the tendency for members of a particular language/ethnic group to socialize with one another.[7] Instead of feeling morally obliged to prefer the company of their co-ethnics, students embraced the opportunity for fellowship and spiritual intimacy across lines of difference. While they did not reject their places of origin or their kin, they felt keenly the pressure to preferentially give their attention, wages, and care to "relatives in the village."

Pasin: An Undertheorized Concept

The anthropology of Melanesia has since the 1970s explored the discourse of *kastom* (custom, tradition, way of life) and its encoding within legal, medical, political, and religious discourses. Most analyses of *kastom* have focused on its roots in colonial governance practices and its subsequent reinvention within postcolonial or de-colonial nation-building practices (e.g., Akin 2005; Keesing 1982; Thomas 1992). The emphasis in these analyses is the dialectical relationship between the construct of the "white man's ways" associated with imported institutions (law, medicine, the modern state, market economy, and Christianity) and the vernacular, indigenized practices glossed as *kastom*. While a lot of ink has been spilled over *kastom*, much less has been said about *pasin*, which in my own field site is intimately linked with—and often supersedes—the notion of *kastom*.

Pasin is a tricky term in PNG Tok Pisin. Related to the English word "fashion," it can be translated as a way of doing, behavior, manner(s) (as in good or bad manners as well as the manner of doing something), style, or tendency. All of these translations suggest that *pasin* is a key term within meta-pragmatic discourse: *pasin* is a word that describes particular kinds of *doings*, ranging from the habitual to the traditional to the idiosyncratic. In nursing education, *pasin* is used as an umbrella term (or euphemism) for witchcraft, sorcery, and associated "traditional" practices. *Kastom*, as it is often used in Melanesianist anthropology, tends to focus on overt cultural productions—symbolic practices or discourses that are primarily "about" the production of group boundaries and various levels of resistance to colonial or postcolonial forms of domination. *Kastom*, one could say, posits the existence of an Other to whose symbolic and institutional forms it can provide an alternative. *Pasin* is more malleable, and less firmly anchored to ideas of the traditional past. "*Em i pasin bilong mipela*," it's our way of doing things, is the explanation frequently offered by rural people for activities or practices that fall outside cosmopolitan norms.

In his early writings on Melanesian *kastom*, Robert Tonkinson noted that while at a local level people can identify the salient images, practices, and norms of which *kastom* is composed, when abstracted to larger scales, like the scale of the nation-state, "the value given to *kastom* must necessarily be largely ceremonial and symbolic" (Tonkinson 1982: 314). The more wide-reaching the institutions involved, the more capacious and "devoid of specific content" (Tonkinson 1993: 600) the category of *kastom* must be. Culture/*pasin*, as it is taught, learned, and used by nurses in Papua New Guinea, subsumes a seemingly limitless set of prohibitions, norms, relationships, practices, taboos, and beliefs. In this respect, it bears a family resemblance to the colonial understandings of native custom that influenced the dichotomy between "custom" and "law" formalized at Independence. Nursing students spend three years or more learning specific techniques of meaning-making associated with their professional role. The vacant concept of culture/*pasin* that is propagated in students' textbooks and other teaching materials must be filled in through other means: through personal experiences, stories from the invisible archive of oral narrative shared within the profession, and through their collective participation in learning activities. In trying to flesh out what "culture" and "*pasin*" might mean for nurses as they worked within the health system, teachers drew on and elaborated students' personal repertoires of knowledge about witchcraft, sorcery, and magic—sometimes asking them to talk about experiences from their own home communities and life histories, or (more often) volunteering their own stories about occult phenomena. These stories were then reinterpreted through two distinct frames. The first, which we might call the professional frame, interpreted traditional beliefs as forms of knowledge that health workers should approach pragmatically and respectfully, understanding their significance as social "conscience." Because the majority of their clients are "rural," and hence bound to a different worldview, the educated health worker should accommodate their beliefs—provided they are not medically harmful—in order to show respect and avoid retribution. The second frame, invoked most often in situations where personal ethical or moral crises were discussed, was a Christian one. In such scenarios, the culture was powerful and destructive, even demonic, and could put the health worker in mortal danger.

Educational experiences create an epistemological ambivalence. Students and teachers learn that witchcraft and sorcery are real and dangerous, but whether they are personally threatening depends on one's location and relationships—not simply their beliefs. Rural settings, where *pasin* was alive and ubiquitous, were thus especially frightening for students—and this is a real problem when one considers the already fragile state of rural health services. Attracting and retaining qualified young public servants to poorly equipped remote health centers is difficult enough without the spiritual threats of *pasin tumbuna*.

In the section that follows, I describe some of the ways that students interpreted their encounters with *pasin* during a rural health practicum in Ivingoi, Okapa district. During the 3-week stay in this remote community, students' anxiety about the dangers of being there became more explicit. I highlight the narrative practices through which students (and their teachers) collapsed different invisible forces into a generic evil associated with locality.

Dangerous *Pasin*

Yearly rural experience practicums were a welcome break from the everyday grind of classroom and hospital learning. Students looked forward to these trips all year, and the trip to Ivingoi was no exception. However, after our departure from Goroka, the excitement about being in a new place and having the chance to work in a rural health center quickly shifted into anxiety about the dangers of being out in the "bush." Among the peoples of Eastern Highlands Province, residents of Okapa—members of the Fore, Gimi, Kanite, and Keyagana language groups—have a longstanding reputation for being aggressive sorcerers. At the outset of the practicum, a student named Daniel, a North Fore speaker born near the district headquarters at Okapa Station, confessed to his classmates: "We are a really sorcerous people (*mipela ol poisin lain stret*). My grandfather was a *poisin man*.[8] It's our *pasin tumbuna*." Students from neighboring districts knew of the region's reputation and had warned their classmates from other provinces that in Okapa, the *pasin* was still strong.

On our arrival, after a difficult 4-h drive over rough highlands roads, we discovered that we had come at the worst possible time—the funeral of a local leader was underway, and the community was deep in mourning. The funeral, and the anxieties it stirred up, set the tone for the rest of the practicum. Forced to modify their plans to comply with local *pasin*, the students and their tutors spent much of their time in Ivingoi discussing sorcery and witchcraft among themselves. Though students and teachers did not explicitly attribute this particular death to witchcraft (at least not to my knowledge), the mere fact that it was located in rural Okapa district summoned the specter of "*pasin tumbuna*".

Adding further to their anxiety, not long after arriving in Ivingoi students learned about *sik kuru*, the degenerative prion disease responsible for a deadly epidemic in the region during the first half of the twentieth century (Anderson 2008; Lindenbaum 1979; Whitfield 2008). Kuru, which had been spread through ingestion of human remains during mortuary rituals but was and remains emically attributed to sorcery, was a new and frightening concept to students, many of whom were unconvinced by my assurances that the disease had been eradicated. The confluence of these two events—one (the funeral) unfolding in the present, the other (kuru) in the past, but both complexly connected with *pasin*—generated an imaginative space that students filled with talk about their own encounters with dark forces.

From mission compound, we could see blue and black tarps fluttering over the temporary structures erected to accommodate the *haus krai* (mourning house ceremony). The size of the tents testified to the importance of the deceased. Pastor Allan, one of the leaders of the mission community, greeted us on our arrival and explained what was going on. A local big man and coffee entrepreneur had died suddenly, and his body was on its way back from Goroka General Hospital. Tomorrow, after the coffin arrived, it would be received in the church, and then taken into the *haus krai* for several days of weeping before burial. Local customs stipulated that people in mourning should not work, so we would have to wait until a respectful period of time had passed before we began our practicum. It was impossible to say how long that would be.

Pastor Allan said apologetically, "We can't work. You know, it's *pasin bilong ples* (our way of doing things) People wouldn't be happy. But you students can come sing a song at the church tomorrow when we receive the coffin, to show your sorrow." The Seventh-Day Adventist student fellowship group, who were always eager to perform, agreed and hurried off to rehearse. Sisters Wange and Biamo, our tutors, announced that we must respect the community's grief. The death of a leader meant that emotions would be running high at the hamlet level, and we did not want to get caught up in any conflict that might surface. This meant major changes to our plans for the practicum: the tutors decided that instead of going to the *hauslain* (hamlets) to do our community health projects, we were to stay inside the fence of the Open Bible Mission and work only with pastors' families, for our own safety.

The next day, after the ambulance arrived from Goroka with the coffin, students clustered together anxiously as it was carried into the church. Behind the coffin walked a long procession of weeping mourners, their skin, and clothes caked with the region's distinctive orange-red earth. The deceased man's close female relatives, held up by supporters as they climbed the small hill, fell to their knees in grief every few steps. We tried to keep a respectful distance.

Once everyone had crowded into the church building, the Adventist students were called forward by the pastor. Priscilla strummed the acoustic guitar while they performed two gospel songs: the first in English, the second in Tok Pisin. As the final strains of "Yu Yet Yu Bikpela Jisas (Jesus You are the Greatest)" faded away, the pastor returned to the pulpit and gave a sermon on the immortality of the soul:

> Our brother has left this body, and taken another body, it is the spirit and it is inside the presence of God in God's Kingdom. Dying and rising again, Jesus opened that road, he died on the cross and this opened the road to show us, all of us men and women on this earth—those with big names, those who are money men, those who are rubbish men, all sorts of people—all of us on this earth will die, there is only this one road that Jesus opened. Our brother here, he has taken this road. … We can mourn, we can cry, but he is not completely dead. There will be a time when he is resurrected, just as Jesus was resurrected, and we will see and we will rejoice. Amen. This kind of [bodily] death, it is not total death. The spirit of the body that is inside your life, the Bible says this spirit will wake you again and you will be resurrected. You will leave the grave. You will take a new body. And you will become something else, as Jesus did. You will not die completely. The body can die and be finished, but the spirit today is with God in Paradise. … The Bible says here, 'The body we bury, it will rot. The body that is resurrected,

> it cannot rot. The body we bury, it's an evil thing. The body that is resurrected, it is truly good. The body that we bury, it has no strength. The body that rises, it has strength. The body we bury, it is a thing of the earth. The body that rises, it belongs to Heaven. There is the body of the earth, and the body of heaven too.

As the sermon continued, I found myself remembering what I had learned of traditional Fore and Gimi cosmology from reading ethnographies of the region: how human life force (*auma* or *auna*) had to be recycled into the forest to regenerate plants, animals, and people through song, weeping, and proper disposal of the corpse (Gillison 1993; West 2005; Whitfield 2008). The anthropologists who had documented these beliefs emphasized that the period immediately after a death was a dangerous time, when the person's homeless, wandering souls could lash out in anger and harm the living. If a person was not properly mourned, its life force would "cling to the body or hamlet forever" (West 2005: 636), causing sickness and death in the living. The Bible verses attested to a different view of death: the body was now an "evil thing of the earth," its loss a cause for rejoicing, not weeping. But if anything of traditional cosmology had survived Christian conversion, it was the danger associated with the liminal time before burial, and the atmosphere of blame and anger surrounding death.

Teachers' fears about exposing students to village conflicts meant that they would only work with particular types of rural people—those who were pastors, who lived in nuclear family households, and who lived inside the mission compound. It seemed ironic to me: the people who benefited from the labor and teachings of the nursing students were those who already lived in relatively safe circumstances and who had the advantages that came with being inside the mission fence. The hamlet was "too dangerous," its people too overwhelmed by anger and grief, too bound to *pasin*; the families inside the mission fence would be better equipped to *daunim bel* (suppress their anger) and cooperate with us.

While the leader's death created a particularly tense atmosphere, the idea that the *hauslain* was an intrinsically risky place because "the *pasin* is strong" was not unique to this occasion. I had accompanied the first year class a few weeks previously on their rural experience in a different district, and students had been vigilant about not transgressing local customs. Female students had kept a particularly close eye on their clothing, food scraps, and sugarcane skins, emphasizing that all of these could be used to harm them. People drew on both of the two interpretive frames described above: students expressed simultaneously a professional concern about offending their hosts' sensibilities and an individual anxiety about personal spiritual harm.

For these second year students, the death brought back bad memories of their own first year trip to Barowagi in neighboring Simbu Province. Though no one from the college had been near the vehicle at the time, they had been blamed when a local man's car was destroyed, their tutor accused of causing the crash with her "hard words." Ellen told me the story of the car crash during an interview. Their tutor, who had retired by the time of my fieldwork, had lost her temper with the pastor in Barowagi who was hosting them.

> One day she 'pressurized' (*presaraisim*) the pastor. We went there in the dry season. The little creek we bathed in was dry, and we had to go to the big river [far away]. No water to cook either. This [tutor] went and yelled at the pastor and said, 'You people, you don't recognize when a good thing comes inside your community. If you take visitors in, you must provide for all their needs. We want to cook and it's hard. You go get water at the big river and fill up this water tank so we can cook.' She pressurized this pastor and [because] he was a pastor, he had trouble responding in this [same] kind of aggressive way… with anger inside him he borrowed the car from a local man. … And he crashed into an ironwood tree in the coffee garden. The community came and cried, cried, came from the hamlet, came crying, crying. The car's owner cried for his car. They cried for the pastor, he was a village leader. All of them were crying and I was really afraid! Now they came and said, 'Why did you cause our man to go and do this? Why don't you settle down (*stap isi*)?'

The intense emotional displays of the villagers—crying over the car as though it were a person—made students fear retribution. They had been taught in the classroom and on the wards that strong emotions, especially anger and grief, could lead the *ples lain* to act out violently. Another student recalled how the car crash incident had made her despair for the entire enterprise of rural nursing:

> At that time I was afraid. Because we were in a strange place, so it was an experience where I felt there was no hope in life. If anything happened it would still happen to us, and I was on guard. I was on guard but there was no hope, they would come and beat us or… . This kind of thought was

> with us. It was an experience I had that made me a little unwilling (*les*) to do rural experience. 'Why did we go so far away? Why didn't we stay at school and go out nearby, go to a settlement [in Goroka] and give health education? Why did we do this?' I thought.

Thankfully, their principal had quickly arranged to give the community several thousand kina as compensation for the damage to the car, and showed up in person to formally apologize and make restitution. Though the compensation and apology bought students safety for the rest of their time in Barowagi, memories of the incident were still strong, and likely colored students' first impressions of Ivingoi as they adjusted to the change in the program.

Our project plans on hold, we unloaded the trucks and explored the mission compound. Ivingoi Open Bible Church Mission comprised several acres of land dotted with Western-style permanent houses and a large church at the center.[9] The mission, established by American missionaries in 1973, included a Bible College and the Ivingoi Health Sub-Center, where we would later do some clinical work. The story we heard from one of the pastors was that the entire compound had formerly been occupied by white missionaries; however, in 2007, they had localized, leaving national pastors in charge of the mission. The health center's patch of land included quarters for resident nursing staff, a cookhouse for patient use, and an empty building in which the male students would sleep. The female students and tutors were assigned to a two-story house deep inside the mission compound, formerly a guesthouse for visiting missionaries. Because we would not be staying in the hamlets, we had access to the luxuries of an indoor bathroom (the water supply had been disconnected, so we still had to haul buckets up the stairs to bathe or flush the toilet), a gas stove, and a door with a hefty security lock.

That night, we set up our sleeping bags on cushions pilfered from the guesthouse's couches and chairs. It was much more comfortable than the bush material mats and platforms we would have slept on in the hauslain. That plus the deadbolts on the door would allow us to sleep easier. Anxious but excited, the girls and their tutors sat up for hours telling scary stories.

Storytelling is an important part of everyday sociality in PNG, both for entertainment and as a mode of sharing news and gossip. But the stories told in Ivingoi, I argue, performed an even more significant role in this particular context: they contributed to a professional archive of first-person accounts of encounters with dark forces. The context of their to deal with the devil was introduced. Barker (1990) has pointed to the significance of the specific discourse on evil for the Maisin of Papua New Guinea. In the encounter between the missionaries and Maisin ideas of sorcery and witchcraft, a space for a re-articulation of Maisin spiritual ideas opened up. Sorcery and witchcraft became an integral part of Maisin Christianity as a representation of evil, much in the same way as Meyer has described it for Ghana.

Returning to Port Vila, one of the key aspects of life in this Pentecostal context is the new significance of evil. As we have seen, social life in Port Vila neighborhoods rotates around ideas, speculations, worry, and preventive action against very tangible and highly present forces of sorcery and demons. Spending an afternoon in any household in one of these neighborhoods one is quickly drawn into this world: in gossip about the neighbor, in discussions about the cause of someone's sickness, or in getting advice about which path to take to the grocery store, or which grocery store to go to in the first place. There is an overwhelming presence of an idea of spiritual danger, which is just around the corner, ever-present and threatening (see also Strong, this volume, where "witches are everywhere").

In our most recent fieldwork in 2014, we worked with a selection of healers, from different denominations, who all work though the Holy Spirit. Although the idea of evil is present in everyday discourse, the healers are more articulate than most people about the nature of evil. The word "evil" itself is not so current in these narratives. It is more talk of "demons," "devils," "poison," or "dirty," "no good" things. The healers develop specific images that they use in their communication with patients to alert them to danger. One of the healers pointed out that the work as a healer is first and foremost about giving protection to people from the roaming danger, a constant presence and threat of malignant spirits always lurking in the vicinity. She and other healers talk about Port Vila as "a jungle." Therefore healing is not only about helping people who are sick, but also doing work in the neighborhood to prevent the moral conditions that cause sickness, death, and misfortune. Because evil spirits are all around, this is constant work, a nonstop effort. By looking at the ways in which the healers talk about the jungle of bad things and how it operates in this world, it is possible to give a portrait of what evil looks like in this context. Understanding what evil is, is also the key to an understanding of how a social order emerges, and thus, as we will show, what the effects of Pentecostal witchcraft are. If Pentecostalism is telling includes the affective tone surrounding students' rural experience trips, and their feelings of vulnerability in a remote, grieving, and potentially dangerous community. While there is no doubt that students found these stories entertaining, they were also serious business.

Ellen's story concerned a woman from Mt. Hagen, in the news recently after she confessed to drowning her six children. This story had been a regular news item in PNG for over a year. People found her story endlessly fascinating and horrifying, and women's commentary on her case often speculated that she had been driven to the act by an abusive husband. The woman was in jail awaiting sentencing, and one of Ellen's relatives, imprisoned for tribal fighting, had told her about the strange sounds he and other prisoners heard at night.

> The children will come, saying 'mummy, mummy.' All of them will come and say, 'mummy, mummy.' The ghosts of the children she killed. Their spirits are restless, that's the true sign [that she killed them].

Sister Biamo, seated on the floor twisting yarn for net bags, was skeptical—not of the presence of the ghosts, but what their presence signified about the woman's guilt.

> She said that her husband was a drug addict. Maybe the husband forced her to kill them, saying, 'if you tell anyone, you will die.' Whether she killed them or not, we don't know. If the ghosts of the children are crying in the prison, that's because someone has worked a satanic action. They need to investigate. People say they drowned, but why was there no postmortem? They must check their bodies.

Sister Biamo's skepticism and calls for a postmortem did not challenge the possibility of supernatural activity. Indeed, the question at hand seemed not to be whether or not the woman had killed her children—she had confessed as much—but who was ultimately responsible for this act, who the true agent was.

Another story, recounted by Sheena, described her personal experiences as a student at Aiyura Secondary School. Everyone was familiar with the fact that Aiyura had particularly serious problems with the "generation system" (school-based cult organizations) mentioned earlier. Seventh-Day Adventist students at the college showed a particular concern with cult activity and talked about it a lot during our interviews.

Sheena described how a young woman in the class above her had been initiated into the system and was subjected to a sort of spiritual rape by her male classmates—they had, apparently, sent their spirits to have intercourse with her while she slept. On becoming pregnant, she procured an herbal abortion and disposed of the fetus in the school toilets. The baby's ghost, Sheena said, would slam doors in the dormitory and afflict girls with seizures and fainting fits.

One scary story led to another, and another. After giving the disclaimer, "I go to church and I don't believe in *sanguma* (witchcraft), but I will tell you this one story," Sister Wange told us about the time she discovered that her brother's death had indeed been caused by a *sanguma*, a woman whose guilt was attested to by her "unusual *pasin*" after the death. When the tutor's story was done, Tina, who had grown up on the border between Okapa and Lufa districts, said in a hushed voice, "These people here, in Ivingoi and nearby, they are the worst ones." If the storytelling had started out as entertainment, things had now become very serious: Tina told us about things she and her relatives had witnessed that attested to the sorcerous *pasin* of the Fore. As I drifted off to sleep, well after midnight, the stories were still flowing.

These stories of strange and supernatural violence were part of the atmosphere of anxiety that students struggled to contain during their stay. When the ban on work ended and students began their clinical practicum hours at the health sub-centre, they were alert to signs of "strangeness" in their clients. The odd young man staring fixedly at them as they worked? He could be mentally disabled or high on marijuana; but he could also be something else. A parturient woman from a distant hamlet laboring for hours with no improvement to her cervical dilation? After nearly a day of stalled labor, a male student asked her if there were any problems in her village—an allusion to witchcraft—that might be keeping her baby from being born. Even the revelations about *kuru* raised questions about the resilience of *pasin tumbuna*.

When an older man in the village who had been a fieldworker for *kuru* scientists told a student about the disease, she had been so shocked that she drove back to Goroka over the weekend, went on the internet, and printed out copies of the Wikipedia page on the disease for her classmates to read. Since I was the only person from the college who had heard of *kuru* before the field trip, I was asked to explain certain things about it; namely, were they at any risk? Might there be prions in the soil, in the local animals and plants, or in the latrines? Had the Fore really stopped eating their dead? I explained that the disease had been carefully studied and declared extinct. Fore cannibalism, I told students, was *pasin bilong bipo tumbuna taim*—a thing of the ancestral past—and had been decidedly abandoned. Some claimed to be unconvinced. If knowledge of the disease and of cannibalism had been kept secret for so long, there were probably other secrets to which I was not party. They knew the people of Okapa district were a *poisin lain*—their Okapan classmates had told them so!

Moreover, there was generally a sort of temporal slippage in remote places that meant you could never be sure that ancestral *pasin* was truly in the past. Because in many parts of PNG the practices classified as "pasin" or "kastom" were abandoned in performative ways at the time of conversion, they have a uniquely problematic status for Christians. Ancestral practices were not classified as ancestral because they were irrevocably in the past, left behind by the impersonal engine of historical progress, but because people had made a choice to repudiate them and become Christians. The Fore living inside the Open Bible Mission fence were probably "safe," but the ones outside the fence in the hamlets might still be secretly conducting evil *pasin*. As Robbins notes, Pentecostal millenarianism posits "the possibility that time with its beginnings and endings may not be continuous, that the present may not lead into the future in a predictable way" (Robbins 2001: 530). Just as one could choose to convert, one could also backslide, or "go backwards," a condition that many Papua New Guinean Christians saw all around them (see Strong, this volume). If humans were by nature both secretive and sinful, then it stood to reason that the Fore might still be up to all sorts of dangerous things.

Conclusion

Here, we can see how social and epistemological practices in higher education, informed by a Pentecostal worldview and social infrastructure, encourage the reproduction of knowledge about witchcraft and sorcery—indeed, the production of *new* knowledge, with new framings and implications. By creating associations and semantic linkages between different kinds of unusual death and illness associated with remote places, students give meaning to the different kinds of danger that they encounter in their personal and professional lives. Triggered by the presence of death in a strange village, and concerned about their own safety, students processed their fears by telling stories about first-person encounters with evil forces. Their scientific and biomedical education does not eliminate talk about witchcraft and sorcery nor relegate it solely to the status of customary belief, something that a modern person must discard in order to manifest an educated, Christian self. Rather, talk about invisible evil may be one of the socially productive technologies that Robbins describes. It allows the ethnically and regionally diverse educated classes in Papua New Guinea to analyze relations between village and town people and to make sense of their own feelings of marginality. Moreover, because they are responsible for mediating between the state and the population, they must be alert to threats of all kinds from disenfranchised people, including threats of spiritual violence. Their debates about spiritual violence, cannibalism, and the persistence of *pasin* out in the bush must be understood within a broader context in which Christianity and professional and class identity are intertwined.

Higher education encourages skepticism about and careful analysis of "traditional beliefs"; however, it also proliferates explanations for death and misfortune that link rural spaces and people to dangerous forces. In the case of health workers struggling to deliver services to underserved communities on the margins of the state, educational experiences amplify their own feelings of vulnerability. Some have been made ill by envious relatives or community members who resent the upward mobility granted them by their schooling (the Christmas holiday, when many secondary, college, and university students return to their natal villages, can be a particularly risky time for educated Papua New Guineans).

What then of Pentecostalism, or Christianity more broadly? Clearly, its role in affirming or challenging witchcraft beliefs is complicated in this instance since health workers learn multiple frames for interpreting misfortune. However, it is important to highlight the alternative geographies of belonging to which Pentecostal churches and fellowship groups give students to access. These support networks give them resources—social, epistemological, and spiritual—for resisting the dangers that they encounter during their educational and professional journeys. While the dangers come from many different quarters, their professional position encourages them to identify village life and village social organization as particularly personally threatening. Pentecostal movements and churches, like colleges and universities, are cosmopolitan spaces, offering individuals new possibilities for connection with a wider world of believers.

Notes

1. My usage of the categories of witchcraft and sorcery in this paper is inconsistent, largely because my informants seldom used these words, preferring terms like *pasin tumbuna* (ancestral practices), *sanguma*, *poisin*, or *bilak pawa*. As Haley (2008: 270 n11) points out, the Evans-Pritchardian distinction between witchcraft and sorcery, while useful in some Papua New Guinean contexts, is not recognized by the law or in media reports, which tend to use "witchcraft," "sorcery," and "magic" interchangeably. The legal definition of sorcery in the 1971 Sorcery Act (repealed 2013), for example, "includes (without limiting the generality of that expression) what is known, in various languages and parts of the country, as witchcraft, magic, enchantment, *puri puri*, *mura mura dikana*, *vada*, *mea mea*, *sanguma* or *malir*a, whether or not connected with or related to the supernatural" (Independent State of Papua New Guinea 1971: 1(1)).
2. This research was conducted between December 2010 and June 2012 in Goroka, Eastern Highlands Province, as part of my doctoral project, "Nursing Education and Gendered Dilemmas in the Papua New Guinea Highlands," funded by the National Science Foundation and the Wenner-Gren Foundation for Anthropological Research.
3. *Wanlotu*, "one church," is a Tok Pisin word indicating membership in the same denominational group and is analogous to *wantok* ("one language group").
4. Because there are so few upper secondary schools in PNG, most students are boarders.
5. Samarai Island is in Milne Bay Province, while Lae is the capital of Morobe Province. As the crow (or the witch) flies, the two places are about 550 km apart.
6. I was told that some schools had closed their dormitories permanently due to cult activity.
7. The so-called "wantok system" is often equated with corruption and nepotism in the context of public institutions.
8. *Poisin man* is one term for sorcerer.
9. Open Bible Church's website states that the church is "a charter member of the National Association of Evangelicals, the Pentecostal/Charismatic Churches of North America, and the Pentecostal World Conference." https://www.openbible.org/about_discover.aspx. Accessed April 10, 2014.

References

Akin, David. 2005. 'Kastom as Hegemony? A Response to Babadzan.' *Anthropological Theory* 5 (1): 75–83.

Anderson, Warwick. 2008. *The Collectors of Lost Souls: Turning Kuru Scientists into whitemen*. Baltimore: Johns Hopkins University.

Api, Unia. 2010. 'Occult 'Sindaun' in a Papua New Guinea Secondary School.' *Catalyst* 40 (1): 65–84.

Drawii, Judy Tatu. 2008. *Cult On The Rise? Students Perspective on Cult Issues In Secondary and National High Schools In Papua New Guinea*. Thesis, University of Waikato.

Foster, George M. 1976. 'Disease Etiologies in Non-Western Medical Systems.' *American Anthropologist* 78 (4): 773–782.

Gillison, Gillian. 1993. *Between Culture and Fantasy: A New Guinea Highlands Mythology*. Chicago: University of Chicago Press.

Haley, Nicole. 2008. 'When There's No Accessing Basic Health Care: Local Politics and Responses to HIV/AIDS at Lake Kopiago, Papua New Guinea.' In *Making Sense of AIDS: Culture, Sexuality, and Power in Melanesia*, ed. L. Butt and R. Eves, pp. 24–40. Honolulu, HI: University of Hawaii.

Independent State of Papua New Guinea. 1971. Sorcery Act. Port Moresby.

Jorgensen, Dan. 2005. 'Third Wave Evangelism And The Politics Of The Global In Papua New Guinea: Spiritual Warfare And The Recreation Of Place In Telefolmin.' *Oceania* 75 (4): 444–461.

Keesing, Roger. 1982. 'Kastom in Melanesia: An Overview.' *Mankind* 13 (4): 297–301.

Kettle, Ellen. 1979. *That They Might Live*. Sydney: FP Leonard.

Lindenbaum, Shirley. 1979. *Kuru Sorcery: Disease and Danger in the New Guinea Highlands*. Palo Alto: Mayfield Press.

Robbins, Joel. 1998. 'On Reading 'World News': Apocalyptic Narrative, Negative Nationalism, and Transnational Christianity in a Papua New Guinea Society'. *Social Analysis* 42 (2): 103–130.

Robbins, Joel. 2001. "Secrecy and the sense of an ending: Narrative, time, and everyday millenarianism in Papua New Guinea and in Christian fundamentalism." *Comparative Studies in Society and History* 43 (03): 525–551.

Robbins, Joel. 2009. "Pentecostal networks and the spirit of globalization: On the social productivity of ritual forms." *Social Analysis* 53 (1): 55–66.

Thomas, Nicholas. 1992. 'The Inversion of Tradition.' *American Ethnologist* 19 (2): 213–232.

Tonkinson, Robert. 1982. 'National Identity and the Problem of Kastom in Vanuatu.' *Mankind* 13 (4): 306–315.

Tonkinson, Robert. 1993. 'Understanding 'Tradition'—Ten Years On.' *Anthropological Forum: A Journal of Social Anthropology and Comparative Sociology* 6 (4): 597–606.

Ware, Michael. 2001. Season of the Witch, Time Pacific. May 7, 2001. Available online: http://www.time.com/time/pacific/magazine/20010507/witch.html.

West, Paige. 2005. 'Translation, Value, and Space: Theorizing an Ethnographic and Engaged Environmental Anthropology.' *American Anthropologist* 107 (4): 632–642.

Whitfield, Jerome, et al. 2008. ' Mortuary rites of the South Fore and kuru.' *Philosophical Transactions of the Royal Society B: Biological Sciences* 363 (1510): 3721–3724.

Author Biography

Barbara Andersen is Lecturer in Social Anthropology in the School of People, Environment, and Planning at Massey University, Auckland, New Zealand. Her research focuses on health care, development, and social change in the Pacific with a focus on Melanesia. She is interested more broadly in issues around inequality, space, gender, and power. Her current research examines the relationship between housing and security in Papua New Guinea.

CHAPTER 11

Witchcraft Simplex: Experiences of Globalized Pentecostalism in Central and Northwestern Tanzania

Koen Stroeken

Introduction

One Sunday in September 2014 in a central Tanzanian town, I attended a Pentecostal service in the church of the Assemblies of God. After a first placid hour of thanksgiving when devotees could publicly share in Swahili their personal experiences of divine intervention and subsequent salvation, a guest pastor came on stage to preach. Before him sat a mixed crowd of inhabitants from poverty-stricken Morogoro region, the few better-off occupying the first rows on his right hand. What could the flashy-dressed Black Canadian have in common with this audience, I wondered. The answer came after 1 hour and a half of preaching in English with simultaneous translation in Swahili, punctuated with the collective choir singing. An entranced audience of 500 hung at his lips as his initial dwelling on the verse Isaiah 6:1–8 'In the year Uzziah died I saw also the Lord sitting on a throne' grew into a series of questions and answers in a scholarly fashion. The dialogue eventually intensified into a commandment exhorting each to become an individual and

K. Stroeken (✉)
University of Ghent, Ghent, Belgium

K. Rio et al. (eds.), *Pentecostalism and Witchcraft*, Contemporary Anthropology of Religion, DOI 10.1007/978-3-319-56068-7_11

take a decision, following the words of the subsequent verse: 'here am *I*. Send *me*!'. 'Yes!' all screamed in reply to his question whether 'you will face the obstacle in your life' and consider 'every trouble as a blessing'; whether 'you will pull God's glory into your spirit', which will fill 'your business, your finances, and your family'—in this order of importance—because: 'WHAT YOU START, GOD WILL FINISH'.

The capital letters flickering on a large screen came at the climax. Everyone visibly agreed that something special had taken place. The pastor called it God-work. Repeating his soulful after-words 'I got a feeling everything's gonna be alright,' which died out in a whisper, he left the stage. The sensory experience was intended to affect each participant. Some cried and a few started to speak in tongues. All cheered. What was initially God's glory had finally become 'Jesus touching your lips, your money, your body, your face, your church, your family.' All participants had as individual bodies merged into a relationship with the personified divinity known as Jesus. Their salvation had led them to enter into the Body of Christ. While imploring the ecstatic audience to now take that first step, and mimicking the physical act repeatedly, the pastor reassured that 'God is obligated to finish the work.'

The work God will finish refers to prosperity, for which the higher salvation known as baptism with the Holy Spirit is a metaphor. But the obligation not even God Himself can escape, stems from the belief in a singular cosmology obeying a universal law. This law boils down to 'return on investment.' We are witnessing a new phase in Pentecostalism, whereby African ripples join a global wave. As noted in the literature review by Birgit Meyer (2004) , the study field of Pentecostalism has been a forerunner in illustrating the intercultural exchange and entanglements between the local and the global in postcolonial Africa, particularly, how African churches indigenized Christianity (Fernandez 1982), without opposing themselves to their 'traditional' forms of religion (Comaroff and Comaroff 1991; Ranger 1986). After decolonization in the 1970s and increasingly so with the intensified globalization of the 1990s, those Indigenous African Churches gave way to a new seminal breed, the Charismatic Pentecostal churches. It, however, meant an ideological inversion regarding capitalism, from resistance to adherence (Meyer 2004: 454). This chapter explores how the adherence in cultural terms became experiential in the current globalized phase of Pentecostalism; how it changed people's experience of the world, particularly of witches and spirits. We cannot ignore the miracle happening daily, of American TV channels as well as a visiting pastor from Canada managing to speak the language of the Morogoro born-again.

The point of view, the reader should know, is that of an Africanist who has mainly worked on witchcraft and with healers, not faith healers. In a first section, I describe the social process of 'nuclearization,' which structurally established a sense of bewitchment that prepared Tanzanians for Pentecostalism. The subsequent sections discuss the epistemological differences with Catholicism and with local traditions of healing as experienced by the healers themselves. The final part applies the concept of simplex relations to the universalism of Pentecostal spirits, whose aversion to parallel cosmologies and whose minimal biographies seem to befit the local process of globalization.

The Pentecostalist Meaning of Witchcraft in Mono-centric Communities

Every ethnographer speaking a local language with an educated Tanzanian, such as a teacher or civil servant, has had the pleasure of being looked upon in sincere sympathy and admiration.[1] Knowledge of local concepts, especially in the field of witchcraft, will be met with more praise and probably laughter and high fives. But it would be a mistake to assume that one's interlocutor is thus attesting to pride over ethnicity. Soon dawns upon the ethnographer the interlocutor's disinterest in reflecting on the local concept. The relationship of Tanzanian and other African elites with their ancestral traditions is ambivalent, fraught with colonial stereotypes as well as with a history of selective recuperation after national independence (Mudimbe 1988). Western Christian education erodes the cultural rootedness of certain concepts, reducing their experiential depth in relation to the rest of the cosmology. Among educated Tanzanians references to medicinal traditions as a rule call for ridicule or exaggeration.

Pentecostal adherents differ from other Christians in that their services take traditional belief seriously, albeit for representing the main evil in their all-out attack on 'witchcraft'.[2] The Pentecostal attack can count on the sympathy of educated elites, who have for a long time wanted to see an end to their compatriots' belief in magic and witchcraft (Geschiere 2013). A remarkable conflation occurs of combating witches and combating the belief in witchcraft, as if beliefs, cosmologies and the frame in which one experiences the world would not make a difference. By proclaiming to exterminate witchcraft, Pentecostal churches do not eradicate the belief in witchcraft. They only reinforce it. Witchcraft's reality becomes stronger with every witch they claim to have converted. A motif staged during church services is the redemptive testimony of new adherents. Ideally, the sins confessed are those of a witch, like in the BBC documentary on a Ugandan pastor claiming to have performed over sixty child sacrifices as a healer before he became a Christian.[3] The conflation of witch and healer is another telling piece of the puzzle. Charismatic Christians treat these figures as interchangeable because they as Christians do not experience the opposition and transition between the two frames, namely between the magical intervention of the healer and the invisible hold of the witch over the victim. In traditional Bantu healing, the witch stands for a disempowering lethal claim rooted in kinship and community ethics, until rituals and initiation conjure up the empowering frame of magic, which renders the curse manageable. After divination has revealed the identity of the witch, the impinging absolute Other of witchcraft becomes an everyday participant in the arena of magical warfare. In the Pentecostalist understanding, however, there is one world, God's kingdom. In such understanding of religion, the emphasis is on the literal content of beliefs and not on the frame of experience, which can generate diverse beliefs. For witchcraft to become culturally globalized and cross-culturally comprehensible, its meaning had to stop shifting between experiential frames. An analogy can be drawn with the early modern prosecutors simplifying the identity of the accused during Europe's witchcraze. The witches supposedly represented the medieval traditions the elites wanted to ban with the slogan 'no charity, no tradition, no solidarity' (MacFarlane 1999). The leveling urge imputed to the witch illustrates the epistemological irritation felt by upcoming capitalist elites.

As we could observe in the mid-1990s, a division grew in Tanzanian rural communities undergoing urbanization and the neoliberal effects of the government's implementation of the IMF's structural adjustment policy. In a period of maximum two generations, educated Christianized groups speaking the national language of Swahili had culturally uprooted themselves to together form a closed informal network, a margin within the villages and nascent towns to live out their modernity, with small benefits such as privileged access to government services offered by their acquaintances. Many of them had formed the vanguard of Nyerere's Ujamaa villagization policy in the late 1970s, which forced peasant communities to centralize around the public services of dispensary, school and cotton store. After a few years, the farmers returned to their old villages (*mahame*) because the artificially created centers had caused land erosion among agro-pastoralists as well as conflicts to fester in the community, culminating in a boom of witchcraft accusations (cf. Hyden 1980). Centralization meant the imposition of a mono-centric residence pattern and social dynamic on farmers who lived in fenced extended compounds at some distance from each other and who were used to dealing cautiously with proximity, in greeting, meeting, herding, and all forms of social exchange. They were used to a polycentric system, integrating in the fairly autonomous 'center' of the homestead (*kaya*) their economy (as farmers and herders), their decision-making (*ha shikome*, at the hearth outside), worship (at the ancestral altars), education (under the tree), and family. Among those multiple centers in each valley, a consensus had to be found for anything collective to happen. A small survey conducted by me in 1997 among 110 farmers in villages where a development project named MRHP cooperated with credit groups indicated the growing gap. Most of the project's participants preferred to live in the Ujamaa centers, in a nuclear family and nuclear house without the hygienic risks of herding. They advocated independence (*kujitegemea*) from clan expectations, freedom from clan solidarity. For help they counted on loans from the anonymous outside world, consisting of NGOs, banks and government administration. They identified with the outside world, which left them marginalized in the rural community. In their eyes, they occupied a structural position of intrusion. They tragically were the ones feeling most bewitched, obsessed with the possibility of witchcraft surrounding them, as later appeared in the religion many of them embraced. Pentecostalism has been their solution to keep on living in the village, for they had bereft themselves of the soothing practices of social exchange of polycentric society (including non-kin alliance via bridewealth, initiatory memberships, cattle-exchange, and divination). The Tanzanian version of modernity seems to have been this nuclearization of the lifeworld: an external orientation combined with a shrunk network nearby, expecting witchcraft from the surrounding community. Many of those in search of social promotion have emigrated to town and city where social expectations are less pronounced.[4] Those staying joined or created a margin for modernity, such as the credit group and the Charismatic church. The price for their courageous act was a cultural invention much less syncretistic than one could have hoped for. They denied themselves the experiential depth of local cosmologies inadvertently built up over centuries of cultural trial and error in polycentric society.

Of particular relevance to our argument is the structural state of Pentecostals feeling intruded upon in their own society. The other members of the community are absolute outsiders: 'outsiders' because they do not see the sin that the converted see; 'absolute' because they will not be relative outsiders, to relate to, exchange with or learn from. The healing of the Pentecostals differs from that of patients going to healers to be delivered of a curse, to thus end their bewitchment and return to ordinary life. In Pentecostalism, the bewitchment is constant, and with it the desire to detect evil, at a weekly, even daily basis, invoking, and repelling it in church, always remembering.

Exorcisms Compared

The above divergence creating profound misunderstandings within rural communities struck me during the first year of fieldwork on Sukuma healing rituals south of Lake Victoria. By coincidence, I had witnessed an experiment, the significance of which I could not have gathered at the time. It was 1995, still before the big wave of literature on Pentecostalism in Africa. Two Pentecostal pastors had come to a healer's compound where I stayed. In my presence they persuaded the healer named Solile, famous for his treatment of *mayabu* mental illness, to let them perform an exorcism on one of his patients in order to prove that the Word of God was stronger than any of Solile's heathen methods. Sudden healing would indeed be a miracle in the eyes of the Sukuma healer, who is used to long-term treatments including ingestion of soothing concoctions, medicinal massages twice daily and regular monitoring of spirit support through divination so that after about 2 years the patients suffering from *mayabu* bewitchment, with symptoms of depression, can return home. The exorcist scene led by the pastors and witnessed by me from a distance should be summed up in the following terms: loud and atrocious admonishments of the patient, repeated references to the devil, panic in the patient leading to a fit, and a bewildered ethnographer barely 3 months in the field, now harshly confronted with the ambivalence of participatory observation. Just before leaving for Solile's place, I had been visited at home by a Tanzanian civil servant and a member of the Seventh day Adventist's church warning me about going to the village where 'the thing called witchcraft' reigns. Unlike his friends in town, the civil servant said, he took the danger seriously. But his experience of witchcraft could not be multilayered like that of Solile's patients.

Wherever 'magic' works in the world, the reason is a sense of differential relatedness. As in the case of Sukuma farmers, the power of *bugota*, medicine, depends on the relatedness or 'kinship' of ingredients with other meaningful parts of culture (Stroeken 2010; see also Myhre, this volume). The ingredients with much symbolical significance are called 'entrances' (*shingila*). The relatedness, among others in the form of metonymic resemblance between ingredient and goal of the remedy, can also be experienced by the user, who as a parent or novice prepares the concoction of ingredients. In the healer's compound, the ethnographer observes the distinction between bewitchment, which is a form of anxiety engendering ideas of persecution, and the making of magic, which is a productive act with therapeutic benefits ending the anxiety. The therapeutic effect of magic depends on cosmological particulars such as symbols that cannot easily be translated across cultures. The globalization of the witchcraft concept thus comes at a price. Subtle shifts of experiential frames get lost. The subsuming of very distinct medicinal, spiritual, and witchcraft-related experiences under 'the occult' by anthropologists and historians alike, criticized in a polemical paper by Ranger (2007), exemplifies the experiential conflation, say 'atrophy,' that comes with the globalization of cultural concepts.

Pentecostal pastors have the same tendency of treating magic, bewitchment, divination, ritual sacrifice, and spirit possession as belonging to one domain, that of 'the occult,' or 'the devil.' Among Sukuma-speaking farmers, however, each of these practices evokes its own type or frame of experience, whereby shifts between them are felt by the participants, a feeling that lies at the very core of Bantu spirit healing and is fostered in life through initiation (cf. Devisch 1993). The different practices magnify experiential frames that cover the wide palette of everyday relations between self and outside world. Exchanging with the world (via magic), feeling intruded by it (in bewitchment), identifying its hidden causes (through divination), expelling the intruder (via exorcism), harnessing the power of externality (through sacrifice) or being in synchrony with the outside world (in spirit possession) are basic structures that accompany experiences in all domains of life, not just religion. Local terms denote existential distinctions such as the one made by Ingold (2000) between a scientist's building perspective and a hunter's dwelling perspective. Yet, these frames appear together in some societies, in all their oppositionality, the first frame linking bewitchment to the logic of commoditization, the second frame connecting magic to economic exchange blessed by the community. The experiential frame crosscuts the domains that our Western education segregates as economic, political, social, religious, and so on. The cultural plurality of these domains blinds us to the fact that in our society the various experiences they produce belong to the same frame. If our economy is capitalistic, so are our religion and politics, because other frames of experience are institutionally discouraged in modern Western society.[5] Therefore, Sukuma healers with their plural frames have been losing terrain fast.

Solile's reaction of scorn not only after but also before their session of 'spiritual healing' was telling. He wanted to give it a chance but never really believed in their miracle cure. The exhorting cries of the exorcists while brandishing the Bible contrasted sharply with the long-term methodic approach of Sukuma medicinal traditions. Pentecostal healing is rather impervious to the both cosmologically and biographically rooted meanings obtained by the patient from the therapeutic rituals, divinatory sessions, historically 'thick' medicines, collective routines of application to the body, and the regularly monitored communications as well as strategic dealings with the spirits. All these practices form a meaningful whole interrelating therapy with the rest of life, which lacked in the Pentecostal attack launched against the devil by those visiting pastors. In the pastors' experience the witch is not biographically specified, a significant other in the victim's life history. The witch remains like all demons that could possess the speaker-in-tongues, an absolute Other.

Catholic Versus Charismatic Cosmologies in Congo and Tanzania

The othering does not mean a choice for simplicity, but rather seems an effective way of dealing with the complexities of life in Africa today. It is thus that I interpret the following discussions on the cultural attraction of Pentecostalism in Lubumbashi, the second largest Congolese city, near the Zambian border. A taxi-driver, whose job exemplifies global–local entanglements for his income depends on the fluctuation of the dollar rate, the oil price, and clients' participation in the urban economy, explained to me why he and his wife have become Pentecostals while their children stay Catholic and go to Catholic schools. He gave me three reasons. The first concerns adults only: sin, which explains the generational division of religious adherence. 'Treating sins is an individual thing for Catholics, to be settled between you and God, whereas among Pentecostalists it is general.' (*Traiter les péchés, c'est individuel pour les catholiques, à régler entre toi et le bon Dieu, tandis que chez les pentecôtistes c'est général*). During the sermon everybody in the audience feels saved. The collectivity of the ceremony reminds of the purification rites with white kaolin among Chokwe and Lamba groups outside Lubumbashi. The collective dimension of Pentecostal services narrows the distance with the precolonial religious past, which Catholic practices precisely tended to magnify. In further contrast, since diviners and healers have to work in hiding in most African countries due to legal prohibition on their trade, their sessions have become private, losing significance at the level of collective release.

The second and third element my interlocutor mentioned in one go: deliverance with the Holy Spirit (*Délivrance avec le saint Esprit*) comprising 'deliverance from demonic possession' (*possession demoniaque*) 'or from family ties' (*liens familiaux*). The latter is a euphemism for bewitchment, typically in a context of unmet expectations or imputed jealousy, calling for black magic or poisoning. Healers without the faith are said to take advantage of those situations to falsely accuse and make money. Then again, Catholic services do not acknowledge, let alone solve these preoccupations of their adherents. Nothing is really 'felt' in those services. But the differences are 'small', he added.

The legacy of Catholicism in these parts of Africa is important to comprehend current local religiosity, as illustrated by discussions between two *Lushois* intellectuals, one still a Catholic, the other a born-again. Both agreed on the Pentecostalist attraction axed on individual sensory experience and group solidarity, *le concret et la solidarité*. The convert takes the gospel literally (*L'évangile est vrai, pas du symbolisme*) in explicit comparison with the Catholic ambiguity about the Bible, a presumably characteristic two-facedness, of saying one thing and doing another. Pentecostal clarity is what the taxi-driver appreciated as well. Everything that is customary is forbidden (*Tout ce qui est coutume est interdit*). He explicitly referred to the sacrifice he had heard a Chokwe chief talk about in my presence. Such is the paradox. The ceremonial deliverance, led by a Canadian messenger of neoliberalism, has the collective and purifying effect in continuity with long-standing local traditions. Only now, what the participants have to be purified of is those traditions.

In the mid-1990s in northwest Tanzania, the epistemological gap was clear between the Catholic priest's idealized sermon and the churchgoers' actual beliefs. It led to a diversity of Christian expressions (Wijsen 1993). Missionaries tried to 'enculturate' the gospel, known as *utamudinisho* in Swahili, to adapt it to local cultures. It seemed a logical strategy of evangelizing. In Pentecostal services in Tanzania, no attempt of enculturation is made. How then to explain its success? How could it captivate so many in its latest version which blatantly ignores the fact of pluralism, of Tanzanians having learned to negotiate between the parallel and sometimes conflicting truths of colonial government, of Islam or missionary Christianity, of precolonial traditions, of new healing cults and religious movements, of national neo-traditionalism, and of postcolonial trends of neoliberalism? The plurality is precisely what the Pentecostalist message resolves. Just as the precolonial interest in the invisible facilitated people's capacity of living with and in many worlds, and allowed Westerners to bring the gospel and erect churches where ideas about a transcendent realm could be spread, the Pentecostalist mass-conversion is made possible by Tanzanians' current immersion in cultural complexity, negatively portrayed in media and popular culture as benefiting the heathen masters of 'cunning,' *bongo*. At the same time, Pentecostalism addresses at the grassroots of society what Catholicism avoided because of the magical connotation: the this-worldly aspect of religion, or 'historiopraxis', the *making of* instead of just invoking history (Coleman 2011). The religion postulates the continuity between the individual believer and God in this life. It mysteriously overshadows the radical contrast with the mentioned plurality of worlds. Whereas Catholicism institutes a dualism of sacred and profane worlds, the Pentecostal message acknowledges only one world. In that world, the believers treat as satanic the many forces that once guided their or their ascendants' lives.

Therefore, it is not surprising to note that today Pentecostalists are unlikely to visit a healer's compound. As I could observe in two field visits in the frame of university exchange in 2012, the researchers belonging to a Charismatic church, who formed the majority, refused to enter the compounds of traditional healers, despite their specialization in community outreach. Unlike 20 years ago, healers are no longer competitors on the same market of belief. The Pentecostalist cosmology trails in its shadow a meta-cosmology, a thinking about cosmologies that excludes certain cosmologies as demonic. Monotheistic religions have an exclusive meta-cosmology that can be contrasted with the inclusive, open truth-claim of magical practices. All over Africa, Christian missions have attempted the ploy of subverting the local belief in ancestral spirits by presenting the latter as demons and using the word *shetani*, devils, for them in sermons and Bible translations (cf. Comaroff and Comaroff 1991). The ploy never prevented Tanzanians from pairing various Christian, Islamic, and other religious expressions. The multiplicity proper to their country is embodied by the Swahili concept of *dawa*, medicine, which has an inclusive cosmology, allowing for multiple frames of experience, and therefore encountered even in hospitals in the facilitating of traditional medicine by the nurses (Langwick 2008). It is indicative about Pentecostalism that magical practice is its ultimate enemy, the destruction of the amulets and fetishes by the pastor a famous sight on TV. There are socio-structural factors that bred the globally financed and increasingly homogenized political ideology of Pentecostalism 3.0. However, in this paper, I am looking for the answer at the experiential level. Pentecostalism in Tanzania shares with magic a this-worldly aspect, the continuity between life and spirit: your belief can make your wish come true. That should make them competitors. Magic loses the fight where its experiential rootedness in the cosmology vanishes. That is the case for customers no longer experiencing the shift between plural frames, from the disempowerment of bewitchment to the empowerment of magic. Thus Pentecostalism can make magic obsolete. Magic can only threaten Pentecostalism in its existence if magic is understood in its local (Sukuma) sense, as containing *shingila*, an ingredient expressing hope (or 'subjunctivity,' cf. Reynolds-Whyte 1997) and thus articulating the uncertainty of belief in its workings. That articulation fits in magic's pluralist cosmology, but obviously not in Pentecostalism. Magic is the killjoy of religious belief.

It is not so much the belief in magical effect that antagonizes the Christian soul as magic's inclusive cosmology perturbing all religious belief. Probably the antagonism does not work in two ways, since magic's inclusive cosmology could not exclude Pentecostalism (even if that belief is exclusive). One conundrum remains. We should expect from all users of magic the same disdain as Solile's. Yet the growing success of Pentecostalism in rural Tanzania is undeniable. Does this attest to the experiential atrophy pervading society? A concrete element is that this region in northwest Tanzania, which secretly kept and adapted its traditions, has since the turn of the millennium largely abandoned its initiations into medicine and divination. The initiations guaranteed the degree of knowledge needed among adults to scrutinize a healer's quality, which indeed depended on that person's ability of cosmologically grounding the medicines and thus providing the users with experiential depth.

Simplex and Multiplex Experiences of Culture

The suggestion of impoverished experiences of life in modernity is not new. The Weberian trope on the iron cage of rationalization sought to identify the dark side of modernity in similar terms. Yet, if studies of globalization have demonstrated anything it is that rationality has not increased, rather that the world has not ceased to produce rationalities as well as irrationalities, a-rationalities, and magic (Kapferer 2005). To depart from Weber's idealist framework and from the materialism of its opponents, we should situate meaning not either in ideas or in social relations or in the experiencing body, but in all three at once. Yet, how to think culture, society, and experience together?

A useful pointer on relating culture and society to experience is Max Gluckman's (1967) distinction between simplex and multiplex societies. The less stratified a society is, the more complex any of its moral issues will be, Gluckman argued. In village communities, which are socially not very stratified, the personal ties with other members are multiple, in the sense of being simultaneously based on the kinship, initiatory membership, corporate alliance, political interests, and so on. Decisions on the right conduct can follow any of these lines of thought, depending on negotiation and palaver. That makes such societies 'multiplex' instead of simple. Rituals inculcating encompassing values can help to manage multiplexity. Prolonged greetings in the morning let Sukuma-speaking farmers take the time to address each other in a biographically correct way, determining the other's line of descent and choosing the kinship position relevant for the encounter, the terms of address the following suit. In the case of joking relationship, people switch to a frame challenging the other's seniority by strategically picking out other social bases than a descent to determine seniority. The multiplex practice resembles a game of chess, quite unlike the anonymous, 'simplex' greetings in modern cities.

To take another example, traffic in the streets and on national roads in Tanzania takes its yearly toll on passengers' lives by reproducing an unspoken rule. Which vehicle can overtake another and claim priority? An a-cultural law seems to prevail, where goods come before people, police have to be bribed, expensive trucks have priority, and the newer brand of vehicle occupies a higher rank. The linear logic resembles the cultural frame of capitalism: the individual invests money and subsequently is entitled to the outcome (Comaroff and Comaroff 2000). It is the universal law even God cannot escape.

Modern, secular, and urbanized societies have less overlap of social roles due to the structural differentiation of society in subsystems, such as politics (State), religion (Church), economy (Market), education (School), and family (Home). The functionalist scheme was perfected in the system theory of Niklas Luhmann (1995). In some sociological applications, the scheme led to a definition of secularization as a process of gradual loss of moral encompassment due to the segregation of religion into a mere subsystem of society (Dobbelaere 1999). For our discussion the upshot of structural differentiation at the level of experience is interesting. From a macro-perspective and in cultural terms the subsystems are very complex, yet at the level of personal experience, the subsystems are designed to facilitate predictable decisions and simplify moral choices. The so-called complex societies appear to be simplex in the experiential sense. People learn to fragment their expectations. Cities, for example, foster the anonymity of navigating between the subsystems, itself a new experience introduced since modernity. It is, however, an experience of simplex society, of personal ties whose multiplicity has eroded and has differentiated into separate roles, thus denying the subject the both healing and bewitching transformation known in rituals and initiations (and perhaps underestimated by Victor Turner), of shifting between opposite frames of experience. Without experiential shifts, a society's power structure becomes fixed and linearly hierarchical. The previous sections illustrated the simplex experience of witchcraft in some Pentecostalist settings. The rest of this chapter compares multiplex and simplex experiences of spirits.

Pentecostal Demons Substituting for Multiplex Spirits

Could Pentecostalism, through practices, such as 'speaking in tongues' and prophecies, be a substitution for spirit cults in Africa? Ethnographers have pointed to correspondences of Pentecostal services with healing rituals, in terms of their ecstatic features (Binsbergen 2004) and their inclination to mimicry, mixing appropriation, and parody of foreign undomesticated powers, including unleashed capitalism (Devisch 1996). Others have emphasized the Pentecostalist convert's 'clean break with the past' (Meyer 1998; Dijk 1997) that demonized clan and precolonial traditions, which in turn facilitated the adoption of underlying Western ideas of individualism and neoliberalism (found in Republican circles in the Southern US among others). The two views do not contradict each other, for indeed the neoliberal message of salvation can flourish in communities whose members are used to depending on invisible forces.

There exist similarities between charismatic and traditional ecstatic religions, an obvious one being the convert's social transformation including detachment from the extended family (cf. Lewis 1971). But the differences seem more fundamental. First of all, the Christian salvation through repentance and belief in God has little affinity with the dependence on whimsical spirits, which are neither good nor bad in the (Bantu) cosmologies of Eastern Africa. The capitalist logic of return on investment frontally collides with the fundamental state of contingency which the healer's patients experience when waiting for the unsure 'arrival' of ancestral voices in oracles, or when engaging in the daily play of magic and counter-magic yielding an uncertain outcome for their life force.

Second, and not in the least, the plurality does not tally with the conversion. Prior to initiation into the Chwezi cult of spirit possession, the medium (*manga*) will wear a bracelet called *ngalike*, a noun derived from the verb *kugalika*, 'to change one's mind.' The change the *manga* must undergo is a shift in experiencing the world, which hinges on the plurality of worlds and the many cults specialized in each of these worlds. In the Chwezi cult, belief in the spirit means a shift of frames and not a change permanent as in a conversion after the descent of the Holy Spirit. What is more: the Pentecostal experience of conversion actually arises from culturally uprooting oneself. That could not work in the healer's pluralist cosmology. The crucial difference with ritual healing and divination is that Pentecostalism allows for one world only. What the Pentecostalist understands by evil is the possibility of many perspectives, which is exactly what the diviner takes for granted. The one encompassing law of Pentecostalism to which even God must obey condemns pluralism. Acceptance of multiple frames of experience amounts to disbelief, which is the ultimate evil.

Bantu divination and healing have a long tradition of integrating foreign beliefs. The *majini* and *pepo* spirits from Islam spread across Eastern Africa in the past century and sometimes they did at the detriment of ancestral spirit cults because those Muslim beings began to infiltrate divinatory diagnoses. The oracle had to choose at some stage which type of spirit was at work: a *djinn* or a clan ancestor. The one lost a client to the other while recognizing the other's skill. The oracle also told whether the spirit-led illness was a curse stumbled on by accident or sent purposively by a witch. In contrast, the Pentecostalist call for conversion never entered the diviner's diagnosis. The oracular frame of experience does not accord with the exclusive truth-claim of Christian conversion.

Only at the cost of experiential depth could Pentecostal exorcism replace local spirit practices. Attesting to the important experiential change, it did replace them, if we interpret the words of Malamala, the leader of the Chwezi cult, well (personal communication 12/9/2015). According to him, the cult has been compelled to move and recruit in the region of Bariadi and Bunda, thus east from its main catchment area 20 years ago, which was southwest from Lake Victoria and a much larger region. The change of catchment area corresponds to the spread of Pentecostal churches from urban centers in Kagera, Kigoma, Kahama, and further afield to the west from Rwanda and Uganda, where the Chwezi cult and its variants, the Kubandwa and Ryangombe cults, died out earlier on.

Just as the concept of witch has been globalized, so as to comprise virtually everything occult, and thus no longer denotes a particular frame of experience to snap out of with the help of the healer's counter-magic, so too has the concept of spirit been globalized, to comprise realities as different as the biographically unique call, the demonic curse and divine grace. This cultural globalization of spirit and witchcraft benefits the dualist Christian frame, separating the normal from the occult, good from evil, over which Bible and priest can decide. The process seems to have had a predecessor in precolonial central Africa. From Rwandan mythology can be derived that the cult of Ryangombe arose at a time, some 500 years ago when King Ndori sought to introduce an autocratic model of the rule (Heusch 1966). The spirit cult originated at the margin of society to maintain the reciprocal, interdependent relation with the spirits, which the king wanted to get rid of. Today, we witness the next phase in the process, as Pentecostalism has entered the margins of society to reorganize people's relations with the spirit world.

Diviners and healers in central Tanzania where Christian and Islamic denominations prevail, live deep within the town center, hidden from view of government officers and educated Christians. In northwest Tanzania, they are located at roadsides or at the periphery of the village to announce their trade and attract customers. Yet, both regions of Tanzania have abandoned the initiatory systems with a public purpose such as social integration. The rite of passage required the involvement of the whole community before and after the teaching in a secluded area of the forest. For very varied reasons, ranging from (neo-)colonial to anti-colonial sentiment, postcolonial Africa has not managed to publicly and unashamedly link up with precolonial traditions. Pentecostalism harbors those sentiments. As a consequence, spirits have lost their history, which was transmitted through oral tradition and oracle, and often dated back many generations. Moreover, the cosmology the spirits partake of is no longer intergenerationally crafted and recrafted, to parallel new cosmologies. As illustrated below, however, in the seclusion of the healer's compound the biographies of spirits and the parallelism of spiritual cosmologies persist.

From Spirit Biographies to the Globalized Frame of Spirit

In Morogoro region, the business of healing takes place in fenced houses, not unlike any other in town. External signs of the trade on the roof or fence are rare. By word of mouth, clients know which one of the many specialties at hand a certain healer offers. Cosmologies parallel each other and interweave. Religious conformity is secondary. The *mganga wa korani* treats by reciting Koran verses, after determining the person's life-force (*nyota*, 'star') through divination techniques unacceptable to orthodox Islam. The *mganga wa kibuyu*, 'healer of the calabash', adopts Luguru traditions of divination, yet combines these with the Islamic concept of *majini*, 'spirits' denoting afflictions, and the related Swahili notion of *mapepo mabaya*, 'evil winds'. The adjective suggesting that there may be good winds too is indicative of the negotiation between registers. Orthodox Islam regards spirits as dangerous and external to society, hence in treatment, the healers of the calabash move away from Islamic cosmology to enter the world of traditional healing where spirits are ancestral and can be protective. This is an indication of the extent to which the plurality of cosmologies inheres traditional healing. The oracles of six different diviners I visited in the region last year confirmed the intrinsic plurality. All healers embraced the continuity between life and spirit agency, but none shared the same cosmology. Most of all, they seemed not to care about forging coherence among their propositions, let alone with those of their colleagues. Each mediumistic vocation has its unique biography; their spirits decide which way is right. The only absent cosmology was Pentecostalism.

One Luguru-speaking healer had a *mzimu*, 'spirit,' *wa kuoteshwa*, 'of being made to grow,' meaning that this *mzimu* permitted the medium to steer and shape it. He developed an original divination technique with a remarkable tool he named Adija: a shiny reddish-brown calabash connected with a palm-size mirror via two thin strings of tiny white and black pearls, each a foot long. The strings carried halfway a pair of small medicinal bottles, covered with a black hair tuft and strengthened with two wooden amulets. Inside the calabash was a transparent liquid with the power to 'pull' the spirit (*kuvuta mzimu*, Swa.). The Adija calabash received the information on the life-force of the client, transmitted 'like an X-ray' said the healer, through the two bead strings and appearing in the mirror. The mirrored diagnosis determined whether the illness is caused by the power of God, *ya Mwezi Mungu*, or by 'superstition,' *ya ushirikina*, literally 'polytheism,' the Arabic notion for heresy and the locally adopted term for witchcraft (also by the healers). The healer emphasized that although his expertise is 'of the calabash,' the liquid in his Adija tool combines the forces of both Koranic and calabash healing (and I would add: radiology). In brief, he saw no need to exclude creeds. God and witches act as if belonging to parallel worlds, the one absent when the other is present. Furthermore, the healer had no qualms about calling witchcraft *ushirikina* with the strong connotation of heresy, even if he knew that orthodox Muslims would consider his counter-magic and rituals a form of witchcraft. Heresy is a void and inconsequential concept in his pluralist cosmology. In short, the disciplining of the adherent's experience, implying control over thought, which the new Charismatic movement stimulates, was absent.

We lack the space here to detail the ways in which Tanzanian communities have perpetuated the biographies of ancestral spirits from the clan and a fortiori, in initiatory cults such as Chwezi, have revived the histories of spirits possessing members (Stroeken 2006). The biography of one's guiding spirit helps to form one's self, often embedded in family history (Lambek 1988). In Christianity, it is the same spirit we are to experience—not an ancestral spirit attached to the history of the clan or of a certain locality. Pentecostalism manages to interweave the believer's personal path of salvation with the one Spirit, through a relationship that evolves (Coleman 2011). It is not the biographically unique embodiment of the path of the subject, as in the cult spirit of the possessed. The communitas of ritual, a collective state famously described by Victor Turner, should not obscure the actual purpose of initiating subjects seeking to become worthy descendants mastering the forest, the plants, and the tools of divination to read personal fortune or expertly consult a healer. The many unique paths of these subjects and their ancestral spirits preclude the existence of a definite, fixed hierarchy (cf. Rio and Smedal 2009).

All reflections in this chapter seem to converge on the view that Pentecostalism is a religious practice befitting the era of globalization, nuclearization, and neoliberalism. Defined as a process that compresses time and expands scales of influence resulting from the free(r) flow of goods, people, and ideas (Brenner 1999), globalization means a greater probability of localities admitting external influences in their midst as well as triggering local ripostes entailing cultural innovation and syncretism (Hannerz 1992), hence producing cultural heterogeneity. My point has not been to reject this claim but to elicit what it conceals: while networks of cultural influences, as effectively drawn up by ANT studies among others, have only grown more complex, the experiential depth of spirit and witch has atrophied. The experiential atrophy has been a corollary of cultural inflation. By depth, I did not mean the intensity of personal experience, which anthropologists are not equipped to measure. I meant the extent to which one practice is related to other practices and thus 'rooted' in history. In the case of much experiential depth, the practice is embedded in a cosmology and co-determining it. Then practices are *differentially* related, that is, born from a strong sense of distinction and allowing for a wide palette of sensation. Among the many faces of globalization, one is to individualize subjectivities, but another paradoxically is to standardize experiences, making their biographical uniqueness disappear. Globalized settings reproduce cultural differences at will, creating so-called superdiversity, which is not conducive to experiencing the symbolic oppositions amidst the diversity, or to experience the shifts between them. Pentecostalism is a multilayered phenomenon but, we have argued, in its most effective popular variants it is the reflection and the driver of this atrophying process, a reflection of its globalized view on the supernatural is hinged on public discourses in African schools, NGO's and churches, yet also a driver as it has found in Christian conversion a universal substitution for the reciprocal, personal, and biographical relations with ancestral spirits. Spiritual warfare has been so effective as to rob the spirits of a history and a name. Both in Africa and Melanesia, evangelism has been confrontational, perfecting the art of 'world-breaking' (Rio, MacCarthy and Blanes, this volume). Surely, no other art could have assisted both God and capitalism against their remaining competitors: the spirit, calling for personal subversion, and the witch, embodying our continuity with the past.

Conclusions

Whence the Pentecostalist obsession with the witch, incorporating in it the spirit as an evil intruding the self? The obsession is that of a whole society. If life is supposed to know only one form, to remain stuck to one experiential frame, then bewitchment is its name. No other religion than Pentecostalism has the meta-cosmology to master that game.

Since Enlightenment, the domains of science, democratic politics, and ethics proceed on the assumption of universal categories, seeking laws or truths governing that one world. However, our one world is allowed to contain plurality within, for it produces truths-under-construction through democratic consensus (Habermas 1985). Monotheistic religions have little room for the contingency of such democracy. Christianity hence established the dualism of worlds, the profane one being reserved for the scientist's cosmology. Contemporary Pentecostalism presents a fourth type of cosmology, differing from magic (many worlds), religion (dualism), and science (one plural world). Its tendency is toward a singular world without inner plurality. The relation between individual and good, or God, is direct. No capricious spirits should come in between. People receive a return on investment. The preachers are the brokers ensuring that people dare the move to that world. While other ideologies, religions, and science present an ideal to strive for that may not be attainable, here is a religion that appeals and excites for projecting its ideal on this world, and claiming the ideal is already attained: it is only up to the individual to embrace it. God will finish, provided that you start.

It is unconventional to distinguish between on the one hand cultural complexity, for example, operationalized as the number of different cultural elements and their interrelations, and on the other hand experiential depth, which refers to the integration of all those elements in a whole, a cosmology (one cosmo-logic) embodied by the subjects. The suggestion of comparing cultures in terms of the members' experiences is almost a taboo in anthropology since subjectivities are supposed to be incommensurable, even more than cultures. It is thus only in a roundabout way that we could put forward indications of experiential atrophy, such as the rising success of Pentecostalism in a globalizing and increasingly neoliberal society, the suitability of Pentecostal sermon to neoliberalism, the simplex experience of conversion, the examples of simplex greeting and traffic, the loss of experiential shifts in magic, the vanishing of spirit cult initiations and their replacement by Charismatic possession, the structural intrusion and the choice for Pentecostalism among the educated, the civil servants, the villagized, the nuclearized families, and other outsiders of the community. An alternative view would seem to be the rejection of the idea of 'experiential depth' altogether and to instead state that spirit cults die out simply because they no longer capture the experience of life in current society, while Pentecostalism does, which would explain its success. But such reasoning boils down to the same conclusion about the relevance today of simplex experience and its fascinating complexity.

Notes

1. This study is based on participatory observation and regular field visits since 1995 in the northwest of Tanzania (predominantly in Mwanza Region) and on annual short research stays since 2012 in central Tanzania (Morogoro Region). Brief field-visits in Kitgum (Northern Uganda) in January 2014 and in Swahili-speaking Lubumbashi (DRC) in November 2015 served as additional points of reference on Pentecostalism in Eastern Africa.
2. During a brief field-visit in Uganda in January 2014 an Acholi diviner told me in an unrecorded interview that she and all healers around Kitgum were the first victims of the LRA's murderous campaign to purify Uganda from witchcraft.
3. The dubitable nature of the claim by pastor Polino Angella was not mentioned by journalist Tim Whewell, who was subsequently summoned for questioning by the Ugandan police, cf. http://news.bbc.co.uk/2/hi/africa/8536313.stm.
4. See the so-called 'Mitchell-Swartz hypothesis' asserting that social competition causes less tension where social ties are loose (Marwick 1970: 380).
5. A (mischievous) explanation for this homogenizing pressure is that experiential plurality, maintaining opposite perspectives, hinders globalization as it would slow down communication and keep influences all too local.

References

Brenner, N. 1999. Beyond State-Centrism? Space, Territoriality, and Geographical Scale in Globalization Studies. *Theory and Society* 28 (1): 39–78.

Coleman, S. 2011. 'Right Now!': Historiopraxy and the Embodiment of Charismatic Temporalities. *Ethnos* 76 (4): 426–447.

Comaroff, J., and J. Comaroff. 1991. *Of Revelation and Revolution: Christianity, Colonialism, and Consciousness in South Africa*, vol. 1. Chicago: Chicago University Press.

———. 2000. "Millennial Capitalism: First Thoughts on a Second Coming." *Public Culture* 12: 291–343.

de Heusch, Luc. 1966. *Le Rwanda et la. Civilisation Interlacustre*. Bruxelles: Université Libre de Bruxelles.

Devisch, R. 1993. *Weaving the Threads of Life: The Khita Gyn-Eco-Logical Healing Cult among the Yaka*. Chicago: Chicago University Press.

———. 1996. 'Pillaging Jesus': Healing Churches and the Villagisation of Kinshasa. *Africa* 66: 555–586.

Dobbelaere, K. 1999. Towards an Integrated Perspective of the Processes Related to the Descriptive Concept of Secularization. *Sociology of Religion* 60 (3): 229–247.

Fernandez, J. 1982. *Bwiti: An Ethnography of the Religious Imagination in Africa*. Princeton, NJ: Princeton University Press.

Geschiere, P. 2013. *Witchcraft, Intimacy, and Trust: Africa in Comparison*. Chicago: Chicago University Press.

Gluckman, M. 1967. *The Judicial Process Among the Barotse of Northern Rhodesia*. Manchester: Manchester University Press.

Habermas, J. 1985. *The Theory of Communicative Action, Volume 1: Reason and the Rationalization of Society*. New York: Beacon.

Hannerz, U. 1992. *Cultural Complexity: Studies in the Social Organization of Meaning*. New York: Columbia University Press.

Hyden, G. 1980. *Beyond Ujamaa in Tanzania: Underdevelopment and an Uncaptured Peasantry*. London: Heinemann.

Ingold, T. 2000. *The Perception of the Environment*. New York: Routledge.

Kapferer, B. 2005. 2003. 'Outside All Reason', In *Beyond Rationalism: Rethinking Magic, Witchcraft and Sorcery*. B. Kapferer ed. Oxford: Berghahn Books.

Lambek, M. 1988. Spirit Possession/Spirit Succession: Aspects of Social Continuity Among Malagasy Speakers in Mayotte. *American Ethnologist* 15 (4): 710–731.

Langwick, S. 2008. Articulate(d) Bodies: Traditional medicine in a Tanzanian hospital. *American Ethnologist* 35 (3): 357–3071.

Lewis, I. 1971. *Ecstatic Religion: An Anthropological Study of Spirit Possession and Shamanism*. London: Penguin.

Luhmann, N. 1995. *Social Systems*. Stanford, CA: Stanford University Press.

Macfarlane, A. 1999. *Witchcraft in Tudor and Stuart England*. London: Routledge.

Marwick, M. 1970. *Witchcraft and Sorcery*. London: Penguin.

Meyer, Birgit. 1998. 'Make a Complete Break with the Past'. Memory and Post-colonial Modernity in Ghanaian Pentecostalist Discourse. *Journal of Religion in Africa* 28 (3): 316–349.

———. 2004. "Christianity in Africa: From African Independent to Pentecostal-charismatic Churches." *Annual Review of Anthropology* 33 (2004): 447–474.

Mudimbe, V. 1988. *The Invention of Africa: Gnosis, Philosophy, and the Order of Knowledge*. Bloomington: Indian University Press.

Ranger, T.O. 1986. Religious Movements and Politics in Sub-Saharan Africa. *African Studies Review* 29 (2): 1–69.

———. 2007. 'Scotland Yard in the Bush: Medicine Murders. *Child Witchesand the Construction of the Occult: A Literature Review'*, *Africa* 77: 272–283.

Reynolds-Whyte, S. R. 1997. *Questioning Misfortune: The Pragmatics of Uncertainty in Eastern Uganda*. Cambridge: Cambridge University Press.

Rio, K., and O. Smedal. 2009. Hierarchy and its Alternatives: An Introduction to Movements of Totalization and Detotalization. In *Hierarchy: Persistence and Transformation in Social Formations*, ed. K. Rio, and O. Smedal, 1–64. Oxford: Berghahn.

Stroeken, K. 2010. *Moral Power: The Magic of Witchcraft*. New York: Berghahn.

———. 2006. 'Stalking the Stalker': A Chwezi Initiation into Spirit Possession and Experiential Structure. *Journal of the Royal Anthropological Institute* 12 (4): 785–802.

van Binsbergen, W. 2004. Challenges for the Sociology of Religion in the African Context: Prospects for the Next 50 Years. *Social Compass* 51 (1): 85–98.

van Dijk, R. 1997. From Camp to Encompassment: Discourses of Transsubjectivity in the Ghanaian Pentecostal Diaspora. *Journal of Religion in Africa* 27 (2): 135–159.

Wijsen, F. J. S. 1993. *There is Only One God: A Social-scientific and Theological Study of Popular Religion and Evangelization in Sukumaland, Northwest Tanzania*. Kampen: Kok.

Author Biography

Koen Stroeken is Associate Professor of Africanist anthropology at Ghent University. He has published on medicine, conflict and witchcraft in the monograph 'Moral Power' (Berghahn) and among others in the journals *Africa*, *Ethnos*, *Journal of the Royal Anthropological Institute*, and *Anthropological Theory*. He (co-)edited the volumes 'Ageing in Africa' (Ashgate) and 'War Technology Anthropology' (Berghahn). He is supervising five doctoral projects and since 2012 coordinates VLIRUOS research exchange with Mzumbe University in Tanzania.

CHAPTER 12

Afterword: Academics, Pentecostals, and Witches: The Struggle for Clarity and the Power of the Murky

Peter Geschiere

One of the many strong points of this collection is that it vividly shows the kaleidoscopic character of phenomena for which people use terms like witchcraft or sorcery. Almost anything seems to be possible: the stereotype for witches in many parts of Melanesia seem to be that they are 'backwards and ugly' (see Introduction, this volume), but in Thomas Strong's contribution on Eastern Highlands of Papua they are envied because they live in a world that people describe as 'highly ordered, flashy and modern'; Congolese Pentecostals suspect that witches now work through modern technology (Katrien Pype, this volume); but Bjørn Enge Bertelsen shows that they themselves can also be suspected—as in Mozambique where German Pentecostal missionaries were suddenly associated with heinous forms of occult violence. Such mulitformity that, moreover, is in constant movement reminds us of James Siegel's seminal insight that witchcraft connects things that should not—or even cannot—be connected, or of Michael Taussig's evocation of the

P. Geschiere (✉)
University Of Amsterdam, Amsterdam, The Netherlands

K. Rio et al. (eds.), *Pentecostalism and Witchcraft*, Contemporary Anthropology of Religion, DOI 10.1007/978-3-319-56068-7_12

power of 'the murky' (Siegel 2006; Taussig 1987). It is, therefore, most fortunate that the Introduction does not try to come to a more or less closed analysis imposing a neat order on such exuberance. The editors rather content themselves to outline certain trends and recurring patterns without freezing that which is constantly shifting.

It is also due to such openness that the regional comparison in this volume—between Africa and Melanesia—works. Of course, such regional comparisons are always risky. An obvious danger is that they lead to stereotypical regional contrasts, and the Africa/Melanesia twinning has some history in this respect. It is interesting to try and understand why this comparison seems to have such attraction for anthropologists, ever since J.A. Barnes' much contested warning against applying African kinship models in the New Guinea highlands (Barnes 1962). Also comparisons on other aspects—for instance, Marwick's 1964 stereotyping of African witchcraft as an inside affair in contrast to sorcery in Oceania as coming from the outside—show a clear tendency to produce binary oppositions, that subsequently are bound to be demolished by colleagues working within each of the regions concerned.[1] Therefore, it is reassuring to see that in this collection, differences cut right through regional boundaries. An overview of the various chapters makes it, indeed, quite hard to conclude that there is something like a Melanesian ontology (let alone an African one).

The collection escapes all the more from the danger of presenting the two regions as blocks since it focuses the comparison on a theme that is both specific and general (at least it is becoming ever more general): the articulation of Pentecostal movements and local forms of knowledge. And on this point all the articles do converge, highlighting one paradoxical trend. Pentecostalism—which is, of course, a panacea term for all sorts of different movements that moreover are constantly splitting up—is victorious because it presents itself as capable of eradicating witchcraft. However, this means in practice that it reinforces the very 'witchcraft' it claims to eradicate. In all the contributions, Pentecostal movements feed on people's fears of hidden aggression, offering relief but at the same time fanning such fears, evoking new and often unheard occult threats. Tom Bratrud shows how child prophets and their attacks on sorcery in Vanuatu emerge from a complex relation with Pentecostal Christianity: it seems to be a relation of opposition but in practice is one of mutual reinforcement. For me, the old notion of *articulation* works wonderfully well to express such a paradox, precisely because it implies that this is a two-sided process. It may be tempting to see the protagonists of new forms of Christianity with their crusades against local witchcraft/sorcery as the main actors. But the action is two-sided, the new religious fervor becoming entangled in local imaginations. Knut Christian Myhre brings out a similar multi-sidedness in his study of albino murders and other witchcraft practices in the Kilimanjaro region (Tanzania) by his notion of 'folding': "Catholicism and Pentecostalism fold into each other to fold out of witchcraft and alternatively fold out of each other as inversions or reversals of one another." A challenging image that asks for detailed, historical studies of how these articulation processes evolved over time: witchcraft, Catholicism and Pentecostalism in their mutual involvement constantly generating new links and oppositions. As challenging is his plea to get beyond a preoccupation with representation (one form of action acting upon the other) but rather to study the relation between Christianity and witchcraft as a relation of 'equivalence'–that is, each modifying the other.[2] Myhre's suggestion to "to allow vernacular actions to act on our [academic] practices and our representational powers" is indeed an urgent one for this whole domain in which the danger of academic interpretations losing contact with people's understandings of how occult forces intervene in their everyday life is particularly great. I certainly agree we must allow for such openness but I would add that we have then also to accept this will have its costs (see below).

In African studies, the paradoxical articulation between Pentecostalism and witchcraft—opposing each other, yet mutually reinforcing—has been observed already for some time (Meyer 1999; Marshall 2009, and many others). It is powerfully condensed in Sasha Newell's notion 'Pentecostal witchcraft' (2007) quoted in several chapters. But, mixing examples from very different regions, this collection highlights again quite different implications of this general amalgamation. For Barbara Andersen's nursing students—upcoming members of an educated elite in Papua New Guinea–Pentecostalism brings relief for practical problems, just as in Michelle MacCarthy's study of Trobrianders embracing Pentecostalism as a protection against 'the old ways.' But for Koen Stroeken, his experiences in Tanzania and Congo rather point to a flattening and a destruction of finely tuned distinctions of the spiritual realm of olden days—a flattening in which anthropologists would have joined for some time already. For Ruy Blanes, the *ndoki* (sorcery) has become a kind of spiritual index for Pentecostal leaders in Angola, comparable to the Dow Jones in economics. Annelin Eriksen and Knut Rio show how the new

Pentecostal religious regime in Porta Vila, the rapidly growing capital of Vanuatu, creates novel fears among the population for a proliferation of novel forms of magic, often with a global background. For Katrien Pype, Pentecostalism seems to have become already a self-evident presence in Kinshasa. Comparing different Pentecostal currents she emphasizes their openness to new developments: in contrast to the classic 'variants' her Branhamist Pentecostals, still preoccupied with *kindoki* (witchcraft), are preoccupied less by its rural background but more by its appearances in modern technology.

Yet, underneath such a flux of variations, there is again a general line, rightly emphasized by Rio, MacCarthy, and Blanes in their introduction: the complex articulation of Pentecostalism and witchcraft means that the universalizing tenor of the former affects also the latter. Rather than eradicating it, Pentecostalism seems to universalize witchcraft by equating it with the devil, a cosmic figure par excellence. On this point, again omnipresent in this book, it is interesting to compare with the work of Joseph Tonda, a Congolese anthropologist, now in Libreville (Gabon), who works on the entanglement of Pentecostal and local forms of healing already since the early 1990s, but whose works has unfortunately not (yet) been translated into English.[3] Tonda has challenging things to say on the interaction between outside influences and local forms of knowledge/perception in Africa ever since the colonial period. He criticizes current views on Africa—also among social scientists and historians—as being marked by the idea of 'the Great Divide': the tendency to oppose, on the one hand, the impact of external factors like the world market, the state and most of all *le travail de Dieu* (the work of God = the mission) and, on the other, *l'esprit sorcellaire* (the witch-spirit). In these current views, the latter is then diagnosed as the real cause of the ongoing crisis in Africa. Over and against such a diagnosis, Tonda develops his powerful vision of one big steaming stream of magma in which all different factors blend. From this nondescript mass emerges the frightening figure of *Le Souverain moderne*—the Leviathan of postcolonial Africa—that Tonda sees as the real cause of Africa's plight (Tonda 2005). Tonda's visionary interpretations are clearly marked by his own horrible experiences of the civil war in Brazzaville in the 1990s which was one of the most violent on the continent since it took place inside the city—a drawn-out war of trenches in which the citizens were at the mercy of warlords and their mercenaries who had dug themselves in, each in one-quarter of the city. Tonda strongly opposes a tendency among anthropologists to interpret the emergence of such frightening leader figures in terms of 'traditional' continuities. For him, it is impossible to separate 'traditional' and 'modern' elements. These *souverains modernes* are as much products of processes of commoditization triggered by the inclusion in global market exchanges—and, indeed, their consumerism is proverbial—, by the authoritarianism of the colonial state and by the missionaries' effort to create a new elite.

Even more importantly is Tonda's warning that present-day 'traditions' have been completely recreated under the colonial impact. In this respect as well, his views are most challenging by their rigor. Especially for what people now call 'witchcraft' he is adamant: people may see this as a tradition but it has been completely recreated and turned inside out by the colonial moment. So, it is futile to oppose *le travail de Dieu* to local ideas about occult power. The missionaries may have seen themselves as crusaders against witches and witch-doctors, but what they produced is an assemblage in which religion and witchcraft are inherently entangled. The parallel with Newell's notion of 'Pentecostal witchcraft' quoted above may be clear. Also, Eriksen and Rio's analysis of a Pentecostal movement capturing Port Vila's population by evoking novel forms of occult dangers corresponds very well to Tonda's vision. In this 2002, book *La guérison divine en Afrique centrale* (Divine Healing in Central Africa) the latter follows a jumble of healers—men and women, old and young, educated and rural—who are quite difficult to classify. *Nganga* ('traditional healers') are in fierce competition with evangelical ones, but they constantly borrow from each other, or even transmute into the other category. In practice, Christian healers have to relate to the very forces they claim to combat. But, vice versa, the very name of 'traditional healer' becomes ironical because their practice is so deeply marked by the changing context.

With Tonda this colonial recreation of 'witchcraft' sometimes seemed to be a quite sudden process. Marshall (2009: 35–38) is even more explicit on this point. Always in for some anthropologists-thrashing, she insists that we have to study this turn as an 'event' in the Foucauldian sense— 'a relation of forces which is inversed, a power confiscated, a vocabulary appropriated and turned against its users…'. The challenge is to look at it as a new beginning, not allowing us to be burdened by the anthropological proclivity to look for continuities underneath all changes.[4] It might be worthwhile, though, to emphasize that this colonial 'moment' was a longer process. Of course, in many parts of Africa, the colonial presence was fairly short. Many areas were only fully 'pacified' in the 1920s, and already in the 1950s independence was already announcing itself. But still, the articulation of local ideas with, for instance, *le travail de Dieu* was a process which often followed a rocky trajectory. For Africa, the most interesting recent developments in the field of 'witchcraft studies' are by scholars—both historians and anthropologists, who take this idea of articulations following specific historical trajectories seriously. As noted in the Introduction to this volume, the long-term debate about the pro's and contra's of using terms like 'witchcraft,' 'sorcery' or *sorcellerie*—a kind of Gordian knot, since these are, of course, distorting western translation of local notions, yet now generally used and appropriated by the population—might be solved in a practical way by such historical studies of how the western terms were introduced: how they became accepted as an ever more current translation of a local term, and how in this process both notions mutually transformed each other. A good example is Andrea Ceriana Mayneri's recent book (2014) on the 'imaginary of dispossession' among the Banda of Central African Republic. A central moment in the book is how the term *sorcellerie* was introduced in a discussion of a French administrator, baffled by the local notion of *ondro*, with a local chief and a missionary who talked about *sorcellerie*; the most important role was (as usual) played by a local interpreter who simply used both terms as equivalents. In his book, Ceriana Mayneri follows the implications of this working misunderstanding for the two notions involved. In her forthcoming book, Florence Bernault follows a related trail by focusing on the convergences between the imaginaries of French colonials and locals in Gabon. Again, both the people involved and many subsequent scholars tend to assume a self-evident opposition here. But Bernault shows that the French struggled with assumptions about spirits and their elusiveness that related in practice very well to the locals' images, while for the latter it was obvious that the French became ever more entangled in the local imaginary.

Such detailed unraveling of historical articulations and their specific trajectories might suggest directions for taking the challenging comparisons in the present collections even further. For one thing, it might be important to place the very idea of 'Pentecostal witchcraft' in a longer time perspective. Present-day articulations of this 'mutually reinforcing relation' are part of a much longer process in which Christianity in its more intolerant forms was confronting local beliefs. In the forest area of southeast Cameroon, where I did my main field-work present-day

Pentecostal fervor seems to bring in some respects a return to the early days of conversion (first decades of the twentieth century) when both Protestant and Catholic missionaries seemed to aim at instituting a sort of theocracy, drawing their converts to the mission post, and imposing a radical regime in order to distance their flock from heathen surroundings—this to the great dismay of colonial administrators who wanted to retain people (and their labor force) for their own projects.

Another interesting alley is opened up by Katrien Pype with her seminal emphasis on technology and science as a new focus in the Pentecostal struggle against witchcraft. Again this evokes a longer struggle. It relates very well to Ceriana Mayneri's emphasis that as long as we can go back, local discourses on occult power where 'provoked' by western scientific discourse—a provocation that led to such determined efforts toward fusion that any idea of a binary opposition becomes futile. Of course, it is standard to oppose Western science as transparent and rational to African (or Melanesian) occultism as murky and irrational. But to the people involved such a contrast is often untenable. 'Traditional' healers will boast of their science and people claim that at night their witches use technology that outdoes by far western equivalents. 'Our planes do Paris and back in one night' as my friend in the village often repeated. And one of the modern *nganga*—who claimed to have a medical degree—was supposed to be particularly successful because he was so good at destroying 'nocturnal air strips' so that the witches' planes could no longer land.[5] People's discourses on occult power have developed for over a century now—and in many areas even longer—in a context where western medicine, technology, and theology were highly present. But this did not lead to an either/or conflict but rather to complex and volatile articulations and assemblages. It is, therefore, important to realize that our informants' discourse on the occult is developing in a long-term articulation with western ideas, not in radical opposition but rather inspiring efforts towards blending and fusion. Tonda's image of a magma-in-flux is very relevant in this respect as well. But despite all this blending—fusing what appears to be separated—the challenge is to study even this diffuse magma as a conglomerate of specific historical trajectories over a longer period of time.

Tonda's magma notion raises similar issues as Michael Taussig's earlier explorations of the power of 'epistemic murk' (Taussig 1987). When I was reading through this collection Taussig's powerful image kept coming back to my mind. Indeed, it seems to be their very fuzziness, allowing for all sorts of explanations, that is important for understanding the resilience of these shifting imaginaries on occult forces, and their capacity to graft themselves upon incisive changes. In Pype's study on Kinshasa, these hidden forces invade new technologies; Eriksen and Rio show that objects from Africa can suddenly become central to horror stories in Port Vila; for Thomas Strong witches in Papua New Guinea evoke jealousy because of their 'ordered modernity.' For Koen Stroeken such volatility seems to be a deplorable effect of modern changes—like the impact of Pentecostal missionary zeal—destroying fine-grained distinctions ordering local society. In my experience, this diffuseness and chameleonic capacities are rather given with basic trends in the discourse on occult powers. The central concern in many 'witchcraft' discourses with dramatic, nightly confrontations place a premium on novel borrowings that can surprise adversaries. Hence their basically unstable and shifting character and a basic ambiguity on what is good and evil: the *nganga* as a healer can always be suspected to turn into a witch. The idea that the same power that can heal can also kill, returns in a wide range of settings. Or, to be more concrete, *nganga* may be healers for their clients, but the witch they attack will claim to be an innocent victim of healers who are themselves witches. Such shifts are also crucial in the interaction of these ideas with Pentecostalism. To these preachers the 'traditional healer' is, of course, a witch—no doubt about that—but this certainty is constantly being undermined by the basic ambiguity of local ideas. As many of the Ghanaian and Nigerian video-films, deeply marked by the Pentecostal message, highlight: the treason may be inside—the most fervent crusader can turn out to be a source of evil (Meyer 2015). It is the shifting character of these imaginaries, marked by deep ambiguities and uncertainties, that make them so resilient despite deep changes.

All this to argue that Knut Myhre's plea for allowing "vernacular actions to act on our [academic] practices and our representational powers" is highly sympathetic but raises also serious dilemmas. It certainly raises enticing perspectives: it is vital not to lose touch with people's ways of seeing things or to try to reduce these to another, more 'real' reality. But it raises also a basic dilemma for us academics. One of the first principles of academia is that we must create clarity, working as much as we can with unequivocal notions. But how to deal then with forms of knowledge that get their power precisely from their un-clarity and their ambiguity? How can we avoid that our efforts to create clarity abscond the very power we are trying to understand? Taussig's solution for gaining insight into the power of the murky was to go along with all these ambiguities: taking the drugs and using his feverish revelations to experience the deep ambiguity and unexpected linkages of this hidden world. I am not reproaching the authors for not following this example. Taussig's book, the sediment of his adventurous journey, is fascinating but also mind-boggling; Tonda's books have the same visionary quality. But we must be aware of the tension between striving for clarity and opening up to the full ambiguities of people's thinking about the invisible forces. The great merit of this collection is that it gives full reign to such transgressive exuberance, not fixing it in an all too firm analytic grid.

Notes

1. See for a recent and spirited defense of anthropology's comparative method (van der Veer 2016).
2. In my view such a double-sided articulation—the impact of global economic changes being profoundly affected by people's imaginaries of occult forces, but the latter in turn provoked by such changes—was exactly what Jean and John Comaroff had in mind with their notion of 'occult economies,' Myhre's main target. But the plea for a view in terms of 'an action upon an action' is of course most welcome.
3. Seagull Press is now preparing a translation of Tonda's *Le Souverain moderne*.
4. See for a similar view from Melanesia, Robbins (2007)
5. Cf. Geschiere (1997); see also Lattas (2010) for New Britain.

References

Barnes, J.A. 1962. African Models in the New Guinea Highlands. *Man* 62: 5–9.

Bernault, F. forthcoming. *Struggles for the Sacred: Power and Fantasy in Colonial Gabon*. Durham: Duke U. P.

Ceriana Mayneri, A. 2014. *Sorecllerie et prophétisme en Centrafrique: L'imaginaire de la dépossession en pays banda*. Paris: Karthala.

Geschiere, P. 1997. *The Modernity of Witchcraft, Power and the Occult in Postcolonial Africa*. Charlotsville: University of Virginia Press.

Lattas, A. 2010. *Dreams, Madness and Fairy Tales in New Britian*. Durham: Carolina Academic Press.

Marshall, R. 2009. *Political Spiritualities: The Pentecostal Revolution in Nigeria*. Chicago: University of Chicago Press.

Marwick, M. 1964. Witchcraft as a Social Strain Gauge. *Australian Journal of Science* 26: 263–268.

Meyer, B. 1999. *Translating the Devil—Religion and Modernity among the Ewe in Ghana*. Edinburgh: Edinburgh University Press for International African Institute.

———. 2015. *Sensational Movies—Video. Vision and Christianity in Ghana*. Berkeley: California Press.

Newell, Sasha. 2007. 'Pentecostal Witchcraft: Neoliberal Possession and Demonic Discourse in Ivoirian Pentecostal Churches'. *Journal of Religion in Africa* 37 (4): 461–490.

Robbins, J. 2007. Continuity Thinking and the Problem of Christian Culture: Belief, Time, and the Anthropology of Christianity. *Current Anthropology* 48 (1): 5–38.

Siegel, J. 2006. *Naming the Witch*. Stanford: Stanford U.P.

Taussig, M. 1987. *Shamanism, Colonialism and the Wild Man: A Study of Terror and Healing*. Chicago: University of Chicago Press.

Tonda, J. 2002. *La guérison divine en Afrique centrale (Congo, Gabon)*. Paris: Karthala.

———. 2005. *Le souverain moderne: Le corps du pouvoir en Afrique centrale (Congo, Gabon)*.Paris: Karthala.

Van der Veer, P. 2016. *The Value of Comparison*. Durham: Duke U.P.

Author Biography

Peter Geschiere is Professor of Anthropology at the University of Amsterdam, fellow of the Royal Netherlands Academy of Sciences and co-editor of the journal ETHNOGRAPHY (with SAGE). Since 1971 he has undertaken historical-anthropological field-work in various parts of Cameroon and elsewhere in West Africa. He has published extensively on issues of citizenship, belonging and exclusion (see, for instance, his 2009 book with University of Chicago Press, *Perils of Belonging: Autochthony, Citizenship and Exclusion in Africa and Europe*). Another central topic in his work is the relation between witchcraft and politics in Africa and elsewhere. This has resulted in *The Modernity of Witchcraft* (University of Virginia Press 1997) and *Witchcraft, Intimacy and Trust—Africa in Comparison* (University of Chicago Press 2013).

CHAPTER 13

Afterword: From Witchcraft to the Pentecostal-Witchcraft Nexus

Aletta Biersack

Framed by an ambitious introduction, this book contributes importantly to the literature on modernity and the occult by highlighting the workings of Pentecostalism in that relationship. It is argued that Pentecostalism wages "spiritual warfare" against evildoers (Stritecky 2001), promoting efforts to identify and punish witches so as to purge persons and communities of Satanic forces and "deliver" them to the Holy Spirit. Pentecostalism is also intolerant of "tradition" and works to abolish it, as in the astonishing episode described in the introduction in which the speaker of Papua New Guinea's (PNG's) national parliament removed emblems of indigenous spirits (carvings, totem poles, etc.) from Parliament House because he deemed them demonic and wanted to dedicate the building and the nation to the Christian Trinity (Rio, MacCarthy, and Blanes, this volume, pp. 1–2; see Eves et al. 2014). The editors see in Pentecostalism a way to explain recent increases in witchcraft accusations and a startling new ferocity in the treatment of alleged witches (see Forsyth and Eves ed. 2015). Taken together the essays provide insight into the functioning of the Pentecostal-witchcraft nexus in various African and Melanesian postcolonial settings at a time of increased market penetration and socioeconomic stratification.

A. Biersack (✉)
University of Oregon, Eugene, OR, USA

K. Rio et al. (eds.), *Pentecostalism and Witchcraft*, Contemporary Anthropology of Religion, DOI 10.1007/978-3-319-56068-7_13

My comments on this collection are offered in two sections: the first, "Witchcraft," and the second, "The Pentecostal-Witchcraft Nexus," a term that is meant to capture the necessary connection between Pentecostalism, which wages "spiritual warfare" against evil forces, and witchcraft wherever witchcraft beliefs are entertained. The first part is largely inspired by Peter Geschiere's *Witchcraft, Intimacy, and Trust* (2013). The second, "The Pentecostal-Witchcraft Nexus," is informed by the Comaroffs' introduction to the edited collection *Modernity and Its Malcontents* (1993) and by their essay on "millennial capitalism" (2000), as well as by Geschiere's *The Modernity of Witchcraft* (1997), Meyer's *Translating the Devil* (1999a), and Robbins's *Becoming Sinners* (2004a).

But first a word about the term *witchcraft*. The title, if not the book itself, blurs the distinction frequently drawn between sorcery, which involves conscious acts of malevolence, and witchcraft, which bears on unconscious attempts to harm. The editors adopt the term *witchcraft* to mean acts of occult malevolence, conscious or not. In these comments, I use the term *witchcraft* in this generic sense as well, but will use the term *sorcery* instead when discussing particular contributors who use that term.

Witchcraft

In an early comparison of Africa and Melanesia, Max Marwick wrote that in Africa, alleged "attacks and accusations of witchcraft and sorcery occur only between persons already linked by close social bonds" (1970: 280),[1] the relationship between the alleged witch or sorcerer having been strained (ibid.), but in Oceania,[2] "the sorcerer ... is believed to direct his destructive magic *outside* his own group" (ibid.), sorcery operating between rather than within communities (ibid.). The Melanesianists Mary Patterson and Michele Stephen challenged Marwick's dichotomy (Patterson 1974; Stephen 1987) and called for a more nuanced comparison, one that acknowledges similarities (as I hope to do here) and not just differences between the two regions.

As this collection shows, witchcraft and sorcery in some Melanesian societies do indeed involve attacks between close relatives. According to Strong, Asaro (PNG) witches kill only their own kin (this volume, p. 74 and passim), and they receive their powers "as a kind of inheritance ..., so that the children and relatives of witches are themselves suspected" of being witches (this volume, p. 73). Reporting on the Trobriand Islands (PNG), the group Malinowski made famous, MacCarthy notes that witches attack members of their own matriline and acquire their powers from their mother in a putative grotesque initiation-like process (this volume, p. 146; see Urame 2015: 26).

Strong's and MacCarthy's accounts echo that of Peter Geschiere for the Maka of southeast Cameroon. In its most dangerous form, *djambe,* an occult force that may be translated as either witchcraft or sorcery, involves "witchcraft from inside the house" (2013: xvi; see also Geschiere 1982: 107, 1997: 38 ff.). Even in contemporary urban contexts, witchcraft is thought "to arise, first of all, from the intimacy of the family and home" (1997: 11). Witchcraft is in fact "the dark side of kinship" (2013: xvi), "the flip side of kinship" (ibid.: 14), "the betrayal of kinship" (ibid.), and leads to "profound ambivalences about intimacy [here Geschiere generalizes broadly] ... all over the world" (ibid.: xxii).

The African chapters in this volume mostly uphold Geschiere's insight that intimacy breeds witchcraft. Pype claims that in Kinshasa, the capital of the Democratic Republic of the Congo, occult powers are transferred "within intimate spheres of belonging (principally the extended family)" (this volume, p. 114). Of urban Angola, Blanes writes that the powers of *ndoki* or sorcery are transferred from maternal uncle to nephew within the matriline (this volume, p. 238). Bertelsen provides the one African anomaly in the collection in recounting how residents of a Mozambican peri-urban area suspected German strangers (missionaries, communists) of witchcraft.

To the extent that witchcraft concerns malice between those related through ties of social and/or geographical propinquity, "the main danger lurks in the very core of sociality" (Geschiere 2013: xxi). In many parts of the world, such ties are developed transactionally, and not surprisingly, suspicions of witchcraft may be aroused by perceived transactional slights, according to some contributors. Asaro, for example, search for some "hidden" resentment (Strong, this volume, p. 75) whenever witchcraft is alleged. "Did the deceased give money to some kin but not others? Was a pig consumed that was not shared?" (ibid.). "Every accusation [of witchcraft] I have encountered revolves around the breaking of the ethos of reciprocity among kin," Strong reports (ibid.). MacCarthy suggests as much in her essay on Trobriand witchcraft. "Gifts and their reciprocation are the basis of all functional relationships in the Trobriands; between kin, affines, friends, lovers, marriage partners, and so on" (MacCarthy, this volume, p. 140). Withholding when indigenous ethics mandate giving constitutes a violation of norms, one that may provoke a witchcraft attack. MacCarthy was warned that if a woman complimented her on her clothing, netbag, jewelry, or other valuable, she should give the item away immediately to forestall such an attack. Refusing even a betel nut to someone who wanted it could result in "retribution," witch-style (ibid.: 139), she was told.[3]

Wherever witches are thought to assault consanguines—or affines, for that matter (see note 3)—witchcraft becomes central in the study of kinship, alliance, and exchange, as their "dark" side. This point was made over two decades ago by Eytan Bercovitch, in his article on Nalumin (PNG) "hidden exchange" (1994). The Nalumin live in small settlements the residents of which are connected through affinal and consanguineal ties. Local norms dictate that peace and harmony be achieved through benign reciprocal transactions. Yet allegations of witchcraft arise within these small, socially close networks. The explanation Bercovitch offers is of general interest. Anyone has too many exchange obligations to meet, putting the person in the position of having to renege on some of these obligations. It follows that to give is also to withhold, the "inescapable" problem of exchange (1994: 520). There is a benefit to giving to others, but this is offset by the risk taken in giving: "the harm that comes from not giving to others" (ibid.: 523). To avoid the conflicts such exclusions could engender, Nalumin conduct their transactions in secret so as not to antagonize non-recipients. Auslander echoes Bercovitch's point, albeit for the Ngoni, an eastern Zambian group. "Ngoni frequently stress that any act of giving or sharing may potentially trigger later dangerous acts of witchcraft or poisoning by those left out ... the witch—as the 'excluded other' (Munn 1990: 3)" reciprocates by retaliating and "endangering the community" (Auslander 1993: 178).

That witchcraft is the dark side not only of kinship but exchange is implicit in the recurring figure of the devouring cannibalistic witch. In Bertelsen's chapter, for example, the Germans are imagined as nocturnal bloodsuckers (this volume, p. 43) and as undertaking "savage hunts for children" (ibid.: 39), who are "kidnapped or devoured" (ibid.). Similarly, Asaro witches are depraved, necrophagous consumers that loiter near graves, where their next meal lies (Strong, this volume, p. 73). They are "figures of unmitigated, cannibalistic hunger or greed" (ibid.) who feed at night "on the internal organs of persons or pigs, slaking their persistent hunger by eating livers, hearts, lungs, and brains" (ibid.). Moreover, the invisible spirit or familiar that is thought to be responsible for a witch's behavior is believed to be lodged in the abdomen, belly, or (in Melanesian creoles) *bel*.[4] Such tropes discursively associate witches with consumption, which is selfish and immoral, not with sharing and prestation, the valorized alternatives. The witch is imagined as "the epitome of maliciousness and antisocial selfishness" (Kelly 1993: 177)—in short, as a transactional pervert (see Munn 1986: 215–233). Something like this interpretation has frequently been proffered. Writing generally of African witchcraft, Marwick states: "It is widely held that beliefs in witchcraft—and the same would hold for sorcery—are an effective means of dramatizing social norms in that they provide, in the person of the mystical evil-doer, a symbol of all that is held to be anti-social and illegitimate" (1967: 124). The witch figure partakes of the logic of exchange and must be understood semantically (rather than functionally), through the morality of exchange, as its inversion.

In *Witchcraft, Intimacy, and Trust,* Geschiere critiques the tendency in kinship studies to assume that the closer the bond, the greater the "self-evident solidarity and trust" (2013: xxi) and the greater the transactional benevolence. But if witchcraft is the dark side of kinship, as Geschiere has maintained, and if it is also the dark side of exchange, as I have argued, witchcraft is integral to these institutions, which must now be rethought in less romanticized terms and with an attention to dynamics (benevolent but also malevolent) rather than structure (cf. Macintyre 1995). Such rethinking would shift witchcraft from the margins to the center of our attempts to grasp human sociality in all its variety, warts and all. The next section pivots to a discussion of what I am calling the Pentecostal-witchcraft nexus, but it never strays far from the considerations of the first section.

The Pentecostal-Witchcraft Nexus

This book is the latest contribution to the study of "witchcraft and modernity" (Geschiere 2013: 7) initiated by the Comaroffs (1993) and which Geschiere (1997) and Meyer (1999a) developed in their respective monograph-length treatments. The witchcraft and modernity paradigm treats witchcraft as a changing and "integral part of people's vision of modernity" (Geschiere 2006: 220) rather than as an ossified holdover from the past. Witchcraft discourses provide "critical commentaries on new forms of wealth and commodification" (Myhre, this volume, p. 156)–in particular "on the new inequalities that have arisen with incorporation into cash and market economies" (Eves 2000: 454). As market-related inequalities have deepened, the witch figure continues to be "good to think with" (Comaroff and Comaroff 1993: xxvii), providing explanations, in some cases, for these inequalities and, in others, for the misfortunes endured by the economically successful, who are presumed to be afflicted by witchcraft. Indeed, Pentecostalism, "one of the great success stories of the current era of cultural globalization" (Robbins 2004b: 117; see also Meyer 2004), with its crusade against the demonic, clearly constitutes an incitement to witchcraft discourse (Foucault 1980), albeit under altered material and symbolic circumstances.

There is evidence aplenty in these chapters of the many connections between the Pentecostal-witchcraft nexus and these altered material circumstances. In Eriksen and Rio's chapter, for example, well-off ni-Vanuatu urbanites worry that jealousy ("for other people's possessions, for other people's wealth" [this volume, p. 187]) will motivate sorcery attacks on them, and they look to Pentecostal churches to provide protection against jealous enemies (ibid.). Elsewhere in Vanuatu, a person who "sees another ... having success relative to and often at the expense of him- or herself" (Bratrud, this volume, p. 208) is expected to engage in sorcery. Meanwhile, on the African continent, urban Angolans view Pentecostalism as the "insurance" (Blanes, this volume, p. 94) needed to shield themselves from the covetousness of others (ibid.; see Meyer 1999a: 188 ff.).

Pentecostalism not only offers to the prosperous safeguards against witchcraft (in the form of "discernment," "deliverance," exorcism, and prayers) but promotes individualism in the face of familial demands for sharing. In Pentecostalism, the individual is the "unit of salvation" (Robbins 2004a: 295): a he or she who is "filled up by Jesus and the power of the holy spirit" (MacCarthy, this volume, p. 147) and who enters into direct relation with the divine as a result (Meyer 1999a: 172). On the theory that "[a]ll family ties are ... potentially dangerous" (ibid.: 170), Pentecostal policy encourages detachment from "the 'corrupting' influence and obligations of kin" (Bratrud, this volume, p. 209). As Trobrianders immerse themselves in Pentecostalism, their attention is directed away from "wide-ranging kin obligations to, instead, the household level" (MacCarthy, this volume, p. 147). To draw on Meyer's *Translating the Devil*, "When witchcraft has been diagnosed as the cause of someone's trouble [among the Ewe of Ghana] ..., all the energy is devoted to cutting the victim's ties with his or her family. Individualization is the main option in the fight against Satan" (1999a: 195).

Pentecostalism undermines the social fabric in another way: by insisting upon a "complete break" with tradition (Meyer 1999b). This can give rise to a generational rift, one that may coincide with an urban/rural fault line. Among the Asaro, for example, the Pentecostal demonization of the past at a time of urbanization produces a fissure between village dwellers, whom the urbanized young identify with "'the way of the ancestors'" (Strong, this volume, p. 72), mainstream, pre-Pentecostal religions such as Lutheranism (ibid.: 70), and witchcraft, on the one hand, and, on the other, city-based Asaro youth, who pride themselves on having been "born in the time of modern technology, the time of 'computerized systems'" (ibid.: 72) and who look down upon villagers for their lack of sophistication. The point is often made that contemporary PNG witchcraft targets vulnerable populations, older people and sometimes women (Urame 2015: 27), and insurgent male youth have been known to take the lead in torturing and killing identified witches and sorcerers in PNG (Gibbs 2012: 129–130; Jorgensen 2014; Urame 2015: 27) and Vanuatu (Taylor and Araújo 2016). The upper Asaro seem to be ripe for this development. Certainly, city-based youth believe that all villagers are witches, and it is easy to imagine that the city-based young men will come to suspect their village-based kinspeople of envying them and engaging in witchcraft to retaliate for felt inequalities.[5]

As the "dark side" of kinship and exchange, witchcraft is symptomatic of the weakness of the grip of these institutions. Pentecostalism exacerbates this weakness by promoting the contraction of social networks, by setting the old against the young, and by offering spiritual protection to those fearful of envious relatives. At the heart of the Pentecostal-witchcraft nexus, then, is a tension between "relationalism and individualism" (Robbins 2004a: 323) in the orientation of converts. The exigencies of new economic circumstances–monetization, market participation—would exacerbate this tension as households become reoriented toward consumption and away from production for exchange purposes (see Meyer 1999a: 207–208).

Much of this book's introduction is devoted to a consideration of the power dimension of Pentecostalism. There Rio, MacCarthy, and Blanes make the strong claim that the "Pentecostal movement, in its many forms and expressions, produces and invigorates a space for invisible powers and it is within this space that Pentecostalism directs all its attention and energy" (this volume, pp. 14–15). Given its involvement with individuals, the kinship and community networks in which individuals are embedded, and their fear of occult events, Pentecostalism presents "a particular form of governance or social ordering" (ibid., p. 26; see also Eves 2011), one that is capable of regulating "the social life of households or the inner person" (Rio, MacCarthy, and Blanes, this volume, p. 26) as "state forms of governance, such as policing or schooling" (ibid.) are not.

In providing "spiritual protection" and "deliverance" from evildoers to those who believe themselves to be vulnerable, Pentecostalism supplies a bulwark against Satan/the witch, something no secular institution can supply.[6] As wielders of secular power, postcolonial states lack the technologies and knowledge thought necessary to defeat malevolent supernatural forces, and must seem utterly irrelevant to those who feel threatened by them. I agree with the editors in their argument that Pentecostalism "invigorates a space for invisible powers" (ibid.: 14), a space of "a particular form of governance or social ordering" (ibid.: 26), and that Pentecostal forms of governance can and do compete with state forms of governance. However, I would resist the idea that Pentecostalism "produces" this space. The space is the space of witchcraft, a space with antecedents that predate Pentecostalism's several decades of activity in Africa and Melanesia. I would attribute Pentecostalism's "success story" (Robbins 2004b: 171) to the way Pentecostalism *re*-invigorated and colonized the space of witchcraft, bringing into its fold indigenes who were desperate for a "deliverance" they had long sought.

Geschiere tells the story of how the Makas of southeastern Cameroon resented the fact that the colonial state protected rather than prosecuted witches, no doubt because its Western culture precluded a belief in witches. In the postcolonial period, however, the protections were no longer there, and, "as the state Africanized itself, the old link between power and the occult was restored" (1997: 15), witchcraft becoming once again rampant. Pentecostalism restores that link, propagating in tandem with its arch enemy witchcraft a zone of power that is at once old and new—"Pentecostal witchcraft," as Newell has called it (2007: 461; see Rio, MacCarthy, and Blanes, this volume, p. 11).

To put the matter this way is to suggest that the success of Pentecostalism, whether in Melanesia or Africa, is best understood not in terms of Pentecostalism per se but in terms of the Pentecostal-witchcraft relationship, through which this zone of power is produced and in which it is lodged. Pentecostalism's globalization is thus simultaneously its localization, to be understood through the interplay of indigenous and exogenous factors (Comaroff and Comaroff 1993: xiii-xiv; Eves 2000[7]; see discussion in Robbins 2001). Such an approach typically accounts for differences. But the real mystery to me is why African and Melanesian witchcraft beliefs, non-Biblical in their provenience, are, even in the era of Pentecostal incursion, so similar to each other.

Notes

1. Marwick first published his views in 1964 in the essay "Witchcraft as a social strain-gauge." Excerpts of this article were subsequently published in 1970 in the collection *Witchcraft and Sorcery*, which Marwick edited.
2. Marwick's term is "Oceania," but his examples come from Melanesia, a region within Oceania, one that contains Papua New Guinea and Vanuatu, about which several contributors have written.
3. Bruce Knauft's discussion of Gebusi (PNG) sorcery provides an example of the use of occult powers in affinal rather than consanguineal relations. As of his initial research in 1980–1982, the Gebusi achieved "balanced reciprocity" (Sahlins 1972) by exchanging women between groups, returning a woman for a woman instead of bridewealth for a woman, as in many other PNG societies. Gebusi "alliance" exchanges were not always balanced, however, and "[s]orcery accusations are especially likely between kin groups linked by a marriage that has not been reciprocated" (2016: 72), a claim Knauft initially made in his first book, *Good Company and Violence* (1985).
4. Geschiere has adopted Jean-François Bayart's notion of a "politics of the belly" (1997:7)—an *imaginaire* that signifies the "dangerous force [of *sorcellerie* or witchcraft/sorcery] that is supposed to live in someone's belly" (ibid.) and that is said to dominate African politics. Melanesian witchcraft discourses also deploy the trope of the politics of the belly by way, I suggest, of signifying the dark side of exchange.
5. As said, Asaro witches only attack kin.
6. In her study of witchcraft and Pentecostalism among the Ewe of Ghana, Birgit Meyer explains Ewe conversion from missionary derived to Pentecostal churches in these terms: the missionary-derived (specifically the Evangelical Presbyterian Church) "failed to deal with demons satisfactorily because its leaders would take neither the Holy Spirit nor the Devil and his demons seriously" (1999: xviii; see also ibid.: 195).

7. Eves's target in "Sorcery's the Curse" is the Comaroffs' introduction to *Modernity and Its Malcontents* which he reads as seeing "local responses as the passive product of exogenous forces" (2000: 454) rather than emphasizing the "dynamic interplay between the local and the exogenous" (ibid.: 455). However, the Comaroffs clearly do emphasize the interplay between the local and the exogenous.

References

Auslander, Mark. 1993. "'Open the Wombs!': The Symbolic Politics of Modern Ngoni Witchfinding." In *Modernity and Its Malcontents*, ed. Jean Comaroff and John L. Comaroff, 167–192. Chicago: University of Chicago Press.

Bayart, Jean-François. 1989. *L'État en Afrique: La Politique du Ventre*. Paris: Fayard.

Bercovitch, Eytan. 1994. "The Agent in the Gift: Hidden Exchange in Inner New Guinea." *Cultural Anthropology* 9 (4): 498–536.

Comaroff, Jean, and John L. 1993. "Introduction." In *Modernity and Its Malcontents: Ritual and Power in Postcolonial Africa*, ed. Jean Comaroff and John L. Comaroff, pp. ix–xxxvii. Chicago: University of Chicago Press.

Comaroff, Jean, and John L. Comaroff. 2000. Millennial Capitalism: First Thoughts on a Second Coming. *Public Culture* 12 (2): 291–343.

Eves, Richard. 2000. Sorcery's the Curse: Modernity, Envy and the Flow of Sociality in a Melanesian Society. *Journal of the Royal Anthropological Institute* 6: 453–468.

Eves, Richard. 2011. "Pentecostal Dreaming and Technologies of Governmentality in a Melanesian Society." *American Ethnologist* 38 (4): 758–773.

Eves, Richard, Nicole Haley, Ron J. May, John Cox, Philip Gibbs, Francesca Merlan et al. 2014. "Purging Parliament: A New Christian Politics in Papua New Guinea?" State, Society and Governance in Melanesia Discussion Paper 2014/1, Australian National University.

Forsyth, Miranda, and Richard Eves. 2015. "The Problems and Victims of Sorcery and Witchcraft Practices and Beliefs in Melanesia: An Introduction." In *Talking it Through: Responses to Sorcery and Witchcraft Beliefs and Practices in Melanesia*, pp. 1–19. Canberra: ANU Press.

Foucault, Michel. 1980. *The History of Sexuality, vol. 1, An Introduction*. Translated from the French by Robert Hurley. New York: Vintage Books.

Geschiere, Peter. 1982. *Village Communities and the State: Changing Relations Among the Maka of South-Eastern Cameroon Since the Colonial Conquest*. Translated by James J. Ravell. London: Kegan Paul International Ltd.

Geschiere, Peter. 1997. *The Modernity of Witchcraft: Politics and the Occult in Postcolonial Africa*. Translated by Peter Geschiere and Janet Roitman. (*Sorcellerie et politique en Afrique-La viande des autres [Sorcellerie and politics in Africa: The Meat of Others*].) Charlottesville and London: University Press of Virginia.

Geschiere, Peter. 2006. "Witchcraft and the Limits of the Law: Cameroon and South Africa." In *Law and Disorder in the Postcolony*, ed. Jean Comaroff, and John L. Comaroff, 219–246. Chicago: University of Chicago Press.

Geschiere, Peter. 2013. *Witchcraft, Intimacy, and Trust: Africa in Comparison*. Chicago: University of Chicago Press.

Gibbs, Philip. 2012. "Engendered Violence and Witch-killing in Simbu." In *Engendering Violence in Papua New Guinea*, ed. Margaret Jolly, Christine Stewart, and Carolyn Brewer, 107–136. Canberra: ANU E Press.

Jorgensen, Dan. 2014. "Preying on Those Close to Home: Witchcraft Violence in a Papua New Guinea Village." *TAJA* 25: 267–286.

Kelly, Raymond C. 1993. *Constructing Inequality: The Fabrication of a Hierarchy of Virtue among the Etoro*. Ann Arbor: University of Michigan Press.

Knauft, Bruce M. 1985. *Good Company and Violence: Sorcery and Social action in a Lowland New Guinea Society*. Berkeley: University of California Press.

Knauft, Bruce M. 2016. *The Gebusi: Lives Transformed in a Rainforest World*, 4th ed. Longrove, IL: Waveland Press.

Macintyre, Martha. 1995. "Violent Bodies and Vicious Exchanges: Personification and Objectification in the Massim." *Social Analysis* 37: 29–43.

Marwick, Max. 1967. "The Sociology of Sorcery in a Central African Tribe." In *Magic, Witchcraft, and Curing*, ed. John Middleton, 101–133. Garden City, NY: The Natural History Press.

Marwick, Max. 1970. "Witchcraft as a Social Strain-Gauge." In *Witchcraft and Sorcery*, ed. Max Marwick, 280–295. Harmondsworth, Middlesex, England: Penguin Books.

Meyer, Birgit. 1999a. *Translating the Devil: Religion and Modernity among the Ewe in Ghana*. Edinburgh: Edinburgh University Press.

Meyer, Birgit. 1999b. "'Make a Complete Break with the Past': Memory and Postcolonial Modernity in Ghanaian Pentecostal Discourse." In *Memory and the Postcolony: African Anthropology and the Critique of Power*, ed. Richard Werbner, 182–208. London and New York: Zed Books.

Meyer, Birgit. 2004. "Christianity in Africa: From African Independent to Pentecostal-Charismatic Churches." *Annual Review of Anthropology* 33: 447–474.

Munn, Nancy D. 1986. *The Fame of the Gawa: A Symbolic Study of Value Transformation in a Massim (Papua New Guinea) Society*. Durham: Duke University Press.

Munn, Nancy D. 1990. "Constructing Regional Worlds in Experience: Kula Exchange, Witchcraft and Gawan Local Events." *Man* (N.S.) (2591): 1–17.

Newell, Sasha. 2007. "Pentecostal Witchcraft: Neoliberal Possession and Demonic Discourse in Ivoirian Pentecostal Churches." *Journal of Religion in Africa* 37 (4): 461–490.

Patterson, Mary. 1974. "Sorcery and Witchcraft in Melanesia." *Oceania* 45 (132–160): 212–234.

Robbins, Joel. 2001. "Introduction: Global Religions, Pacific Island Transformations." In *Charismatic and Pentecostal Christianity in Oceania*, ed. Joel Robbins, Pamela J. Stewart, and Andrew Strathern. Special Issue, *Journal of Ritual Studies* 15 (2): 7–12.

Robbins, Joel. 2004a. *Becoming Sinners: Christianity + Moral Torment in a Papua New Guinea Society.* Berkeley: University of California Press.

Robbins, Joel. 2004b. "The Globalization of Pentecostal and Charismatic Christianity." *Annual Review of Anthropology* 33: 117–143.

Sahlins, Marshall. 1972. *Stone Age Economics.* Chicago: Aldine.

Stephen, Michele. 1987. "Contrasting Images of Power." In *Sorcerer and Witch in Melanesia*, ed. Michele Stephen, 249–340. New Brunswick, NJ: Rutgers University Press.

Stritecky, Jolene Marie. 2001. "Israel, America, and the Ancestors: Narratives of Spiritual Warfare in a Pentecostal Denomination in Solomon Islands." *Journal of Ritual Studies* 15 (2): 62–78.

Taylor, John P., and Natalie G. Araújo. 2016. "Sorcery Talk, Gender Violence and the Law in Vanuatu." In *Gender Violence and Human Rights: Seeking Justice in Fiji, Papua New Guinea and Vanuatu*, ed. Aletta Biersack, Margaret Jolly, and Martha Macintyre, 197–227. Canberra: ANU Press.

Urame, Jack. 2015. "The Spread of Sorcery Killing and its Social Implications." In *Talking it Through: Responses to Sorcery and Witchcraft Beliefs and Practices in Melanesia*, ed. Miranda Forsyth and Richard Eves, 23–35. Canberra: ANU Press.

Author Biography

Aletta Biersack is emeritus Professor at University of Oregon. She has post-graduate training in both anthropology and history and focuses on the culture and history of Pacific peoples, primarily on the Ipili speakers of the Porgera and Paiela valleys, Papua New Guinea, whom she has been studying since the 1970s. She has published extensively on the topics of political ecology, historical anthropology, and sex/gender, making contributions of an ethnographic and/or theoretical nature. She is co-editor of *Imagining Political Ecology* (Duke University Press, 2006), *Emergent Masculinities in the Pacific* (The Asia and Pacific Journal of Anthropology, 2016), and *Gender Violence & Human Rights: Seeking Justice in Fiji, Papua New Guinea & Vanuatu* (Australian National University Press, 2016), and editor of *Ecologies for Tomorrow* (published in *American Anthropologist,* 1999*), Papuan Borderlands* (University of Michigan Press, 1995), and *Clio in Oceania* (Smithsonian Institution Press, 1991).

Index

K. Rio et al. (eds.), *Pentecostalism and Witchcraft*, Contemporary Anthropology of Religion, DOI 10.1007/978-3-319-56068-7

CPSIA information can be obtained
at www.ICGtesting.com
Printed in the USA
LVHW051828270519
619156LV00008B/142/P

9 783319 560670